To,
Rama

He did it

SWAMI CHINMAYANANDA

A LEGACY

With Best
Compliments

Mohan Peri

Published by

Chinmaya Mission West
P.O. Box 129, Piercy, CA 95587 U.S.A.
Tel: (707) 247-3488
Email: publications@chinmayamission.org
Website: www.chinmayamission.org

First Edition: May 2011, 25,000 copies

Very special thanks to Pujya Guruji Swami Tejomayananda for his love and guidance, Swami Shantananda for his loving support and guidance to the Mananam team, and Swami Ishwarananda for conceiving the idea of the book series and guidance to the Mananam team.

Grateful acknowledgment and very special thanks to Shibani Khorana, Anjali Singh, and devotees who have contributed towards the text, research, and photographs.

Grateful acknowledgment is made to the following for permission to use material from their books:

Nancy Patchen: *The Journey of a Master: Swami Chinmayananda: The Man, the Path, the Teaching*. Copyright 1989 by Nancy Patchen.

Rudite Emir: *At Every Breath a Teaching: Stories about the Life and Teachings of Swami Chinmayananda*. Copyright 1999 by Chinmaya Mission West and Central Chinmaya Mission Trust.

Grateful acknowledgement and special thanks to Swami Advayananda, Jujhar Singh, Dr. D.V. Prafulla, and Madhabi Paul.

Edited and supported by the Mananam team

Margaret Dukes, David Dukes, Neena Dev, Rashmi Mehrotra,
Arun Mehrotra, and Padmashree Rao

Design, Layout, and Typography by

Preeti Pahwa, Meenakshi Singh, and Jai Mangal

Printed by

Silverpoint Press Pvt. Ltd., India

Library of Congress Control Number: 2011924225

ISBN: 978-1-60827-006-4

THE mananam SERIES

CHINMAYA BIRTH CENTENARY CELEBRATION SERIES

He did it

SWAMI CHINMAYANANDA

A LEGACY

CHINMAYA PUBLICATIONS
CHINMAYA MISSION WEST PUBLICATIONS DIVISION

HIS LIFE ITSELF IS A SCRIPTURE,

HIS WORDS ARE HYMNS,

HIS ACTIONS ARE BLESSINGS UPON THE WORLD.

HE IS THE FULFILLED, THE PERFECT.

IN SUCH AN ACCOMPLISHED MAN,

WE WATCH GOD AND HIS PLAY.

| SWAMI CHINMAYANANDA |

An offering of love,

at the sacred feet

of Pujya Gurudev,

Swami Chinmayananda.

Contents

SPECIAL PAGES

ॐ

Foreword

Dear Reader,

Hari Om!

He alone lives to become immortal, in whose *living* millions of people derive inspiration to live a life of nobility, sacrifice, and service. Blessed indeed are those who have the opportunity to live in the company of such great men of spiritual enlightenment. In the absence of such company, we can come to know and be inspired by enlightened masters through their writings as well as through various spiritual literatures, which show the way to live an elevated life. Here, in this book, is an opportunity to learn about the world-renowned Vedantic Master of the twentieth century, Swami Chinmayananda, whom we reverently call Pujya Gurudev.

What makes a person become great is a moment of inspiration, culminating in a clear vision of the goal, brought to fruition with relentless hard work. Then, a person's life becomes one of extraordinary achievements in both inner and outer worlds, inspiring and motivating others to follow.

This is also the story of Pujya Gurudev. We felt that his story needed to be told, for it *must* be read and known by all. It has the power to purify and light a spark of inspiration in open minds. Read it and be blessed! Come to realize that there is a vast and abundant existence just waiting to unfold within you.

I am very happy that *Mananam* is bringing out this special edition — *He did it: Swami Chinmayananda, A Legacy* — as the first of a series of twelve books to herald the celebrations leading to Pujya Gurudev's birth centenary in 2016. May Pujya Gurudev's blessings always be with you in your quest for Self-knowledge and abiding happiness.

With Prem & Om,

Swami Tejomayananda | May 8, 2011
Head, Chinmaya Mission Worldwide | CCMT, Mumbai

Introduction

Ādi Śaṅkara is the perfector of what had come before. Swami Vivekananda is Vedānta's brightest single shining moment. Swami Chinmayananda is Vision; he built — or rebuilt — the path to scripture for modern man.

Comparisons between saints can only be on the outside. Each of India's spiritual giants has had a unique character and personality. Each has brought to play a specific role in the revelation of the eternal Truth for mankind. And, in the modern age, Swami Chinmayananda is acknowledged as the saint who pioneered a renaissance within Hinduism — that knocked on doors, swept homes — and ended the monopoly of orthodox priests over Vedānta, handing the priceless knowledge of the scriptures to the masses of India and the world.

On May 8, 2016, we celebrate the birth centenary of one of history's most dynamic saints — 100 years old — his legacy 100 years young. As a tribute to him, and as a testimony to his lasting legacy, we present this first book of the Chinmaya Birth Centenary Series, as a humble gesture of our reverence and appreciation, and as the first of many celebrations towards his birth centenary. To the readers of this Series who share in that legacy, we welcome you to this celebration.

Swami Chinmayananda has been honored, loved, and revered all over the world by leaders and ordinary people alike. Enraptured by all this praise, we might sometimes forget the vision, hard work, and long struggle that made all of this possible. Thus, this book is also an attempt to understand a divine saṅkalpa conceived a century ago, on May 8, 1916 — where the journey begins with his birth. And through the passage of time, we will see how his life has stood the measure of love and inspiration, multiplying many-fold the impact he had on his world, and on ours.

But if we think we get a true taste of the real Master — then perhaps we are doing what the Zen master said, "eating pictures of rice cakes." Can memories at any time adequately compare themselves to the mystery and reality we hold at this very moment as living, breathing human beings? No. Yet, to leave this earthly realm, and not avail ourselves of an opportunity to glimpse into one of the greatest inspirational journeys of the twentieth century — why, then we haven't really left our confines at all.

We present to you some glorious moments from the original memories of Swami Chinmayananda, in the hope that once reconstructed, these fragments will yield their share of history's gold, and make his life and legacy meaningful to you in this ever-present moment.

PART ONE

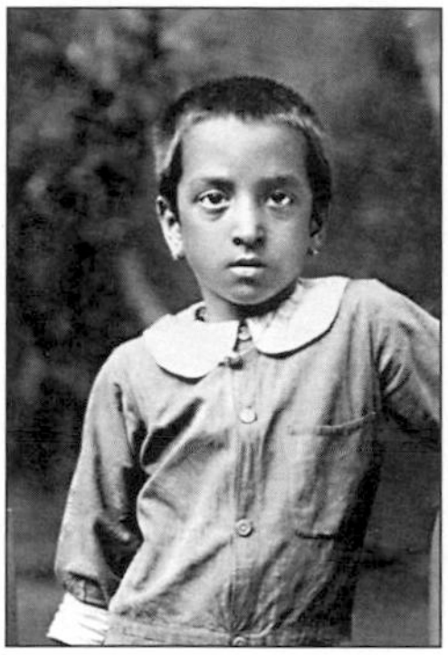

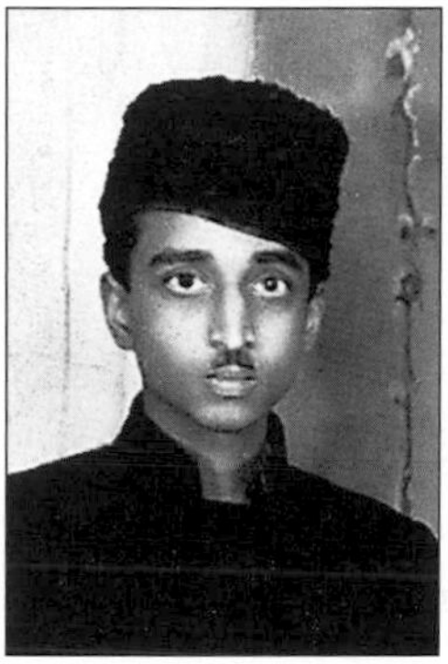

Born in the Land of Saints

◂ **Overleaf:**
Left:
Balan, 8 years old, Ernakulam, 1924
Right:
Balan at Lucknow University, 1940

I

The Stage is Set

The "big story" of man at the dawn of the new millennium is the same as that of all men in past millennia: how is he to be happy? Through the ages, history has shown that answers to all questions on happiness — if it is to last, are to be found only with men of God. There is no other way.

When is it that men of God come upon this earth? It is from the divine Will. Whenever goodness declines and the unbridled growth of adharma, that is, the unrighteous, materialistic and diabolical forces become too strong, then the Almighty God sends a Master to revive the culture. Such men of God are pioneers; they set a vision for generations to come, and often repackage the existing religion to make it viable for the new man. Veda Vyāsa was such a pioneer. He documented Hinduism from the spoken to the written word. Ādi Śaṅkara systematized it by making it a compact ideology and giving it a rationale. Swami Vivekananda took it beyond the shores of India. And, Swami Chinmayananda brought the Truth hitherto kept only with a select few scholars and made it available to all mankind. He took it to every city, every home, despite great opposition from the prevailing orthodoxy, and gave it to the common man in a simple language that he could easily understand.

Saints and sages have never come to create anything new. Their only goal is to expound the Truth. Mohammad, Jesus Christ, Buddha, Guru Nanak have each come to protect the culture and religion of their time. Which Master has said anything other than this Truth? Whenever men of God appear, they endeavor to explain the true significance of the practicing religion and reveal this essential knowledge of Truth which is universal.

And, in the early twentieth century, India was a very troubled corner of the globe. Nay, the entire world went to war in the first quarter of the century. For some time, the Indian subcontinent had been fraught with oppressive rule, foreign invasion, princely squabbles, and internecine strife — and, on occasion, full-scale war. During the mid-nineteenth century A.D. (after the 1857 Indian Rebellion), the subcontinent was officially under the British Empire. India also experienced some of the worst famines ever recorded, including the Great Famine of 1876–78 in which ten million people died, and the Indian Famine of 1899–1900 where another ten million are said to have perished. The effects of these famines are largely attributed to British policy in India. By 1916, the land was in continuous upheaval to free itself from the rule of the British. Was it time for Providence to strike its hand?

On May 8, 1916, nine months after Mahatma Gandhi landed into the foray of India's freedom struggle after twenty years abroad — near the backwaters of Kerala, a child of destiny was born — who, as Swami Chinmayananda, would accept the challenge set by Providence. With an authority that reached from the Pacific to the tips of southern Australia, his name would spread far beyond the land of his birth. He would become an erudite scholar, practitioner — and one of the most powerful orators of Truth who ever lived — who *would* live long after his time. The vision of his work would inspire generations after him, not on a new route to the ancient Truth, but in the rediscovery of one long forgotten.

The common man owes his spiritual awakening — that was once the portrait of a distant dream — to the Malayali baby born in the climax of India's freedom struggle.

The boy was Kuttan and Parukutti Menon's son, Balan.

II

Of Havens and Heritage

Kerala, the land of coconuts or "God's own land" is located on the west coast in southern India. Barely 22–75 miles in width and 367 miles of coastal length, Kerala is proudly wedged between the Arabian Sea to the west and the majestic heights of the Western Ghats to the east from where the land ripples westward presenting a vista of silent valleys clothed in the richest green.

The generosity of Kerala is inherent in its culture and, over time, it has embraced several ethnic and religious groups. The seaports welcomed those who came to trade. In ancient times they exchanged goods with Egypt, Babylonia, Greece, and Rome. The Chinese arrived from the Far East leaving their fishing nets, which can still be seen today. The Jews first landed as traders during the reign of King Solomon and, later, as refugees fleeing the persecution. In the first century (52 A.D.), St. Thomas the Apostle landed in Kodungallur and began his missionary activity. It is assumed his initial converts were the Cochin Jews who had arrived in 526 B.C. after the destruction of Solomon's Temple. In 644 A.D., Malik bin Deenar arrived to build mosques and spread Islam. And, in the eighth century, Ādi Śaṅkara was born in Kerala, who consolidated the doctrine of Advaita-vedānta. Kerala has been an open field for missionaries of all religions.

In Thiruvananthapuram, the capital of Kerala, a temple, a mosque, and a cathedral can be seen standing side by side.

And that's not the half of it. Add to this the Dutch, Portuguese, and British in the eighteenth century and infiltrations from the states of Tamil Nadu and Karnataka and a large number of Gujaratis, Marwaris, Konkanis, Gowd Saraswat Brahmins, Parsis, and Kudumbis — all who migrated to Kerala.

There's nothing like a mix of ethnicity to reveal hidden emotions. There's nothing like time to reveal distortions in the name of religion. Although Kerala is a bizarre anomaly among states — even nations — still, this small state shows the beating heart of all Indian people.

By the nineteenth century, orthodoxy and caste discrimination had taken strong roots within all parts of society. Religion was no longer synonymous with spirituality, much less an expression of Truth. When Swami Vivekananda toured the state in 1897, he remarked, "I have walked into a lunatic asylum of castes." He was appalled by the horrors of the caste system practiced at the time. The many groups bickered and quarreled over rights and privileges, arguing over who stood higher on the caste ladder. The miserable custom of untouchability existed, and a large majority of people were denied entry into temples. The brahmins had come to acquire a hereditary monopoly over scripture and had bungled up its meaning and significance for personal interests.

Why orthodoxy existed in Indian society is not the point in question — at least, not here. The point is that it prevailed within ethnic groups and religion. This is a natural consequence of all things of the world — to become polluted with time. Every religion has faced this dilemma — if they have survived, it is because a man of God came and shook things up. Jesus Christ, Guru Nanak, Buddha, Rāmānuja, Madhavācārya — to name a few — not only threw away polluting traditions and practices, but also remolded them to suit the new times. And thirty-five years later, India would once again bring forth a Master who would turn its people towards the age-old values of Sanātana-dharma. The prevailing attitudes were about to discover that their reach had rather exhausted its limits.

One thing you notice in Kerala: the women command attention. They have a bearing, an assurance, which is more natural than the empowered New Yorker. The home and property are jointly managed by the women in the family. This practice is unlike anywhere else in India, except perhaps Meghalaya. The joint family lives, works, and prays together in mutual cooperation that affords extra mothers and fathers, and many sister-and-brother cousins for each child.

With so much wealth and heritage beneath one cover, Balan was born on 26 Meṣam, 1091 of the Kollam era (May 8, 1916) at 7:30 P.M. to an aristocratic family. His father, Vadakke Kurupath Kuttan Menon, was landed gentry from the Kurupath House, and his mother, Parukutti (Manku) Menon, came with exalted relations. Her sister, P. Neelakanta Menon, was married to the Chief Justice of Cochin; and her cousin, Sittassi, had married the Maharaja of Cochin. Biographers are often inclined to have their subjects begin life in abject poverty — a rags-to-riches story makes a grand adventure — but with the baby Balan, this was a far cry. The Poothampalli House, Manku's family home, rejoiced with happiness and festivities. The birth of their first child was an occasion for great joy — a boy who would follow in the footsteps of his father with a career in law. Yogiraja Bhairananda, the kula guru (spiritual preceptor of the household) and a regular guest at the Poothampalli House, was immediately called to the home to cast the baby's horoscope. He candidly informed them the baby would become a great man. There was even potential for worldwide repute!

Balan's maternal grandfather, Choppully Kunjkittu Menon, was particularly devout and known for his kindness and generosity. Many holy men stopped for a rest during their travels at the Poothampalli House because of its serene atmosphere. One such distinguished guest was Chattambi Swamigal. He was renowned as a great yogī, and said to have the power to be in three places at one time. However, his true love was the study and understanding of Vedānta. He was one of those rare saints through whom the true essence of the Hindu scriptures has been preserved as a living experience. The parents requested him to bless their son and give him a name. And so, with the grace of such a holy man in his first week, the child was named Poothampalli Balakrishnan Menon, meaning "the child Kṛṣṇa."

Balan was welcomed into a loving and religious family with all ancestral rites and rituals. On the twenty-eighth day, he was bathed, and each day for six months given a mixture of locally grown herbs with a dash of powdered gold to give him a clear complexion. His first outing was to the temple, and it was conducted with great fanfare with the entire family accompanying him. To ensure a long life, his head was officially shaved. At six months, there was a ceremony when he took his first solid food. By the end of the year, his ears were pierced and gold earrings were inserted. This practice served both for decoration and the prevention of disease, particularly hernia. His first years passed with all the attention and affection possible, with five mothers in the household to take care of his every need.

When Balan was two years old, Chattambi Swamigal returned to the Menon home. Every evening the family and neighbors would gather around him for a satsaṅga, which was often followed by a vīṇā recital lasting hours. Chattambi Swamigal would speak on Sanskrit and Tamil scriptures and relate stories from Hindu mythology. His vast knowledge along with his own personal experiences and meetings with other holy men made him a fountain of inspiration.

But this visit by Chattambi Swamigal is especially remembered because of a unique exchange between the yogī and the toddler Balan.

One day, after his midday meal, the yogī had retired for his customary rest, lying on a cot in the wide, shady verandah. He then called Manku to bring Balan to him. Taking the boy, he set him on his chest and began to tease and jostle him in a playful manner. He spoke to the boy in a strange language, an occurrence that is reported to have happened several times during this visit. Manku did not know whether it was just childish gibberish or a language that was foreign to her, and her curiosity prompted her to ask the yogī, "What language are you speaking?" "Don't worry, this is only between him and me," replied the yogī with a bright smile. "Look at his face! See! He understands what I am saying." But towards the end of his stay at Poothampalli House, Chattambi Swamigal is said to have remarked, "I have taught him everything."

I ONLY HAVE A VERY DIM MEMORY OF HIM.
AND YET, THE FLASHES THAT RISE IN MY BOSOM
ARE UNFAILINGLY CLEAR. THEY HAVE BEEN A
SILENT INSPIRATION. THEY HAVE HELPED ME
MORE OFTEN THAN I DARE TO CONFESS.

| SWAMI CHINMAYANANDA |

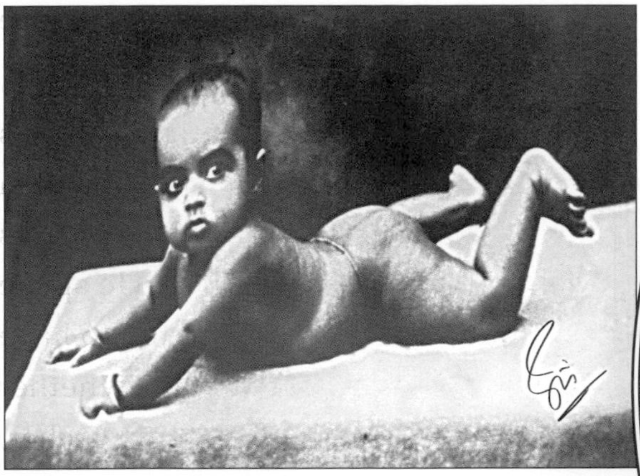

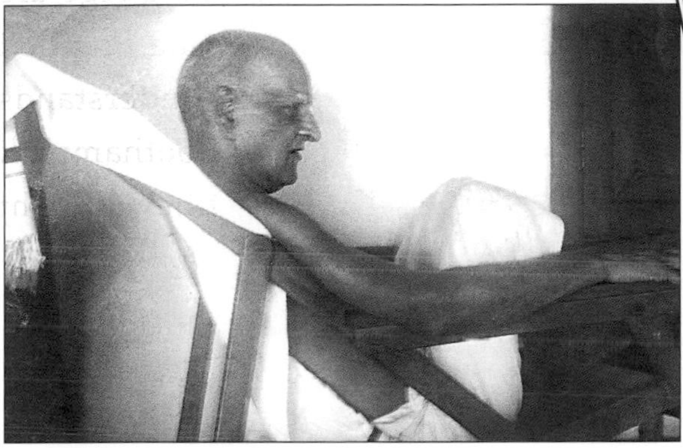

Clockwise from above:
Balan, 4 months old,
Ernakulam, 1916
Parukutti (Manku) Menon,
Balan's mother, 1920
Poothampalli House, Balan's maternal
ancestral home, Ernakulam
Chattambi Swamigal (1853–1924)
Kuttan Menon, Balan's father, Ernakulam

III

Infamous Adventures and the Non-negotiability of the Lord

Before moving forward with our story, we must pause at the period when his mother, Manku, died. Balan was five, and he had become an unusually attractive and intelligent child. He now had a younger sister, Padmini. When Manku was blessed with a third child, Kanakam, Manku's vital signs suddenly failed after the birth of the baby girl. The doctor reasoned that she had died of a heart attack.

Balan soon adjusted to the new situation. He had great affection for his eldest aunt, Kouchi Amma, who was a widow and lived in Poothampalli House with her four children along with several of his mother's other sisters. Balan called her "mother." He later said of her, "My mother had her own welfare department. Anyone in need knew where the door of Poothampalli House was. She never had to leave her own home and family to do volunteer work like the women of today. She practiced her charity right at home."

Throughout his early years, Balan was sure of himself and managed to get what he wanted. His aunts cared for his every need to ensure that he did not suffer any emotional deprivation from the loss of his mother. If Kouchi Amma did have to discipline him for coming home late, he would win her over with his sunny disposition, massaging her back until he was forgiven. Not only did he bask in the attention given at home, but as the son of a District Judge and the nephew of a Police Commissioner, he enjoyed a special status. The inevitable happened — Balan became spoilt.

At thirteen, he began studying at Maharaja's College in Ernakulam. He would play pranks on the teachers and instigate mayhems — a loud noise when the teacher looked away, a book or paper taken from the teacher's desk and hidden, a ball tossed to a friend across the room — anything for a little merriment to break up the boredom of class.

One of Balan's cohorts was Shankar Narayan, an orphan. Balan made him a deal — he would furnish the books if Shankar supplied the homework. He also loved to play ball with his classmates, or just hang around street corners. He would often gather the boys to make an audience and give them a discourse, extempore. His friend Shankar recalls, "He was always full of ideas and advice, given out on any subject at random, and full of gestures and jokes. We were always in peals of laughter." These street corner packs were frowned upon by Balan's family. His uncle even warned some of the boys not to follow in his nephew's example, but his friends thought he was the greatest — there was always some boisterous fun going on when Balan was around.

I HAD EVERYTHING I WANTED IN MY CHILDHOOD.

I NEVER THOUGHT OF THE FUTURE.

| SWAMI CHINMAYANANDA |

Yet, his friends could not deny that he had a compassionate side. He would pay Shankar's school fees on their due date, telling him to pay back whenever he had it. But when the money did not materialize, Balan would still pay his next term's fees without even a comment to his friend. Also, there were moments when he questioned life itself and could not find any meaning or purpose to it. "That he even thought about such deep questions," says Shankar, "I thought it indicated a spiritual bent of mind, and I even told him so."

Chattambi Swamigal visited regularly during these years and his presence in Balan's life grew with time. On warm, spring afternoons, with the smell of jasmine floating in the air, he would sit out in the shady verandah. Balan was drawn to the aura of peace surrounding the swami. He would often sit next to him, and during these stays, all the children seemed to think the sannyāsī favored Balan.

Some things are non-negotiable. And for Balan, attending the evening pūjā at Poothampalli House was one of them. But after the first fifteen minutes of singing bhajans, his mind would drift. His daydreaming took many forms, including studying the various gods in the colored paintings in the altar and making up stories about them. The deity who best suited his adventurous temperament was a picture of Lord Candrakalādhara, a form of Lord Śiva. Years later, he described this beautiful form of the Lord saying:

> The crescent moon poised on his broad forehead, the smiling eyes of compassion, the serpent coiled around his neck, the beaming mouth that seemed to be ready to speak of tenderness and affection from behind the moustache. This ideal Śiva was the ideal of my own heart, and, somehow, I had stumbled onto a new game — I would look at the picture — then shut my eyes to see Lord Śiva exactly as he was in the picture, in the darkness within. This gave me a game so sweet and pleasant that it became a habit to call up this picture onto the mental screen behind my closed eyelids at all hours of the day. The picture came readily as soon as it was ordered, and my wonder grew at my success. It was in those days of waiting for the conclusion of the worship service that Swami Chinmayananda was born in Balan.

Inadvertently, Balan had discovered a technique of meditation. As time would show, like all upāsanās (spiritual practices), it would reach its zenith and dissolve into the one absolute Reality.

Clockwise from above:
Kouchi Narayani, Balan's foster mother, 1920
Balan with father, Kuttan Menon, and sisters, Padmini and Kanakam, Ernakulam, 1924
The pūjā room in Poothampalli House, Ernakulam

IV

The University of Direct Experience

Over the years, Balan had grown into an arrogant teenager and considered himself to be quite an intellectual. When he thought of God, it was only with negative doubt. Who is God? Where is God? He also rejected all superstitious rituals. All those baths, that was another stupidity, he claimed. In his opinion, one bath in the morning was enough unless you got dirty during the day. He had taken to wearing silk shirts rather than the traditional cotton ones. He wore gold chains around his neck, waist, and arm. But it was his oily hair that most irritated his father. "So much hair dressing is bound to make you bald," he would chastise his son, "and then you'll see how much oil you will need." But these remarks had no effect on Balan, who had no use for the older generation's opinions on fashion.

When Balan had just completed intermediate school, his father was transferred to Trichur to a higher position in the regional courts. Kuttan Menon had moved into a large, rambling two-storied house along with his second wife, Devaki and their four children, as well as Balan, Padmini, and Kanakam. Although Kuttan Menon had a serious side, he was a generous and affectionate father. In the evenings, one could often hear the roar of loud laughter and disputes over a card game coming from the verandah of Patinjaresrambi House.

Kuttan Menon had put down an ultimatum that Balan must study during the time his father was gone to work on Saturday mornings. One time, he returned home early, thinking he would give Balan a break from his studies. Instead, he found Balan and Kuttappan having a gala time playing badminton. Kuttan Menon was quite shocked at such an overt display of disobedience and gave his son a thorough scolding, but his anger never lasted long. Within ten minutes he was out in the verandah with a chessboard and playing a game with his smartest opponent, Balan. Kuttan Menon loved his son's charm, intelligence, and wit, but he also feared for his future. What would become of this arrogant lad who had no interest whatsoever in studies — and no ambition at all?

One of the few persons in town who owned a car was Neelakanta Menon, Balan's uncle. He was the Police Commissioner of Cochin (and later Chief Justice), and absolutely no one was allowed to touch his car — except the driver, and Balan. Everyone wondered how Balan had managed to talk his uncle into letting him drive the vehicle. Naturally, Balan's inquisitiveness soon got the better of him, and he began tinkering with the car — he would often be seen under the hood of the car removing and adding parts, much to the mortification of the driver. But his uncle never seemed to mind. He had the confidence that his brilliant nephew would one day — somehow — find his place in society. And secretly, he hoped the lad would follow in his footsteps. He would often send a messenger to call Balan to his home for dinner with the greatest intention of getting the "dedicated loafer" straightened out. Determined to fire up some ambition in him, he would start off a sermon on the evils of laziness, the virtues of hard work, and the absolute necessity of having a career to pay for all the things that Balan enjoyed.

As the years went by, Kuttan Menon became more distressed and openly disappointed in his son's performance. On one occasion, the Inspector of Schools in Cochin came for a visit. The man was a bachelor, strictly self-disciplined and financially successful. Kuttan Menon called his son. "I want you to meet this man, because at forty-two years of age he does not have one bad habit!" He then proceeded to give a thorough lecture to Balan right in front of the guest. "At barely twenty-two years, you have all the vices possible. ..."

In one last attempt to make his son qualified for a job in the Indian Civil Service, Kuttan Menon dismissed the home tutor and moved the studious Shankar right into their home. Now, Balan's behavior affected Shankar's grades as well as his own.

The family gave up.

Balan's interest in religion did not improve either. He would use Hindu concepts to carefully rationalize his position as an agnostic. Yet, even in those days, pocketing all self-dignity, he would secretly do his japa in bed. He did not let go of his relationship with Lord Candrakalādhara. The spiritual Balan persisted, if only as a shadow in the background of the unconvinced sophist, through to the day when he left home to enter Lucknow University. And so, officially, Balan's teenage years ended, not with a bang of enthusiasm and hope, but in a show of pride and defiance.

MY EARLY HABIT OF ASKING QUESTIONS
ABOUT EVERYTHING, INCLUDING GOD,
GREW WITH THE BONES. I CAME TO ASK
SUCH DANGEROUS QUESTIONS AS,
"WHY SHOULD THERE BE A GOD?"

| SWAMI CHINMAYANANDA |

Clockwise from above:
Balan as a student, 1937
Balan in his nightsuit at midday, September 1940
Balan at Lucknow University, 1940

PART TWO

The Turning of a Dream

◀ **Overleaf:**
Left:
Balan ready for the Himalayan Char Dham yatra, 1948
Right:
Swami Chinmayananda, soon after sannyāsa, Rishikesh, 1949

V

Struggle and Strife

We now enter upon the summer of 1942 when the fate of Indian independence hung in the balance. The "Quit India Resolution" declared by the All India Congress Committee at Gowalia Tank Maidan, Mumbai, in August marked a turning point in the freedom struggle. It called for immediate independence — a fight to the finish. In a stirring speech Mahatma Gandhi told the people of India, "There is a mantra, a short one that I give you. You imprint it on your heart and let every breath of yours give an expression to it. The mantra is *do or die.*" Within twenty-four hours of Gandhiji's speech all leaders of the All India Congress, including Gandhiji, Nehru, Patel, and Azad — along with 14,000 satyāgrahīs (Gandhian nonviolent freedom fighters) — were imprisoned in the usual manner: no trial, no sentence. The arrests set off an electrifying response from the Indian people. Everyone from laborer to housewife took to the streets singing nationalist songs and demanding the release of their leaders. Students poured out of universities and instigated a campaign of sabotage throughout the Northern provinces — benches with the sign "For Europeans Only" were removed, taxes withheld, and protest marches in every city.

But now, to review where things stood with Balan in the summer of 1942: He studied Liberal Arts at St. Thomas College, Trichur.

Liberal Arts was not his first choice — but since he had not prepared himself adequately for his final intermediate exams, he had reproduced the question paper on the answer sheet in the science section and turned in the exam — that marked the end of any career in science.

In 1940, he joined Lucknow University. The University had offered him the opportunity to obtain a Masters Degree in English Literature and, at the same time, take a secondary course in Law, which had possibly pacified his father.

Balan excelled in his literature courses, covering all the classics including Shakespeare, Swift, and Milton. He particularly admired George Bernard Shaw and was somewhat influenced by his Shavian manner of social and religious criticism in his own journalism later. Balan loved to talk on his favorite books and would often corner the distinguished scholar and professor of literature, Sir Vilasan Nair, for long discussions.

On the other hand, he ignored the subjects that didn't appeal to him, so he had plenty of extracurricular activities — the university tennis team (he had represented Lucknow University in the singles against Ghaus Mohammad Khan, the Indian competitor at Wimbledon), the literary committee, and the debating team.

How did Balan ever pass his exams? It's anybody's guess — but he managed. Once, through a little research, he found out that the professor of a course, in which his attendance was inadequate, was very religious and always went to a particular Hanumān temple. The very next day, Balan waited with folded hands in front of the deity until the professor arrived. "Do you come here often?" asked the surprised professor when he saw Balan. "Yes, especially now, as I have a particular problem — and if Lord Hanumān cannot help me, then .I fear no one can," said Balan. Not surprisingly, his lack of attendance was taken care of by the professor.

Surely, no one but the Creator himself could have known the mission designed for this unlikely servant. Yet, on closer look, it would seem that, as a collective foundation with his pious and sheltered upbringing, the years that followed would, in fact, have the makings of a different story altogether.

We left the freedom struggle, approaching August 1942, in the midst of wide-scale fervor with an all-out attempt by the Indians to make the British "quit India." Balan was one of the students to join in writing and distributing leaflets to stir up national pride. He gave many speeches with the intent to generate awareness of the inability of the British to understand, much less solve the problems of India. Such "thinkers" commanded a certain respect — not just with Indians, but also with the British, who considered them as the instigators behind the threat to their rule. The British countered every demonstration with whips, guns, and arrests. Within weeks, 10,000 Indians were arrested nationwide, mass fines were levied, and thousands were killed in police and army shootings. Nevertheless, many national leaders went underground and continued the struggle by broadcasting messages over clandestine radio stations and continuing to distribute pamphlets. During these massive lock-ups, a warrant was issued for the arrest of Balakrishnan Menon, a Madrasi. Balan was actually from Ernakulam, but the British did not recognize the distinct states and cultures of South India. To them, it was all "Madras" — the central city of their southern trade headquarters. When word of his impending arrest reached Balan, he went undercover.

He spent the next year moving around in the state of Kashmir, out of range of British officials. However, he did take several trips to visit his former college roommate and close friend, Shroff, at his family home in the outskirts of Delhi. Except for these brief respites to get fresh clothes, some decent food, and catch up on the latest political news — there was neither the time nor place for Balan to rest. Constant movement was necessary in case word got around in this predominantly Muslim state, that a "Madrasi" — easily noticeable by his accent, dark skin, and thin stature — was in the area.

After a year, Balan left Kashmir and moved towards Delhi. At Abbotabad, he boarded a bus that was headed for the capital. But at the next stop, an officer stepped into the bus and started questioning passengers, "Did anyone see a Madrasi enter here?" Balan immediately scooted out the back door of the bus. He knew nothing about the town he was in and had no idea where to head for safety. Momentarily disorientated, he noticed a sign that read: "Earn While You Learn." Balan quickly ducked inside the door below this invitation.

He found himself in the military quarters of a British intelligence communications center responsible for receiving and relaying coded messages for the Allied war efforts in World War II. Balan was hired immediately, and since he intended to stay only a few days, the menial nature of the job did not bother him. But within a week, his superior officer had noticed that this young man was too intelligent for the job, and he promoted Balan as his personal assistant. After eight months of working, Balan departed with a train ticket, plus a considerable cache of rupees from his accumulated salary.

It was now almost two years since the British had issued his arrest warrant. Thinking his case was long forgotten, Balan arrived in Punjab and started mingling with several freedom groups. He began advising students on distributing leaflets and organizing public strikes. The British officials soon learned of the "Madrasi" stirring up trouble. Balan was promptly picked up and thrown in prison.

Winters in Delhi are cold and damp, and the Indian revolutionaries were kept in a makeshift prison in the capital where conditions were miserable. The cells were dark and overcrowded, with no heat or light. The cracks in the walls provided the only ventilation; the food was of poor quality and given in small rations. Once a day, the revolutionaries would be taken out of their cells and interrogated. This was accompanied by beatings with iron rods on the ankles, where no telltale scars would be left. Before long, disease became rampant and many inmates died.

Balan spent several months in these unhygienic conditions and soon caught the typhus. He quickly fell into a stupor; at this stage, there was little hope for survival. The large scale deaths in prison became known to those in the city as they made arrangements for cremating bodies. Fearful of an impending investigation, the British officials decided to avoid any more in-prison deaths. Consequently, Balan was among those who was carried out into the night and tossed beside a road on the outskirts of the city.

It all so nearly came to nothing, but for an Indian Christian lady who was passing along that route the next morning and happened to notice a young man lying on the roadside. On impulse, she stopped her car to investigate, and noticed that the youth was very sick, delirious, and burning with fever. It seems she was sympathetic to his plight, for her own son was with the Indian troops in Europe. The lady took Balan to her home and immediately called for a doctor who insisted that the young man be taken to a hospital without delay. But once his torn clothes (the remains of the one suit he had worn during the several months in prison) were changed to an old suit of her son's, and the suspicious flogging wounds were made visible, it was decided that Balan would be safer at home, and possibly better cared for by the lady.

After several difficult weeks Balan slowly recovered and regained enough strength to make a short journey to Baroda, where he spent the next several months fully recuperating from his ordeal in the home of his cousin, Achutan Menon (Kouchi Amma's son). The Christian lady, who had saved Balan's life, never knew that she had saved the life of a future Hindu sage, for she died a few years later. Her only son was killed in action in World War II and buried in Europe.

IT WAS MY NOSE THAT SAVED ME ON THE ROADSIDE THAT DAY — IT LOOKED EXACTLY LIKE HER SON'S!

| SWAMI CHINMAYANANDA |

Balan recuperating in Baroda
after being released from jail, 1942

VI

The Earnest Mr. "Mochi"

Achutan Menon was thirteen years older than Balan and an officer with the Indian National Forest Service, which meant that he was away for weeks at a time. His wife would come and go; she preferred to spend the time that Achu was away with her parents in Cochin. However, the couple had made sure that Balan was well looked after by a dutiful servant, Narayan. He made sure that Balan had fresh fruits and vegetables along with plenty of fresh milk and yogurt each day. He would also cook in the style of Balan's home state — the diet of rice and dāl, instead of roṭī and potato. Balan would affectionately call the servant, "Baroda Narayana," meaning the Lord of Baroda.

This period in Achutan Menon's home opened a new chapter for Balan. Left to his own devices, he dug out Achu's typewriter and began a career in journalism under the pseudonym "Mochi," meaning "street shoe cobbler." Along the pathways that skirt the city, the mochi sits under a tree, with bits of string and a simple metal punch, repairing shoes in exchange for a few paise. Consigned to a life of poverty, he barely earns enough money to buy food for his family each day. Thus, Mr. Mochi became an apt symbol through which Balan would express the poor man's point of view. He wrote a series of articles — short, critical satires by Mr. Mochi — where he put forth his own views on the imperative of socialism in a society where the vast majority of people were poor. These were soon published regularly in Indian national papers. Each time Achu returned to Baroda, he was surprised to find that more articles had been published and even paid for.

However, the series of articles was not quite the end. The convalescence in Achu's home marks a turning point, when Balan began to rethink, in short sojourns, a subject he had left behind some fifteen years ago — the Hindu religion. The months in prison had made him reflect on the precarious nature of life. He had seen too many lifeless bodies carried out to ignore the reality of death — his own death had seemed inevitable.

The impetus for this rediscovery came from an unlikely source — a woman's magazine. During her last visit, Achu's wife had brought a stack of magazines, no doubt meaning to amuse herself with enough reading material during the lonely periods. In one of the bound volumes of *My Magazine,* with themes from gardening to cooking to religion, there was a particular series of articles on the lives of saints in the Himalayas. Balan leafed through the pages with only a meager interest. On the surface, he was not awed by these so-called holy men who lived in caves and huts, completely detached from the problems of their fellow countrymen. But there was one article on the president of the Divine Life Society of Rishikesh that piqued his interest. It described him as a dynamic, intelligent, and educated swami dedicated to the spiritual upliftment of his countrymen. Balan's recent thoughts on the meaning of life, made him briefly wonder if this holy man really did have the answers he was looking for, but then he thought better of it.

The philosophical wanderings of Balan's mind were quickly checked by the practical realities of life. Eager to get on with a career and gain success in the world, he left Baroda as soon as he felt strong enough and returned to Lucknow University, where he took several courses in journalism and completed his Masters in English Literature with Honors.

By the end of 1945, he had started to write for *The National Herald,* a popular Indian newspaper, on subjects ranging from history and culture to social and political issues. Articles such as, "Honor to Released INA Men," "In Praise of the Postman," and "The Mochi — Symbol of Craftsmanship," quickly gained him a reputation as a controversial character, willing to speak out against anyone, even the news media. In 1947 he began a new series of articles for *The Commonweal* under another pseudonym, Mr. Tramp. The themes continued to center on the subject of social and economic justice for a free India, and he remained sensitive to the plight of the poor and underprivileged.

Balan might simply have continued on this path, and remained a footnote in history, but the articles in *My Magazine* on the lives of saints in the Himalayas continued to trigger peaceful memories of long forgotten days — when he had bounced on the knees of various holy men who had visited his childhood home — when he had slept well after doing his japa.

In his journalistic days, Balan was lean and tall, with his hair oiled and combed perfectly in place. He was a zealous follower of fashion, and the homespun cotton of his student activist days had given way to the British-made sharkskin suits. He was an up-and-coming journalist, with an extroverted personality, and a skill on the tennis courts that was impressive. Not surprisingly, one day he found himself invited to a grand ball in one of the Delhi palaces, where the guest list included top dignitaries of government and business magnates. At this point, it is worth noting that, up until now, Balan was a fervent advocate of economic growth as the obvious answer to an ailing humanity. But on that fateful evening, he observed firsthand the lives of the rich and famous, and almost instantaneously, the "good life" that had seemed so grand turned into a house of cards. The experience left an indelible imprint in his mind.

Balan describes the impact of the grand ball:

> A roaring welter of unnatural values! Impossible behaviors! Sick and suffering was this generation of hollow, lifeless creatures in the hustle and bustle within those stuffy palace walls. In their studied smiles were dormant tears; in their insincere, made-to-order laughter were sighs of voiceless, deep regrets. Their heartless love concealed stormy hatreds, grudging sympathies, and poisonous rivalries. Each suffered and contributed lavishly to the suffering of others.
>
> This was sufficient for Mr. Balakrishnan Menon. At that ball, he saw what a godless animal life could be, at what most considered to be the best. He decided on the very first day of gate-crashing into this "Palace of Life" to quit it for good.

And henceforward, the spiritual life would again come sharply into focus, as Balan mustered all his courage, determination, and intelligence to start on a new course of action in pursuit of a true and more lasting happiness.

For three years, Balan pursued a life of strict spiritual practices, while remaining in the mainstream of journalistic life. He moved in with an uncle, V. K. Govinda Menon and his son B. Gopinath, who had both come to Delhi for an extended stay to transact some business. Over the next several months, Balan pored over books hoping for some insight to dispel his doubts about life. He studied philosophy, mainly European thought, but it gave little consolation. He read books written by and about great saints, until one day

Uncle Govinda informed his inquiring nephew, "I know a Ramana Maharshi … ."

Earlier, in the summer of 1936, Balan had had a darśana of this great saint. He was traveling on the Southern Railroad — to no destination in particular, and with no schedule. He had been offered a student pass for a nominal fee, so he had just taken off. As the train passed through a desert area in Tamil Nadu, a barren, red mountain loomed in the distance. The people in the coach jumped up and ran to one side of the train to look in the direction of the mountain. When Balan inquired about the fuss, he was told of the famous Arunachala Hill, mentioned in the Purāṇas as the center of the universe. He was also informed that a great sage now lived at its base. Intrigued by all this enthusiasm, Balan jumped out of the train to investigate:

> I made my way up to a large thatched hut and sat down there to await whatever it was that everyone else was awaiting. When my eyes adjusted to the dim light, I discerned the form of a human body stretched out with his feet in my direction. My eyes began to slowly scan the body, starting at the feet, part by part — his legs, his hips (he wore only a simple loin cloth), his chest, his arms. He had one forearm up and was resting his head on that hand. As my eyes traveled they finally reached his face, then the area of his eyes. They were closed; he seemed to be sleeping. But just at that moment, my eyes focused on his eyes; his eyes popped open and he looked straight into mine. I knew, in that one moment, with that one look, that he knew everything about me, even things I did not know myself. I sat there transfixed as if seeing my whole life go up in a wave. Then he quietly closed his eyes again. I continued to sit there for a short time; I really don't know how long. When I was again aware of my body and surroundings, I forced myself to get up, wondering just what had happened to me.

> I shook my head to clear my thinking — *Nothing has happened to me, I rationalized. This man is a hypnotist.*

And as they say, the rest is history. Recalling this memory with his uncle, Balan reasoned this was the right time for him to make his move. "I'm going to the Himalayas to see what those holy men are really up to," he informed Uncle Govinda. "I'm going to get the inside story!"

[illegible]DAY, DECEMBER 20, 1946. NATIONAL HERALD

The Mochi, Symbol of Craftsmanship

(By P.B.K. Menon)

[illegible] curfew is only up to 6 a. m. [illegible] even two hours later, but for [illegible] few frightened and panicky [illegible]-by, the entire city looks de-[illegible]ed. These few, mostly mill-[illegible] and coolies, soon pass, and [illegible] streets in the 'disturbed areas' [illegible] again retire into their omi-[illegible] silence.

[illegible] the da[illegible] grows, first the police [illegible] then the citizens start flocking [illegible] the bazar streets. In the grim [illegible]mercial strife by noon their [illegible] get drowned.

[illegible] nine you come out of your [illegible]. On the wayside you see [illegible] frail creature sitting under the [illegible]ltering shadow of a straggling [illegible] the very symbol of Crafts-[illegible]ship. He is, squatting on the [illegible]path, bent double, with his [illegible] hanging low over his work, [illegible] his naked knee rising far above [illegible] Propped up thus, this weather-[illegible]n, dark, dear thing sits all day [illegible] at that very spot. Around [illegible] are scattered a few crumbled [illegible]her pieces, footweare of vari-[illegible] types many years ago. A few [illegible] in a castaway tin, a crude [illegible]mer, some yards of thread and [illegible] needle, a dirty bag containing God knows what—these are all the [illegible] be b[illegible]. This is our hero, the [illegible], honest and silent, modest and cheapest.

All mochis of the last generation are alike. They never attract at-[illegible] nor do they get attracted

free for an old and suffering, wrinkled and neglected way-side beggar; and makes it good from a rich Babu. Even in this policy of careful discrimination he is always Just. Neither the rich nor the poor could ever complain seriously at his rates.

• • •

If only the so-called modern industrial nations, bewildered and lost in their own progress, were to copy his system!! Then these reposted wars for world markets, this terrible curse on the world threatening man and man-made things, could so easily be averted! Progress conceived and set in motion by man's own intellect, has by slow degrees acquired such a devastating momentum that today it threatens him with total atomic annihilation.

Mothers burst out in agony at the

palmy days of a fast disappearing system in business based on honesty, hard work, patience, discrimination and tolerance. Today uncontrolled industrialization and the consequent ever growing out-put has set the producing countries in a vicious race for market. They are furious in their impatient lust for gains. Savagely they jump at each others' throat. Killing and burning, they shamelessly leave the world empty and poor. The winner, himself half dead, in the end CAN claim all the markets....... but, all the same, putrifying corpses and mutilated trunks can have no need for his finished products!!

Every action of a mochi bears a message for the world. Bent double at his work, he allows all the daily worries of life to pass over him. At the rest of the foolish folk, who suffer themselves away in a hell prepared for them by themselves, he with folded-feet, indulgently smiles. He has no sign board of his own. If he were to have one, the most appropriate would be *A Dirty Shoe Gripped Tight Within Folded Feet!!!*

This crest would then represent not only his trade, but also his philosophic contempt for the modern world rotting with its own false sense of values......its meaningless strifes, and its ridiculous prejudices.

As he deftly wields his blunt

The Mochi, Symbol of Craftsmanship, December 20, 1946

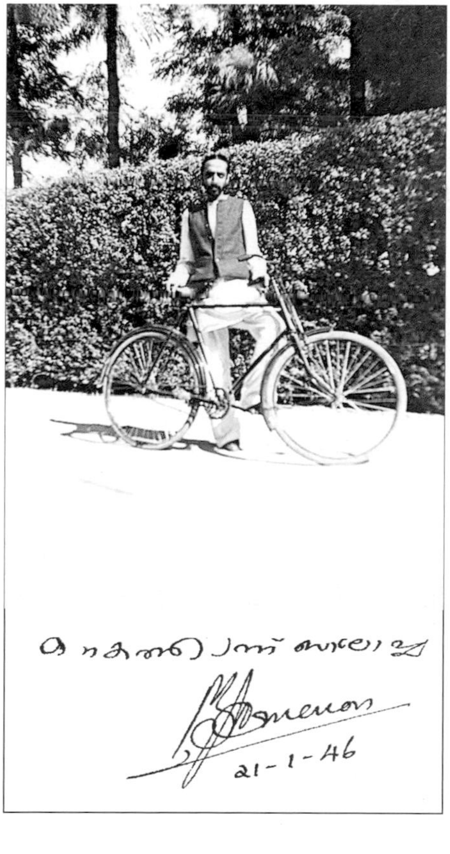

Clockwise from above:
The well-dressed Balan, with his hair oiled and combed perfectly in place, 1945
Balan as a journalist in Delhi, February 6, 1946
Balan as a journalist in Delhi after the impact of the grand ball, January 21, 1946
In Praise of the Postman, March 10, 1946

INDIAN VIGNETTES

IN PRAISE OF THE POSTMAN

It is a strange truth. All things in this world that serve Man, according to the degree of their usefulness, get injured, broken and destroyed, but in their very smothering they serve the best. The postmen, in serving society with soulful devotion, are the living prophets of our age.

From tomorrow onwards, they would have struck work had it not been for the wiser among the authorities thinking better of it. Now the threat is no more. But the havoc that it could have created had they struck work is a measure of their usefulness. The entire society would have come to a stand-still; the springs of affection and love would have got choked; even the nearest village would have been rendered miles away. In short we should have been forced to realise that a postman is

"Messenger of sympathy and love,
Servant of parted friends,
Consoler of the lonely,
Bond of scattered family,
Enlarger of common Life"

There can be but a rare few among us now who do not feel the relief that the proposed strike is called off. I for one dread to live in a society sans postmen.

From the moment a dak reaches the post-office till the arrival of the next, postmen are busy sorting, carrying, enquiring and distributing the innumerable

tenderness. In his last lingering scrutiny of the address before he leaves each cover at the door, he seems almost to hesitate to part with it.

The postman is supremely impartial and completely impersonal. Like destiny he deals equal-

today an accomplished artist. With callous indifference, copied directly from the Civilisation around him, he brings hopes, blessings and compliments to one, curses, distress and sorrows to another. It is not his habit to compliment or to condole. He is a product of our ill-conceived Progress: beneficial and a thousand times evolved from his messenger days, and yet, pitiless and ugly, empty and soulless.

Whatever be the nature of the message he is delivering, the postman bears a habitual well-poised outlook on life and a face beaming serene in his immutable nonchalance. Professionally he refuses to look beyond the address.

Gopal is my postman. In the course of his duties he has been bringing consolation in my loneliness, hope into my dark despair. Yet never has Gopal, even for once, paused to watch my gratification and smile. When it is a money-order he counts the amount more than once, examines my signature, hands over the 'notes' and contrives to linger round in eloquent hesitation, watching my face for some [illegible] and charity on my [illegible]. Either he salaams in passive gratitude and walks off or he struts out with the quick gait of an outraged

VII

A Saint for All Seasons

In every age, there are a handful of winners who reach the finish line. But only one amongst them can be called "first" among equals. Few will disagree with putting Swami Sivananda first.

From posh drawing rooms to remote villages, Swami Sivananda of Rishikesh has gained unprecedented glory, and any conversation or reading material on saints and sages of India is only complete with the mention of his name.

They say that he was an exemplary karma yogī, who blended wisdom with action, service with love, and brought true meaning to the yoga of selfless action.

In his lifetime he wrote 296 books on a variety of subjects: Vedānta, metaphysics, yoga, western philosophy, eschatology, fine arts, education, mythology, health, and anthology. His works reflect his insight to be on such an immeasurably higher plane, that at his bidding spirituality seems at once to have stepped out of closed doors and into the open.

His ideology was simple — it condensed the entire gamut of spiritual teachings into four small words: *Serve, Love, Meditate, Realize!*

He had endless energy and enthusiasm for reaching out to diverse sections in society — be it running a free hospital for the poor, giving spiritual discourses to the educated, or teaching yogāsanās to ashramites. This earned him widespread appeal, and he truly is a saint for all seasons, and properly belongs high on a list of the World's Most Loved Persons.

Swami Sivananda sparked a unique devotion from spiritual seekers in the last century. Most of them can trace their lineage to him one way or the other — as their Guru or Parama Guru.

He is an inspiration to all would-be preachers. Several of his direct disciples gained world-repute as Masters of their time, and between them they dominated the world's spiritual arena in the second half of the twentieth century. Ten went on to create new organizations, multiplying the greatness of their Guru a hundredfold.

In the face of such a distinguished resume, Balan didn't stand a chance. In the summer of 1947, he arrived in Rishikesh, by the banks of the Gaṅgā, and confidently made the one-mile hike to the Divine Life Society, the ashram of this legendary saint. Before leaving, he had boasted to his friends, "I am going to find out how these holy men are keeping up the bluff. I am prepared to expose the whole racket!" In truth, Balan was searching for something more than he was willing to admit. Was it possible for a man to find peace and tranquility? He was not even sure what a "spiritual life" meant, but since denial was no longer possible, he was determined to find out.

The desire for Truth is a decisive point in the spiritual life of man. The moment he starts to question the pursuits he has been following, he becomes a seeker. Once that desire arises, it is then a natural progression to the final destination. Just as rainwater flows through the river and merges into the sea from where it originated; in the same way, the jīva (individual ego), that has sprung from the supreme Self, rests only when it reaches its Source. Events were about to catapult out of Balan's control. By going to the mountains in search of Truth — any truth — he had effectively about-turned his future from a "dedicated loafer" to a sincere seeker.

On reaching the grounds of the ashram, Balan eagerly went about introducing himself to the Master's disciples. He informed them that he had come to meet an authentic sage in person. He was warmly received, and arrangements were made for him to stay in a guest hostel. He left his luggage in a small sparsely furnished room and returned to join a group of residents sitting under the shade of a mango tree. Around noon, Swami Sivananda approached the group from the rear. Everybody arose, including Balan. He had recognized the saint from a photograph in one of the magazines. After the customary introduction, Swami Sivananda asked him a few personal questions. Balan explained that he was a journalist from Delhi who had come to see the land of the holy sages. He added that he wanted to do a story on the area, and since he had read some of Swamiji's works, he had specifically come to the ashram to interview him.

"How long will you be staying?" asked Swami Sivananda.

"I'll probably be able to get everything I need in a day or two," replied Balan.

"What's your hurry!" exclaimed Swamiji. "It's a long journey from Delhi. You should take your time and satisfy yourself. Stay at least a few days. Anyway, you are welcome to stay as long as you like."

Balan was astonished to observe that Swami Sivananda was no hermit sitting in the retirement of meditation. He was busy seven days a week, without holidays or vacation. His daily routine started at 4:00 A.M. with a bath in the cold waters of the Gaṅgā, which was followed by a session on meditation with disciples. During the day, he attended to a huge stack of correspondence received from spiritual seekers around the world, wrote articles and books on religious subjects, received visitors, and administered the running of the hospital. He would sit in the main hall each evening with disciples and guests to answer questions and clear doubts. Then he would conduct a service of chanting scriptures and singing bhajans, after which there was always a discourse on a spiritual text. In spite of such a busy schedule, he found time to take tea to a visiting swami, or carry fruit or sweets to patients in the hospital. He was the humblest of men — there seemed no job too small for him, and no day too short to complete his work. Swami Sivananda exuded a dynamic peace through all his activities, and Balan found himself drawn to this enlightened saint. He extended his stay by a few days — then a few more — and then some more.

One month passed. It seems Balan had quickly become a favorite with Swamiji — at least, that was the general opinion in Ananda Kutir. In turn, Swami Sivananda would nudge him saying, "God has blessed you with such intelligence. Why don't you use it? Analyze and see that worldly life is only misery. Observe. Think about the life you live down in the plains. Then draw your own conclusion!"

During Balan's initial stay at Ananda Kutir, one of the events being planned was a big celebration to mark the sixtieth birth year of Swami Sivananda on September 8, 1947. To commemorate this occasion, it was decided to bring out a souvenir book. This book would include articles on Swamiji's life and work as well as various spiritual subjects. Disciples and devotees would write the material, but no one seemed qualified to edit the book. Mr. Dar Rao, who was Swami Sivananda's secretary at the time, suggested Balan take on the arduous task of editing.

Balan began work on the souvenir. He ruthlessly cut the articles, some written by important persons. When the book was complete, Swami Sivananda felt that the original writers might be offended. But Balan stood his ground. He assured him, that although a newcomer

Below:
Swami Sivananda (1887–1963) by the banks of the Gaṅgā, Rishikesh

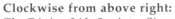

Clockwise from above right:
The Divine Life Society, Sivananda Ashram, Rishikesh, 1949
Balan with Swami Sivananda, Sivananda Ashram, Rishikesh, 1947
Balan in Sivananda Ashram, Rishikesh, 1948
Balan in Sivananda Ashram, Rishikesh, 1948
Balan in Rishikesh, 1947

to the ashram, he had nevertheless maintained the essence of the articles. In fact, the message was even clearer now that he had removed the extraneous material! So, the articles were printed as edited by Balan.

A few days later, Balan's self-image was given a reality check. Out of the blue, Swami Sivananda called him during an evening satsaṅga and asked him to give a talk to the ashramites.

"Me?" inquired Balan. "What will I talk about? I don't know this spiritual subject like you, or some of the others. Isn't that why I'm here?"

"So talk on anything, something you do know about — your trip to Rishikesh!" suggested Swami Sivananda.

"Well ... I came up from Delhi ..." His mind flashed to the villages, the wide plains of wheat racing by the train window. But there was nothing special about that! What was he going to say?

It was one of those rare occasions when Balan was at a loss for words. At last, Swami Sivananda interrupted the silence. "It's okay ... you'll get another chance," he said. The satsaṅga was concluded with the chanting of *Om Namaḥ Śivāya*. As Balan made his way out of the hall, Swami Sivananda stopped him and commented, "What is this, an M.A. and a successful journalist unable to give a short impromptu discourse? You had better prepare yourself for tomorrow evening's satsaṅga as I am sure to call on you again." Then he started to walk towards his cottage, but turned back to add, "Say, why don't you take the theme of 'śreyas' and 'preyas' as your first topic."

The talk on the path of the morally good (śreyas) versus the path of the sensually pleasant (preyas) would not qualify as his most brilliant discourse, but with it Swami Sivananda had launched Balakrishnan Menon on a life of giving spiritual talks. In due course, he would be immortalized as one of the most compelling orators in history to shake the world out of its spiritual slumber — a remarkable transformation for a man fumbling for words on his first day on a spiritual subject.

Over the next several months, Swami Sivananda continued to call on Balan to give short talks on various spiritual topics. Thereafter, Balan would spend a portion of each day studying and reviewing a particular topic, and then he would carefully assimilate his thoughts into a clear, succinct presentation. One of the senior disciples, Swami Maunananda, would go over his notes to clarify or elaborate on some of the points. To the swami's surprise, Balan often did not use his suggestions. He felt that it was better to use the ideas of his own reflections and contemplations, rather than blindly imitate someone else's words.

One evening, the performance of one short drama on the life of Gautama Buddha brought more than its share of joy and wisdom in the ashram. The story to be enacted was of a distraught mother who comes to the Buddha holding a dead child in her arms. Weeping over her loss, she implores the Great One to give life to her only son. In his wisdom, the Buddha instructs her to go out into the village — inquire in each house, and bring back a mustard seed from any household that had escaped the tragedy of death. If she brought back even one mustard seed, he would surely give life back to the child. The woman leaves for her investigation but does not return, since she never finds a house where death had not visited.

Balan was selected to play the role of the distraught mother. With a scarf draped around his head and a cloth-bundle baby cuddled in his arms, he made such a caricature of the dejected mother, and elaborated such a display of weeping and wailing, that the whole audience exploded into laughter. Swami Sivananda was delighted with the performance. "The best I've seen," he declared, wiping away tears from his eyes. Some days later, when a special guest had come to the ashram, he asked for a repeat performance with Balan in the same role. Once again, he roared with laughter until tears flowed from his eyes. "I have derived the greatest joy from this repeat performance," he announced.

And every so often, Swami Sivananda would continue to say to Balan, "God blessed you with such intelligence, why don't you use it for Him? You can join us — become a swami like us! Keep this idea in mind, even when you continue with your life in the world."

Over the next year, Balan did shuttle between Delhi and Rishikesh, spending a few months in the ashram each time he came. Whenever he returned to Delhi, he would carry a bundle of books written by Swami Sivananda, so he could continue with his studies. Many were verse-by-verse commentaries written on various scriptures of Vedānta.

One of the reasons he would regularly visit Delhi was to spend time with his college friend, Shroff, who was suffering from a terminal illness. After several years of intense pain, Shroff passed away with Balan near him. The elder Mr. Shroff was quite old, and since Balan was like a second son to him, he requested the boy to immerse his son's ashes in the Gaṅgā.

The twenty-four hour train-ride to Rishikesh, with the sole remains of his once vibrant friend, were some of the longest hours of Balan's life. He tried to pass the time by reading, but his attention kept going back to the urn near him. He had spent many happy hours with Shroff in a train compartment just like this one — those were happy, carefree hours, coming down to Delhi from Lucknow University to spend the holidays with Shroff's family. A recurring thought kept going through his mind:

> The man who is usually with me is now in that small basket — a few bones and ashes are all that remain. Flesh and life are gone. Flesh and life are gone ...

Although Balan continued with his journalistic career in Delhi, his writings now included reviews of spiritual books. The review on "The Streamers of Light from the New World," published in Los Angeles, California, deserves special mention, since it clearly illustrates his views on a world spiritual renaissance.

> Altogether, "Streamers of Light" is an exceptionally decent volume, providing a vivid picture of the author's vision of a new, ideal world: a new race characterized by width of tolerance, height of vision, and depth of insight, and of an enduring peace passed from generation to generation. To work out the dream, we will have to train a generation to be perfect, a generation who are masters of themselves. In this, I find no impossibility; perhaps, some millenniums will be necessary to achieve this degree of perfection — but the goal is worth the attempt and the ultimate achievement worth the waiting.

The words read like a prophecy of events to come a decade down destiny's road. No doubt such ideals and confidence were strengthened by his encounter with a master of Swami Sivananda's exalted spiritual stature. In him, Balan could envision a concrete example that such actual self-perfection was indeed possible.

By the spring of 1948, for all practical purposes, Balan had taken up permanent residence at Ananda Kutir. From here, he continued with his journalistic career by mailing his articles to Delhi. At this time, another of his cousins, Bhaskar Menon, came to the ashram and was initiated into sannyāsa by Swami Sivananda. Bhaskar Menon, now Swami Jnanananda, had a great desire to go on a pilgrimage to the Himalayas and invited Balan to join him.

On April 24, 1948, just days before Balan's thirty-second birthday, the two cousins and Ramesh Gautam (a householder devotee of Swami Sivananda's) and a local young man (who carried the necessary cooking utensils, supplies, and so forth) left for a grand pilgrimage to the Char Dham, the four great Himalayan temples in Yamnotri, Gangotri, Kedarnath, and Badrinath. They reached their first destination, Yamnotri, after nine days of relentless climbing, traveling 120 kilometers northwest of Rishikesh along the footpaths that skirt the Yamunā river.

Balan took great delight in the breathtaking beauty of his surroundings. The Himalayas are considered to be the most spectacular mountain ranges on the planet. They are often referred to as the "abode of the gods" or the "roof of the world." These majestic snow-capped mountains, leaping rivers, and flower-decked plateaus have inspired awe and devotion from mankind for centuries. And for Balan, the coming months would leave their mark on him, made more glorious by the blessings of the many extraordinary saints he would encounter during his journey.

En route to Gangotri, the group passed through Uttarkashi, the dwelling place of Swami Tapovanam. He was reputed to be amongst the wisest of sages in the Himalayas — a master of scripture, as well as austerity. In the following year Balan would become his student. But lest our story stray ahead of itself, we will only outline Balan's first meeting with Swami Tapovanam at this point.

On reaching Uttarkashi the three pilgrims immediately sought out this renowned master, and consequently spent the evening in satsaṅga with him. It seems that Swami Tapovanam knew of Balan through his articles published in *The National Herald*. However, Balan never suspected that Swami Tapovanam might have heard of the newspaper, let alone read English. This fact only became known to him several years later, when an Australian devotee passed by Tapovan

Clockwise from above:
Balan ready for the Himalayan Char Dham yatra, 1948
Balan enacts the role of a weeping mother in a play with Swami Chidananda, Sivananda Ashram
During morning class with Swami Sivananda, Rishikesh, May 20, 1949
Balan before sannyāsa, Sivananda Ashram, Rishikesh

Kutir, and, to Balan's complete surprise, Swami Tapovanam had conversed with the man in perfect English. Anyhow, the next morning, when Balan returned to bid the sage farewell, Swami Tapovanam advised him, "During the entire journey, keep a continuous Brahman-vicāra (reflection on Truth) — just as when a person is walking, he remembers a loved one who is far away."

As the pilgrims trekked farther towards Gangotri, they met Sri Phalahari Baba, a natural renunciate who dressed only in a loin cloth and spent his days in continual meditation and maunam (silence). Balan and his party approached him for his blessings. He was observing a one-month fast and appeared somewhat weak to them, so they asked after his health, to which Sri Phalahari Baba replied by writing in the sand, "It is the nature of all flesh to be now healthy, now sick, now fat, now lean. We are not to be concerned by transformations of the body, for we are the indestructible supreme Spirit."

Nearby, they also visited the slightly larger hut (one was able to stand up straight in it) of Sri Raghunath Das. After asking the three seekers where they came from, Sri Raghunath Das sat facing them in total silence for the rest of their duration in his presence. Balan concluded that if he had not understood the meaning of this silence, there must be something wrong with his understanding.

The next morning, the group went to meet Sri Krishnashram, a naked ascetic. He also remained silent when they sat in his presence. Before leaving, Balan asked him for a message, to which the ascetic wrote:

> Drink the true pure Gaṅgā water, not this river water. Visit the inner source. The guide to lead you is in you. You must only develop faith and love. There is no God beyond, nor beside you. God's grace is really your own efforts.

> Karma Yoga is not for renunciates. Writing books, opening schools — these are the duties of a charitable householder. One need not take to the spiritual path for this purpose. Nowadays, everybody writes. But what for? They are only culling ideas from old books and expressing them in their own language. This is a sheer waste.
>
> Write when new experiences and truths gurgle forth from the inner consciousness. Ādi Śaṅkara wrote and he was justified. In such instances, the author is only an instrument. It means the time has come for those particular ideas to be given to this generation. Accept renunciation and end all outer activities. Delve within and reach the inner source. Drink the true Gaṅgā water.

By the end of May, the travelers had begun the beautiful but treacherous 105-mile trek from Kedarnath to Badrinath, the last holy shrine on their pilgrimage. On a typical day, they would get up at 3:00 A.M. and immediately set out on the trail, covering approximately fifteen miles each day. Balan's simple sandals had given out, and the absence of anything resembling a shoe store forced him to continue the journey barefoot. Yet, in the peaceful moments of twilight, when the sun disappeared behind the mountains, leaving the valley in a cool shadow, he would sit in meditation for hours on end. The daily reports in his journal best describe the joy he felt during these months:

> Wonderful! No words to describe the inner peace I enjoyed, the concentration I achieved, the entire world forgotten. Forgotten are all worldly contacts, for I have come to live in myself. For the first time, I tasted a bliss in meditation, which I know is but an iota of what one can have from deep, long, steady, and powerful meditation. My only prayer to my divine Guru and to the divine Lord is that by their grace I may never fall and that I may drink deeper at the fountain of the Eternal Divine Nectar.

Once the group reached Badrinath, Balan decided to stay behind an extra month, while the rest of his group returned to Rishikesh. One day, he hiked to the cave of an aged sādhu. The sādhu was in poor health and had an ulcerous sore on his leg. Balan was horrified to see that there were maggots on his wound. Just at that moment, one of the maggots fell off. The sādhu promptly picked up the creature and placed it back on his leg. "There, my son," he said to the maggot. Then he looked straight into Balan's eyes, and said to him, "Don't you know that it is all only matter — matter feeding matter."

There is no question that the ethereal beauty of the Himalayas is amplified by the remarkable ascetics that dwell in its land. These enlightened beings live in a state of absolute fullness, with no cravings or interference from worldly things. Their presence alone speaks volumes — and their words are without frills and fancy — without the trappings of passing unrealities. With every fiber of their being, they unequivocally echo the ultimate teachings of all scriptures: *That Thou Art* — It is YOU — the infinite Self.

It was during these forty days spent alone in Badrinath that Balan recognized the absolute necessity for his next course of action. It became absolutely clear to him that the death of the ego was the only way of awakening to the infinite Self. He knew that he could no longer get by with half measures, and the time for his own renunciation ceremony had come. When he returned to Ananda Kutir in late August, Swami Sivananda seemed to know it, too, for he told Balan to write to his father and ask for his permission to become a sannyāsī.

Sannyāsa is the renunciation of the ego and desires for the world. In the literal sense, when an individual takes sannyāsa, he performs his

his last rites in the world as an individual. From a spiritual standpoint, true sannyāsa implies Self-knowledge and an awakening to the Knowledge that the world is an illusion.

The elder Mr. Menon was quite shocked at this turnaround of events, and although he was not overjoyed at the prospect of his son giving up a successful career, and possibly a good wife and some dear children in the near future, he nevertheless gave his permission. "This boy always does exactly what he wants. It is useless for me to stand in the way!" he informed the stunned family members. But in his reply to Balan, he wrote, "You must have met a very great saint indeed to have influenced you so. Go ahead, I give my permission."

On the auspicious day of Śivarātrī, February 25, 1949, Balakrishnan Menon was initiated into the holy order of sannyāsa by Swami Sivananda. He plunged three times into the chilly waters of the Gaṅgā, chanting the vows of renunciation with each immersion. His past life washed away like the wisps of a faded dream, he emerged the epiphany of a man reborn.

There is something luminous that surrounds the renunciation of a spiritual seeker. And on that auspicious Śivarātrī day, for one moment in time, all opposites were reconciled, all tensions resolved; that luminous moment was Swami Chinmayananda.

I WAS BORN ON THAT ŚIVARĀTRĪ DAY,

THE PAST OF THIS BODY AND MIND

HAS NOTHING TO DO WITH ME.

| SWAMI CHINMAYANANDA |

Right:
Swami Sivananda with the new sannyāsis after dīkṣā, Śivarātrī Day, February 25, 1949 (Swamiji third from right)
Below:
Swami Chinmayananda, soon after sannyāsa, Rishikesh, 1949

Center (left to right)**:** Swami Sashwatananda, Swami Chinmayananda, Swami Krishnananda, Swami Chidananda, Swami Sivananda, Swami Raghavananda, Swami Harisharanananda, February 25, 1949
Right:
Swamiji seated next to Swami Sivananda in the forest, Rishikesh, 1949

Clockwise from above:
At the railway station during Śrī Sivananda Yatra from Rishikesh to Rameshwaram
Swamiji with Swami Jnanananda (previously Bhaskar Menon)
Studying in the Forest Vedānta Academy, Sivananda Ashram, Rishikesh
Swamiji sitting with fellow disciples, Forest Vedānta Academy, Sivananda Ashram

▸ **Facing page above:**
Swami Chinmayananda's sannyāsa dīkṣā announcement, 1949
Below:
Swami Sivananda with Swami Chinmayananda and other disciples under a peepal tree, Sivananda Ashram, May 18, 1949

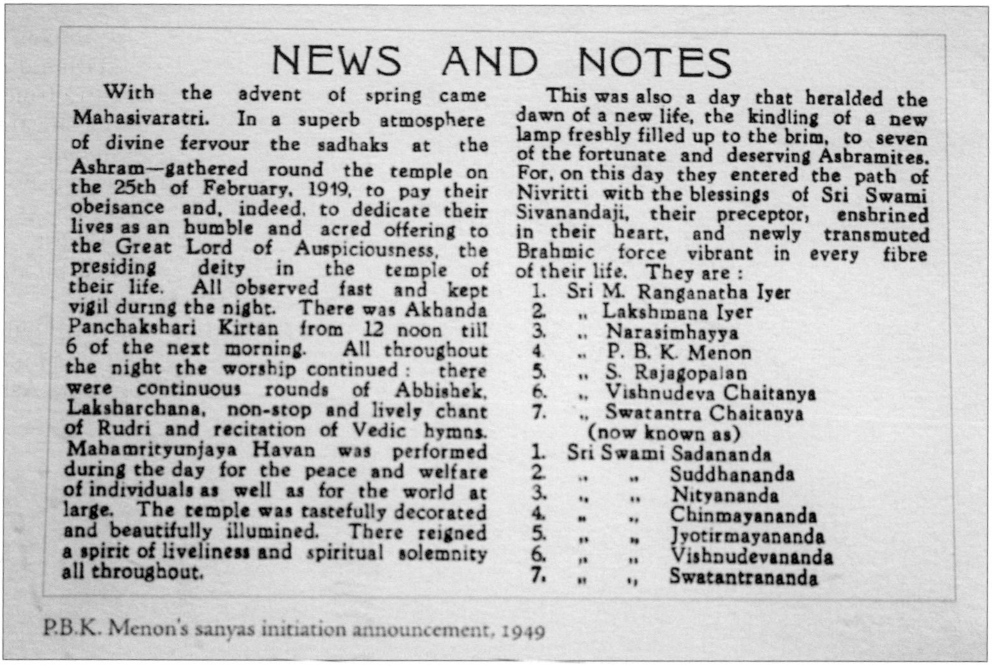

NEWS AND NOTES

With the advent of spring came Mahasivaratri. In a superb atmosphere of divine fervour the sadhaks at the Ashram—gathered round the temple on the 25th of February, 1919, to pay their obeisance and, indeed, to dedicate their lives as an humble and acred offering to the Great Lord of Auspiciousness, the presiding deity in the temple of their life. All observed fast and kept vigil during the night. There was Akhanda Panchakshari Kirtan from 12 noon till 6 of the next morning. All throughout the night the worship continued: there were continuous rounds of Abhishek, Laksharchana, non-stop and lively chant of Rudri and recitation of Vedic hymns. Mahamrityunjaya Havan was performed during the day for the peace and welfare of individuals as well as for the world at large. The temple was tastefully decorated and beautifully illumined. There reigned a spirit of liveliness and spiritual solemnity all throughout.

This was also a day that heralded the dawn of a new life, the kindling of a new lamp freshly filled up to the brim, to seven of the fortunate and deserving Ashramites. For, on this day they entered the path of Nivritti with the blessings of Sri Swami Sivanandaji, their preceptor, enshrined in their heart, and newly transmuted Brahmic force vibrant in every fibre of their life. They are:

1. Sri M. Ranganatha Iyer
2. „ Lakshmana Iyer
3. „ Narasimhayya
4. „ P. B. K. Menon
5. „ S. Rajagopalan
6. „ Vishnudeva Chaitanya
7. „ Swatantra Chaitanya

(now known as)

1. Sri Swami Sadananda
2. „ „ Suddhananda
3. „ „ Nityananda
4. „ „ Chinmayananda
5. „ „ Jyotirmayananda
6. „ „ Vishnudevananda
7. „ „ Swatantrananda

P.B.K. Menon's sanyas initiation announcement, 1949

VIII

The Glory of the Himalayas

He's history's few, God's own ascetic, a beacon of knowledge, and a Himalayan jewel — all rolled into one. Beyond that, he is known to only those who have studied scripture in the last century. Even to them, Swami Tapovanam is a symbol of complete abidance in Truth, the light that never descended — philosophically, literally, and figuratively.

Swami Tapovanam was a recluse. He lived in a one-room mud hut, with no belongings, no comforts, and no involvement whatsoever with the world. He encouraged no students, nor supplied them with anything. He was a strict disciplinarian who stayed in severe climates. Each day, he ate one meal (a watery lentil soup and roṭī) and took two baths in the freezing Gaṅgā. In all, thirty-five or so students came with enthusiasm at one point or another to study under him. They all ran away. Save one.

He was also, of course, an incredible teacher of Vedānta. It might have been impossible to live under the same exacting conditions, but it was equally impossible to resist his brilliance, outside and within. His teachings came from the innermost depths of his illumined being, and, as such, they were the quintessence of pure, unalloyed Self-awareness.

Swami Tapovanam represents the ideal, even amongst saints. He is one of those rare sages who personifies the Absolute in every sense of the word — eternal and infinite — radiant and resplendent, dazzling with the effulgence of a million suns. Swami Sivananda called him "Himavat Vibhūti," meaning "the glory of the Himalayas"; and in the world of sages and ascetics, Swami Tapovanam is acknowledged as one of the four great enlightened masters of Vedānta to live in those mountains during the time, along with Swami Vishnudevananda, Brahmaprakasa Udasina, and Devagiri Swami.

SWAMI TAPOVANAM WAS AN INSTITUTION UNCAUSED,
AND HE, TOO, CAUSED NO CAUSE.
HE CAME FROM NOWHERE, EXISTED EVERYWHERE,
AND ULTIMATELY WENT TO BE EVERYWHERE.

| SWAMI CHINMAYANANDA |

But first, back in Ananda Kutir, Balan had been given the new name Swami Chinmayananda. "Chinmayananda" is a compound word of three units — cit-maya-ānanda (consciousness–full of–bliss) — meaning, "one who revels in bliss which is full of pure consciousness." Very often, the name given to a sannyāsī indicates the goal he is seeking, or it might represent a predominant quality in his character (*yathā nāma, tathā guṇa* — as the name, so the qualities). It was in Swamiji's (as we will now call Swami Chinmayananda) nature to question everything, to be intellectually satisfied, and to accept nothing simply on faith. At the same time, he had the courage to accept the truth once it was revealed to him. He had a remarkable ability to be honest with himself, and to be uncompromising in his quest for truth. His pursuit of Knowledge is the highlight through his entire life, and it ultimately culminated in the realization of the absolute Truth.

As a result, it was only natural that Swamiji would want a thorough grasp of scripture, that is to say, a word-by-word analysis of their meaning rather than a mechanical recitation of something he did not understand. Swami Sivananda was well aware of Swamiji's disposition and directed him accordingly. "You want to master the scriptures?" he said to Swamiji one day. "Go to Swami Tapovanam, the great teacher from Kerala, your own home state."

Swami Tapovanam was originally from the state of Kerala. But his deep love for the sights and sounds of nature had brought him to the Himalayas, where he became renowned as a scholar of scripture, a sage of extraordinary spiritual experiences, and an intuitive poet. "As he roamed the Himalayan peaks, his pen was constantly scribbling down the beauties he discovered and the thoughts passing through his sacred bosom," wrote Swami Chinmayananda. However, Swami Tapovanam was most renowned as an authority on the Prasthānatraya, that is, Upaniṣads, *Bhagavad-gītā,* and Brahmasūtras.

During springtime, Swami Tapovanam would come down to Rishikesh and spend a few months in Brahmananda Ashram, on the opposite shore of the Gaṅgā from the Divine Life Society. It is here that Swamiji approached him, and requested the sage to teach him the subtleties of this highest philosophy and clear his doubts on some of the seeming contradictions in scriptures. Swamiji also presented him with a letter and a package sent by Swami Sivananda. "I can teach, but it is you who must understand," replied Swami Tapovanam. "I will be returning to Uttarkashi before the monsoons begin in mid-June. You can follow then and begin classes."

In the summer of 1949, Swamiji set out by foot for the long trek to Uttarkashi. When he reached the tiny village, he found that Swami Tapovanam was not one to provide any room or board for his students. This sage left such details in the capable hands of the Lord! Sure enough, Swami Govindagiri offered accommodation to the new student at Dev Giri Ashram, just down the path from Tapovan Kutir. A local villager, Jagdish, who often served Swami Tapovanam by cleaning and delivering milk, reports the happenings of that day:

> The greatest, most glorious event of my thirty years service to Swami Tapovan Maharaj happened with the arrival of a sweet boy full of ardor, every part of him throbbing to learn Vedānta under the Master. Looking at the frail, tall Swami Chinmayananda, one wondered whether he could stand all the weight of knowledge that his Master was going to unload on him.

But there was no hurrying Swami Tapovanam. "We'll start next month after we go up to Gangotri," he replied in answer to Swamiji's enthusiastic inquiry as to when classes would begin. "You contemplate on what you have already studied. Get those ideas clear before you add on more!"

One sunny day not long after, he called out to his new disciple. "Chinmaya, make a garden for us here, in front of my hut," he said. "Some fresh vegetables would be appreciated by all of us."

"But Swamiji, there's no water supply up here on the hill," replied Chinmaya.

"What! The mighty Gaṅgā is roaring down at the bottom of the hill — and here's a bucket. You can bring plenty of water for a garden."

"Yes, of course," said Chinmaya.

From then on, Swamiji would climb the 100-foot steep path to Tapovan Kutir from the banks of the Gaṅgā, carrying buckets of water for the vegetable garden.

When the warm summer season started, Swami Tapovanam packed his kamaṇḍalu (begging bowl) and an extra cotton robe and left for the colder climate of Gangotri, away from the influx of pilgrims who came to the lower Himalayan ranges in the summer months.

Left:
Swami Tapovanam (1889–1957)
Below:
Swami Tapovanam
and Swami Sivananda

Above:
Swamiji walking with kamaṇḍalu in the Himalayas
Right:
Swamiji resting on his way to Uttarkashi, 1949

Clockwise from above:
Swamiji (right) with Swami Govindagiri (center), Uttarkashi, 1949
The young sannyāsī, Swami Chinmayananda, 1949
Steps to Tapovan Kutir, Uttarkashi, 1949
Studying in Uttarkashi, 1949
Entering his hut in Gangotri, 1949

Swamiji braved the difficulties without complaint because he had an intense desire to study and understand the philosophy of Vedānta. He would have a bath in the icy waters of the Gaṅgā each morning, and although this caused excruciating pain to his body, it also woke him up for the morning class at 6 o'clock like no other exercise could.

ACROBATS AND AUSTERITIES

Fifty years back, Swamiji carried a kamaṇḍalu and wore wooden khaḍau (sandals with a knob between the first and second toe). His hair was tied with a saffron scarf in a knot at the back of his head. His kuṭiyā in Gangotri was dug near Swami Tapovanam's cottage. It was difficult to enter it, since it was dug below ground level, and one had to bend to enter it. I always wondered how a tall person like Swamiji used to go in and out of that entrance for years. It had a low roof, and anyone with a decent height could neither stand straight nor sleep with legs stretched. The roof was thatched, and it had a matching thatched door to keep out the howling cold wind of Gangotri.

Once, I asked Swamiji how he managed with such a tall frame. He answered, "Acrobatics are not allowed for sannyāsīs. For sitting, meditating and relaxing the back, it is sufficient."

Sheela Sharma
Chinmaya Mission Delhi
[She organized Swamiji's first Jnana Yagnas
in Rewa, Allahabad, Kanpur, and Agra]

The classes began in Gangotri. The first text was Pañcadaśī, written by Svāmī Vidyāraṇya, the eleventh Śaṅkarācārya of the Shringeri Matha. Swami Tapovanam would read out one verse of the text, and then explain the word meaning of the Sanskrit, giving the rules of grammar and the equivalent translation in Hindi, as well as the possible misinterpretations. He would follow with a commentary, and perhaps an example to illustrate the meaning. As he spoke, Swamiji would meticulously translate everything into English, because he wanted all his notes to be in the language most familiar to him. Swami Govindagiri remembers those first classes:

> The subject matter of *Pañcadaśī* is so subtle that it takes a brilliant, penetrating mind to comprehend the contents, and grasp the abstruse meanings that lie hidden beneath the words themselves. At that time, I had studied several texts with Swami Tapovanam and had not once dared to question him during class. But not this Chinmaya — he would put so many questions to the Master. He was not willing to move on to the next topic until every doubt on the present subject was removed by the teacher.

Swami Tapovanam often concluded the class by saying, "Remove the conditioning and realize the Self." After contemplating on these words for several days, Swamiji felt compelled to ask a question, "Why not remove the conditioning and explain the pure Brahman? Why do you say that it is the *eye* of the eye without the eye-conditioning?" All of a sudden, Swami Tapovanam said to him, "Chinmaya, get me some water to drink."

Swamiji brought a glass of fresh water and placed it in front of his teacher.

"What is this?" asked Swami Tapovanam.

"Swamiji, this is the water you requested," murmured the disciple.

"But did I ask for a glass?" enquired Swami Tapovanam, "or for water? Take the glass away and bring me the water."

"But Swamiji … how? Without a glass … how?"

"Exactly! Nobody can bring water without a vessel. It is the same with the knowledge of the Truth. We cannot convey the Truth with words, but it can be expressed through the medium of one or the other of its conditionings, in this case words."

By the end of October, Swami Tapovanam returned with Swamiji to Uttarkashi. The discussions continued in such an intense manner that other students were often intimidated to approach the two as they sat in the verandah of Tapovan Kutir. There was no electricity for reading, and Swami Tapovanam discouraged talking among students. If students were seen in the verandah at any time, other than class, he would chide them, "What are you doing here? Don't waste a minute! You go to your own reflection. It's all in you!"

In fact, Swamiji did not waste any precious minutes. Swami Govindagiri recalls, "Chinmaya practiced an intense sādhanā (spiritual discipline) all during his period of study with Swami Tapovanam. I often saw him sitting all night in meditation in a quiet corner of the forest or sometimes on a boulder beside the Gaṅgā."

Every so often, Swamiji would cook the meal received in bhikṣā for everyone (since the bhikṣā received was often uncooked wheat flour and dāl). Swami Tapovanam would give a quizzical look at the questionable nature of the misshaped, thick roṭīs brought to him. One time, he was particularly amused. "See, one never gets to give up tapas (austerities) in these Himalayas. Not with Chinmaya's roṭīs!" Nevertheless, he would always eat them with good humor.

One fascinating incident, which took place in Uttarkashi, involved a plain cotton cloth which was given to Swami Tapovanam as a gift. He had asked Swamiji to make a robe out of it for him. The fabric was dyed with saffron, and carefully cut and stitched by hand. It was then laid out, Indian style, to dry over some bushes. Finally, it was wrapped and presented to Swami Tapovanam. But when he took it out of the wrapping, it had a tear in it.

"Look! You tore it. You were careless when you took it off the shrubs!" he said to Chinmaya.

"No, I was very careful, Swamiji", replied the student. "I don't know how that happened!"

"You were careless. Your attention was not on what you were doing," replied Swami Tapovanam. "And now you are surely lying!"

This was a heavy blow to Swamiji — to be called a liar — especially when he knew he was telling the truth. What's more, whenever Swamiji approached Tapovan Kutir after that, Swami Tapovanam would taunt him, "Liar!" Swamiji could bear it no longer and he made up his mind to leave. Luckily, an older swami pointed out in time to Swamiji that Swami Tapovanam was in fact testing him. So the next time Swami Tapovanam called out "Liar," Swamiji was prepared with an answer.

"Perhaps," he replied to his Guru.

"Oh, so now you see!" said Swami Tapovanam with a chuckle. "This whole creation is a lie, why make a big deal over one little lie!"

Another story which is retold again and again with various versions, since it happened on multiple occasions, is about a box of sweets which would invariably be offered to Swami Tapovanam. If the package of sweets or biscuits came by post, he would direct the postman to set it on the corner of the verandah. Without opening the packet, he would then instruct a student to carry it down the winding path to the Gaṅgā, where it was unceremoniously dumped. Swami Tapovanam did not allow comforts for himself, nor did he sanction any for his students. If anyone even suggested a tiny idea for a nonessential, he would huff, "What do you think we have here, a dharmaśālā!"

On one particular afternoon a box of laḍḍus (Indian fresh sweets favored by many holy men) arrived just as class begun. "Put it inside!" he ordered a student. A few days passed. The students became disturbed. Their minds kept going to the laḍḍus. Why was their Guru allowing the sweets to rot? Did he plan on distributing them? Why had he not already done so? On the fifth day, the attendance in class had abruptly dropped.

"What's happened? Where are the other two?" asked Swami Tapovanam.

"They left," came a timid reply.

"Chinmaya, come here. Now bring that box from my room."

Swamiji followed the order, thinking as he went, *Now he is going to distribute them to us, the ones who stayed!* He promptly took the laḍḍus to his Guru.

"To the Gaṅgā! Throw them out!" ordered Swami Tapovanam. "When you take sannyāsa you are supposed to have control over your senses. Just look at the quality of your minds, agitated over a paltry box of sweets. I saw the distractions and knew what was going on, and I don't want to encourage it. We're here to study the Upaniṣads, not to eat laḍḍus!"

Swamiji was enthralled with the *Māṇḍūkya Upaniṣad* and its *Kārikā.* He enjoyed the sureness and completeness with which the transcendental Knowledge had been expounded in this text. As was his custom, he took careful notes — spending hours after each lesson going over each word, making sure nothing was forgotten, no thought was incomplete, no insight undigested. In a letter to Swami Chaitanyananda (a fellow disciple in Ananda Kutir) he wrote, "This is the most thrilling text that you could ever imagine! When I arrive we will study it together."

Swami Tapovanam would silently observe his student. He was not one to directly compliment his students, but he would tell others, "Chinmaya is very intelligent." He was also alert to the necessity of eradicating a student's ego, so to Swamiji he would say, "Chinmaya, you are so carried away by the dual philosophy! In the morning you are studying the non-dual Reality in the *Māṇḍūkya Kārikā*, and yet at 4:00 P.M. you are in duality writing letters!"

Eighteen months passed. It became a practice for Swami Tapovanam and Swamiji to move up to Gangotri for the summer months (July–October), and come down to Rishikesh during the winter period (February–March). These journeys with his Guru were very special. Swami Tapovanam was such a pure soul that he saw God in everything. Along the way, he would often stop and point out the magnificent scenery, "Look at those clouds, Chinmaya! So beautiful is all of nature. How can anyone not believe in the grace and beauty of the Lord when they see His form manifested in this wonderful world of nature." Swamiji later wrote of those blissful days with his Guru:

> When we used to move back and forth from Uttarkashi to Gangotri, Swamiji would often stop abruptly in the trail, alert and thrilled, tense and silent. I watched him — now lost in wonder at the snow peaks, now aghast at the thundering laughter of the Gaṅgā in her panting speed — even a long-tailed tiny bird fluttering across the path was sufficient to tickle Swamiji into a visible rapture. At these times, he would stand bathed in a vivid glow of joy, whispering silently his homage to the Creator.

Swami Tapovanam would stay in his usual quarters at Brahmananda Ashram in Rishikesh, but Swamiji would return to Ananda Kutir and spend time with Swami Sivananda. He left this routine on one occasion in February1950 (a year after his sannyāsa initiation), when his father wrote to Swami Sivananda and requested to see his son since he was very ill.

A decade had passed since Swamiji had last seen his family. At first, they were slightly hesitant of this new person, who was now a swami. But Swamiji acted like his old self within minutes. "See, I had my head shaved, so you don't have to worry about me going bald," he joked with his father. Everyone had a good laugh.

Swamiji stayed a few weeks in Kerala, and during this time he was invited to give several lectures on behalf of the Divine Life Society. His father had recovered sufficiently to accompany him to one of the talks. Afterwards, in a letter to Swami Sivananda he wrote that he was "utterly surprised by the knowledge his son had gathered in so short a time." Kuttan Menon ended his letter with the following words:

> I feel myself much honored and blessed by having such a son for whom God has been pleased to give such a saintly Guru. I have no regret at all, that I had given my free consent to him to be a pupil under you and to serve you for all time.

In the winter of 1950–51, Swamiji flew on wings of exhilaration to his old lodgings at Ananda Kutir. It is reported that he would express his sense of revelation with those enigmatic statements often treated as signs of wisdom: "The world is unreal! It doesn't exist!" During this time, the writings in his daily journal also reflect a change of quality and a palpable sense of assuredness. One entry written in Uttarkashi in early 1951 reads as follows:

> I know no Sanskrit. I know no Hindi. I know no language to express what I know. In brief, I know that I know not how to make you know what I know.

> I know that I know not, yet I know that I know. My Gurus know that I know. But I know not how to make you know what my Gurus know. Knowledge is unknowable; yet, the unknowable becomes known when a knower explains it to be the knower's own Self, which illumines for him the very urge to know.
>
> Serene in the recesses of the bosom — when Knowledge comes to know itself — the Wisdom Light is one homogeneous whole, in which the unknown becomes known without the distorting intervention of the Knower knowing the Knowledge.
>
> In short, unless you are ready to take a plunge into your own within and move up beyond the mind and the intellect to the very source of light, power, and wisdom, I know not how to make you know what I know.

Listening to these echoes down the changing corridors of time, we're a long way from Balan's adventures as a child. But it was he who gave the yell that started it all, and we know that he would have been satisfied. What might once have seemed a puzzling line on a graph, had strengthened and soared over the years to astonishing conclusions:

If the measure of happiness is pure joy, Swami Chinmayananda qualified.

If it is eternal peace, he qualified.

If it is Self-awareness, he qualified.

If it is Truth, he qualified.

Clockwise from above:
Swamiji with Swami Tapovanam,
Tapovan Kutir, Uttarkashi, 1956
Swamiji's notes written neatly on the textbook
Swamiji with his family during his first visit
to Ernakulam after sannyāsa, 1950

PART THREE

Life on the Renaissance Road

◀ **Overleaf:**
Left to right:
Portrait of Swamiji, 1957
Portrait of Swamiji with head scarf, 1957
Portrait of Swamiji, Sangli, 1967

IX

Operation Faquiristan

There is a strip of land in Gangotri called Faquiristan, or the "place of the wise." The Gaṅgā emerges from a gorge of high rock surrounded by tall trees, and makes a wide turn, cutting out a small peninsula. This land is embraced by the holy river on three sides, and over the years, it became a favorite spot for all visiting sādhus, who would sit out in the sun for hours on end and debate a variety of Vedāntic subjects. Too often, these discussions were competitions of intellectual superiority, rather than a means to quieten the questioning mind (which is the true outcome of any healthy spiritual debate). When Swamiji returned to Gangotri in the summer of 1951, he would sit amongst the sādhus in "the place of the wise" and listen to their arguments. Before long, he began to notice some serious flaws within the prevailing system of merely "intellectualizing" scriptures.

An entry from his journal during this time reads:

> We called it the "Faquiristan" (place of the wise). There the elderly mahātmās discussed Ādi Śaṅkara's commentaries among themselves and asserted vehemently some conclusion or other, often without much logical argument. It was out of court to interrupt the divine prattlers, even if it be to inquire for the logic of a deduction. I was often snubbed by them as "one who will never understand Vedānta."

> These daily discussions gave me a peep into what these mahātmās were saying in the cities, and how much their words must be affecting, adversely no doubt, the educated, thinking class. I was terribly disappointed. Slowly, I left them for my own personal reflections and meditation.

It was after one of these encounters in Faquiristan, when Swamiji was sitting on a large boulder on the banks of the Gaṅgā, that he had a flash of inspiration. It seemed as if Mother Gaṅgā was saying to him, "Son, don't you see me? Born here in the Himalayas, I rush down to the plains taking with me both life and nourishment. Fulfillment of any possession consists in sharing it with others."

At this monumental moment, Swami Chinmayananda decided to take the truth of the Hindu scriptures, as taught by the Master and realized by the student, to his fellow countrymen. He would take this knowledge in all its pristine glory to the plains below for the enrichment of humanity. Why should Vedānta only be taught in holy places and to only a select few? Why should its true meaning continue to be misinterpreted and misunderstood? These were some of the questions he was about to answer.

But it was not quite that easy. His first challenge was to convince Swami Tapovanam, who was a staunch believer that a sannyāsī should lead a life of retirement (from the world) and only remain active in studying the scriptures, taking pilgrimages, and teaching those who come to him. Swami Tapovanam felt that the highest philosophy of Vedānta could be taught to only those who are pure at heart, and not to all and sundry — the ordinary public — for such people were so consumed by manifold desires that they lacked the subtle mind to comprehend the deep import of the scriptures. Moreover, if the time was right, would not a person develop true vairāgya (dispassion for the world) and automatically leave everything and go to the mountains in search of Truth, and discover their Guru? Swami Tapovanam had not once left the Himalayas since his renunciation. As a result, when Swamiji approached him with what he called his "afternoon dream," Swami Tapovanam admonished him. "You can't treat this knowledge like your newspaper business. It is useless to carry Vedānta to the market place!" he exclaimed. With these words, the "afternoon dream" remained just that — a dream of an afternoon — or at least, so it would seem for another six months.

It is not that Swami Tapovanam did not have sympathy for those who were living without the blessings and guidance of their ancient culture. He deplored the plight of men, who were so busy with worldly concerns that they had no time to consider and discover the inner Spirit. A passage from his book, *Wanderings in the Himalayas,* portrays his sentiments:

> I must confess, I can hardly pass through the solitary valleys in the lovely Himalayan region without casting a long, lingering look at the past, and without being saddened by the changes that have come over our motherland. I believe that no man who loves his native land and who has some power over thought still left in him can traverse these regions without feeling a touch of melancholy for the loss of our great culture.

By the summer of 1951, Swami Tapovanam was no longer holding daily classes with Swamiji. He had developed a severe cough on his return to Uttarkashi in the spring, and had consequently told his student, "I have taught you the Upaniṣads, now you study the *Gītā* on your own. If you have questions, we'll discuss them." Thus, Swamiji continued with his own studies in Gangotri.

But a month later, Swami Tapovanam made a suggestion. He told Swamiji to make a trip to the plains, and wander around as a renunciate, living as a beggar among those he had once emulated. "This will rub out your ego! To have the experience of the Divine is not enough.

You must be able to keep that vision through all your activities. Go down to the plains and keep your mananam (continual reflection), where it is the most difficult. Adversities of life will prevent you from falling into the dangers of complacency and self-contentment in your spiritual discipline."

Swamiji wrote of this journey:

> Thus, it was in May 1951, I walked down from the heights of Gangotri to Rishikesh, and from there moved on to Delhi with a plan to set out on an all-India pilgrimage, visiting all the important spiritual centers, to see how others were serving the Hindu brethren. I traveled on foot some six months; living on bhikṣā (begged food), sleeping in ashrams, temples, and under wayside trees. Swamiji was correct — it was quite an experience in rubbing off the ego. Education, social status, family connections, prejudices, sham values — these were no longer mine. When people do not know who you are, they consider you an inconvenient beggar, a worthless monk, an unproductive member of the community. And they insult you with looks of abhorrence as if you were something the cat dragged in. If you ask me, this kind of discipline is the best cure for the ego-disease.

Before we continue with our story, let us take a moment to reflect on the import of Swami Tapovanam's words. The dawn of Knowledge is the awareness that Brahman alone is the Reality, the world is an illusion, and the jīva (individual ego) is nothing other than Brahman (*Brahma satyaṁ jaganmithyā jīvo brahmaiva nāparaḥ*). This Knowledge is not a mere passing intellectual understanding, but it is an abiding conviction based on one's own direct divine Experience. When Swami Tapovanam said, "To have the experience of the Divine is not enough," he indicated that Swamiji had such an experience of the Self. However, this should not only be at the seat of meditation, but it should also continue to be present at all times, even when perceiving the world of names and forms. Hence, he advised, "You must be able to keep that vision through all your activities."

Also, Swami Tapovanam said, "This will rub out your ego!" What does this mean? Does not the ego cease at Self-realization? Indeed, at Self-realization, the ego is dead. But, to *be* and function in the world, for example, to even eat food, the ego is necessary — for it is the ego that is the doer, and not the Self. The man of Self-realization functions in the world with a "falsified ego" which is incapable of creating bondage. Such a falsified ego is compared to a burnt rope; it is incapable of binding anything. It is with this false ego that saints and sages continue to display various personalities in their play with the world, even after Self-realization. Even this false ego — Swami Tapovanam felt — had to be rubbed and polished in his beloved student!

In short, Swami Tapovanam had wanted what was best for his student. He wanted Swamiji to consolidate his newfound Self-knowledge before he plunged into a world of activity, so that he would be able to keep his higher vision at all times.

Swamiji began his journey in Delhi, from where he traveled to Chennai through the state of Andhra Pradesh, and finally across South India. He mostly followed the route of the railway lines, and all through his journey he would talk and listen to his countrymen, observing and assessing their aimless and dejected lives, despite their newly gained independence from British rule. Those who did practice some religious discipline, had no understanding of why or what they were doing, and they derived little spiritual benefit from such mechanical rituals.

When Swamiji left Chennai, he turned southward and returned to Arunachala for his second visit with the celebrated saint, Ramana Maharshi. This time, Swamiji had a one-on-one satsaṅga with the saint. They discussed the various spiritual centers in the Himalayas, and Ramana Maharshi fondly recalled Swami Tapovanam, who had visited the Ramana Ashram during his early travels. Ramana Maharshi had also received news from time to time, from other sādhus who had visited Swami Tapovanam.

Swamiji then went farther south to Kanyakumari at the southernmost tip of India, where in 1892, Swami Vivekananda had been inspired to begin a dynamic exchange of values between a spiritual India and the materialistic West. "In America is the place, the people, and the opportunity for everything new," said Swami Vivekananda. "The Americans are quick, but they are somewhat like a straw on fire, ready to be extinguished."

Circling up the west coast, Swamiji finally reached his hometown in Kerala. His family gave him a warm welcome. A former schoolmate of his stepmother, Shankaran Marar, organized some public talks for him to give to the locals. Five rupees was spent on advertisement (the cost of printing flyers), but the attendance was more likely out of curiosity. Could this swami possibly be that worthless Balakrishnan Menon of Trichur?

By the end of October 1951 — some six months after he had begun his journey — Swamiji had completed his tour of India and returned to Uttarkashi. He had witnessed firsthand the spiritual and economic degradation of his homeland, and his resolve to bring the knowledge of Truth down to the plains was even stronger. He again approached Swami Tapovanam for his blessings to implement the "Gangotri Plan" (as he now called his "afternoon dream," since the inspiration had dawned on him in Gangotri). He informed his Guru that a Mr. Nanda, whom he had stayed with during his India pilgrimage, had suggested having a series of talks on the Upaniṣads in Pune. Swamiji had first met Mr. Nanda in Ananda Kutir, and they had hiked together to visit an ascetic saint, Vasistha Gupta, who lived in a cave beyond the hills in Rishikesh. "Pune! There are so many brahmin scholars in Pune!" exclaimed Swami Tapovanam. "How will you tackle them? They will never allow a swami talking on scriptures!" At the same time, Swami Tapovanam also knew his student well, and his determination and will to serve as the Lord's instrument. And so, he gave his permission, but warned Swamiji, "Consider yourself lucky if you find five to six listeners for Vedānta, especially when you take the Upaniṣads as textbooks." With these very cautious words, the renaissance of the Hindu religion had officially begun.

All together, Swami Tapovanam must have seen the signs of enlightenment on Swamiji's face. The text *Yogavāsiṣṭha* outlines these qualities as being the following: saumya, which is calm and serene as the moon, with the mind constantly in reflection on the Self; prasanna-vadanam, which is a glow of absolute satisfaction on the face; and rasāsvāda, which is fullness of reveling in bliss. At such a moment, the person is no longer a student to be guided, but he becomes a master himself. It was now time for Swamiji to start sharing what he had himself experienced.

During the first leg of his journey, Swamiji made a stop in Rishikesh to take the blessings of Swami Sivananda, who was overjoyed and heartily approved of Swamiji's plan. "Go roar like Vivekananda," the Master proudly said to Swamiji. He even presented him with a message to be read aloud in his first talk. Some of the other swamis in Ananda Kutir were not as confident. "What if the response is not good and they don't appreciate what you say? What will you do?" they questioned. "Do? I'm a sannyāsī! I keep my bags packed. If they like what I say, I'll stay. If they don't, I'll leave. It's as simple as that!" replied Swamiji.

With four annas in his pocket and a trunk filled with notes and books (the words DIVINE MISSION carefully lettered on the trunk's top), Swamiji arrived in Pune on December 23, 1951. He had left the peace and security of the mountains, and the traditions of the

Himalayan masters who spent their lives teaching only those who came to them. Swami Chinmayananda now dared to go to the people, live amongst them, share the life they lived, and address the problems they encountered.

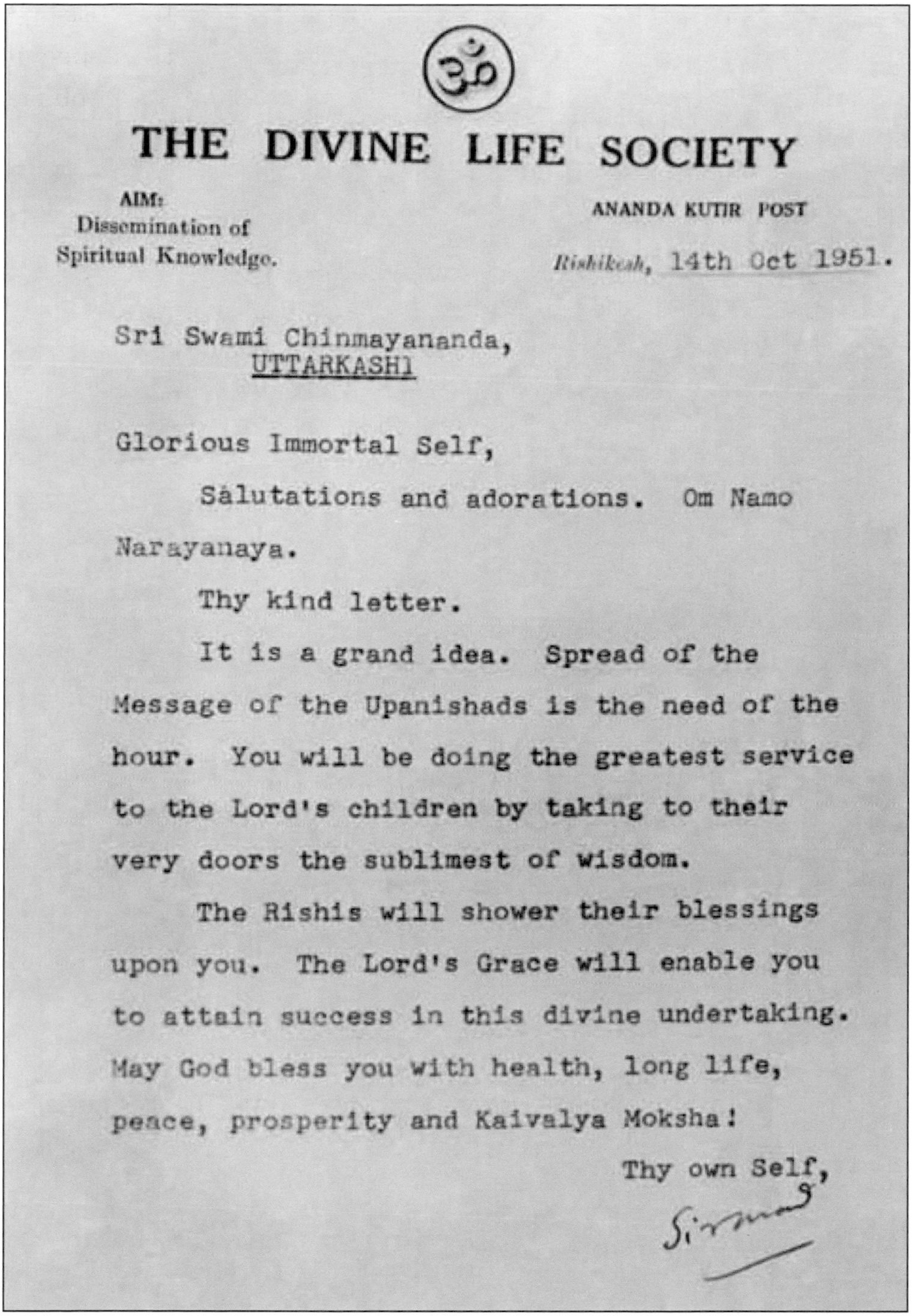

THE DIVINE LIFE SOCIETY

AIM:
Dissemination of
Spiritual Knowledge.

ANANDA KUTIR POST
Rishikesh, 14th Oct 1951.

Sri Swami Chinmayananda,
UTTARKASHI

Glorious Immortal Self,

Sàlutations and adorations. Om Namo Narayanaya.

Thy kind letter.

It is a grand idea. Spread of the Message of the Upanishads is the need of the hour. You will be doing the greatest service to the Lord's children by taking to their very doors the sublimest of wisdom.

The Rishis will shower their blessings upon you. The Lord's Grace will enable you to attain success in this divine undertaking. May God bless you with health, long life, peace, prosperity and Kaivalya Moksha!

Thy own Self,
Sivananda

Swami Sivananda's letter to Swami Chinmayananda, October 14, 1951

Portrait of Swamiji, 1950

Clockwise from above:
Sitting in meditation in a temple
Swamiji in Kanyakumari
Portrait of Swamiji, 1952

X

Let Us Be Hindus: The Jnana Yagnas Begin

The satsaṅga in Sushila Mudliar's garden in Pune on December 23, 1951, consisted of six listeners, besides Swamiji and the host. Swamiji was delighted. He wrote to Swami Tapovanam and informed him that there was one more person than expected!

Sushila Mudliar was a telephone operator, and Swamiji had met her when she had come to Uttarkashi to meet Swami Tapovanam. Along with Gopal Reddy of Hyderabad (a devotee of Swami Sivananda), they were the two contacts who would prove invaluable in organizing Swamiji's early Jnana Yagnas. Swami Sivananda had given a letter of introduction for Gopal Reddy, who was thrilled to get a letter from his Guru, and had hosted Swamiji for a few days in Hyderabad before buying him a train ticket to go to Pune.

The 1st Upaniṣad Jnana Yagna was held at the Vinayak Temple in Rastha Peth in Pune, and started on December 31, 1951. It lasted 100 days. Since there were no workers to publicize the Yagna, Swamiji wore a turban and vest and went around the town on a cycle with a megaphone, shouting, "Come and listen to the swami who has come from Uttarkashi and is giving good talks in English!" He himself inaugurated this Jnana Yagna, since in his own words, "there was no one else who was prepared to do so." The texts were *Kenopaniṣad* and

Kaṭhopaniṣad. Residents of Pune recall that Swamiji spent 60 out of the 100 days just on the introduction. This introduction is considered to be Swamiji's best on the subject. In his enthusiasm, he had only spoken from the highest standpoint.

> ON THE OPENING DAY, I HAD
> AN AUDIENCE OF EIGHTEEN TO ADDRESS,
> AND THEREFORE MY HEART JUMPED WITH JOY.
>
> | SWAMI CHINMAYANANDA |

Swamiji began his lecture as if the entire hall were filled with interested listeners. He put aside all concerns for success or failure, and spontaneously expounded the wonders of the scriptures. During the first seven days, he prepared the audience by introducing the terms and language of the Upaniṣads. His delivery was wonderful and powerful as his voice rang out the eternal truths of life in a straightforward, modern, and witty style. The listeners were astounded. Madhukar Veeraswami of Pune recalls that he was "compelled to attend the talks after the first day." Day by day, the crowds swelled; army officers from the Southern Command came on their bicycles to listen to the eloquent swami; and the audience overflowed into the lanes near the temple.

The first day had been an introductory talk for the 100-day Upaniṣad Jnana Yagna. It was titled, "Let Us Be Hindus," where Swamiji outlined his plan for the spiritual revival of the Hindu religion. And this remained his goal throughout his life. His dedication is clearly expressed in his introductory address; excerpts are given here:

> A Hindu swami to talk. A Hindu temple for a background. A Hindu audience, and the subject for discussion: "Let Us Be Hindus." Strange! It sounds like a ridiculous paradox and a meaningless contradiction. I can very well see that you are surprised at the audacity of this swami!

It has become a new fashion with the educated Hindu to turn up his nose and sneer in contempt at the very mention of his religion in any discussion. No doubt, Hinduism has come to mean nothing more than a bundle of sacred superstitions, or a certain way of dressing, cooking, eating, and so on. Our gods have fallen to the mortal level of administrative officers at whose altars the faithful Hindu might pray and get special permits for the things he desires, that is, if he pays the required fee to the priest.

This degradation is not the product of any accidental and sudden historical upheaval. For two hundred years, Hinduism has remained an unwanted orphan without any patronage from the state and with little encouragement from the rich. Once upon a time, the learned philosophers were rightly the advisers of the state. But then the quality of the adviser class (brāhmaṇa) and the ruler class (kṣatriya) deteriorated. By slowly putrefying themselves in the leprous warmth of luxury and power, they have taken us to the regrettable stage in which we find ourselves now.

At the present state of moral, ethical, and cultural degradation in our country, to totally dispose of religion would be making our dash to ruin even quicker. However decadent our religion may be, it is far better than having none at all. My proposal is that the wise thing for us would be to try and bring about a renaissance of Hinduism, so that under its greatness — proven through many centuries — we may come to grow into the very heights of culture and civilization that was ours in the historical past.

Hinduism is not this external show that we have learned to parade about in our daily life. Hinduism is a science of perfection. There is in it an answer to every individual, social, national, or international problem.

The Upaniṣads declare in unmistakable terms that, in reality, man — at the peak of his achievement — is God himself. He is advised to live his day-to-day experiences in life in such a systematic

> and scientific way that, hour by hour, he is consciously cleansing himself of all the encrustation of imperfections that have gathered to conceal the beauty and divinity of the true Eternal personality in him. The methods by which an individual can consciously purify and evolve by his self-effort to regain the status of his true nature — is the content of Hinduism.
>
> During these 100 days of the Upaniṣad Jnana Yagna, we shall try to discover the eternal happiness and bliss that is the succulent essence of all true religions. In the light of the principles of Truth declared in the Upaniṣads, we shall try to get at the scientific significance of the various practices that are considered part of our religion. In the spirit of communal living for these 100 days, we shall come to discover the science of Perfection, the true essence of Hinduism.
>
> Let us know what Hinduism is! Let us take an honest oath for ourselves, not only for our own sake, but for the sake of the entire world; that we shall, — when once we are convinced of the validity of the eternal Truth — try honestly to live as consistently as possible the values advocated by this ancient and sacred religion.
>
> Let us be Hindus, and thus build up a true Hindustan, peopled with thousands of Śaṅkaras, hundreds of Buddhas, and dozens of Vivekanandas!

As Swamiji moved into the text of *Kenopaniṣad*, his vivacity and animated explanations captured the interest of the audience. He would rouse them with thundering declarations, and then coax them into a blissful silence with profound subtleties. Swamiji answered questions about life that had long been in their hearts and minds. Questions that come to a "thinking man" observing his daily life: Is life only a journey between the office and home for the purpose of sleeping and eating? If so, is it worth it? Is there another meaning to life? Is there a higher purpose?

Swamiji had taken the words "Jnana Yagna" from the *Bhagavad-gītā,* wherein Lord Kṛṣṇa praises both the teacher and student of the *Gītā* by saying, he who studies the sacred dialogue or shares this knowledge is performing a worship of Knowledge, and, hence, is very dear to Him. After his 40th Jnana Yagna in Bangalore, Swamiji admitted to the Śaṅkarācārya of Shringeri Sri Abhinava Vidyatirtha that "Jnana Yagna" was a term that he had adapted from the *Bhagavad-gītā* for his work in contemporary times.

MY MISSION IS TO CONVERT HINDUS TO HINDUISM.

| SWAMI CHINMAYANANDA |

As the Jnana Yagna continued, Swamiji incorporated a program of spiritual development to accompany the discourses. However, this outline was subject to much experiment and change in the early years, until it developed into a structure that best suited the modern temperament. "The Yagna scheme was not fully clear to me then. It became more and more revealed as I worked ahead with my daily lecture programs," said Swamiji. "Some of the programs which I then went through were later on rejected, and new schemes were envisaged and incorporated into it from time to time, expanding, enlarging, widening, and deepening the Yagna technique."

Swami Rampremi arrived from Ananda Kutir to lead bhajans before the lecture, so that the mind could be brought to a peaceful state after the day's activities. Meditation and akhaṇḍanāma-saṅkīrtana (continuous singing of the Lord's name) for the concentration of the mind began after the first introductory week, and continued for forty days. Participants were asked to sign up for at least one hour a day of chanting in front of a small altar. In this way, the chanting was unbroken except during the class each day. At the midpoint of the Yagna, a four-day traditional vaidika-havana (fire sacrifice ordained in the Vedās) was initiated, where Swamiji explained the meaning and significance of the elaborate rituals. Brahmin priests were called to conduct the sacrifice, and to their utter surprise, everyone in the audience, including women, businessmen, and lower castes, were asked to participate in the rituals. At the end of the Yagna, everybody went on a spiritual picnic. Buses were engaged, and the group left amidst chanting and bhajans towards a holy place. This was to encourage community living.

There was one unforgettable ceremony at the conclusion of the Jnana Yagna. On the last day, Swamiji would walk up and down the aisles with a kalaśa (pot) in hand, and sprinkle Gaṅgā-jala (holy water) with a stem of three leaves on all who had gathered — many of whom had never seen the Gaṅgā, but knew of her lore through legend. This was a form of "holy bath," or spiritual cleansing, and one wonders at the remarkable turn of events from Balan's younger days when he thought all baths were unnecessary! Sheela Sharma of Delhi recalls this memory:

> It was a sight for the gods to see. In the twilight of the setting sun with innumerable devotees chanting *Om Namaḥ Śivāya,* Swamiji's tall, splendorous, orange-clad figure — silhouetted against the light — walked through the crowd as if in a trance, sprinkling Gaṅgā-jala on all those gathered there. It is a sight imprinted in my memory forever.

The holy Gaṅgā was Brahman (the infinite Self) itself in liquid form to his Guru, Swami Tapovanam. And indeed, it was Gaṅgā herself who had inspired Swamiji to share the timeless wisdom of the Himalayas with the masses in the plains.

All through the Jnana Yagna, the seekers were asked to maintain a spiritual discipline outside of the yajñaśālā (place where yajña is performed). They were told to keep their attention focused on whatever

Right:
During the evening discourse,
1st Jnana Yagna, Pune 1951–52

Below:
Hari Har Bhajan Samaj,
venue of 1st Jnana Yagna, Pune,
December 31, 1951–April 8, 1952

Above:
Portrait of Swamiji

Left:
Swamiji with Sushila
Mudliar who invited him
to Pune and organized
his talks, Pune, 1952

Clockwise from above:
Havana ceremony midway during Jnana Yagna
Distributing prasad at the conclusion of the 4th Jnana Yagna, Palghat, 1954
On the march with devotees
To Guruvayur on foot in a disciplined line
Sprinkling Gaṅgā-jala at the conclusion of a Jnana Yagna

task was at hand during the day. In addition, they were asked to abstain from sexual contact, movies, and rich and spicy foods, so that the mind could concentrate towards the spiritual goal. Swamiji would also give personal initiations into the practice of meditation every Thursday morning before sunrise. "Have a bath. Take your usual cup of tea. If you come with a completely empty stomach, you'll only be meditating on the rumblings of your stomach," he instructed the initiates. This later evolved into early morning group meditation classes, which have remained a part of the curriculum for all spiritual retreat camps in Chinmaya Mission.

Both Swami Sivananda and Swami Tapovanam were extremely pleased with Swamiji's progress. A letter dated January 20, 1952, addressed to "Sri Swami Chinmayanandaji," was quick in coming from Swami Sivananda. It read:

> You have asked the aspirants to observe brahmacarya (celibacy), and a sāttvic diet (pure, simple and light food), and not go to cinemas during the period of the grand yajña worship. It is very good; this is tapas (austerity).
>
> May the Lord bless you and your work!

A letter also arrived from Swami Tapovanam dated January 22, 1952. After succinctly pointing out the transcendental goal to be reached, the causes for missing it, and the methods for reaching it, he closed his message with these loving words:

> Therefore, diligently and constantly practice with a long and intense pursuit the Paths of Devotion, Selfless Action, and Yoga. One who has thus purified and disciplined his inner personality comes to experience intimately the Absolute Truth beyond all qualities, conditionings, and limitations, and attains Godhood.

May you all reach that Eternal State of Perfection and Divinity in this very birth.

May the blessings of the Upaniṣad ṛṣis be ever upon you all!

1951–52 PUNE JNANA YAGNA:
THE BEGINNING OF IT ALL

When I went to the temple in Rastha Peth in Pune, there was a Swamiji giving a speech in English. Only a few people were in the audience; you could count them on your fingertips. His talk was fascinating, and he spoke very sincerely, and in excellent English. He said, "If you can't live the *Gītā* in the marketplace, then throw the book in the dustbin."

Swamiji would sit to the right of the Gaṇeśa idol and speak. Within a week, the temple was full of people, and there was no place to sit inside. People started to sit in the lanes outside. And many of the army officers came on cycles from their camp to the Rastha Peth temple. After a few days, even the lanes outside were fully occupied. People then started to sit at the junction where the temple lane meets another street leading to the main road. We could hear Swamiji's voice through the loud speakers outside.

Swamiji would go everywhere on foot. His walk was brisk and fast. Even in the afternoons, when the sun was very hot, he would go for bhikṣā on foot, whatever the distance.

He had an ordinary small metal trunk (not much larger than a school bag) with him. He would take down the address of anybody who visited him, and make a card. Then he would alphabetically arrange this in the trunk. He sent Yagna Prasad to everyone, and wrote all the addresses with his own hand.

Sometimes, he was given a piece of cloth along with gurudakṣiṇā. Since it was white in color, Swamiji would dye his own clothes. His hands remained stained for days.

An akhaṇḍanāma-saṅkīrtana had been organized in front of the Madrasi Dharamsala. We would sign up to chant: *Hare Rāma Hare Rāma, Rāma Rāma Hare Hare, Hare Kṛṣṇa Hare Kṛṣṇa, Kṛṣṇa Kṛṣṇa Hare Hare.* Swamiji had prepared a schedule for the chanters, and cyclostyled it [the method of making copies at the time]. People would come according to their specific time. Between 2–4 A.M. there were no volunteers, so Swamiji would chant at this time. He would ensure that there was always enough oil in the lamp, and would give many practical tips; for example, he would put dry camphor powder on the wick of the lamp to make it light easily.

On the last day, Swamiji took out a procession through the entire city of Pune. He did not hesitate to pass through certain sensitive areas which had witnessed riots post-India's independence.

Swamiji told us that when he had got down at Pune station (on December 23, 1951), he had bought a newspaper — *The Times of India* — and was reading it. There was one local man who came up to him just to check if he was holding the newspaper right, since in those days nobody expected a sannyāsī to read English. Many days into the Jnana Yagna, I went with him to Radhakrishnan's house for bhikṣā. There was a bhikṣu (beggar-like) sannyāsī, who was not very knowledgeable, who had also come for bhikṣā. One of the guests asked Swamiji, "What is your opinion about these types of sannyāsīs?" Swamiji replied, "Ours is the redshirt union! No comments!"

M. V. Naidu
Chinmaya Mission Chinciwad (near Pune)
[He was sixteen years old when he attended
Swamiji's first Jnana Yagna in Pune, 1951–52]

It was only a matter of time before Swamiji faced criticism from orthodox brahmins. Their relentless complaint was that he had no regard for caste, status, and profession. He allowed everybody to equally participate in everything, whereas, the sacred scriptures were only to be taught to brahmins, and not to all. And why was he teaching in English, the language of the foreign devils ... unheard of! Undaunted, Swamiji continued with his work and showed great patience. He firmly responded that Mother Śruti (Vedic Wisdom) knew how to take care of herself. She did not require any security guards to protect her from unworthy students. If a student was unfit, he would simply fall asleep or walk away from a talk.

At one point, the brahmin priests went in a group and complained to the saint of Kanchi Kamakoti Mutt, but it seems that the saint reprimanded them, "You don't know what Upaniṣads and *Gītā* are all about. Here is a person who not only knows them, but has come to interpret them for people." In fact, the brahmins had no reason to protest, since our own history shows that some of the wisest sages of India had been kṣatriyas (warrior class) — Rāma, Kṛṣṇa , Janaka, and Buddha, to name a few. Even Rājā Parikṣita was given the knowledge of *Śrīmad-bhāgavatam* by Maharṣi Śuka. And where indeed are such superficialities of caste or creed for the saints who have risen beyond them!

Swamiji was most fluent in English, which was also the most practical language for holding discourses in Indian cities post-independence. The English language was a common bond between educated classes in cities like Delhi, Chennai, Bangalore, Madurai, and Calcutta where the Jnana Yagnas took place. It was also Swamiji's mission to reach out to the English-educated masses who had no appreciation of their religion and scriptures. Swamiji said, "I have assessed the mood of the educated classes in these cities and found that they have, in their ignorance, an aversion to Sanskrit, a great language." At the end of a Jnana Yagna, people were interested in learning Sanskrit, and special classes were very often started to teach Sanskrit. Later, in 1989, Swamiji would establish the Chinmaya International Foundation in Adi Sankara Nilayam, Kerala, an institute for research and study of Sanskrit and Indology. This practical, albeit visionary, approach is one of the primary reasons Swamiji was so successful in spreading the knowledge of Vedānta, despite the unsurpassable language barrier that modern man faces when he studies Indian scripture.

From the very first Yagna onwards, Swamiji had careful rules of discipline. Ten minutes before the talk, a large group would assemble outside the house where he was staying, and accompany him to the yajñaśālā. He would walk in a dignified manner, straight and tall, yet at such a speed that it was hard to keep up with him. He always entered the dais exactly on time. Once the discourse started, if anyone caused a disturbance, Swamiji would stop the talk and make his displeasure known. He would either be completely silent, which made everyone feel awkward, or he would make some sort of remark. Anjali Singh reports an incident from a Delhi Jnana Yagna in 1977:

> Swamiji was taking the 11th chapter of the *Bhagavad-gītā,* which describes the "Virāṭ" (macrocosmic) form of the Lord. The audience was so inspired during these sessions that on the last day, Swamiji thanked them for their attention saying, "I, too, felt very inspired."
>
> There was one moment, however, when Swamiji had just started the 31st verse, and a lady got up in the middle of the hall and started to look around to see how she could leave. Everybody stared at her. They all knew that Swamiji would fire up anyone who caused a disturbance.
>
> Sure enough, Swamiji's voice thundered across the hall, "Who are you? Have mercy on me! Who are you in this form?" The audience was momentarily stunned; then, just as Swamiji started to explain,

"It is in the book! Arjuna asks the Lord, 'Who are you?'" Everybody burst out laughing. The lady still had not realized what had happened, and Swamiji continued to address her, "I do not indeed know your purpose (for being here) …" And the audience laughed even harder. Finally, some way was made for the lady to walk out!

DISTURBANCE IN THE ANDAMAN ISLANDS

On the inauguration day of a Jnana Yagna in Port Blair (in 1991), a three-year old girl was running about in a playful mood. Her mother was seated in the front row. When Swamiji's talk started, the child ran up to the dais, looked at everyone, and then ran back to her mother. When she did this for the third time, Swamiji scolded the mother, "Do you know the harm you are doing to your child? Every time the child runs to the front, everyone looks at her with irritation because she has disturbed their concentration. There are 2,000 people sitting here, and if they all project unconsciously, even a tiny ray of anger at her, the collective force of their anger will form a very powerful vibration and harm your child. So please don't allow her to do this. This is a serious hall of study, where people are trying to gather their disarrayed minds and focus it on the Self."

Narrated by Anjali Singh
Chinmaya Mission Delhi

For the most part, everyone was very impressed with the discipline maintained in the yajñaśālās. The punctuality, orderliness, and silence were especially appreciated after the noisy gatherings that most had become accustomed to in Hindu temples. Swami Brahmananda (Regional Head, Chinmaya Mission Karnataka) says that Swamiji once explained, "The yajñaśālā is my pūjā room and the audience is my Īśvara, whom I worship for one and a half hours."

The 2nd Upaniṣad Jnana Yagna was in Chennai, and started on April 25, 1953. The text was *Muṇḍaka Upaniṣad*. Swamiji had arrived early to help the Yagna Committee that had been formed to look after the organizing duties of a Jnana Yagna. He stayed with an uncle, Kuttikrishna Menon, who had offered to help him find a suitable place for the talks. Each day, Swamiji and his uncle would go out to look for a place, starting with the most logical places, which included temples. But the brahmin orthodox priests would have none of it. They firmly refused to allow a non-brahmin to talk on scriptures, much less allow him to speak in English. From one end of Chennai to the other, even in the surrounding villages, the response was the same — No!

Just when it looked as if Chennai would have to be put on hold, a Muslim friend, who had a large vacant palace, offered the use of his property for forty-one days. There was just one problem — the Arni Palace was haunted. "Well, I've never seen a ghost," said Swamiji, quite amused. "This looks like a good opportunity!" Sure enough, the flickering kerosene lanterns did call up strange images as the group of listeners dissolved into the night. The disappointed look on the faces of the Yagna Committee was obvious. "Don't worry; others will come tomorrow night. You'll see!" reassured Swamiji. "You have done your part; now leave the rest to the Lord." Within a week, the crowd had grown beyond all expectations, and the hall in the palace was abandoned for a canvas shelter on the spacious palace grounds, complete with platform and microphone. V. Nagarajan expresses the sentiments of the audience:

> Every evening at half past five, whether I was at home or in the office, I would have a great urge to run to my room, get out of my long pants, dress in the traditional Indian dhoti, and hasten to the Palace. Never had I found, nor can I ever find elsewhere, the effect that perfect silence and discipline can produce. Precisely at 6:00 P.M. — one could set his watch accordingly — Swamiji would enter the

> platform. At his appearance, a feeling arose in each one of us that was inexpressible and incomparable, and produced a joy greater than when one meets a beloved family member after a long absence.

In the introductory letter for the Chennai Yagna Prasad (detailed in the chapter "The Indisputable Good Sense of Package! Print! Publish!"), the editor, Kesavlal Takharwadi, wrote:

> For the number of practical tips we are getting here, this Yagna is an unprecedented opportunity for every one of us. Each speech of Sri Swamiji is an exhaustive treatment of the subject chosen for the day, replete with examples from everyday life, and riveted with perfect logic and good sense. Ever practical and always scientific, Sri Swamiji is proving himself to be the final answer to the materialists' turn to atheism.

Two aspects of Swamiji's discourses instantly endeared him to all who listened. First, he was presenting the highest philosophy of the scriptures, and this was entirely unknown to the general populace. Second, he was presenting it in a way they understood and could apply it to their own lives in the immediate circumstances, not after retirement. Moreover, his witty and down-to-earth examples had the audience in peals of laughter. To introduce the commentary of the first verse of the *Muṇḍaka Upaniṣad,* Swamiji related the following story:

> Gopal Iyer is a poor insignificant member of a big family. In his own house, he is a victim of the mischief of even his youngest son. Now, Mr. Iyer earns his livelihood on a paltry pay which he gets as a police constable in the local precinct. Thus, he has, in fact, more than one personality operating through him — the father, the unhappy husband, and the mighty policeman!
>
> Now, when exactly does the ineffectual Gopal Iyer become the mighty "hand in law" as a policeman, a dread to the mischief-

> makers, a phantom for our criminals, and an ever-present threat to every rash driver? Certainly the policeman in him is not when he is in a dhoti and shirt, lolling about on the verandah of his house, persecuted by the pranks of his son, or bullied by the demands of his wife. The moment Gopal Iyer gets into his khākhī shorts and puts on his red turban — out of that very same personality — the policeman appears. Thereafter, he is a potent power to be reckoned with by every citizen!
>
> Similarly, my friends, each one of us is not merely an ineffectual, fearful, ever-sighing, limited creature, but has within himself a personality supremely omnipotent, fearless, unlimited, all-blissful, and godly. Just as Gopal Iyer becomes a policeman by a process of self-invocation — and, thereafter, the policeman forgets to act and live the weaknesses and limitations of the father and husband — so, too, can we, through meditation and prayer, invoke the Divine in us and come to transcend our own personality with its defects and limitations. These are the techniques by which we tune ourselves to the highest perfection and, thereby, come to invoke in ourselves a greater perfection of both mind and intellect.

Sushila Mudliar and Devaki Menon had come from Pune to assist Swamiji with the organizational work of the Jnana Yagna. And Mr. Shukali had come from Delhi to help him with his secretarial work. From then on, Mr. Shukali accompanied Swamiji to each Yagna, as his secretary-treasurer until his death in 1959. At noon, and after the evening talks, one of the local families would bring bhikṣā (a food offering) for Swamiji and the three assistants. After the meal, everyone would stay for an evening satsaṅga to ask questions. But when Swamiji chanted three loud OMs, satsaṅga was over. As time past, the crowd and interest grew, and the satsaṅgas lasted longer and longer.

Kouchi Amma came to hear her Swamiji during this Yagna, which made it especially poignant. Everyone happily took care of the tiny eighty-year old lady, treating her with the reverence due to a saint. The Chennai devotees arranged a pāda-pūjā (worship of the Master's feet) for both Swamiji and his mother. Kouchi Amma was to live for another ten years, but this was one of her proudest moments as a mother.

On the last day of the twenty-four hour japa chanting, Swamiji took out a procession through the city with everybody chanting together. They were to remain in a neat file, and he walked along beside them, moving from front to back to make sure all were paying attention to their own action. At the conclusion of the forty-one days, a spiritual picnic was organized to Rameshwaram. The group boarded six buses at 6:00 A.M. for the 200-mile trip to Rameshwaram, a full-day's journey. They were asked to carry no toiletries, except a toothbrush, comb, and coconut oil for the hair. Swamiji wanted to give the group a taste of renunciation. The night was also spent in a dharmaśālā near the temple. In the evening, he gave the pilgrims a talk on the importance of meditation.

The 3rd Upaniṣad Jnana Yagna started in Delhi on September 12, 1953 (near Kashmiri Gate). The choice of text, *Māṇḍūkya Kārikā,* must definitely have shocked a good many. An entry from Swamiji's journal on the eve of the inauguration reads:

> Only twenty-four hours remain for me to find myself undertaking yet another great endeavor — a ninety-one day Yagna with one of the toughest text books of Vedānta to explain. Mother Śruti's (Vedic Wisdom) grace alone is my wealth, my courage, my strength. If she fails me, why should I worry? She alone fails.

Mother Śruti did not fail Swamiji. She lit his words with wisdom. The average daily attendance was 800 listeners. "Even the students of Delhi have accepted the swami," wrote one person. Since this Yagna treated the most subtle of Upaniṣads, Swamiji particularly emphasized meditation; and the first phase of the Yagna was devoted to the explanation and practice of meditation. Shakuntala Bindra describes the impact Swamiji had on her:

> Swamiji was speaking on the sacred syllable OM (A-U-M) as described in the *Māṇḍūkya Kārikā*. The way he explained upāsanā (worship) on OM touched my heart deeply. From that day onward to this day, I have followed this method of worship and all other things that he explained to me.

However, starting with the 13th Jnana Yagna, which was once again held in Delhi (in September 1955), Swamiji began to take the *Bhagavad-gītā* during the evening lectures. He had realized that a lot of study and preparation was needed before the masses could understand the import of the Upaniṣads. In comparison, the *Bhagavad-gītā* was simpler to understand and more practical to implement in day-to-day life. Thereafter, the Upaniṣads became the text for the morning class, which was usually attended by the more serious seekers.

Swami Jyotirmayananda (later Regional Head, Chinmaya Mission Delhi, 1972–2003) recalls, "Swamiji did not take the *Māṇḍūkya* again until 1969. Even when I joined the Vedānta Course in 1963 in Sandeepany Sadhanalaya Powai, the students could not lay hands on this Upaniṣad, as it was kept under lock and key. Swamiji did not want unprepared students to misunderstand the philosophy, for they might give up sādhanā (spiritual practice), dhyāna (meditation), japa (repetition of Lord's name), karma yoga (devoted service), and bhakti yoga (devotion unto the Lord), at the early stages itself."

Anjali Singh also says that Swamiji would not sign her *Aṣṭavakra-gītā* book when she first took it to him in 1975, since it was another advanced text. It was only on her insistence that Swamiji finally signed it in 1977. Even then, he cautioned, "Don't lose your head. This is at the moment and after the exploding 'experience' of Oneness."

During this 13th Jnana Yagna in Delhi in 1955, Swamiji also began formal morning classes on the *Vivekacūḍāmaṇi* (by Ādi Śaṅkarācārya) at his Karol Bagh residence. In fact, it was at this time that he first introduced the world-famous BMI chart as a visual aid. Although in the first stages of development, there was an X instead of an OM at the top of the chart. The X represents the Source (the very substratum of the three states of experience — waking, dream, and deep sleep — the primal cause of the entire cosmos). With this chart and a long pointer, Swamiji would illustrate that Vedānta was indeed a scientific method-of-investigation that led the individual back to his Source. In the years to follow, the BMI chart became synonymous with Swamiji's Gītā Jnana Yagnas. It captivated both serious seekers of Vedānta and children alike. Children would invariably be dressed up as Swamiji in a Balvihar play, and imitate him pointing to the world of OET (objects, emotions, and thoughts), telling the audience to "THINK!" The celebrated American cartoonist, Jim Coffin, also took great inspiration from Swamiji and his BMI chart. Many of his cartoons depict Swamiji avidly explaining the logic of spirituality with a pointer and chart.

Swamiji insisted that each person bring a copy of the *Bhagavad-gītā,* so that the entire gathering could chant the verses in unison to help the audience stay alert. Swamiji explained:

> There will be a dullness of the intellect after a period of silent attention. A quiet mind has a tendency to go to sleep because that is what it has been doing for years. Therefore, we have to restrain it from sleeping, while at the same time, we must sustain the quietude and keep it as alert as possible. In the talks, I keep you awake with a joke, or by chanting the *Gītā*. That's why I insist that everybody has a *Gītā* in his hand to participate in the chanting.

Clockwise from above:
Swamiji making a point during 2nd Jnana Yagna, Chennai, 1953
During the 5th Jnana Yagna, Madurai, 1954
Impromptu satsaṅga in an alley
Satsaṅga anywhere, anytime!

◂ **Facing page clockwise from above:**
A dip in holy waters during avabhṛta-snāna
Satsaṅga in a park, 1954
Avabhṛta-snāna in Mother Gaṅgā's lap (Swamiji front centre),1955
A dynamic teacher, Jnana Yagna in Palghat, 1957
Satsaṅga on the way during a spiritual picnic

Top left:
Welcome in Tatmangalam, January 1969
Top right:
Being welcomed with pūrṇa-kumbha by temple priest, Chennai, June 1955
Left:
Traveling in Trivandrum, 1958

Above left:
Satsaṅga outside the temple space, Allahabad, 1957
Above right:
Bhikṣā in Alandi, 1957
Left:
Boat journey from Palghat to Kanyakumari, 1957

Clockwise from above:
On the dais during morning class in Ellisbridge, Ahmedabad, May 1966
Sitting on a trunk during satsaṅga in Alandi, 1957
M. Parukutty translating Swamiji's address in Tunjar Gardens under the Presidency of P. Kesav Menon, Editor of *Matru Bhoomi*, a Kerala newspaper
Spiritual picnic to Kanyakumari after Palghat Jnana Yagna, 1957

From Above:
Crowds following Swamiji as he walks through the city
Crowds following Swamiji on cycles, 10th Jnana Yagna, Mattancheri, 1955
The Divine Pilot, cars following Swamiji as the procession grows, 10th Jnana Yagna, Mattancheri, 1955

Clockwise from above:
One Thousand Steps, 4th Jnana Yagna, Palghat,1954
Eating fruits with devotees in a boat at Triveni, Allahabad, November 1957
Group photo with devotees after avabhṛta-snāna
In the bus during spiritual picnic

ENCOUNTER WITH AN ELEPHANT

The year 1958 marked a revolutionary change amongst the orthodox ritualistic people of Tirunelveli District (Tamil Nadu). All the arrangements for the 38th Jnana Yagna had been perfectly streamlined and meticulously planned. Swamiji was to arrive from Alleppy by car along the rickety ghat-section road, which would take him seven hours to reach Tirunelveli.

At the outskirts of Punalloor, driver Pillai suddenly braked the car. There was a huge elephant standing in the center of the road, and Pillai got very panicky. Immediately, Swamiji exchanged places with him. He took control of the steering wheel with one hand, and, with the other, he held a bunch of plantains (bananas), which were all his eatable possessions. He threw them at the elephant saying, "Inda edutho!" meaning "Take this!" in Malayalam. The elephant swallowed the whole bunch, then turned about and left sideways for the jungle.

"Patent non-possession is the way to succeed and survive!" exclaimed Swamiji.

Dr. N. Krishnaswami
Chinmaya Mission Ooty

MUMBAI BEGINNINGS

On a visit to Delhi in 1957, I asked Swamiji at the MLA quarters where he was staying, "Do you ever come to Mumbai, Swamiji?"

"If you call me, I will come," replied Swamiji.

"But, I don't know what all needs to be done!"

Swamiji assured me that Sushila Mudliar from Pune would come and help us with all the details. The 1st Mumbai Jnana Yagna was arranged on the terrace of K. C. College in December 1957. It was for twenty-one days, and Swamiji stayed with us at Omar Park, Warden Road.

He never went to the dais till the scheduled time. If we arrived at the venue early, Swamiji would walk around the venue till 30 seconds before the appointed time. At the end of the Yagna, everyone went on a spiritual picnic to Alandi, a temple dedicated to Sant Jnaneshwar. I remember Swamiji teaching us how to make queues at the entrance of the temple.

In those days, there were not many workers, so we used to pack all the books, which we then sent to other places. Swamiji would show me how to do it neatly. Everything was taught by example, by doing it himself.

There were only a hundred people for that first Yagna, since we had only done the publicity by word-of-mouth. But when Swamiji came again in December 1958, there were at least five-hundred people. This Yagna, held in Shriniketan, Marine Drive, was also for twenty-one days, but there was no spiritual picnic. I think the picnics ended in 1957.

By the 3rd Mumbai Jnana Yagna (in 1959) the crowd had become an astonishing twenty-thousand people. I was not in Mumbai at the time, and this was arranged in Matunga. The Chinmaya Mission had really grown.

Sheel Dewan
Chinmaya Mission Mumbai

RAIN OR SHINE

Jnana Yagna plans were being made in Rourkela in October 1985. Before the time of the Yagna arrived, Swamiji had written to me and said, "The Yagna will go on, come what may."

Although it was not the rainy season, arrangements had been made to cover the open-air lecture area. And indeed, it rained heavily the night before the concluding lecture. Water swept in from the surrounding area onto the straw mats on the ground where people were sitting, and the cover also collapsed under the weight of the rain, destroying the dais.

Immediately, arrangements were made to hold the last talk inside the college auditorium next to the grounds. The last lecture was held inside a closed hall lit with petromax lights, and the Jnana Yagna continued uninterrupted.

After the Yagna, Swamiji wrote, "I'm so happy that the Yagna went on — despite all storms!"

K. C. Patnaik
Head, Books and Publications Division,
Central Chinmaya Mission Trust

SUBRAMANIAM VERSUS SUBRAMANIAM

On the inauguration day of a Jnana Yagna in Chennai (in 1988), there were many eminent persons sitting on the dais with Swamiji. Among others, there was Mr. A. Subramaniam (the President of Chinmaya Mission Chennai) and Mr. C. Subramaniam (a former cabinet minister and statesman). Swamiji smiled at both of them, and began his address, "To my left is A. Subramaniam, to my right is C. Subramaniam; so I must B(e) Subramaniam! You also *Be* Subramaniam!" [Subrahmaṇyaḥ or Kārtikeya is the son of Lord Śiva, a favorite deity in South India. Subrahmaṇyaḥ here refers to Divinity or Godhood.]

Narrated by Swami Mitrananda
Acharya, Chinmaya Mission Chennai

The early days were not easy. The days were long and packed with activity. Swamiji spent up to three hours answering a mounting pile of daily letters from devotees. The morning and evening lectures had become a standard for all Jnana Yagnas, and they were often preceded by a group meditation class. There were also question and answer sessions, satsaṅgas, pūjās, bhikṣās, and book projects to attend to during the day. In addition, Swamiji was on constant alert, improving and building on these requirements. Shivraman, who began serving Swamiji from 1963, reminisced of the early days:

> Swamiji had given me standing instructions to always keep clothes ready for travel. He only traveled by bus or train as funds were limited. Many days he went to sleep at 1:00 A.M., but he would always be up by 3:00 A.M. to start the new day. I would sometimes oversleep, and when Swamiji came out of his room he would lovingly wake me up.
>
> In 1963–64, during the Mumbai Jnana Yagnas, Swamiji would go to the city for bhikṣā after the evening talk. The distance from Powai ashram was great, and it would take him one and a half hours just to drive back at night. It used to get very late, so he would sleep in the van.

From 1952–60, many cities all over India started to organize Jnana Yagnas: Palghat, Madurai, Coimbatore, Kozhikode, Mattancheri, Ooty, Bangalore, Calcutta, Rewa, Tanjore, Ernakulam, Trichur, Hyderabad, Allahabad, Mumbai, Tirunelveli, Aurangabad, Mangalore, Tripunithura, Cannanore, Tiruchirapalli, Mysore, Trivandrum, Secundarabad, Nagpur, and Vijayavada.

Swami Jyotirmayananda remembers the challenging days of the 4th Upaniṣad Jnana Yagna in Palghat (in 1954):

> Damodar Nair and I had extended the invitation to Swamiji to come to Palghat when we were in Guruvayur. We came in a bus with Swamiji, and it would get stuck at every climb. Swamiji would come down with the other passengers and push the bus. And because there was not enough seating room, Swamiji and I huddled in a little corner where the spare tire was kept, for the entire journey.

> Swamiji was so full of energy and enthusiasm. He never bothered about discomforts. We would share one mat to sleep on, and there was no bedding or pillows. Very often, the three of us would share one banana. And that was our meal.
>
> Towards the end of the Yagna, Swamiji drove through the town in a truck and sprinkled Gaṅgā-jala on everybody. Other trucks, cars, and cycles would follow him. He led all the devotees all over the town, and finally performed the avabhṛta-snāna (bathing in the river). Word spread from town to town and the circle of devotees grew. Things began to move.

Up until now, Swamiji had been broadly known as "the swami from Uttarkashi." But as word of his spiritual brilliance and marvelous oratory spread — intellectuals, professionals, scientists, politicians, the young and old, rich and poor — all gathered at Jnana Yagnas in their cities.

In 1956, the 23rd Jnana Yagna in Delhi was inaugurated by the President of India, Dr. Rajendra Prasad. He spoke in glowing terms of the work Swamiji was doing to restore India's cultural glory.

In 1961, Delhi's Community Hall on Panchkuin Road was packed with people despite the heavy monsoon rains. When there was no seating room available, men stood against the wall and women sat on top of shoes.

In a span of five years, Swamiji had provided a happier life for over 50,000 of his countrymen through twenty-five Jnana Yagnas in the country. Each year the invitations had grown: In 1951–52, one Yagna; in 1953, two Yagnas; in 1954, four Yagnas; in 1955, eight Yagnas; and in 1956, ten Yagnas. After the second Jnana Yagna, an invitation to Swamiji to conduct a Yagna was always backed by a group of dedicated workers who organized the activities.

When Swamiji was in Ananda Kutir in the summer of 1953, Swami Sivananda had advised him that 100 days was too long for a Yagna. Swami Sivananda felt that shorter doses at regular intervals would be more beneficial. Thus, when Swamiji conducted his 12th Jnana Yagna in Chennai in June 1955, the number of days had come down to twenty-one. This Yagna was also the first "Mobile Jnana Yagna." Over twenty-one days, Swamiji moved between three localities — Egmore, Saidapet, and T. Nagar — covering portions of the *Vivekacūḍāmaṇi. He had taken the scriptures to everybody's doorstep.*

As he went from city to city, town to town, new ideas to incorporate into the Yagnas occurred to him. By 1967, Swamiji had conducted 150 Jnana Yagnas. The spiritual renaissance of India was turning out to be quite a mission! Over the next thirty-five years, this figure would become 773 Jnana Yagnas — an impressive achievement in itself for just one lifetime. Not surprisingly, Swami Sivananda had proclaimed to all present in Ananda Kutir in 1953, "There are many disciples here, but none so daring and courageous as Chinmaya." Swami Govindagiri had expressed a similar sentiment in Uttarkashi, "One thing I can definitely say the entire time I have known him — Chinmaya is fearless!"

> IT WAS AN AFTERNOON DREAM THAT TOOK ME
> TO MORE THAN A HUNDRED CITIES IN INDIA,
> TO ADDRESS ABOUT 50,000 DEVOTEES,
> IN TWENTY-FIVE JNANA YAGNAS.
>
> | SWAMI CHINMAYANANDA |

It is an extraordinary dream, and surely the most fearless of all of Swamiji's transformations: In youth, from self-proclaimed agnostic to spiritual seeker — in maturity, from fumbling speaker to brilliant orator— and now, to visionary and man of God.

CHINMAYANANDA

Phone: Perumalpuram 63.
138, PERUMALPURAM
TIRUNELVELI-7

My Programme
(Gives here to leave you.)

August

15th — Yagna concluded here.

16th — Madurai (Civic Address)

17th — Tapovanam (Meditation)
evening Rotary Club.

18th — Trichy (Public Reception &
Civic Address).

19th — Nagercoil (Public Reception) Sleep
at Cape.

20th — Visit Vivekananda Rock — Temple
building. Evening: Mission
meeting Trivandrum.

21st. — Ernakulam — (Civic address):
with members of C.C.M.T. Advisory
Board from all over India visits
to Kaladi.

22nd. C.C.M.T. Advisory Board meeting

23rd. Bangalore (Civic Address). The
largest reception — in Glass House,
Lalbagh. Seats for 25,000 people!

24th. Mysore (Reception)

25th — 29th. Hyderabad — Usmania

University Colleges: 4 Colleges —
4 meeting each day for
4 days!

30th Bombay — V.H. Parishad meeting

September
31st — 2nd Sept — Baroda: University.

4th Sept — Coimbatore (Reception)

5th — 19th — Yagna Ooty & Conoor.

20th — Reception Palaghat —
Evening Civic Address Kozhikode.

21st — Mangalore (Bala Vihar)

22nd — 25 — Bombay (College)

26th — Delhi — Lunch Bindra —

26th Evening — 30th morning: Meerut.

30th — Lucknow J.P. evening
Rotary Club
"Secret of Efficiency".

October.
1st — to Madras.
2nd — to Trivandrum — by car to
Dharangadhara Chemicals,
Sahunagar....
2nd Evening — 5th Evening: 7 talks on Indian Culture.
drive to Trivandrum —
6th jet to Bombay
7 Calcutta — Yagna - - - - Gita

◀◀ **Overleaf:**
"Given here to tease you,
Swami Chinmayananda's
itinerary, August–
October 1965

Above:
Welcome at a railway station, 1959
Center:
Swamiji honored in his own state — Kerala (Swamiji standing in the car), 32nd Jnana Yagna, Trichur, 1957
Below:
Last day of Jnana Yagna, Bangalore, 1957

◀ **Facing page clockwise from above:**
Audience during Jnana Yagna, South India
Dr. Rajendra Prasad, President of India, inaugurates a Jnana Yagna, New Delhi, 1956
97th Jnana Yagna, Mumbai, November 1961
During a Jnana Yagna in Juhu Beach, Mumbai

Clockwise from above:
Jnana Yagna in Kollengode, Palghat, 1960
Swamiji with devotees during 7th Jnana Yagna, Delhi, 1954
Morning class in Mumbai, (Jnana Yagna inaugurated by Cardinal Gracias), 1964
Swamiji arrives at the yajñaśālā with kamaṇḍalu, Palghat, 1957
During 86th Jnana Yagna, Hyderabad, May 1961

Clockwise from above:
aily crowd in Hyderabad Jnana Yagna for *Bhagavad-gītā*, Chapter 3, May 1961
Portrait of Swamiji, Ooty, June 1955
Audience in Raja Annamalai Hall, Chennai, July 1965
One section of gathering in Hyderabad, January 20, 1964

XI

Everything Coming Out "Young" and Wise: The Birth of Chinmaya Mission

The taste of Truth is a mysterious thing. It leaves you unsatisfied and wanting more — at least until you've got the whole truth and nothing but the truth. At the end of the 2nd Jnana Yagna in Chennai (in 1953), a handful of people expressed the desire to create a forum for study and discussion. They wanted an ongoing program to clarify their understanding of Vedānta, and to keep up the inspiration of the fourty-one days spent with Swamiji.

Swamiji was aware that he needed a bigger plan. At present, whenever he left a city at the conclusion of a Jnana Yagna, everything folded up. And if a seeker was to gain success, śravaṇa (listening) would have to be followed by mananam (reflection), and cintanam (thinking).

In the summer of 1953, a Chennai group had written to Swamiji in Uttarkashi to inform him of their plan to call the new forum "Chinmaya Mission." Swamiji's reply came without delay. He agreed in principle. But, he said:

> Don't start any organization in my name. I have not come here to be institutionalized. I have come here to give the message of our ancient sages which has benefited me. If it has benefited you, pass it on.

The dozen people insisted that the best way to "pass it on" was through the support of a group. They wrote back stating that the word "Chinmaya" did not have to indicate Swamiji's name, since the word itself meant "pure Knowledge," which they were seeking. "As seekers of the Truth" they concluded, "we are calling ourselves Chinmaya Mission."

It made excellent sense.

Swamiji relented.

On August 8, 1953, Chinmaya Mission was formed. And the seekers of Truth lived to study another day.

THE PERFECT NAME

When Swamiji started his work in 1951, he called it DIVINE MISSION, since he had been with Swami Sivananda in the Divine Life Society. But I am so glad the Chennai people persisted and called our organization Chinmaya Mission, because this is the perfect name.

Swamiji was devoted to the study of "pure Knowledge." He was a true jñāna-niṣṭha — one who abides in Truth — and this is the central aspect of his life and work. Everything that he did was for the propagation of Knowledge, in which he himself was firmly established. Abiding in Self-knowledge, he brought about the legacy we see and experience today. Whether it is in the field of education, medicine, society, or spirituality; whether it is for children, youth or adults, all his work arose from this Knowledge and was done for this Knowledge. Until the very end, even when his health deteriorated, he remained steadfast in his love for and abidance in "pure Knowledge."

When I first met him in 1969, it was only for 2-3 minutes. He was recuperating in Mumbai after a heart attack, and I had been allowed into his bedroom for my Vedānta course interview. He had said to me, "Yes, I know you have come here to study. You stay in the ashram." With just these two lines my interview was over! But during this period of so-called rest, he completed his lengthy commentary on *Vivekacūḍāmaṇi.*

Later, when I went with him to Uttarkashi in 1971 (June–August), his health had again deteriorated. And this rest period resulted in the commentary on *Aṣṭavakra Gītā.* Every morning he would dictate the commentary to the stenographer, who typed it and showed it to him. Swamiji would then correct it and have it retyped. And again, he would check it. He also attended to his correspondence, and that was voluminous — I know, because I was given the charge of posting the letters. The post office in Uttarkashi treated me like a special guest, because Swamiji gave them good business. In the evenings, Swamiji would conduct satsaṅga and take classes on *Vivekacūḍāmaṇi.* All this was supposed to be rest.

Swami Tejomayananda
Head, Chinmaya Mission Worldwide

At the end of the 17th Jnana Yagna in Delhi (in March 1956), Swamiji emphasized the necessity for meeting regularly with a definite venue and study scheme. From then on, towards the end of each Yagna, he would distribute a form to the audience (which later coincided with the gurudakṣiṇā envelope). Those who were interested in continuing the study of Vedānta were asked to fill their contact details, after which they were allocated to a "Study Group" in a venue near their home. Each week, the group met for one and a half hours, to study the various scriptures of Vedānta together, in a methodical and systematic manner.

The focus of the Study Group is "śāstra-cintanapradhāna," where emphasis is given to the study and "logical reflection" on the teachings of scriptures. The aim is to gain Self-knowledge. To explain the importance of constant reflection, Swamiji gave the example of a cup of coffee with a spoon of sugar at the bottom. Unless, and until, the sugar is stirred, the coffee remains bitter. Similarly, knowledge is only absorbed when it is properly stirred by the intellect. The role of the Study Group is to stir knowledge so that its sweetness becomes one with the personality. Thus Swamiji said:

> Mere listening will not add to your beauty. These ideas are to be reflected upon deeply, and digested slowly. This process is hastened only when you discuss what you have studied with others. Study Groups constitute the heart of our Mission. The ideas, when discussed with others, not only become deeply rooted in you, but as they become clearer in your own understanding, they also inspire those who listen to you.
>
> Each student, while trying to strengthen his own understanding, can become an instrument for the spread of knowledge. This process is the dynamic study scheme followed in Vedāntic tradition. This is not a Chinmaya methodology; it is the most ancient Vedāntic tradition of study.

The Study Group has been the strength of Chinmaya Mission from its inception. In the early years, members of Study Groups were the organizers of Jnana Yagnas. They also formed the Executive Committees of the 307 mission centers that have since come into existence. Not only have Study Groups been responsible for the foundation of Chinmaya Mission, but they are also credited with its sustenance and expansion.

DO YOU WANT TO JOIN A STUDY GROUP?

When I was posted to the Army headquarters in Delhi in 1979, Swamiji asked me what I was doing after office hours.

"Nothing in particular, Swamiji," I replied. "Please give me some work. Any work! I'll do it."

"When I started out from Uttarkashi, I did not ask anyone, *What should I do?*" Swamiji said to me. "I saw the need of the hour, *and I did it.* You, too, look around you, and see what needs to be done. Then go ahead *and do it.*"

Soon afterwards, at the end of Swamiji's Jnana Yagna (the texts were *Bhagavad-gītā* Chapter 3 and *Nārada Bhakti Sūtra*), we filled up our gurudakṣiṇā envelopes "inside and outside" as directed by Swamiji. On the cover of the envelope, we were asked to write our name, contact details, and tick the boxes next to the activities that we wanted to join. For example, "Do you want to join a Study Group?" Tick.

Many days passed, but I did not hear from the organizers. So I went to meet Br. Radhakrishnan (later Swami Jyotirmayananda) who was the ācārya stationed in Chinmaya Mission Delhi. I asked him if the gurudakṣiṇā envelopes had been sorted out.

"Not yet!" There are too many envelopes, and I have not been able to sort them all," he said.

"Brahmachariji, let me help you," I replied.

It took me a week to sort out the envelopes and contact individuals via postcards (those were the days of snail mail). Then, I again went to meet Br. Radhakrishnan.

"Who will take the Study Groups?" he asked me.

"I will," I replied.

And that is how eight Study Groups started in Delhi in 1979. I would rush back from work in Sena Bhavan, change out of my uniform, drink a quick cup of tea, and vanish into the night for a daily Vedānta class.

Ajit Sukhtankar
Chinmaya Mission Belgaum

But why only teach grown-ups? If children were groomed with noble values from a young age, it would be natural and easy for them to step into a life of vision when they grew up. And what about instructing the youth? Swamiji himself had said, "The youth have the greatest potential. Had it not been necessary to first change the mindset of adults, I would have focused on the youth straight away." There was also the elderly to think about, who had reached a stage in life that called for specific needs. And, women had talents and interests that also required a distinct outline.

Thus, a complete set of programs were initiated, to take care of everybody. As early as 1955, Swamiji had directed Janaki Seth to organize a special program for children in Delhi, where they could learn values with fun. Janaki Seth gathered thirty-five children to begin the "Children's Well-being Center." Within months, the number of children had doubled and they ran out of space. Janaki Seth moved the classes from her home to a public park. In the spring of the same year, the children gave a performance of a Rādhā-Kṛṣṇa dance depicting Holī; and although only two hundred invitations had been sent out, a crowd of three thousand showed up. Soon after, another devotee, Janaki Menon, started a second center in Ernakulam.

Swamiji led the children of Chennai on an excursion to the Guruvayur Temple in 1956, where the main idol is a child Kṛṣṇa.

Enthusiastic children filled an entire train car for the overnight trip to Trichur, where everyone was packed into a bus to finish the remaining twenty miles. The children marched in pairs down the palm-decorated corridor to the entrance gates of the temple chanting *Hare Rāma, Hare Kṛṣṇa* in unison. The entire parade was headed by Swamiji, and accompanied by devotees from all over India.

Due to the growing demand by parents in many cities, the "Children's Well-being Center" was incorporated into a more formal program for children called "Balvihar" in 1957. Balvihar is centered on "saṁskāra pradhāna" (emphasis on inculcating noble values and right disposition in life). Once a week, children between the ages of five-to-twelve years (further separated into groups of juniors and seniors) meet at a common place for 90 minutes, and are exposed to India's cultural and spiritual heritage by trained and dedicated teachers. "We employ various interesting techniques to bring to these children the flavor and beauty, the light and melody, of the Bharatiya culture — the Hindu philosophy of thought and action," wrote Swamiji in *Gītā for Children.* A typical Balvihar class includes bhajans, Gītā chanting, story-telling from the Bāla Rāmāyaṇa, Bāla Bhāgavatam, Purāṇas and Pañcatantras, and a talk on subjects like, "Why pray?" or the "Significance of Festivals." Dr. N. Krishnaswami remembers that "during a Yagna in Thirunelveli in 1958, each evening Swamiji would tell one story to the children."

Swamiji gave great importance to India's Purāṇic literature. He often said:

> Tell ... never teach a story. The very story in the growing child will, by itself, instill the great truths and higher values of life as time passes on. Children learn more by a well-told story than what we teach them through a story.

In olden days, such values were taught at home by elders. But, modern life — with all its complexities, hurry, tensions, and confusions — has denied such benefits to the children of today. They are often stunted by an over-zealous education that gives precedence to material gain. In a manual for teachers, Chinmaya Balvihars: *How to Organize and Run*, Swamiji wrote:

> When a child sheds his milk teeth, this is found to be the most appropriate time to venture forth, from the limited world of his imagination and fancy, into a more solid world of creative thinking, endless curiosity, and irrepressible wonderment at all that is happening around and about. Thereafter, never can a child feel this much of intense hunger to investigate, to enquire, and to know the nature and beauty of the world into which he has entered. Thus, it is a crucial and quickly passing dynamic stage when the child moves from the "lap of the mother" to the "courtyard of his house," and from there, onto the "playfield." If, at this juncture, we can flood him with ideas, and mold him with a little discipline, it will be the greatest service man can do for his child; for at this stage of the child's growth, mishandling can create a devil out of a child; but when rightly handled, we can make a saint out of even a crooked, underdeveloped child.
>
> A tender plant with right support can be trained to grow correctly; but after a stage, when the tissues have hardened, a curvature in the same plant cannot be straightened. Character-building of a nation must start from the cradle and the playfields. Therefore, the simple and unpretentious efforts that have been started by the Chinmaya Mission in organizing Balvihars in the private homes of the very sevikās and sevakas, though at present may seem to be of little significance to all, yet I foresee them as history-making programs for the country — nay, man-making schemes for the world.

> In these workshops, we are conceiving and molding the leaders of tomorrow, and as such, a great and onerous responsibility rests upon the shoulders of the Balvihar workers.
>
> Children are the architects of the future world. They are the builders of humanity. It is the most sacred task of parents and teachers to mold these lives in accordance with the sublime Indian tradition. The seed of spiritual values should be sown in their young hearts, and the condition should be made favorable for its sprouting and steady growth by the exercise of proper control and discipline. Cared for with warmth of love and affection, such a tree shall blossom forth flowers of brotherhood, universal love, peace, bliss, beauty, and perfection.

Anil Sachdev of Delhi beautifully sums up his inspiration:

> When I was a Balvihar student in 1969, Swamiji gave me a signed copy of his book, *Vedānta Through Letters,* as an award for standing first in every subject in my class. In the book, he wrote, "Never yield the first rank in any field to anybody." As a result, I have always been the youngest leader, at every level, in the company where I worked, and also became a director on the board of Eicher at the age of thirty-five years, and went on to become the founder of three leading organizations: Eicher Consultancy Services, Grow Talent Company, and the School of Inspired Leadership (SOIL). I have always had the inner confidence that I could excel anywhere, and in anything, because I have grown up believing that we are all blessed with the same inner Truth.

Swamiji loved children, and his love was wholeheartedly reciprocated by the wide-eyed, self-assured Hindu children. Thousands of adults in India and abroad happily claim the honor of having sat on Swamiji's knee when they were toddlers. He never turned down an opportunity to talk to children. Often, he would start his presentation at a school with the question, "Everyone tells you that you must be good, but did anyone tell you *how* to be good?" When he had gotten their attention with these words, he continued:

> Of course, you all want to be good. You don't need mommy and poppy to tell you to be good, because you all want to be good. But then something happens, and we don't act like we want to. Why?
>
> A bad action means that, at that moment, we had a bad thought. Think about it. It's true, isn't it? I must have had a *kicking* thought before I kicked my little brother. So, here we have our clue. If bad thoughts mean bad actions, then good thoughts must mean good actions. So, we must change our thoughts.
>
> So, how do we get good thoughts? First, we can think of someone who is very good. It could be someone you have heard about from the scriptures, like Rāma or Sītā, or it could be a person you know now who you feel is very good. You remember them and think how they would behave if they were in your situation. If I think that I am as good and kind as Rāma, I will not have a kicking thought when my little brother takes my toy truck. If I do not have a kicking thought, then I will not kick my dear little brother who only wanted to play with my toy.
>
> It is the same as when we call a pot by what it contains: a pot with honey is called a honey pot, a pot with milk is called a milk pot, and a pot with ink is called a ... what? (The children shout — "ink pot!") Yes, an ink pot! In the same way, your mind is called by the thoughts that it contains. Bully thoughts mean a bully mind, so the actions will be those of a bully. Good thoughts mean a good mind, so the actions will be . . . ? (The children shout "good!") Yes! So, now you know how to be good! Good thoughts — good actions! As the thought, so the mind; as the mind, so the child!

THE STORY OF A STORY

During a Gītā Jnana Yagna on Curzon Road in New Delhi (in March 1968), I heard Swamiji for the first time as a teenager, and offered my entire life in service to Chinmaya Mission.

Swamiji was very amused and gave a full laugh, chuckling with his shoulders in merriment. He ruffled my head, and said, "My dear girl, you must not take decisions of a lifetime in an emotional moment. We will talk about this after two years."

When Swamiji left for Uttarkashi after the Yagna had ended, I felt empty; and in this mood, I wrote him a six page letter. He immediately

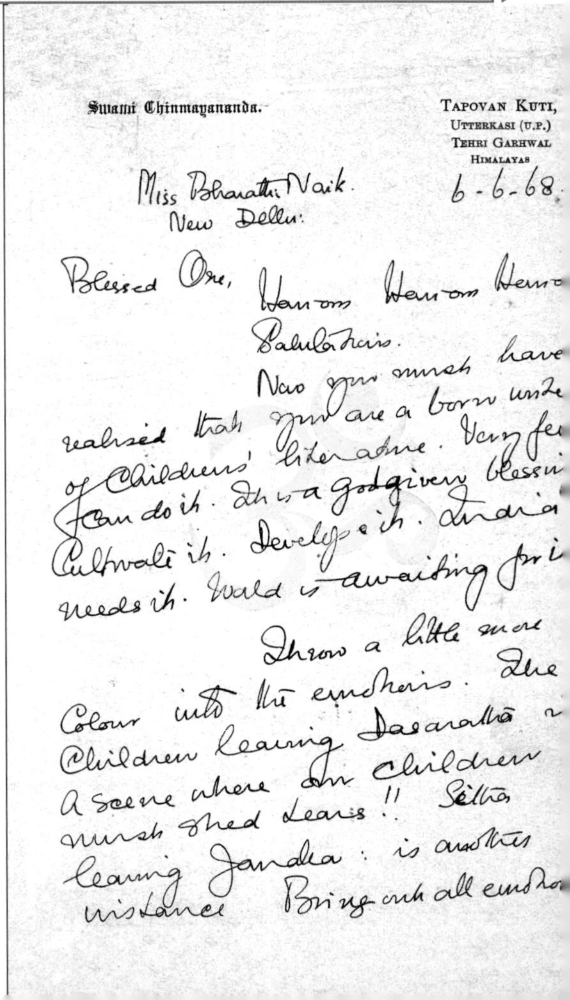

Swami Chinmayananda.

TAPOVAN KUTI,
UTTERKASI (U.P.)
TEHRI GARHWAL
HIMALAYAS

Miss Bharathi Naik. 6-6-68.
New Delhi:

Blessed One, Hariom Hariom Hari
Salutations.
Now you must have
realised that you are a born write
of Childrens' literature. Very fe
can do it. It is a godgiven blessi
Cultivate it. Develop it. India
needs it. World is awaiting for i

Throw a little more
Colour into the emotions. The
Children leaving Dasaratha
A scene where our children
must shed tears!! Seetha
leaving Janaka: is another
instance Bring out all emotio

wrote back, saying, "Write a *Bāla Rāmāyaṇa* for children." Me? Write for children? I was a science student! Nevertheless, I started the work, and would send him 20–25 pages at a time to correct. The printed book was released by Swamiji a few months later in November 1968 during his Gītā Jnana Yagna in Shivaji Park, Mumbai.

And then, another letter arrived from him. It said, "Read *Śrīmad-bhāgavatam.* We will take it up after August. Say, in September middle. Okay?"

Bharati Suktankar
Chinmaya Mission Belgaum
[Writer of children's books Bāla Rāmāyaṇa and Bāla Bhāgavatam]

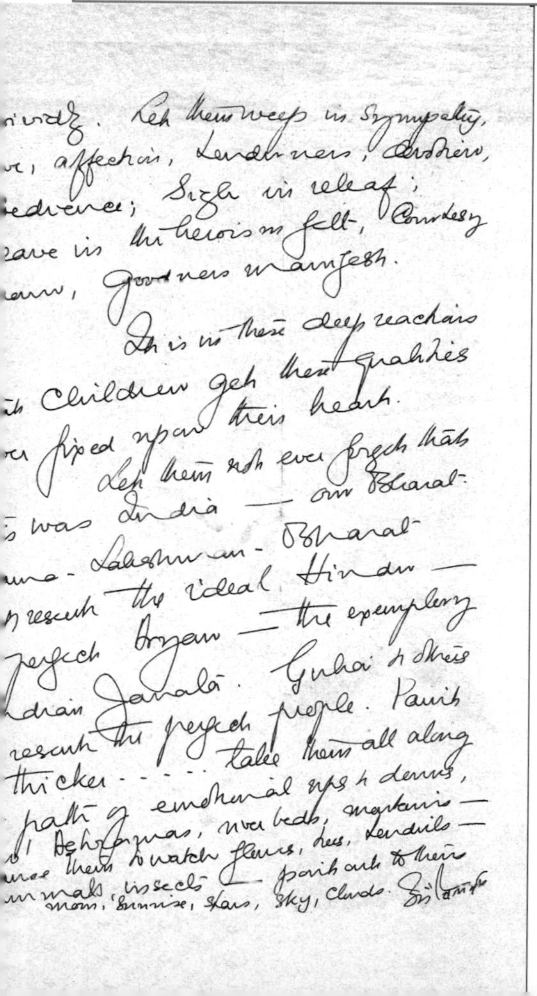
...wardly. Let them weep in sympathy,
...e, affection, tenderness, devotion,
...bedience; Sigh in relief;
...rave in the heroism felt, Courtesy
...own, goodness manifest.
It is in these deep reactions
...th children get these qualities
...er fixed upon their heart.
Let them not ever forget that
...s was India — our Bharat-
...ma-Lakshman-Bharat-
...present the ideal Hindu —
...perfect Aryan — the exemplary
...dian Janata. Guha & others
...resent the perfect people. Point
...thicker . . . . take them all along
...path of emotional ups & downs,
...! Ashramas, river beds, mountains —
...use them to watch flowers, trees, tendrils —
...nimals, insects — point out to them
moon, sunrise, stars, sky, clouds. Swami...

Clockwise from above:
Swamiji with children in Kerala,1953
Swamiji with child, 1967
On a trip with Balvihar children, Kolkata, 1973

▶ **Facing page above:**
Swamiji with children in Kerala,1953
Below:
Addressing children in Chennai, 1966

◀◀ **Overleaf above:**
Swamiji with children in Kolkata, 1964
Below:
Swamiji with child in Raveli, 1962
Centerfold:
Letter to Bharati Suktankar, June 6, 1968

◀ **Overleaf above:**
"You want to see a trick?" says Swamiji, Balmahotsav in Kollengode, 1962
Below:
Then, "See the Swami disappear!" Balmahotsav in Kollengode, 1962

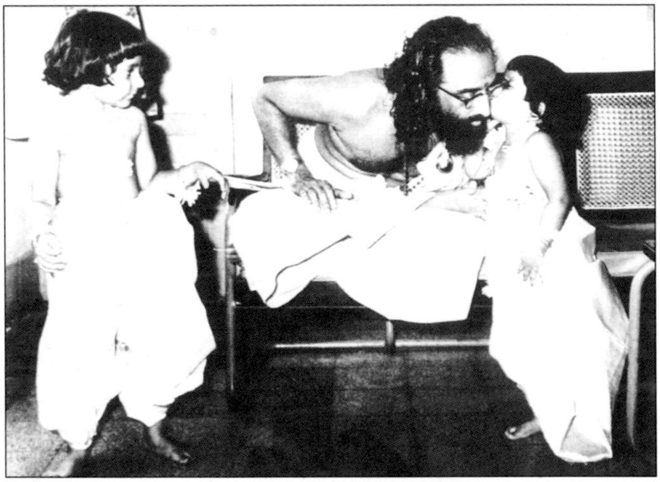

Clockwise from above:
Telling a story to children, 1965
Giving a prize to "Vāmana Bhagavān," Trichur, 1974
All Kerala Balmahotsav, Kollengode, 1962
A child expresses love for Swamiji after a Balvihar cultural program, 1966

Clockwise from above:
Thirteen year old Jujhar Singh mimes Swamiji in Sidhbari, June 1983
Swamiji leading the parade during Balmahotsav in Cannanore, 1962
151st Jnana Yagna, Matunga, Mumbai, 1967
Swamiji watches a cultural program by Balvihar children, Indore
Swamiji with children in Kollengode, 1964

There is a need for each new generation to argue and discuss where their present actions are taking them in the future. Where such discussion is encouraged, better destinies are made. Not surprisingly, Swamiji often said, "The youth are not useless or careless, but used less and cared less." Thus, the "Chinmaya Yuva Kendra" (CHYK) is a special forum that gives attention to the needs of youth all over the world between the ages of thirteen-to-twenty-eight years, and this environment centers on "vicāra pradhāna" (emphasis on enquiry).

Swamiji encouraged youngsters to enquire and ask questions:

Q: Swamiji, is spirituality relevant to young people like me? Can it qualitatively improve my life?

A: Yes! It is far more relevant to you because you are young. You must learn the art of living as early as possible. If you can understand your real nature today, then why wait till life has passed you by. Qualitatively, it means being infinitely happy today, and staying that way to infinity!

Q: But, do I have to give up things I like?

A: When you want to pass an exam, you have to temporarily give up some fun time to study. But once you have passed, you don't have to continue to do so. Understanding who you truly are is the ultimate exam. Once you have this Self-knowledge, you become a law unto yourself.

Q: But, don't you think taking sannyāsa (renunciation) is escapism?

A: Let's get one thing straight. If a black coat on you does not make you a lawyer, and a white coat does not make you a doctor, then an orange robe will certainly not make you a sannyāsī! Sannyāsa means retirement from the distractions of the world in order to apply the mind with complete attention in one specific line of study. If Einstein had not taken sannyāsa from the ordinary world, he would not have achieved anything. All people who have contributed anything in the world have taken sannyāsa. All research scholars, all artists are sannyāsīs, in the sense that they have no time for the ordinary things of life. When the great lawyer, Tej Bahadur Sapru, was asked for the secret of his success, he said, "In order to be successful, you must work like a horse, and live like a hermit." Without tyāga (giving up), sannyāsa is impossible; and without sannyāsa, achievement is impossible.

Q: In one of your lectures, you said that Nārāyaṇa in the form of thought strikes Eintein's mind; and the theory of relativity is the result. Why? How?

A: Nārāyaṇa is ever-present, just as electricity is ever-present. Yet, the radio does not play music until it is switched on; and even then, the electric current produces only that music which is played by the station to which the radio is tuned. Einstein was tuned to relativity, Newton to gravity, Sir V. C. Raman to the Raman rays, and Ādi Śaṅkarā to Saccidānanda.

Q: Then what should be *my* tuning?

A: Tune your mind to the Self within. Remove your individual pettiness (ego) from all your actions. Your whole world will expand; you will see the "bigger picture," so to speak. Then whatever you do will be perfect.

A TRICKY QUESTION

One day in Sidhbari (in 1992) when I was 19 years old, I put a handkerchief on my hand and asked Swamiji, "Does God know which side of my hand I am going to drop (as in tilt) this handkerchief?"

Swamiji looked at my mischievous face and solemnly said, "God is sarvajña (all-knowing). He definitely knows!"

"If God really knows, then it means he has already decided where it should fall! So where is the question of free will?" I asked. "If there is free will, God cannot be all-knowing; and, if God was all-knowing, there cannot be any free will."

I thought I had trapped Swamiji. He had already said God is sarvajña, so how could he now say there is free will without first retracting his earlier statement? Swamiji gave me many examples to explain the point. The others around him possibly thought I had been very audacious, but Swamiji seemed to be very pleased with my questioning. He told me, "Keep studying. Keep enquiring. Keep asking questions. Good!"

I had not been satisfied with any answer that day, but if anyone were to ask me the same question today, I would say exactly what Swamiji had said to me then. Swamiji knew what was best for the student, and this is something I have only understood with time: Teaching is Love. The Truth has to be revealed when the student is ready to benefit from it. Or else, such a teaching may fail to benefit. It may even cause serious difficulties for the spiritual novice.

Swami Advayananda
President, Chinmaya International Foundation
Ādi Śaṅkara Nilayam, Veliyanad

The youth are symbols of energy, dynamism, creativity, and courage. CHYK aims to channel these qualities with clarity of thought and higher ideals. Vedānta study classes lie at the very core of CHYK, and the youth are encouraged to apply their knowledge in all their multifarious activities — be it "Awakening Indians to India" (a television quiz show with a participation of 280,000 students), Youth Empowerment Programs, motorcycle rallies, cultural performances, or compiling books and magazines. Such "Dynamic Spirituality," as Swamiji phrased it, "equips the youth to build their life, and to deal with life as it comes."

THE AUTOBIOGRAPHY OF EVERY MAN IS:
RUN TOWARDS WHAT YOU WANT AND RUN AWAY
FROM WHAT YOU DON'T WANT. THE IRONY OF LIFE IS
THAT WHATEVER YOU DON'T WANT RUNS AFTER YOU,
AND WHAT YOU WANT RUNS AWAY FROM YOU.

| SWAMI CHINMAYANANDA |

During the 1st Upaniṣad Jnana Yagna in Pune (in 1951–52), young students had begun to shoulder many of the organizational tasks. A year later, Swamiji received an invitation from Jaybala Gujjar, a student of Fergusson College, Pune, to speak for four consecutive evenings at the campus. Swamiji called the lecture series: "The Creative Power Under the Lens of Logic and Science." To the delight of the organizers, the auditorium was packed with students; and the following week many of them gathered at Swamiji's residence to air their doubts.

One girl had asked him a simple question, "Why is it that even though we know a child is innocent, we are attached to the clean one and repelled by a dirty one?" Someone in her group criticized the girl for asking such an unimportant question. But Swamiji corrected them. "No! No question is unimportant. You are just beginning to question the nature of the mind. You have to start with simple questions." Swamiji later remarked, "This will be one of the greatest experiences in my work to look back upon for all times."

MIND THE MOBIKE

A group of CHYKs went on a cycle rally in 1985 to Tamaraipakkam, which is 35 kilometers from Chennai. When Swamiji later came to our city, we excitedly told him about our rally. He laughed, and whispered, "Ssssh!! Don't say it loudly. The milkman goes there daily with his two cans of milk. If you go to the Himalayas, then you may call it a rally."

Swamiji's words had a deep impact on the CHYKs. And this is how we started our mobike rallies all over India. Since then, the CHYKs have done rallies to the Char Dham (Yamnotri, Gangotri, Kedarnath, and Badrinath); and to Amarnath via Ladakh, where we biked on the highest road on earth; and to Khardungla Pass. We have also done five rallies to Sidhbari in Himachal Pradesh. All these rides have made us tough, and in their own way, they have taught us how to meet life.

During one of his Yagnas in Chennai in the late 1980's, we started to pilot his car with our mobikes. We would clear the traffic in front of the car; Swamiji proudly called us "His escorts." On the last day, when I was standing outside his door (looking very glum since Swamiji was leaving the next day), he remarked, "Tomorrow onwards, you escort your mind towards Him. If any obstacles come, you say 'Move!' and it will obey."

Swami Mitrananda
Acharya, Chinmaya Mission Chennai;
Director, All India Chinmaya Yuva Kendra (AICHYK)

SPIRITUAL WARFARE

In 1961, the Jnana Yagnas used to last twenty-one days. "Shoot!" Swamiji would say after the morning class and shake his crossed-over leg while waiting for people to ask questions. I was eighteen years old and liked firing missiles from the audience line, which he would proceed to blow into smithereens each time. After two weeks of "warfare," I formally surrendered and went to see him at his Ashoka Road residence in Delhi.

"Where do you manufacture them?" he asked, referring to the ammunition I had been sending out in the form of questions.

"My uncle said you liked explosives!" I said with a smile.

I again went to meet Swamiji with my mother on Guru Pūrṇimā day (dedicated to worship of the Guru). He asked my mother what I was doing. She told him that I had given up my studies midway in order to study Vedānta.

"Anjali has even spent one and a half months in Uttarkashi, and from there has gone on-foot to Yamnotri and Gangotri," she concluded.

Swamiji seemed not at all impressed. "How will you master the subjective science of the Self, which is far more difficult, if you are not able to cope with the objective world, which is much easier? First, master the objective science, then you master the subjective science. Go and get a degree!" he said to me. Then he again turned to my mother, and scolded her, saying, "Go and put her back into college!" This was Swamiji's first gift of grace to me on that sacred occasion of Guru Pūrṇimā.

Anjali Singh
Chinmaya Mission Delhi

Swamiji wanted the youth to be well educated — simultaneously, he wanted them to start thinking about the religious ideas presented in his talks. During the 13th Gītā Jnana Yagna in Delhi (in 1955), the students had presented a short satire which was set in modern life based on his *Gītā* talks. Thereafter, Swamiji had announced a student essay competition on the subject of "My Religion" based on the ideas of *Bhagavad-gītā,* Chapters 3 and 4. Later that year, in Calcutta, he announced another student competition on the theme, "More Light on My Religion," based on his classes on *Īśāvāsya-upaniṣad.* The first prize was a generous 100 rupees, with 50 rupees for second place.

Given the smallest opportunity, Swamiji would address students at various colleges. On one occasion, he drove all night after the evening lecture to give a presentation at a college graduation ceremony in the morning, and returned that same afternoon just in time for the evening *Gītā* talk. The book *Meditation & Life,* compiled from the 13th Jnana Yagna in Delhi, was given to all graduates of Madras University and Delhi University through a nonprofit trust.

By the time CHYK developed into an organized body in Bangalore in 1975, Swamiji had begun to challenge the youth, demanding a higher standard of excellence from the more experienced CHYK members. Swami Chidrupananda (Acharya, Chinmaya Mission Noida, and Director of All India CHYK North Zone) relates an incident from the CHYK Camp in Trichy in January 1988:

> It was during a question and answer session, when one of the CHYK members asked, How to exhaust vāsanās (desires)? Swamiji remarked, "Such simple questions on Vedānta are not expected from our senior members. They are thoroughly supposed to know the basic concepts." Of course, Swamiji then went on to answer the question, but his point was clear to all.

On another occasion reported by Dr. D. V. Prafulla of Bangalore, a CHYK student had written a letter to Swamiji requesting his blessings before starting a new business venture. Swamiji wrote back, "With so much lethargy, you will not succeed in business." The youth was confused. He did not understand why Swamiji had thought he was lethargic. But days later, it struck him that his letter to Swamiji had been posted almost a week after it had been written. Swamiji had noticed the date on the postage stamp! Once again, the point had been made loud and clear.

BE ALERT. BE VIGILANT.

LET YOUR MIND BE WHERE YOUR HANDS ARE.

| SWAMI CHINMAYANANDA |

Swami Mitrananda recounts an incident with Swamiji in Sidhbari (in 1986). The CHYKs had recently completed a "Relay Yagna" on *Śrī Rāma-gītā* in Chennai under the guidance of Swami Dheerananda (then Br. Sudhir Chaitanya). They would each speak on the topic for twenty minutes before handing the microphone over to the next youth member. When the group of CHYKs arrived in Sidhbari, Swamiji asked them to conduct their Relay Yagna for the entire camp. The CHYKs conclusively decided Swamiji must have been joking! But the next day, Swamiji ended his evening talk forty-five minutes early, and handed the mike to the CHYKs. Raju (now Swami Mitrananda) was the first speaker, and his topic was "Māyā" (cosmic delusionary power of the Lord). When he finished fifteen minutes later, Swamiji clapped his hands and said, "What I have been trying to explain for thirty-five years, my child finished explaining in fifteen minutes!"

Swamiji was no stranger to self-assured women either. He had grown up amidst them, and was in complete agreement with furthering the cause of their liberation and education in Vedānta. Many talented and energetic women had been the chief organizers of his Jnana Yagnas, starting with Sushila Mudliar, Devaki Menon,

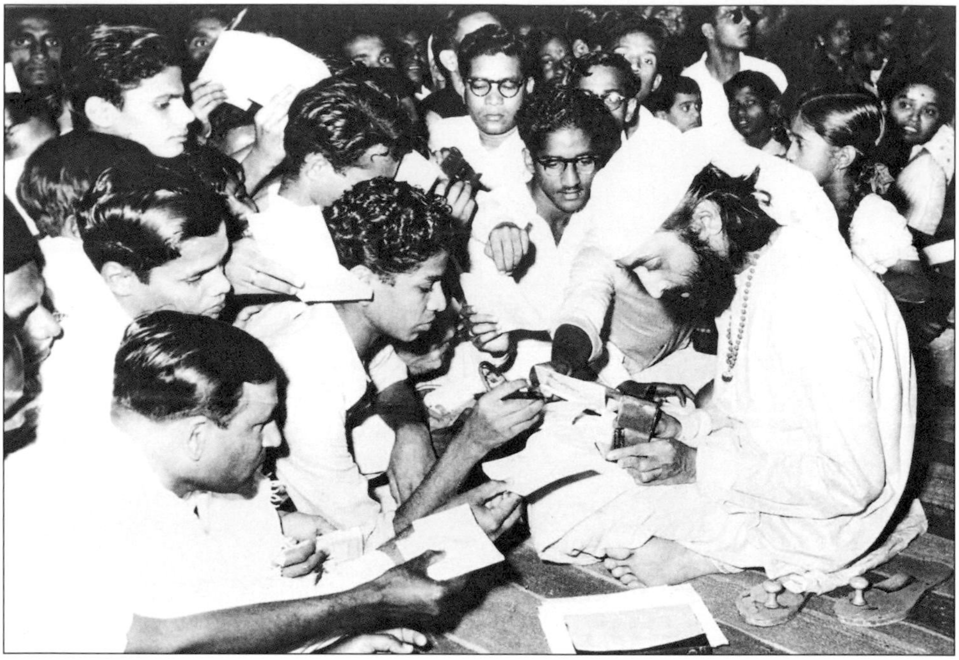

Above:
Swamiji's last youth camp in India (with 700 participants), Sidhbari, May 1993
Center:
Teenagers flock around Swamiji in the courtyard, Sidhbari, 1983
Below:
Swamiji talks to students, Sidhbari, 1983

◂ **Facing page above:**
A rush for autographs, 1956
Below:
With children in Mangalore, 1967

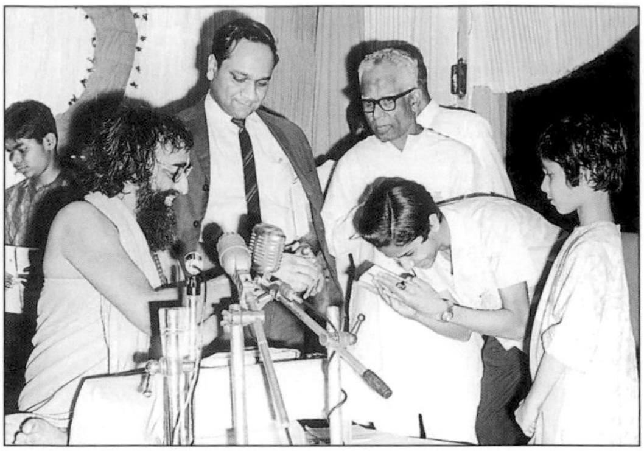

Clockwise from above:
CHYK Meet in Vishakhapatnam, March 1993
A teenager wins a prize on an essay on "The Vision of Gītā"
Meeting youth in Kuala Lumpur, 1989
Meeting youth in Indore, March 1993

Below:
CHYK Camp, Sandeepany Sadhanalaya Powai, 1974

and Sheela Puri. As early as 1954, the 7th Jnana Yagna in Delhi had been organized by an all-female committee; and in 1962, the women of Chennai had organized his 100th Jnana Yagna.

Consequently, when Ma Sundaran approached him in Chennai on November 2, 1958, with a request to start a Study Group of like-minded ladies, Swamiji heartily encouraged her, and named them the "Chinmaya Devi (Goddess) Group." This format allowed women to study scripture as well as apply its concepts to their specific problems at home.

The activities of the Devi Group were given a real boost in January 1960, when several hundred women delegates from twenty-three towns gathered at the Venguhad Palace at Kollengode, Kerala, for a Chinmaya Devi Conference. The Raja of Kollengode personally saw to the comfort of every person. Each day was filled with classes on scripture, instruction, and practice of bhajanas, and satsaṅga with Swamiji. His message to women centered on the importance of the women in the family. "When a mother is a true seeker, the whole environment of the house changes," said Swamiji. "Your family does not have to go out to hear a swami. You change, and your environment will follow suit. You are the mother, the model, the Guru."

THE EFFEMINATE MIND

Q: Swamiji, are women and śūdras (lower castes) prohibited from chanting Gāyatrī Mantra?

A: Thousands and thousands of ladies and śūdras are chanting Gāyatrī under Arya Samaj. When the śāstras (scriptures) declare so, the declaration is true, but our understanding is wrong. Japa (continuous recitation of the name of the Lord) is undertaken by the mind and not the body, and, therefore, the "woman" in the śāstras does not indicate the physical sex, but it is the "effeminate mind" which is full of attachments, fears, passions, and lusts.

Śūdra also means those who are tāmasic (slothful and sleepy) in their mind. To such people, the Gāyatrī japa would be ineffective and a waste of time, since they will not be able to gain the full benefit of the japa.

You go through the book *Meditation & Life;* completely study it; and if you still have the same doubts, please come back to me in a letter.

Q: In your talk on *Nārada Bhakti Sūtra,* you pointed out the difference between "love" and "devotion." You said "devotion" is love towards the higher, and "love" is love towards the lower. When a mother sacrifices her own life for the sake of the child, is this higher or lower love? How can one distinguish between the two?

A: This question is answered by Nārada himself in the Sūtras. In a nutshell, the love that leaves you with agitations in the mind is lower. And the love that leaves you with profound peace and joy is higher.

When you love material objects, and entertain emotions and thoughts for your own selfish pleasures, this love gives rise to desires and agitations in the mind. Fulfillment of these desires will only create a demand for more of the same, whereas disappointment of such desires gives rise to sorrow, anger, and a whole lot of other emotional agitations.

People speak of "falling in love." Since it is a fall, it is obviously lower. On the other hand, when you love the higher; every action, every sacrifice you make towards the object of your devotion, is prayer — a dedication that reduces your egocentric desires and calms the agitations in the mind. Only the mind that has become peaceful and tranquil is fit for meditation. And a mind at meditation knows pure devotion and higher love.

Clockwise from above:
Akhil Bharatiya Chinmaya Devi Sammelan, Kollengode, 1960
Portrait of Swamiji, Madurai, 1954
Akhil Bharatiya Chinmaya Devi Sammelan, Kollengode, 1960
Group photo with Devi Group during 72nd Jnana Yagna, Bangalore, 1960

SHASTRI'S SHASTRA

On one of his visits to Chennai, I gave Swamiji a commentary which I had written on the first ten verses of *Nārāyaṇīyam*.

Nārāyaṇīyam is generally considered to be a devotional work, but it contains all the principles of Vedānta. Swamiji went through the entire commentary in great detail, and even gave me permission to publish the book.

Later, I requested him to write a foreword for the book. He sent me a beautiful forward, where he says in a rather humorous way, "Even senior bureaucrats understand Vedānta. I did not know this till I saw Shastri's commentary on *Nārāyaṇīyam*."

S. N. Shastri
Chinmaya Mission Chennai

Aging gracefully is an art, and very few are naturally good at it. One incident with Swamiji delightfully brings this point home. A group from the *Senior Citizens Association for Technocrats* happened to be passing through Sandeepany Sadhanalaya, Powai in Mumbai in 1986. Anant Narayan (aka Uncle Mani, as he is fondly called in Chinmaya Mission) made an appeal to Swamiji:

> "Please give darśana to these *older* people," I pleaded with him. Much to my surprise, Swamiji replied, "I shall also address them. Assemble them in the hall." Then, he turned to the others present and said, "Mani has brought some vṛddhas (old people). He thinks that I am young!" Then it hit me! I had not wanted to call myself or Swamiji old! (Swamiji was seventy years old at the time).
>
> In his address to the group (which was for thirty minutes), Swamiji said, "Never say you are (so many) years old. Forget

> the dead past! Think of the future and say (so many) years to go. What we have is a gift from the Lord. What we *do* with what we have is our gift to Him."

During the Vivekacūḍāmaṇi marathon camp in Sidhbari (in 1992), Swamiji was relaxing in the rose garden outside his kuṭiyā the day after the camp had ended. As devotees trickled in and out, saying their goodbyes, one elderly person asked him:

> Swamiji, I have lived a successful life as a householder. My children are well settled. Now, I have deep desire to live the life of vānaprastha, but how can I do it in modern times? There are no forests near about. Plus, I have lived a luxurious life, and I cannot even think about the prescribed lifestyle of vānaprastha. Moreover, I feel the benefit of my long experience will be lost to the younger generation.

Swamiji was thoughtful. After a pause, he said:

> You need not go to the forests to become a vānaprastha. You can start the life of a vānaprastha immediately, while living in your own house. Our scriptures are flexible enough on the subject.
>
> Decide firmly that you want to lead the life of vānaprastha. Vacate the master bedroom for your oldest son, and shift to the outer room of your house. Separate the bed, and get your food in your newly occupied room. Start spiritual studies and satsaṅga, try to complete your cherished hobby, and discharge the remaining responsibilities towards your family. Finally, take to selfless social work in association with other elderly people around.
>
> After some years of living this way, you will be inclined towards a peaceful ashram life, and will develop spiritual yearnings. You will then become fit to shift to an ashram, along with your wife or without her, and that ashram need not be a forest.

Accordingly, the Central Chinmaya Vanaprastha Sansthan (CCVS) aims to give a comprehensive vision to senior citizens, and improve the quality and style of their life through learning and selfless service. CCVS assists and trains senior citizens to make a smooth transition from their life in gṛhastha-āśrama (householder) to a life of a vānaprastha (retirement).

The back cover of *Graceful Aging*, a Chinmaya Mission publication for senior citizens reads:

> Before life corners you with a bent back, how about rounding off its rough edges with a smooth understanding? Remember, maturity is a stage and not an age. It doesn't just come with time and grey hair. You have to work towards it.

In the early years, Jnana Yagnas, Study and Devi Groups, Balvihar, and CHYK (followed by Vanaprastha Sansthan in 1996) laid the foundations for Chinmaya Mission. Even today, they form the grassroot activities of Chinmaya Mission. Swamiji's "afternoon dream" had conspicuously become a Mission in rapid succession. What's more, it was fast becoming apparent that this was not the will of an individual, but the collective will of the Indian people who yearned for a happier life and had once again turned to the ancient truths of their forefathers.

At the same time, "Īśvara-saṅkalpa or collective will is not enough," says Swami Purushottamananda (Regional Head, Chinmaya Mission Maharashtra, Goa, and Gujarat). "It requires an instrument to 'plan out the work, and then work out the plan.' Swami Chinmayananda was the perfect instrument. His every action was an indication of conviction powered by the experience of Reality."

During a temple tour in South India, 1957

JNANA YAGNAS

The core of the Hindu religion is its philosophy of Vedānta. Vedānta is a science. Just as physics, chemistry, biology, etc. are sciences of the objective world, Vedānta is the science of the subjective world. It is the science of life. It provides answers to questions such as: *What is the goal of life? How should one live life so as to achieve that goal? What is God? What is man, and what is the relationship between God and man?* The principal forum through which Chinmaya Mission disseminates this man-making knowledge of Vedānta is Jnana Yagnas and Spiritual Camps.

SPIRITUAL CAMPS

Jnana Yagnas are a five-to-seven day series of public discourses (60 or 90 minute evening and/or early morning daily talks) on a Vedāntic scripture given by an ācārya of Chinmaya Mission. Jnana Yagnas are regularly organized by all Chinmaya Mission centers. In the *Bhagavad-gītā,* **Lord Kṛṣṇa, uses the term "Jnana Yagna" to refer to the student who performs the ritual of worship at the altar of Knowledge through the study of scriptural texts.**

Spiritual Camps are weeklong retreats organized by Chinmaya Mission in various ashrams and other locations in India and around the world. A typical day during a camp consists of classes on the scriptures (for example, Upaniṣads, *Bhagavad-gītā, Śrīmad-bhāgavatam, Ramāyaṇa*)**, group discussions, meditation sessions, and cultural programs.**

| JNANA YAGNAS, SPIRITUAL CAMPS & YOU |

Attend a Jnana Yagna to rejuvenate and inspire yourself. Bring your family and friends. Jnana Yagnas are free of charge and open to the public. Spiritual Camps are a great opportunity for you and your family to take a break, learn, reflect, and relax. Special programs are organized for children and youth.

| CONTACT US |

Contact your nearest Chinmaya Mission Center.
Central Chinmaya Mission Trust, Sandeepany Sadhanalaya,
Saki Vihar Road, Powai, Mumbai 400 072, India
Tel: +91 (22) 2857 2367, 2857 2828, Email: ccmt@chinmayamission.com
Website: www.chinmayamission.com
www.chinmayamission.org (in North America)

STUDY GROUPS

A Study Group involves five-to-fifteen people who meet at a mutually agreed time, place, and day for ninety minutes each week. The group studies and discusses scriptural texts according to a prescribed syllabus that offers the seeker a systematic exposure to Vedānta. The emphasis of the Study Group is to help seekers in the practice of "logical reflection" in order to achieve abidance in Knowledge.

Devi Groups are exclusively for women. These groups meet weekly for scriptural study, devotional singing, and a variety of cultural and social activities. Devi Groups also provide an opportunity for women to express themselves freely and frankly, identify their problems, and solve them in the light of their discussions.

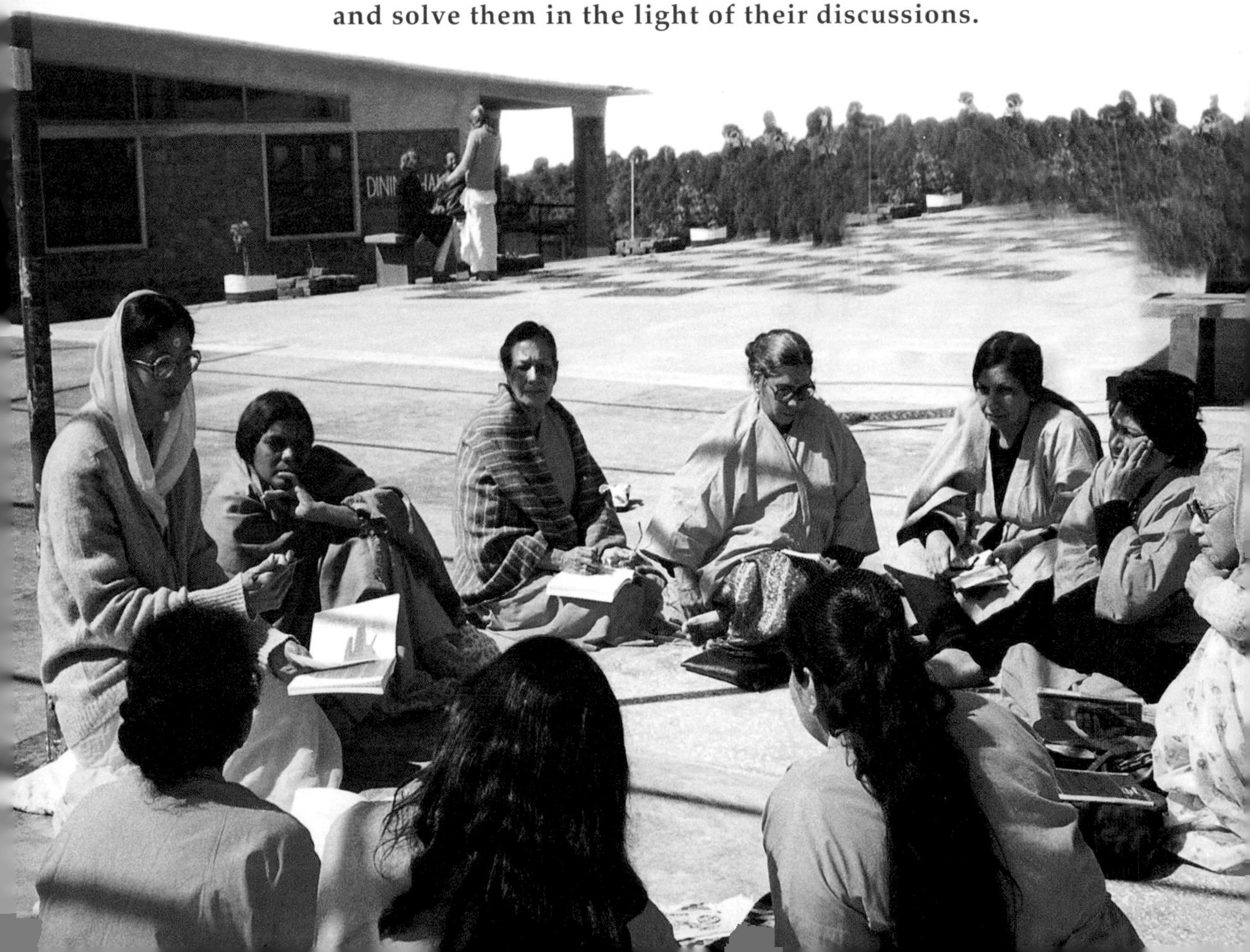

DEVI GROUPS

SCHEME OF STUDY

- *Kindle Life*
  (by Swami Chinmayananda)
- *Bhaja-govindam*
  (by Ādi Śaṅkarācarya)
- *Tattva bodhaḥ* (by Ādi Śaṅkarācarya)
- *Manaḥ-śodhanam*
  (by Swami Tejomayananda)
- *Ātma-bodha* (by Ādi Śaṅkarācarya)
- *Upadeśa Sāra* (by Ramana Maharshi)
- *Nārada Bhakti Sūtra*
- *Meditation & Life*
  (by Swami Chinmayananda)
- *Bhagavad-gītā*, Chapters 1 & 2
- *Jñāna-sāra*
  (by Swami Tejomayananda)
- *Kenopaniṣad*
- *Bhagavad-gītā*, Chapters 3–6
- *Dhyānasvarūpam*
  (by Swami Tejomayananda)
- *Kaivalya-upaniṣad*
- *Bhagavad-gītā*, Chapters 7–9
- *Īśāvāsya-upaniṣad*
- *Bhagavad-gītā*, Chapters 10–12
- *Bhakti Sudhā*
  (by Swami Tejomayananda)
- *Bhagavad-gītā*, Chapters 13–15
- *Muṇḍaka-upaniṣad*
- *Bhagavad-gītā*, Chapters 16–18
- *Saddarśanam* (by Ramana Maharshi)

FOR ADVANCED STUDY GROUPS

- *Yogavasiṣṭha-sārasaṅgraha*
- *Advaita-makaranda*
  (by Śrī Lakṣmīdhara Kavi)
- *Aitareya-upaniṣad*
- *Dakṣiṇāmūrti stotram*
- *Kaṭhopaniṣad*
- *Praśnopaniṣad*
- *Taittirīya-upaniṣad*
- *Māṇḍūkya-upaniṣad*

STUDY, DEVI GROUPS & YOU

Enhance your knowledge of Vedānta by joining a Study or Devi Group in a locality near you.

CONTACT US

Contact your nearest Chinmaya Mission Center.
Website: www.chinmayamission.com
www.chinmayamission.org (in North America)

BALVIHAR

CHILDREN ARE NOT VESSELS TO BE FILLED, BUT LAMPS TO BE LIT.

| SWAMI CHINMAYANANDA |

Balvihar is a weekly gathering of children (between the ages of five-to-fifteen years) that takes place in Chinmaya Mission Centers or in private homes, under the supervision of trained teachers. The aim of Balvihar is to help children learn values through fun-filled activities — to delight like the moon and shine like the sun. In an atmosphere of love, children are imparted cultural and ethical values through the singing of bhajanas (devotional songs), chanting of scriptures, hearing and narrating of Purāṇic stories and other delightful activities. There are a few thousand Balvihars in India and abroad operating under the guidance of Chinmaya Mission.

BALVIHAR

| BALVIHAR & YOU |

Enroll your children in a weekly Balvihar class.
Give them the opportunity to grow with time-tested,
ever fresh values that are at the heart of
India's rich cultural heritage.

| CONTACT US |

Contact your nearest Chinmaya Mission center.
Email: balavihar@chinmayamission.org (in North America)
Visit the website at www.chinmayakids.org,
www.chinmayamission.org (in North America)

CHYK CHYK

SUCCESS IS THE TRIBUTE LIFE PAYS TO EXCELLENCE.

| SWAMI CHINMAYANANDA |

Chinmaya Yuva Kendra (CHYK) is the global youth wing of Chinmaya Mission (ages thirteen to twenty-eight years). It aims to empower youth with vision, values, and dynamism for success in all fields. The motto of CHYK is: Harnessing youth potential through dynamic spirituality.

CHYK conducts weekly classes where young people are made aware of their potential through the study of scriptures. After they have gained this awareness, their potential is directed towards creative channels. CHYK organizes and executes cultural, social, and spiritual programs. When young people execute such programs, their individual capacities unfold. It brings out various abilities latent in them — abilities that they perhaps didn't even realize existed within them. There are hundreds of CHYK centers in India and abroad.

CHYK CHYK

| YOUTH EMPOWERMENT PROGRAM (YEP) |

YEP is a value-based leadership program for college graduates who have a desire to learn Indian culture and serve India. Over a fourteen-and-a-half month period, this residential program incorporates Vedāntic studies, training in a variety of service projects, and hands-on internship, all of which are designed to promote individual inner strength and holistic transformation for a balanced lifestyle of personal growth and selfless service. At the end of the internship, YEP helps to find employment for its students in their chosen fields.

| CHYK & YOU |

Join CHYK. Participate in multifarious activities to discover your hidden potential and tap into your infinite source at will.

| CONTACT US |

All India Chinmaya Yuva Kendra (AICHYK)
No. 2, 13th Avenue, Harrington Road, Chetput,
Chennai 600 031, Tamil Nadu, India
Tel: +91 (44) 2836 5300, +1 (734) 663 8912 (in North America)
Email: aichyk.info@gmail.com
Email: chykwest@chinmayamission.org (in America)
Website: www.chyk.net

VANAPRASTHA

SANSTHAN

Central Chinmaya Vanaprastha Sansthan (CCVS) is the senior citizens wing of Chinmaya Mission. It unites people over sixty years of age. The CCVS encourages senior citizens to pursue the final spiritual goal of life and shows them the means to achieve it.

CCVS motivates them to reduce their dependence on society. It also tries to qualitatively improve the lives of senior citizens through community projects, health check-ups, financial advice, and other activities. CCVS participated in the formulation of the National Policy for Older Persons issued by the Government of India. There are over 200 units of CCVS spread around India.

Chinmaya Mission has eight Pitamaha Sadans (senior citizens homes) in India. They are located in Allahabad, Kanpur, Rewa, Tamaraipakkam, Coimbatore, Ellayapalle, Kothapatnam, and Kolhapur.

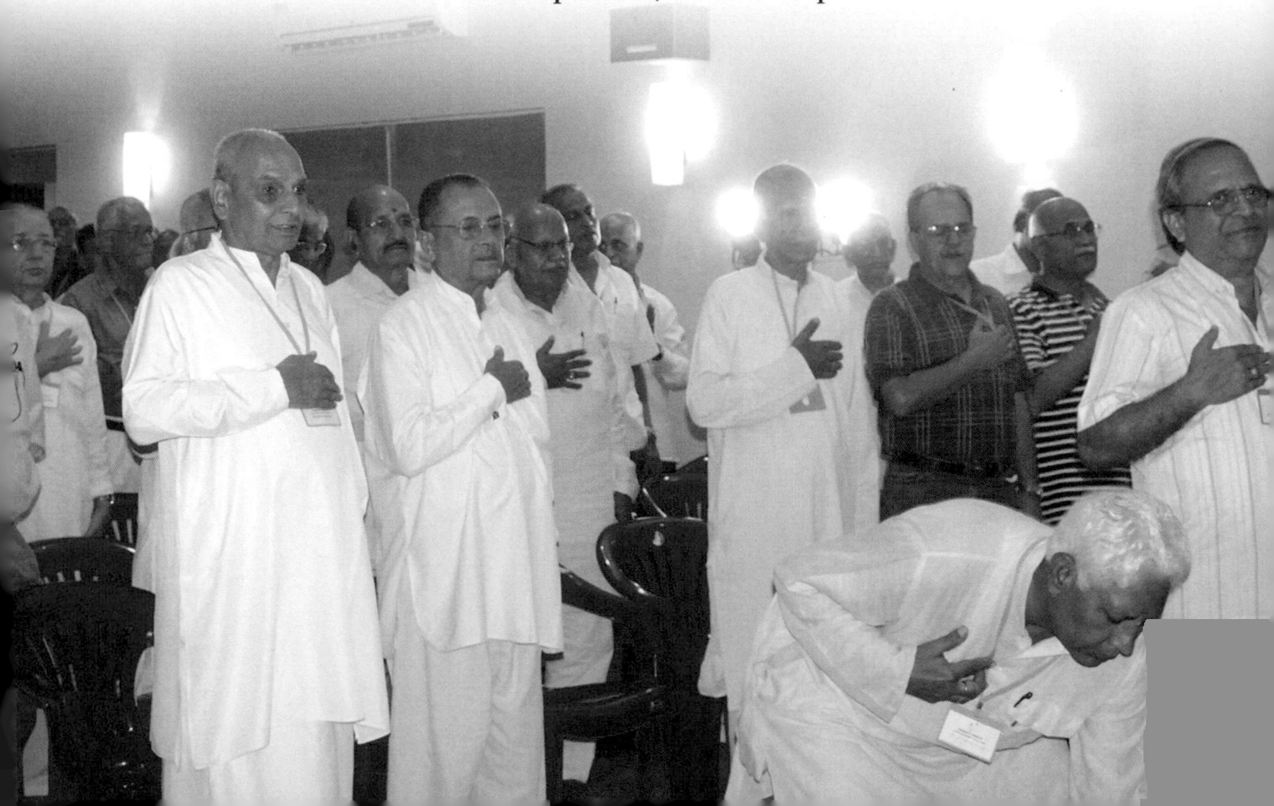

SADANS
PITAMAHA

The Pitamaha Sadans provide affordable and comfortable accommodations, nourishing vegetarian food, libraries, medical and other facilities. The focus of the Pitamaha Sadans is on spirituality. They organize many spiritual activities and provide an excellent ambiance for spiritual unfoldment.

| CONTACT US |

Central Chinmaya Vanaprastha Sansthan
Navin Sewa Ashram, Rasoolabad Ghat Road
Allahabad 211 004, Uttar Pradesh
Tel: + 91 (532) 254 6602, 254 6540
Email: shivswarupalld@indiatimes.com
Visit the website at www.ccvs.in

XII

The Indisputable Good Sense of Package! Print! Publish!

The only time Swami Tapovanam was *actually* heard laughing was after Swamiji was successful with his "Gangotri Plan." Each monsoon season (June–August), Swamiji had continued to go up to Uttarkashi to be with his Guru. Swami Tapovanam would quietly listen to the bubbling reports of his disciple. Swami Govindagiri says:

> From that time onwards, Swami Tapovanam always treated Chinmaya as a friend, and not as a student. Chinmaya had the total blessings of his Guru, which could only have come from his own merit. They would sit on the verandah of Tapovan Kutir and be engrossed in discussions. By the peals of laughter and the looks on their faces, I could tell that the two were really enjoying each other's company. On one occasion, Swami Tapovanam even teased Chinmaya, "A little ambition is good, but this young man wants to carry the whole Himalaya!"

Swamiji would also spend time in Ananda Kutir with Swami Sivananda, who was always overjoyed to see him. He was particularly impressed with his idea of recording all his lectures, which were then compiled into booklets and posted to a wider audience. "This kind of innovation is necessary if we are to succeed in bringing the truths of the Upaniṣads to the modern world, where this wisdom is so urgently needed," he said to Swamiji. It was not so much the mailing of printed books, but the foresight in recording *all* his talks in shorthand (which could then be transcribed and posted) that had impressed Swami Sivananda, who was himself illustrious for sending spiritual messages by post. Swamiji had taken this one step further.

From Day 1 (starting with the "Let Us Be Hindus" talk on December 23, 1951), Swamiji had requested that each of his talks be taken down in shorthand. By Week 2, a handful of dedicated workers had established a routine for the 1951–52 Pune Jnana Yagna. Mani Iyer would take down the lecture, transcribe it, and type it out the following day. The same day, S. Seshadri would edit the manuscript and rush it to the printer. Three or four daily discourses were then combined into booklets called, "Yagna Prasad." Thereafter, whoever came to see Swamiji was immediately put to work — putting Yagna Prasads into mailing wrappers, addressing them, and stamping them for mailing. These Yagna Prasads were later combined to make up the text book of *Kenopaniṣad*. Hence, its introduction and appendix is a record of the introductory talk given during the 1st Upaniṣad Jnana Yagna in Pune, and the commentary section is the actual transcript of Swamiji's first public talks on this Scripture.

The first mailing list was made up of friends and relatives of the Pune audience but requests for the publication started arriving in surprising numbers. An appeal for donations to cover the mailing costs had to be made. The budget was 1,000 rupees (approximately $20), and the necessary amount began arriving from all parts of India: Mumbai, Delhi, Chennai, and many towns in Kerala. The mail bags continued to grow in number, but the first two Yagna Prasads of every Yagna were unfailingly addressed to: "Śrī Swami Tapovanam, Tapovan Kutir, Uttarkashi" and to "Śrī Swami Sivananda, Ananda Kutir, Rishikesh," with the words "With prostrations, Chinmaya"

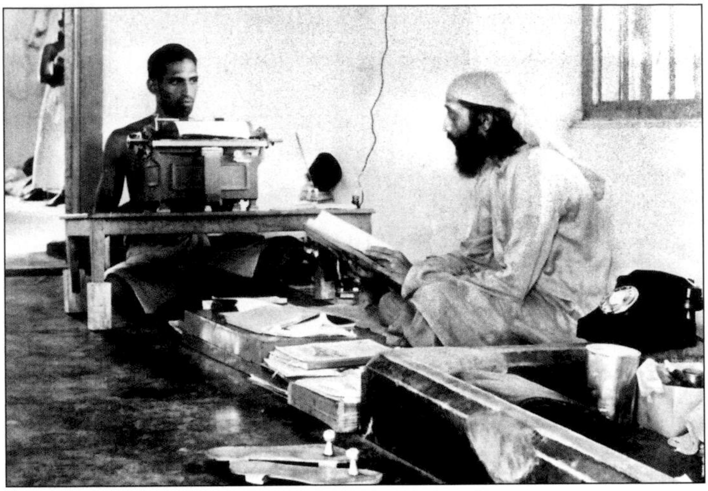

Left:
Swamiji's "office" in 1955
Center:
Swamiji checks the typing of his daily discourses while Mr. Kharbanda looks on, 3rd Jnana Yagna, Delhi, 1953

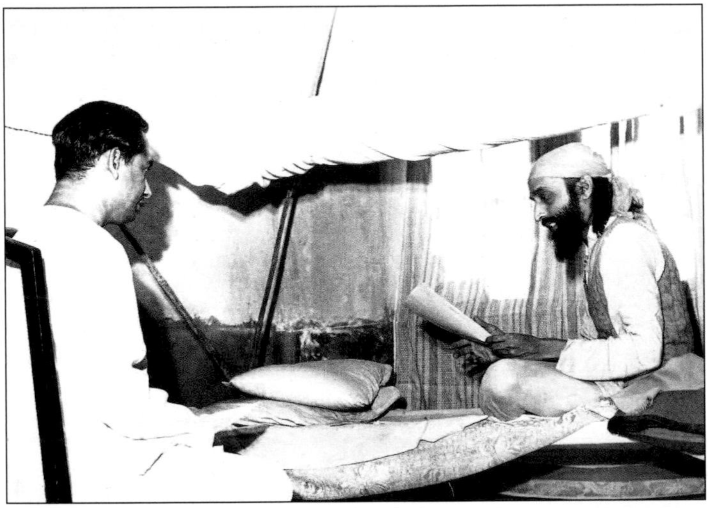

Below left:
Swamiji distributing Yagna Prasad, Tirunelveli, 1960
Below right:
A thick queue for Yagna Prasad on the last day of 16th Jnana Yagna in Mylapore, Chennai, January 29, 1956

scrawled in Sanskrit across the title page. When Swami Tapovanam read the *Māṇḍūkya Kārikā* discourses in his weekly Yagna Prasad mail, he was very pleased. "Yes, this certainly was spoken by Chinmaya," he said. He meant that the person Chinmaya had stepped aside, and the wisdom of the true Chinmaya (pure Knowledge) had come through him. Swami Tapovanam replied with a three-page message dated October 26, 1953, to the Delhi Yagna Committee. Excerpts are given here:

> Brahman is the only Reality. Nothing else is real. The entire universe, consisting of the ever-shining sun, moon, and stars, is a dream — a long, long dream. How can this everlasting universe we perceive in the waking state be a dream? In the great *Māṇḍūkya Kārikā*, the illustrious teacher and seer Śrī Gauḍapāda tries to answer this question. The *Kārikā* explains clearly and proves with various methods of logic that this universe is nothing but a dream.
>
> Śrī Gauḍapāda leads us to that eternal Bliss, the eternal Brahman, by the most direct shortcut — straight, as an arrow flies, not by a serpentine twisting path. That is the greatness and distinction of this wonderful work *Kārikā*.
>
> The English-educated people of our capital city are very fortunate to have the opportunity of hearing the discourses on this *Kārikā* from the lips of Swami Chinmayananda, a modern sannyāsī of contemporary education. I believe that he will explain to you the subject of the text in the modern and scientific methods, rather than in the orthodox way of the Sanskrit paṇḍitas (priests).
>
> I hope the Delhi people will be highly benefited by this Jnana Yagna ceremony now being conducted by Śrī Swami Chinmayanandaji. May God bless you all for the successful completion of the Jnana Yagna, and for the successful practice of Knowledge which you attain from it.

In addition to the lectures, the Yagna Prasads included other items of interest concerning the Jnana Yagna. The front page of the first booklet contained the only words with which Swamiji had ever spoken of his enlightenment:

Chinmaya's work is dedicated to the Śrutis (Vedic Wisdom)
That told me what Reality is;
To Swami Tapovanji Maharaj of Uttarkashi
Who guided me to the end and pushed me into the Beyond;
And to Sat Gurudev Swami Sivananda Maharaj of Rishikesh
Who showed me in this life how to live and act
In God as God!

By 1955, the Yagna Prasads were being mailed to 12,000 spiritual seekers in India, and requests for more continued to pour in every day. They were always sent out free to anyone who requested them, and the cost of mailing them to so many seekers each week had become a burden for the organizers of Jnana Yagnas. A group of Chennai devotees suggested that Swamiji publish his discourses in a fortnightly journal which would be made available by subscription at a nominal cost. Swamiji agreed and the journal was named *Tyagi*. He further recommended that *Tyagi* include articles by such great saints as Swami Sivananda, Śrī Aurobindo, Swami Vivekananda, and European thinkers as diverse as Aldous Huxley and St. Francis of Assisi. In the inaugural issue dated September 1955, Swamiji wrote:

> May *Tyagi* hold the torch high, so that our generation may walk out of the jungle into which they have wandered unwittingly.

Swami Tapovanam was equally optimistic, but for different reasons. After carefully noting the inexpensive paper and dreary black and white text, he sent the following message:

> I am glad to say that *Tyagi* deserves its great name because it looks like a tyāgī (renunciate) itself, with no extra ornamentation about it. Such a journal is entitled to preach tyāga (detachment), vairāgya (dispassion), and jñāna (knowledge) to others. May it protect and follow the greatness of its name.

From 1955–1960, the location of the editorial office of *Tyagi* changed several times. The printers in Chennai were unable to print the journal in time, and very soon there was a huge backlog of issues. Swamiji found another printer in Bangalore and moved the editorial

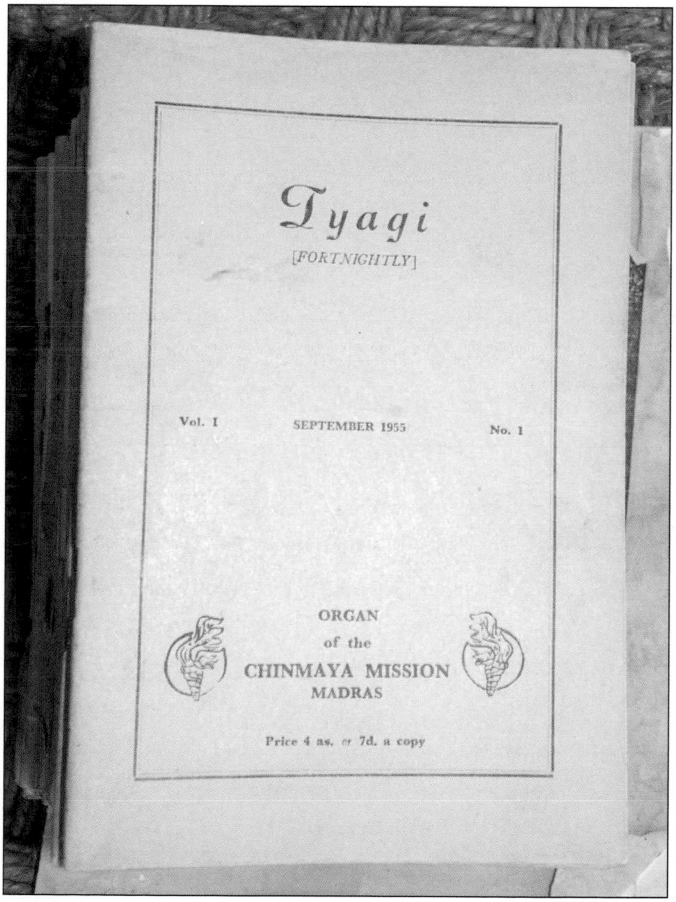

Tyagi, September 1955

office there; but as it turned out, the editorial team in Bangalore was not as committed. In 1960, he again shifted the office of *Tyagi* to Chittoor.

In September 1958, Swamiji introduced a second publication *Usha*. This was a monthly newsletter which typically carried Jnana Yagna and Study Group reports, articles on spiritual picnics and satsaṅgas, photographs, and maybe a letter to children to highlight moral and ethical values. Swamiji made it mandatory for Yagna Committees to publish an account of their Jnana Yagnas in *Usha*. In effect, *Usha* was able to coordinate and monitor activities of Chinmaya Mission, crystallize Swamiji's thoughts, and spread the code of conduct given at yajñaśālās. It also allowed Study Group members to keep abreast of all Chinmaya Mission events in India. Thus, *Tyagi* and *Usha* were complimentary publications, the former covering spiritual knowledge and the latter carrying the administrative details of Chinmaya Mission.

During this period of growth, certain swamis in Ananda Kutir took issue with Swamiji because, in one of his talks, Swamiji had criticized "weekend devotees." The swamis insisted that this was a direct affront to many of Swami Sivananda's city devotees who came to Rishikesh during the weekend. They also felt Swamiji was using Swami Sivananda's name to make his fame, especially since some of the early organizers of his Jnana Yagnas had been devotees of Swami Sivananda. But Swami Sivananda had no such qualms and continued to openly praise Swamiji. "Chinmaya is doing good work; he has thrilled the whole of India!" he commented when a newspaper clipping of a Jnana Yagna was shown to him.

Throughout the development of Chinmaya Mission, Swamiji had remained loyal to both his teachers. There was always a picture of both Swami Tapovanam and Swami Sivananda reverently placed on the stage in all yajñaśālās. But the jealousies continued, and according to one disciple in Ananda Kutir, it was for the sake of peace in the ashram that Swami Sivananda at last wrote to Swamiji, "From this moment, let us worship each other in our hearts."

As a result, Swami Tapovanam became the symbolic figure of Parama Guru (Guru's Guru) for all devotees of Chinmaya Mission. Swamiji's love for Swami Sivananda did not abate, and neither did his communication with him. A few years later, when he published his commentary on the *Holy Gītā* (in 1959), Swami Sivananda lovingly volunteered the use of the Sanskrit translations from his own published *Bhagavad-gītā*. They had been composed by accomplished Sanskrit scholars with exacting accuracy, and this saved Swamiji many hours of work.

Swamiji's discourses on the *Bhagavad-gītā* were regularly published in *Tyagi*. But he had only taught up to Chapter 9 in the Jnana Yagnas. And in March 1956, when he received word that Swami Tapovanam had fallen ill, he had taken a month off from his Yagna schedule and rushed to Uttarkashi. During this period Swamiji took up the arduous task of finishing the entire eighteen chapters. He even borrowed lanterns from other sādhus, so he could continue working long into the night. Ultimately, it was on October 23, 1957 (Divālī day), that Swamiji announced in Hyderabad, "The *Bhagavad-gita* commentary, all 2,085 pages of manuscript, is complete."

It was time to move ahead. From 1959–60, *Tyagi* and *Usha* had frequently carried announcements publicizing the availability of Swamiji's *Bhagavad-gītā* discourses in three volumes. In March 1961, Chinmaya Publications Trust was established in Hyderabad to publish books on scripture and to further spread the message of Vedānta. The May 1961 issue of *Usha* carried a notice to this effect (see overleaf).

DISCOURSES ON

THE BHAGAWAD GEETA
BY
SWAMI CHINMAYANANDA

First Volume is getting ready

This contains the first five chapters—Stanzas in *Devanagari* script with Roman transliteration—Word for each stanza followed by paraphrase
The exhaustive discourse by Swamiji covers a wide field of human knowledge religion, culture, society and human psy commentary on Life! Beautifully got handle size of ¼ crown.

GEETA IN THREE VOLU

Ordinary edition : Vol. I—Rs. 7/-, V
Vol. III—Rs. 4/-.

De-lux edition : In Real Art—Rs.
sale-proceeds of th
to make the ordina

Rese

Ch

(Post
The
not
of th
sets,

DISCOURSES ON

THE BHAGAWAD GEETA
BY
SWAMI CHINMAYANANDA

First & Second Volumes are ready

These contain the first eleven chapters— Stanzas in *Deva-nagari* script with Roman transliteration, word for word meaning for each stanza followed by paraphrase and commentary. The exhaustive discourse by Swamiji on each human knowledge like philoso- and human psychology. It is utifully got up in an easy-to-

REE VOLUMES

/- per set."

l Art—Rs. 50/- per set. (The oceeds of this edition go to he ordinary edition cheap).

tting Rs. 15/—or Rs. 50/-

ovindas B. Parikh,
aliar Rd, Kilpauk Madras-10.

E FREE

are stocked only at the above ad from any of the Branch unt to Sri Govindas B. Parikh

Discourses on

SRIMAD BHAGVAD GEETA
By
SRI SWAMI CHINMAYANANDA

(GEETA in Three Volumes)

Ordinary Edition : Rs. 15/–

De-Lux Edition : Rs. 50/-

(Packing & Postage Free)

Volume III will be ready by March 1960.

Available at :

Sri Govind Das, B. Parikh
3, Dr. Guruswami Mudaliar Road,
M A D R A S – 10.

All the Orders should be sent to the above address only.

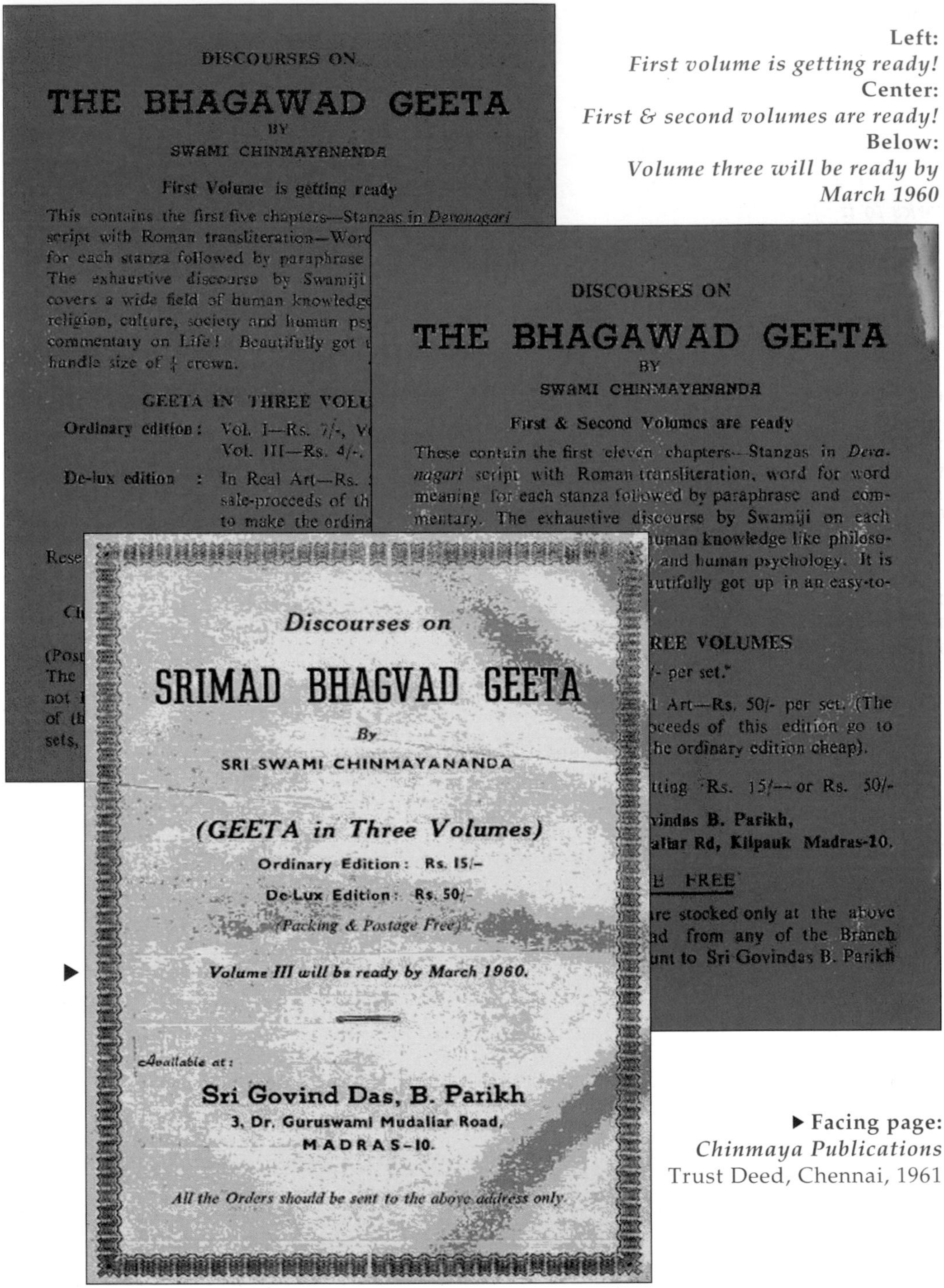

Left:
First volume is getting ready!
Center:
First & second volumes are ready!
Below:
*Volume three will be ready by
March 1960*

▶ Facing page:
Chinmaya Publications
Trust Deed, Chennai, 1961

Chinmaya Publication Trust (Reg.)

Madras

Sree Swamiji Maharaj has constituted the above Trust and has given away all his works to it for future publication of the volumes. Some interesting points from the Trust deed we give here under.

Whereas the devotees of Swami Chinmayananda are desirous of creating a Trust for the purpose of publishing books, periodicals, in all languages, and such other literature expounding Bharath culture and Hindu Philosophy and allied subjects as propounded by the great scriptures and whereas devotees have offered to donate books already published to a Trust.

Whereas for the aforesaid purpose, publications of Swami Chinmayananda, ▶ numbering in all to 59 books have been handed over to the Trustees herein by Sri G.B. Parekh for the purpose of forming the nucleus of this Trust.

The name of the Trust shall be **"Chinmaya Publication Trust"**, with its principal place at Madras. Its office will be at 175 Rasappa Chetti St. Park Town, Madras-3.

Objects of the Trust.

The objects of the Trust are:-

1. To acquire, retain and possess copyrights for such books, periodicals and literature dealing with Bharath Culture, Hindu-Dharma and Hindu Religion and Philosophy.

2. To acquire copyright with full or reserved rights on such books and publications of Swami Chinmayananda and such others in consultation with Swami Chinmayananda.

3. To print, publish and sell or distribute such books or literature.

4. To establish libraries, institutions for Sadhana and propagation of Bharath Culture in the interest of revitalising Hinduism and to do all such other things as are incidental to aid and assist in the propagation of Bharath Culture.

5. To educate the masses in Bharath and the world at large in the right direction as propounded by the great scriptures of the World.

Constitution of the Trust Board.

1. Swami Chinmayananda shall be the Founder-Patron of the Trust, with 2. Sri V.N. Subbarayan, as the *President of the Board and the Managing Trustee;* 3. Sri M. CT. M. Pethachi as the *Vice-President of the Board of Trustees.* 4. Sri V. Sethuraman, as the *Publications Trustee*; 5. Sri Govindadas B. Parekh, as the *Administrative Trustee;* and 6. Sri P.V. Parthasarathy as the *Sales Trustee.*

Swamiji's books can be had from the Trust at 175 Rasappa Chetti St; Park Town, Madras and its branches hereafter. For all particulars relating to Swamiji's books and allied publications the Trust may be contacted.

All Mission Branches are requested to intimate the stock position of Swamiji's books with them to the Trust in the following proforma.

S. No.	Name of the books	Language	No of copies.

This will be done by the end of May 1961 So that the Trust Office can know its full Stock-position.

Clockwise from above:
Chinmaya Mission bookstall at Vivekananda Rock Memorial Temple, Kanyakumari, 1970
At the bookstall counter, Chennai, 1980
At the bookstall counter, Delhi, 1977
At the bookstall counter, Chennai, 1980
During a Jnana Yagna, Ranchi, 1962

▸ Facing page clockwise from above:
At the bookstall counter during a Jnana Yagna, Bahrain, 1972
Women of rural India reading the Hindi translation of *Manual of Self-Unfoldment*
At the bookstall counter, 3rd National Jnana Yagna, Jamshedpur, 1974
During Silver Jubilee Year of the Chinmaya Movement, 5th National Jnana Yagna in Parel, Mumbai, 1972
Women of rural India reading the Hindi translation of *Manual of Self-Unfoldment*

MUMBAI BLUES

On the bedside table in my hotel room at the Taj in Bombay (in 1979), there was a copy of the *Holy Bible* and the *Holy Gītā*. I casually picked up the *Gītā*. It was a commentary by Swami Chinmayananda. I got engrossed in the book and read it the entire evening. When I got back to Chennai I bought a copy for myself.

It was after this that I started attending Swamiji's Jnana Yagnas in Chennai. When Swamiji spoke on *Vivekacūḍāmaṇi* in 1980, I requested him to sign a book of his commentary for me. He wrote, "Read and reflect again and again." During a Yagna in 1984 on *Māṇḍūkya Upaniṣad*, he again gave me a beautiful message. This time, he signed, "World is not unreal. The world as we now understand is not real. *Māṇḍūkya* explains this riddle. Carefully read and reflect on the text some 6 times."

H. R. Pandurang
Chinmaya Mission Chennai

This was the beginning of the present-day "Books and Publications Division" of Central Chinmaya Mission Trust, which is today one of the largest publishing institutions in the world for Vedāntic literature. When we consider the life and legacy of Swami Chinmayananda, the incredible volume of work he produced in so *few* years must be recognized, as well as his individual works of magnificence. Swamiji authored fifty-nine manuscripts in just nine years (1952–1961), and ninety-seven in his lifetime. His commentary on the *Holy Gītā* has reverberated throughout the world as one of history's best in English. Saints, sages, intellectuals, and critics of the twentieth century have not yet found enough superlatives in their assessments of his work. Swami Haridhos Giriji Maharaj of Thennangur Namasankeerthanam declared, "He must have been that Arjuna to whom Lord Kṛṣṇa gave the *Gītā*. How else can someone understand and explain it with such clarity?" And Swami Chidanandaji Maharaj of Divine Life Society pronounced, "Swami Chinmayananda is 1,000 Lord Kṛṣṇas put together."

Over the years, luxury hotels in India started to keep a volume of Swamiji's commentary on the *Bhagavad-gītā* in all their guest rooms. *Meditation & Life* is another one of Swamiji's fascinating expositions on the theory and practice of meditation. Without going into abstruse technical explanations, it gives the logic behind meditation, as well as the practical exercise of applying it in modern times. In light of the enormous response to "new-age meditation" in the last century, the mind reels with the possibilities as it stands in awe of Swamiji's far-reaching vision.

The Hindi translation of *Manual of Self-Unfoldment* is read in remote villages by minimally educated women of rural India. Again, the simplicity and practicality with which Swamiji brought the highest knowledge of the scriptures to all sections of society is astonishing.

It didn't stop there. Books were translated into all regional languages: Hindi, Tamil, Malayalam, Marathi, Telugu, Kannada, Oriya, Bengali, Sindhi, and Urdu. Sheela Sharma of Delhi started the first translations. She translated eight Upaniṣad commentaries in Hindi: *Kena, Kaṭha , Praśna, Māṇḍūkya with Kārikā, Muṇḍaka, Taittirīya, Aitreya*, and *Īśāvāsya.* She also translated the commentary on *Nārada Bhakti Sūtra*, a devotional text.

Over the years, devotees abroad translated Swamiji's books in French, German, Polish, Spanish, Russian, and Taiwanese. The Parisian Swamini Umananda, who translated Swamiji's *Bhagavad-gītā* commentary in French, says:

> The French translation was published on June 14, 1998, exactly five years after Swamiji's last visit to Paris in 1993 (June 10–12). The book

has now become a reference in bookshops here in France, and was reprinted in pocket format in 2008.

After the book was published, Pawan Gupta, an Indian gentleman from Bangalore (married to a French lady, Elizabeth Gupta) told me, that way back in the 1970's, Swamiji had said to him, "It *must* be translated in French, so that everybody can know the beauty of the *Gītā*." This message came directly to my heart across time and years! I felt amazed to see that Swamiji's words had become true through us in this wonderful way.

With the Publication Division firmly in place, *Tyagi* became redundant. Consequently, in 1962 and 1965, *Usha* and *Tyagi* were successively absorbed into one voice, *Tapovan Prasad*, which started in December 1962, after the creation of Tara Cultural Trust (see "The Making of 100 Vivekanandas"). The motto for this new monthly was taken from

Chinmaya Vani Book Store in Sandeepany Sadhanalaya Powai, Mumbai

the *Bhagavad-gītā*: "O Kaunteya, know for certain — my devotee will never perish" (Chapter 9, verse 3). Since its inception, *Tapovan Prasad* has served as the central magazine for Chinmaya Mission worldwide, carrying news and spiritual articles from centers around the world.

Earlier, in 1955 Swamiji also took his teachings to the air waves with a three-part series on All India Radio. The first topic was "Symbolism in Hinduism." Swamiji explained the various Hindu symbols, rituals, and temple worship and the reason why all forms of classical art — for example, classical music and dance — served the function of glorifying God. The second topic was "Science of Life," which included a challenge to self-develop through self-discipline. The third talk, "Work as Worship," included the ideas of karma yoga (devoted service) as explained in the *Bhagavad-gītā*, Chapter 3.

Although many of Swamiji's talks were recorded in audio-spools starting in the 1960s, a formal body called Chinmaya Video Dham was set up in March 1992. This is Chinmaya Mission's audio-visual division. It publishes discourses, bhajans, and Vedic chanting in cassette, CD, and DVD format. Over a twelve-year period (1980–1992), many of Swamiji talks were recorded on video, and for those who did not meet him in person, his unique and potent influence can be felt in these recordings, showing him in full, eloquent flight, on the teacher's podium. Most noteworthy are Swamiji's talks on "The Logic of Spirituality" and his commentary on the *Bhagavad-gītā* (all eighteen chapters), recorded in Piercy, California (May 29–July 3, 1991); and his commentary on *Vivekacūḍāmaṇi*, which was recorded during a two and one-half month marathon camp in Sidhbari (in 1992). During this time, the bright lights pointed at Swamiji had created much heat and light, which caused irritation to his eyes, making them water. When some devotees expressed their concern for Swamiji, he dismissed it saying, "Fifty years later, *this* is what you will have!"

Toward the end of 1956, Swamiji received word that Swami Tapovanam's health was much worse. On December 8, he drove up to Uttarkashi with several devotees from Delhi to bring Swami Tapovanam back for a proper diagnosis and medical treatment. A few devotees suggested taking him to London or New York for treatment. But Swami Tapovanam would hear none of it:

> Are there not people dying in London, in New York, and in Delhi with all the *best* facilities for diagnosis and treatment? Then why should I not end my life in peace amidst the Himalayas where I have lived for so many years.
>
> Chinmaya, you go and continue the work .... Come now, don't weep!

On a full moon day, January 16, 1957, Swami Tapovanam breathed his last at 4:30 A.M. (brahma-muhūrta) in Uttarkashi. Swamiji was given the news via telegram four days later (on January 20) during a morning satsaṅga in Palghat. His eyes filled with tears. At that time, Sheel Dewan asked him, "Swamiji, are you crying?"

"Yes. Do you think that because a man is a renunciate, he is devoid of feelings? I have emotions just like anyone."

Swami Tapovanam's body was immersed in the icy waters of the holy Gaṅgā a few hours after his mahāsamādhi. He was taken in a grand procession along the winding path from Tapovan Kutir down to the lap of Mother Gaṅgā, whom he had so dearly loved throughout his life. His body was adorned with marigold garlands and carried in a palanquin by a multitude of sādhus who had gathered to pay their final homage to this most perfect embodiment of God, who would ever be remembered as the glory of the Himalayas. After the last rites were over, Swamiji spent many days in Rishikesh, in quietude and meditation.

Swami Tapovanam, in his last years, had been full of pride and admiration for his disciple, Chinmaya. He had commended the idea of Chinmaya's Jnana Yagnas to a group who had accompanied Swamiji to Tapovan Kutir in March 1956. "Taking the teachings of Vedānta to the hearts of the people is the highest service a man can do for his fellow men. Chinmaya's method and interpretation of the scriptures is exemplary. It is a good thing Chinmaya is giving all his classes in English, because this message of Vedānta is to be taken to the spiritually starved people of Europe and America."

Left:
Group that accompanied Swamiji to Uttarkashi, 1956 (clockwise from above: Sheela Puri, Swami Tapovanam, Swami Chinmayananda, Nano Atal, Chanchal Khosla, Janak Kapoor, and P.L. Khosla)

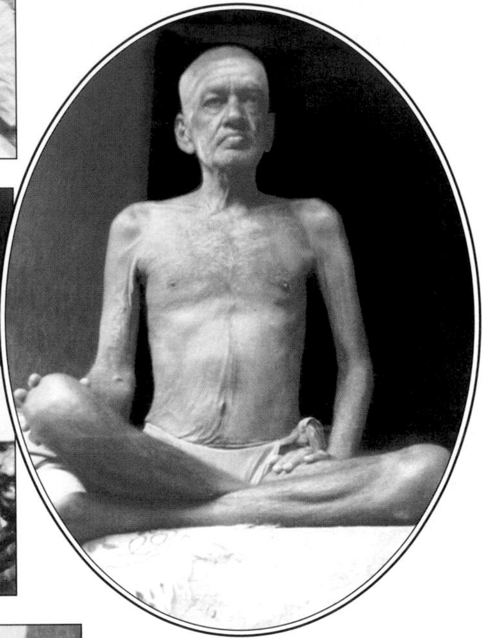

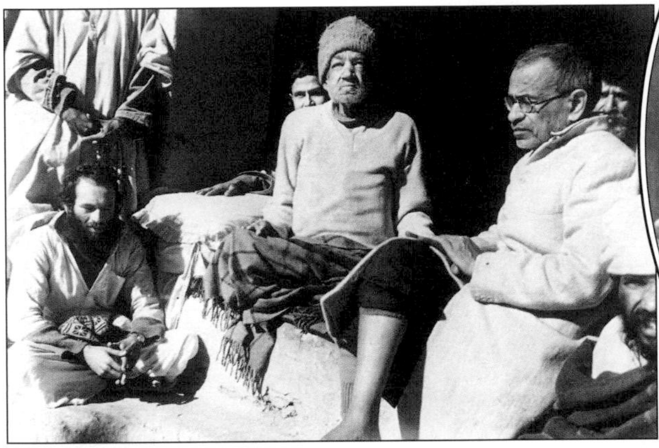

Above:
Swami Tapovanam, Uttarkashi, 1956

Center:
Swami Tapovanam relinquishes the support of a pillow whenever he could (two weeks before mahāsamādhi), Uttarkashi, December 1956

Left:
Swami Tapovanam looks at a śiva-liṅgam in front of Tapovan Kutir (two weeks before mahāsamādhi), Uttarkashi, December 1956

Clockwise from above:
Swami Tapovanam carried in a pālkī to Gaṅgāji after mahāsamādhi, January 16, 1957
Swami Tapovanam before jala-samādhi into Gaṅgāji, January 16, 1957
Swamiji with shaven head after mahāsamādhi of Swami Tapovanam, 1957
Swami Tapovanam before the jala-samādhi into Gaṅgāji, January 16, 1957
Swamiji after mahāsamādhi of Swami Tapovanam, Kolkata, 1957

BOOKS

Chinmaya Mission has a vibrant publications division that produces books, audio tapes, CDs, DVDs, mp3s, periodicals, and photographs. It has published over 900 titles in English, Hindi, Gujarati, Kannada, Malayalam, Marathi, Tamil, Telegu, French, Spanish, German, Polish, Russian, and Taiwanese.

These include:

- Swami Chinmayananda's widely-acclaimed commentaries on the *Bhagavad-gītā* and the main Upaniṣads.
- Commentaries on other scriptures like *Ātma Bodhaḥ, Bhaja Govindam, Dṛg-dṛṣya Viveka, Nārada Bhakti Sūtra, Saddarśanam, Upadeśa Sāra, Vākya Vṛtti, Śrī Viṣṇusahasranāma, Vivekacūḍāmaṇi, and Yoga Vasiṣṭha.*
- Original works on Vedānta like *Bhakti Sudhā, Dhyānasvarūpam, Jñāna Sāra, and Manaḥ Śodhanam.*
- General Books on Vedānta, culture, ethics, and morality like *Hindu Culture, Kindle Life, On Wings & Wheels: A Dialogue on Moral Conflict, Self-Unfoldment, Symbolism in Hinduism, The Art of Man-making, In Indian Culture: Why do We, and Vedānta Through Letters.*
- Books on meditation such as, *Art of Contemplation and Meditation & Life.*
- Children's books like *Bāla Bhāgavatam, Bāla-Rāmāyaṇa, Gītā for Children, Tell me a Story, Parables.*

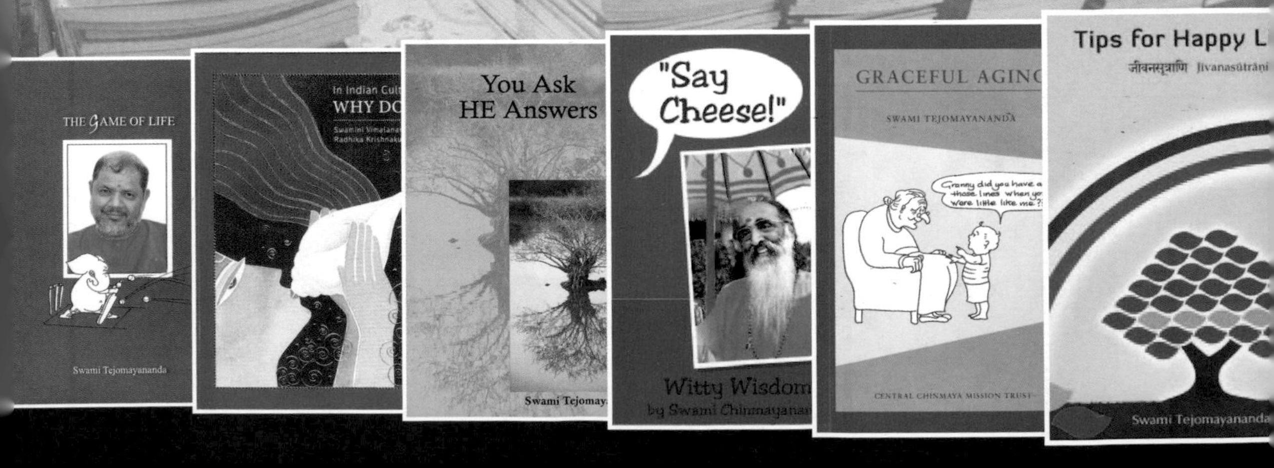

PUBLICATIONS

- Books for youth such as, *Awakening Indians in India, Say Cheese: Witty Wisdom, The Ah! Wisdom Book: Conversations with Swami Tejomayananda, Victorious Youth, and You Can: Inspirational Insight.*

| CONTACT US |

Central Chinmaya Mission Trust,
Books & Publications Division,
Sandeepany Sadhanalaya, Saki Vihar Road,
Mumbai 400 072, India
Tel +91 (22) 2857 2367, 2857 2828
Email: ccmtpublications@chinmayamission.com
Website: www.chinmayasmission.com

(In North America)
Chinmaya Publications, 560 Bridgetown Pike,
Langhorne, PA 19053, U.S.A.
Tel: +1 (215) 396 0390
Email: publications@chinmayamission.org
Website: www.chinmayamission.org

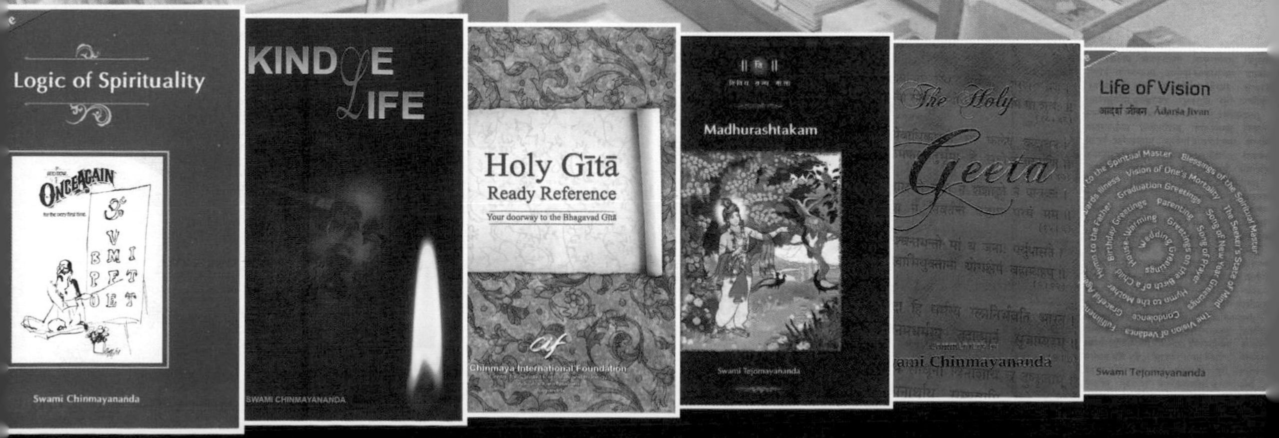

XIII

The Making of 100 Vivekanandas

Retrace the momentous trail of your spiritual journey, and you will eventually find yourself back in Sandeepany Sadhanalaya, where either you — or the ācārya who inspired you — studied Vedānta. The idea of a "modern day gurukula," to teach the philosophy of Advaita Vedānta to young men and women who would then take the knowledge back to their community, began forming in Swamiji's mind as early as June 1955. During an inaugural address in Chennai, he said:

> What we need is more spiritual teachers. The message of the Upaniṣads is to be interpreted, taught, and broadcast — carried from door to door.

He again mentioned his plan in Mumbai, then again in Delhi, and again in Hyderabad. He kept at it until he gathered enough supporters:

> We want an army of Vivekanandas all over the country. The problems are so severe that they can no longer be remedied by even a handful of persons. Thus, I have to start many training centers, and our hopes are that all of them will bring forth true Vivekanandas.

This *is* Vision. Swamiji wanted full-time, well-educated trained preachers, without worldly ambitions or vested interests — brave and courageous — who were willing to leave personal ties and concerns behind, for a life of surrender to the Divine through service to mankind.

The turning point occurred in January 1963 — and it may well mark the birth of the long-term ripples of Swamiji's farsightedness — when construction of the first ashram, Sandeepany Sadhanalaya Powai, in Mumbai was completed. The gurukula was named after Lord Kṛṣṇa's guru, Ṛṣi Sandīpaṇi; and it is Chinmaya Mission's first residential training academy of Advaita-vedānta. Here, students study various scriptural texts over a two-year period, primarily the Prasthānatraya (Upaniṣads, *Bhagavad-gītā* and Brahma-sūtras) based on the commentaries of Ādi Śaṅkara. They are also taught Sanskrit grammar, Vedic chanting, and select devotional masterpieces (*Tulasī Rāmāyaṇa, Śrīmad-bhāgavatam, Nārada Bhakti Sūtra* to name a few) and original compositions of spiritual masters like Sant Jnaneshwar and Ramana Maharshi. The students withdraw fully from worldly life for the two-year period, and follow a disciplined schedule of classes and activities in an ashram setting to promote spiritual learning, reflection, and contemplation. Thereafter, they are encouraged to work in the field as missionaries to their own people, although this is not a stipulation for joining the Vedānta Course.

Sandeepany Sadhanalaya Powai was built entirely through Yagna collections and private donations offered by the numerous supporters of Swamiji's mission. The land was donated by Tara Swaroop. In December 1962, the Tara Cultural Trust was formed to look after its day-to-day transactions.

On April 11, 1963, the classroom, dining hall, kitchen, and hostels were completed, and the training course was begun with full fanfare. All Swamiji's Yagnas were canceled for a three-year period, and he became the Acharya for the 1st Vedānta Course in Sandeepany Sadhanalaya Powai. Thirty students together hoisted a flag with a large OM symbol, amidst Vedic chanting, ringing of bells, and the blowing of a conch. Turning to the students, Swamiji said, "Look, I have not hoisted the flag, it was you. Now it is up to you to keep the flag flying." He never expressed any disappointment about the number of students although it was fewer than what he had expected.

Each prospective student had a preliminary interview with Swamiji. Swami Purushottamananda, who was a student of the 1st Vedānta Course, remembers his interview with him, "I will watch you. You will watch me," said Swamiji, and wound up the interview.After watching Swamiji for three years, Swami Purushottamananda concluded:

> Swamiji has the discipline of a father and the love of a mother. One time, I interrupted him during class to ask, "Swamiji, this ignorance that Vedānta is always pointing out, where did it come from?"
>
> "Are you here to learn about knowledge or ignorance? I think you are all masters of ignorance without studying it!" remarked Swamiji. The whole class exploded in laughter.
>
> But, Swamiji could also be strict. A few students left the ashram without permission while Swamiji was away, and went to the city. (Thank God, I was not one of them!) Swamiji came to know about it, but did not say anything to anyone at the time. The routine continued and everyone thought Swamiji had forgotten. After a few months, when he had a camp in Surat, and all the students were to accompany him — the tickets were booked, the bags packed, we were all very excited. But just before boarding the bus, Swamiji asked, "Who were the boys who left the ashram without permission? Cancel their tickets!" We were all stunned. Swamiji saw the long looks on our faces and again said, "You are here to learn, and I am teaching you the best way I know. The gate is always open, but once you walk out, there is no coming back."

Each afternoon, walking tall and straight with his measured pace, Swamiji made a round of the ashram to check the ongoing construction.

His astute mind was quick to see a better way to do the job, and he had not lost his flair for mechanics! Sandeepany Sadhanalaya Powai is located on a hill, and one of the immediate problems was reaching the water underground. "Dig until you strike," he told the workers and pointed out an area to dig. Water was encountered at four hundred feet. After that, Swamiji began to tease the students with the same slogan for their spiritual quest, "Dig until you strike!"

The foundation stone for the Jagadeeshwara Temple in Powai was laid on April 10, 1964, by the Śaṅkarācārya of Kavir Matha. The ninety-nine year old Swami said that Sandeepany Sadhanalaya was exactly the type of institution that he himself had contemplated establishing, and his cherished desire had now found fulfillment.

By the end of the first year of classes it became apparent that Swamiji would have to continue with the Jnana Yagnas, since the operating funds for the ashram could only be sustained by the gurudakṣiṇā he received from all over the country. With his "one square inch of assets" (the phrase with which he often referred to his tongue), Swamiji would be gone for ten days at a time. "Don't waste a single minute!" he challenged the students on his way out of the gate. "After listening to the teacher, you must do your own contemplation. The time that I am away is a God-given opportunity for you."

During the monsoon season, when no Jnana Yagnas were scheduled, Swamiji took the students to Uttarkashi. One day, he happily announced while rubbing his palms together with a broad grin, "Now, it's your turn to start talking." Each day, several students would explain the *Gītā,* taking it verse by verse, each one speaking for ten-to-fifteen minutes on each verse. Then, Swamiji expanded the time to thirty minutes per person. "Now, you know how to talk ... it's time to listen," he beamed as he brought out a tape recorder. About the same time, he pulled the plug on their rotation system. After several days, when the students were able to figure out which verse would

Clockwise from above:
Unfurling the flag in Sandeepany Sadhanalaya Powai, 1982
Emblem of Sandeepany Sadhanalaya
Swamiji with students of 1st Vedānta Course, 1970
Students of the 1st Vedānta Course (left to right: Swamini Sharadapriyananda, Swamini Gangananda, Swami Jyotirmayananda, Swami Purushottamananda, and unidentified), 1967
Swamiji with brahmacārīs of 1st Vedānta Course, Uttarkashi, 1970

fall on their turn (so naturally they had prepared exclusively for that verse), Swamiji began a new system. The selection would be done by pulling straws, and the speaking time was extended to one hour each. Then, some months later, he informed them, "Okay, now you can explain the *Gītā*, but can you talk to an audience? Let's see!" he would give them some hypothetical case of a certain type of audience which they were to address: a businessman's seminar, an old-age home, giggling college girls — Swamiji's imagination ran rampant as he challenged their flexibility.

One day, he hit Kutty (a student of the 1st Vedānta Course) with the impossible — a night club! Neither Kutty nor any of his fellow students had ever entered a night club. Nevertheless, Kutty forged ahead with a lengthy discussion on the three states of consciousness.

"Look," Swamiji interrupted him, "you are surrounded by dancing girls and a drunk manager. You only have three minutes before the beer bottles start to fly. Now, what will you have to say? You must be prepared for whatever the world throws at you!"

Uncle Mani (Acharya, Chinmaya Mission Chicago 1991–94) remembers his anxiety on the eve of his first Rāmāyaṇa Jnana Yagna in Bangalore in 1978:

> Swamiji happened to be passing through the airport the day before. He could tell that I was really nervous and took me firmly in hand. "Mani, close your eyes and fire off!" he commanded. And that is what I have been doing all these years as His instrument.

In another episode, Swami Mitrananda describes a scene from his student days during the 7th Vedānta Course in Sandeepany Sadhanalaya Powai (1989–91):

> Swamiji was coming down the stairs of the temple and it was quite steep. I just stretched my hand for him to rest. He gave me his hand,

> but then deliberately took it back and got down by himself. "Don't depend, walk alone," he instructed.

The following monsoon season, Swamiji again took the students to Uttarkashi. During one evening satsaṅga, when Swamiji walked into the classroom, he noticed that the students had forgotten to chant the Gaṅgā Stotram (hymn to Mother Gaṅgā) which is a daily ritual in Tapovan Kutir. As a result, he declared, "Everyone fasts today!" Later that night, dinner was served to Swamiji, but he would not eat it. "When I said everyone, I meant everyone. If my students don't eat, I don't eat either," he said. And the next day, he warned the students against becoming dry intellectuals, and made them sing bhajans for four days straight, canceling his lectures. "The spiritual ideas of the intellect must trickle down and melt the heart," he admonished them.

Swamiji's own exemplary life of alertness and vigilance, and conscious living each moment through *all* his actions, were in themselves the greatest teaching for disciples and devotees. Vilasini Balakrishnan (Acharya, Chinmaya Mission, Washington, DC) beautifully describes him:

> During Swamiji's years of service, hundreds of thousands of people delighted in hearing his talks on Vedānta. What people saw and heard when they sat for his discourses was an amazing presence, a force of inspiring dynamism, an energy that swept into one's heart and opened it to greater wisdom. But there is one strong quality of Swamiji's that was not so apparent on stage — and that was his deep, penetrating, soul-stirring silence.
>
> Swamiji taught this silence off-stage. It is this teaching that made him a living Upaniṣad. It is in this silence that the mind gets hushed, and the joy lying within one's being comes forth. Swamiji was always in this silence.
>
> One of his earliest teachings to me was very powerful. He had said, "When you find your teacher, jump behind him, like he is on a

motorcycle, and hold on tight, but never let him know you are there!" Swamiji was telling me that the relationship with the teacher is very subtle. He was also saying that I should try to get my ego out of my attachments (hold on fast, but never let him know you are there).

Swami Tejomayananda articulates:

I saw him as a perfect Jīvanmukta-puruṣa — a person liberated while living. Many a time I have felt that it is easier to describe Brahman (the supreme Reality) than to describe a jīvanmukta. We find very many verses in our scriptures in praise of such an enlightened soul. One such characteristic that comes to mind is that the enlightened person is one who is free from worrying over the past or being anxious about the future. Swamiji himself used to speak about such a person as someone like a mirror. A mirror accepts everything, rejects nothing. Swamiji indeed was that Jīvanmukta-puruṣa.

A HUMBLE MAHATMA

When we were studying in Sandeepany Sadhanalaya Powai (1972–75), one day Swamiji said that another swami was coming to visit the ashram. His name was Swami Gangeshwarananda. He was very old and completely blind. On the previous day, Swamiji had come to supervise the preparations to make sure everything was all right. We arranged all the flowers and other details on the speaker's podium.

Swamiji saw two chairs on the stage and asked, "What is the other chair for?"

"It is for you, Swamiji," we replied.

"For me? On stage? A great mahatma is coming. When he was a swami, I was a nobody! I was nothing! When he comes, I won't sit on stage."

The next day, when Swami Gangeshwarananda came, everybody

Left:
Swamiji seated
at the feet of Swami Gangeshwarananda, 1979
Center left:
Swamiji with
students and devotees, Powai, 1974

Above:
Morning class on
Māṇḍūkya-upaniṣad
at Ellisbridge residence (students of the 1st Vedānta Course accompanied Swamiji), 159th Jnana Yagna, Ahmedabad, May 1966
Left:
Group photo
of students, at Powai, 1982

went near the entrance. Swamiji ran across the temple steps like a child to receive him. The visiting Swamiji was taken to the temple, and garlands were placed around his neck.

Swami Gangeshwarananda sat on a single chair on the stage. Swamiji, who sat just below him, started massaging the Swamiji's legs. We can never forget that scene. Such a great mahātmā "came down" (became so humble) when he was in the presence of another mahātmā. On that day, the eyes of many of the brahmacārīs were opened to the glory of Swamiji.

Swami Siddhananda
Acharya, Chinmaya Mission Philadelphia;
In-charge, Chinmaya Publications West
[Student of the 2nd Vedānta Course
in Sandeepany Sadhanalaya Powai, 1972–75]

GOD'S WORK

On one occasion, when I was mailing Swamiji's correspondence, I did not have the correct-size envelopes. I solved the problem by taking a larger envelope and folding it over at one end.

Swamiji saw what I was doing and said, "No, that's not how it is to be done."

He then showed me how to do it. He cut the envelope carefully at the open end and fashioned a flap to fold over for closure. The procedure took a lot of time, but Swamiji was determined the task be done right, not just expediently.

"This is God's work," he said. "It must be beautiful."

Brni. Robyn Thompson
Acharya, Chinmaya Mission Vancouver
[Student of the 5th Vedānta Course
in Sandeepany Sadhanalaya Powai, 1984–86.
She served as Swamiji's secretary in USA from 1987–93.]

Sandeepany Sadhanalaya was Swamiji's dream institute, and it is no secret that during his travels, he was always on the alert to recruit new students. However, parents the world over would routinely plead with him to find their son or daughter a splendid marriage with one of the children of his many devotees. "Swamiji travels everywhere, he *must* be the *best* person to find a match," they would boldly suggest.

"I want brahmacārīs! A hundred Vivekanandas!" roared Swamiji.

Yes. Swamiji, did do a *lot* of matchmaking, which many of his married devotees will vouch for happily (and unhappily) But that's a story for another day!

When Swami Advayananda (student of the 8th Vedānta Course in Sandeepany Sadhanalaya Powai, 1991–93, and currently President, Chinmaya International Foundation) decided to join the Vedānta Course at the young age of fifteen, he had an extraordinary exchange with Swamiji. Swami Advayananda details the events leading to 1991:

> It was during the *Vivekacūḍāmaṇi* camp in Sidhbari in 1988 that I made a decision: I wanted to realize this Brahman, and for that I needed to go to Sandeepany. It took me twenty-five days to understand what my goal in life was. It was a deep calling.
>
> I decided to tell Swamiji. Just as he got up from his chair outside Tapovan Hall, I found him walking alone with his walking stick.
>
> "Swamiji, Swamiji ...," I said. "I want to meet you in private."
>
> "Private?" he questioned.
>
> "Yes. PRIVATE."
>
> "Come tomorrow at 4 P.M."
>
> The next day, I went at 4 P.M. to his kuṭiyā, but Swamiji was not up from his afternoon rest. I waited till 5 P.M. with no luck. Later, I again asked him, "When can I meet you? You asked me to meet you yesterday, but you were not ready, so I could not meet you."
>
> "Come tomorrow after the morning class."

The following morning, after class and then bhikṣā, Swamiji put some food into my mouth. There were a lot of people around him, but I waited. When the bhikṣā was over, he said to the others, "I want time with him." Everybody immediately cleared out.

Swamiji sat on the swing in the hall in his kuṭiyā. "Hān!" he said signaling for me to begin my private talk.

"Swamiji, I want to join the ashram. I want to study Vedānta, and I want to realize this Brahman what you are speaking of," I said.

"What are you studying?"

"I am in 11th standard. I will *not* go back home. I want to go to the ashram straight," I said.

"Why?" asked Swamiji.

I explained, "You said vāsanās (desires) become stronger. Once I go home, worldly vāsanās will become strong, and I do not want to give a chance to them."

"As long as the mind has a higher goal to which it is attached, vāsanās cannot have a grip on us," Swamiji patiently explained to me.

"Fine, but I don't want to go back home."

"Your English is good, you can join Powai ashram," agreed Swamiji.

I relaxed.

Then, he said, "At least finish your 12th standard. After that you immediately join Sandeepany. Don't waste any more time. But I want you to get very good marks — an 'A,' distinction!"

"Swamiji, I want to realize this Brahman what you are talking about, *not to speak about it.*" I meant that I was not interested in giving discourses. I don't know why I said this, but it came out unplanned.

"First, you must study, and then you must *teach* as well," Swamiji said firmly. "If I had not come down from the Himalayas and taught all of you, would you be here asking for Self-knowledge? It is your duty to also teach."

That day, I was in a different world. The mind was altogether in a different plane. Swamiji seemed to have broken all the barriers of my mind and thrown "me" out. I prostrated to Him, and the tears would not stop flowing from my eyes. I had found my Guru.

Swamiji said he would speak to my parents. "Bring them to my kuṭiyā at 4 P.M. tomorrow," he said, as I was leaving.

The next evening, Swamiji asked my parents, "Were there any saints in your family?"

My father shook his head.

"He wants to join the Vedānta Course. I have asked him to come after 12th standard. I want him. I hope I have both your permissions."

Both my parents gave their consent. I was in ecstasy. Later, my mother tried to persuade me to take up medicine. She put pressure on me through an aunt and other family members. But, I secretly wrote to Swamiji and asked him to help me put an end to this kind of pressure. Swamiji wrote back to me with a note for my mother. The note said, "His calling is here, so do not try to stop him. Five years of medicine for *him* is a sheer waste of time. Śaṅkarā's mother had only one son and she permitted. You have four children!"

And that is how I joined the ashram.

A gift from God, be it material or spiritual, must be shared. Swamiji repeatedly emphasized that the student *must* give the knowledge he had been taught to others. "Your life's work is to discuss and impart the essence of Vedānta, and to inspire others to live the dynamic, courageous chaste life of love and dedication. Be yourself a 'Sandeepany' who lights the lamp of Truth in others," he said.

On yet another occasion in Sidhbari in 1989, Swamiji was asked during a satsaṅga:

Q: "Swamiji, you have been preaching in India for the past few years. Do you think you are successful?"

A: "As a sādhu, it is my dharma (duty) to teach. My Guru was teaching all through his life — the *Gītā*, the Upaniṣads, and other scriptures. Similarly, I, too, teach what I have learnt. I don't consider my work 'success' or 'failure.' I teach, and I am happy."

Three months after the inauguration of Sandeepany Sadhanalaya Powai, on July 14, 1963, at 11:15 P.M., Swami Sivananda attained mahāsamādhi in Ananda Kutir, Rishikesh. He had witnessed ten outstanding years of Swamiji's life of service to God, guiding him through this crucial period, celebrating in his efforts, and smiling at his success. He had even seen the birth of the dream institute. In the early morning of July 15, his body was taken to the banks of the Gaṅgā where the last prayers began. He was then placed in a palanquin adorned with flowers and carried through the streets of Rishikesh amidst the chiming of bells and the sound of Vedic chanting. All of Rishikesh, and hundreds of devotees from surrounding areas, poured onto the road to accompany his procession as it made its way to the Satsang Mandir, where he was given a bhū-samādhi. Along with the other disciples in Ananda Kutir, Swamiji had his head shaved as a mark of reverence for his most beloved Guru.

Exactly a year later, when Swamiji came back to Ananda Kutir for the Puṇya tithi-arādhanā (first anniversary of samādhi) of Swami Sivananda, he said, "My inspiration to work in the world outside, I received from Sri Swami Sivanandaji. He exhorted the disciples to come out into the world and speak the spiritual message. We have the responsibility of carrying out the life-giving ideas of Vedānta to our brethren throughout the country."

COURTING THE DISCIPLE

One day in London in 1988, I went to see Swamiji in Laju and Kavita Chanrai's home. At the time, I was a yoga teacher in Bitche, France and had come to London for Swamiji's Yagna.

Swamiji was working in the study. But he suddenly got up from his desk, walked directly in front of me, and sat down.

"Yoga is not enough, you must learn philosophy!" he said looking straight at me.

I told Swamiji that I did wish to attend several camps over one month.

"Not one month! Several months!" responded Swamiji. "You will be my guest. You will see how I work, and you will learn."

I told Swamiji that I had a job …

"Drop the job!" he said with force. "The Lord will give you another one!"

A few days later, I received a letter from him informing me that he was expecting my arrival in India. I replied to him confirming that I was ready.

Then, in November 1988, he sent me another letter, where he wrote, "Since you have decided to leave your job and come to India, why not you plan to be a student here for 2 ½ years."

I joined the 7th Vedānta Course in Sandeepany Sadhanalaya in 1989. When Swamiji saw me in Powai ashram the day after I landed in India, he exclaimed, *"Really, you have come!"*

A few months into the course, Swamiji asked me, "How are you?"

"Swamiji, I am very happy," I said.

He laughed. "You will refuse to leave the ashram," he said.

One of the guest students told him I was able to chant the Vedās (since I am French, this was initially difficult).

"I know, I know … Selected ones! The first day I saw her, I knew that she would come to me. I thought I would have to court her, but she came by herself. But I would have courted her."

Swamini Umananda
Acharya, Chinmaya Mission France
[Student of the 7th Vedānta Course
in Sandeepany Sadhanalaya Powai, 1989–91]

PILLARS OF THE WORLD

My father was not happy when I wanted to join the Vedānta Course. So I took him to meet Swamiji, who was staying at the Varier's home in Coimbatore in 1990. When my father mentioned his hesitation, Swamiji roared, "Don't ever worry about your son. He is like a pillar. He will stand on his own to support my cause!"

My father was speechless. Thereafter, he never stopped me.

Swami Ishwarananda
Acharya, Chinmaya Mission Tustin and Bakersfield
[Student of the 8th Vedānta Course
in Sandeepany Sadhanalaya Powai, 1991–93]

SEALED WITH A HANDSHAKE

At the Pocononos camp in Pennsylvania (in 1981), I went up to Swamiji in the first week of my meeting him, and said to him, "I would like to make an appointment with you."

"You want an appointment? What for?" asked Swamiji.

"I want to ask you something," I replied.

"You want to ask, ask now!"

I had wanted to prepare for my appointment, to impress Swamiji, so I kept on insisting he give me an appointment later.

Swamiji was equally insistent. "No, you ask now," he said.

"I think you can take me out of body awareness," I blurted.

Swamiji gave me a deep look. "Who told you that?" he asked.

"That much I know," I said confidently.

"Then you come to India with me," said Swamiji.

"That's all I wanted to hear," I said. Then, to the dismay of the devotees around us, I stretched my hand out to Swamiji. He responded with a handshake! Ten days later, I was on an airplane to India.

Swamini Shivapriyananda
Acharya, Chinmaya Mission Toronto
[Student of the 5th Vedānta Course
in Sandeepany Sadhanalaya Powai, 1984–86]

LIKE FATHER, UNIQUE SON

In 1968, Swamiji had written in my father's *Holy Gītā*: Read five verses daily and meet me after three years.

Twenty years later, I gave the same book to Swamiji at a Yagna in Tirupati and asked him to autograph it for me. He saw the old signature and asked, "Whose book is it?"

I told him it was given to me by my father. Swamiji smiled and wrote on the same page, "Son also, advice the same."

To the people sitting around him, he said, "This is our culture. The book should be handed from father to son."

When I graduated from Sandeepany Sadhanalaya Powai in 1991, I showed the same book to Swamiji once again. This time, he signed, "Father missed, but son got it!"

Swami Mitrananda
Acharya, Chinmaya Mission Chennai;
Director, All India Chinmaya Yuva Kendra (AICHYK)
[Student of the 7th Vedānta Course
in Sandeepany Sadhanalaya Powai, 1989–91]

Sandeepany Sadhanalaya is acknowledged as the single greatest achievement of Chinmaya Mission. The open question is whether it is the single greatest achievement for the spread of Advaita-vedānta in the modern era.

The 1st Vedānta Course started with thirty students — sixteen survived the grueling five years. Four stayed on to work as missionaries for Chinmaya Mission — Swami Purushottamananda, Swamini Sharadapriyananda, Swami Jyotirmayananda, and Swamini Gangananda. Among them, the "Magnificent Three" exert enormous influence in their states — Maharashtra, Andhra Pradesh, and Uttar Pradesh — and on the spiritual revival of India in the late twentieth century.

Swamiji's direct disciples became ācāryas of forty-seven successive Vedānta Courses in seven Sandeepany Sadhanalayas, setting in motion a multiplier effect with 741 students graduating in fifty years.

On November 7, 1979, "Sandeepany West" (also known as Krishnalaya) was founded in Piercy, Northern California, for students abroad. Chinmaya Mission has thirty-seven ācāryas alone in the USA, Canada, and Trinidad-Tobago. A Vedānta Course is currently in progress in Krishnalaya, and another fifteen students are expected to graduate on July 28, 2011.

On April 25, 1981, Sandeepany (HIM) was inaugurated in Sidhbari, Himachal Pradesh, at the foothills of the Himalayas for Hindi-speaking students. The first ācārya for the 1st Vedānta Course in Hindi (1981–83) was Br. Vivek Chaitanya. He is a student of the 2nd Vedānta Course in English (1972–75) in Sandeepany Sadhanalaya Powai. We know him as Swami Tejomayananda, head of Chinmaya Mission worldwide. Swami Chinmayananda described him as an "exquisite teacher." Beyond that, this disciple can only be described by one who *knows* Him.

On February 8, 1982, "Sandeepany Andhra Pradesh" was inaugurated in Chinmayaranyam, Ellayapalle, Andhra Pradesh, for Telugu-speaking students.

On February 16, 1988, "Sandeepany Kerala" was inaugurated in Kasargod, Kerala, for Malayali-speaking students.

On May 9, 1988, "Sandeepany Tamil Nadu" was inaugurated in Siruvani, near Coimbatore, Tamil Nadu, for Tamil-speaking students.

On May 10, 1988, "Chinmaya Sandeepany" was inaugurated in Deenbandhu Devasthanam in Bangalore, Karnataka, for Kannada-speaking students. It was shifted to Chokkahalli in 1990.

On August 24, 1997, "Sandeepany Kolhapur" was inaugurated in Kolhapur, Maharashtra, for Marathi-speaking students.

Chinmaya Mission has 293 inspired ācāryas worldwide who are actively spreading the knowledge of Advaita-vedānta. Moment-to-moment, this number multiplies. Moment-to-moment, a common person — like you and me — is benefited. Moment-to-moment, the supreme goal is reached by someone, somewhere. Moment-to-moment, ultimate liberation is experienced in regular homes by working people around the world.

This *is* Vision!

MESSAGE TO ACHARYAS

by Swami Chinmayananda, Ghatkopar, 1978

It is interesting to note how the elderly mahātmās living in the Himalayan valleys look at the missionary zeal of the young mahātmās. Once, I had to face one of the elderly mahātmās in Uttarkashi. When in conversation I reported to him, with a naive enthusiasm and a sense of pardonable satisfaction, that my work of spreading the contents of our scriptures is being slowly recognized and appreciated by the younger generation, the ancient brows were slightly raised to express an impossible surprise. There was an excruciating silence for a few minutes, and my flow of words stopped the moment I saw the screaming criticism on those sacred brows. After a time, the revered Swamiji said, "Chinmaya, you had better stay here now, and no more need you go out in the world."

No doubt, I was at a loss to understand what he meant. Explaining his idea, the revered Swamiji continued, "If you think that you are spreading these spiritual ideas — my boy, by the time you have spread the sacred ideals of Vedānta among the people, you will be a lost soul; because you will have by then developed a terrible amount of irrepressible ego! Our ācāryas have advised us that after sannyāsa we have one sole duty in life — to reflect upon the truths of the scriptures and thus meditate upon the Infinite."

How can the dissemination of knowledge bloat one's ego? I was not convinced. When I expressed my inability to follow his line of thinking, that revered old saint of knowledge and wisdom kindly smiled, and patting me paternally on my back said:

> "Son, devotees might come and ask us their doubts. You may give your discourses in the cities; there is none who is doing it as efficiently as you are. But one thing we should do. Never talk to the audience;

talk to your own mind and make it a louder reflection in yourself to yourself. Thereby, you will not only stop the growth of your ego in you, but also will be talking to the mind and heart of your audience. May your missionary lectures and inspired preaching be a homely talk and a fruitful discussion between your own intellect and the lower mind. If those who are around you are benefited by your own self-reflection, it shall be the glory of the Lord and not your personal efficiency."

I was smothered down by the beauty and depth of significance of this sacred attitude of the ideal Hindu missionary in India. "Glory to the Ṛṣis!"

WHEN MAN IS ABLE TO TEMPORARILY OVERCOME
HIS BASER TENDENCIES, HE DEVELOPS AN EGO
THAT HE DID IT, FORGETTING THAT IT WAS
NĀRĀYAṆA'S GRACE THAT MADE IT HAPPEN.

| SWAMI CHINMAYANANDA |

Clockwise from above:
Visiting brahmacārīs from Sandeepany Sadhanalaya Powai in Sidhbari, 1985
Swamiji with Prakasam family (clockwise: Vijayalakshmi Prakasam, Guruswamy Prakasam, Roger, Saraswati [who is now Brni. Shruti Chaitanya], Ambalavan, [who is now Swami Advayananda], Raja Rajeshwari, Ramana)
Swamiji with students of 5th Vedānta Course, Powai, 1986
Swami Tejomayananda garlanding Swamiji, Kanpur, 1978

Left:
With students of the 8th Vedānta Course in Sandeepany Sadhanalaya Powai in Sidhbari (after Hanumān Abhiṣekam), October 10, 1992
Center:
After Dīkṣā ceremony, students of the 7th Vedānta Course, 1991
Below:
With students of the 5th Vedānta Course, Sandeepany Sadhanalya Powai

▶ **Facing page clockwise from above:**
Swami Tejomayananda with students of the 6th Vedānta Course, Powai, 1988
With disciples (Swami Brahmananda, Swami Purushottamananda, and Swami Tejomayananda), in Thangkam Varrier's house, Coimbatore
Swamis and brahmacārīs with Swamiji after Hanumān Mastābhiṣekaṁ, Sidhbari, October 10, 1992
On sannyāsa dīkṣā day with Swamiji (left to right: Swami Jyotirmayananda, Swami Tejomayananda, and Swamini Gangananda), Sidhbari, October 10, 1983

SANDEEPANY

Sandeepany Sadhanalaya is a modern day gurukula to teach the philosophy of Advaita-vedānta to young men and women who can then take the knowledge back to their community. The gurukula is named after Lord Kṛṣṇa's guru, Ṛṣi Sandīpaṇi, and it is Chinmaya Mission's residential training academy of Advaita-vedānta, where students study various scriptural texts over a two year period, primarily the Prasthānatraya (Upaniṣads, *Bhagavad-gītā* and Brahma-sūtras) based on the commentaries of Ādi Śaṅkara. Students are also taught Sanskrit grammar, Vedic chanting and selected devotional masterpieces (*Tulasī Rāmāyaṇa, Śrīmad-bhāgavatam, Nārada Bhakti Sūtra* to name a few) and original compositions of spiritual masters, such as, Sant Jñāneśvara and Ramana Maharshi.

SADHANALAYA

| SANDEEPANY SADHANALAYA & YOU |

Sandeepany Sadhanalaya is the ideal institute for all students who want a thorough grasp of scripture, regardless of their upbringing and faith. Its traditional teaching method is fully dedicated to the seeker's spiritual education and growth. Vedānta Courses are in English, Hindi, and several Indian languages.

| CONTACT US |

Tara Cultural Trust,
Sandeepany Sadhananalaya, Saki Vihar Road,
Powai, Mumbai 400 072, India
Tel: +91 (22) 2857 0368
Email: tct@chinmayamission.com
Website: www.sandeepany.chinmayamission.com

XIV

Mission and Vision

Let us briefly move out of the life-changing events of the last decade and delve deeply into Swamiji's vision for Chinmaya Mission. No mission can successfully function or produce positive results unless it has a vision — the higher the vision, the greater the mission.

Was it Swamiji's goal to start Jnana Yagnas, Balvihar (for children), CHYK (for youth), Vanaprastha Sansthan (for senior citizens), Sandeepanys, and so forth?

No.

These are the activities of a mission — not the goal. Activities are a means to a goal, and action without vision has no meaning. Likewise, a vision without action remains an imagination. But when both vision and action come together, they bring about a transformation.

The vision of Chinmaya Mission is to reach the Supreme — to attain the state of "Chinmaya" or "pure Knowledge." The mission is to translate this vision into action — to provide a means for individuals to purify their hearts and reach the inner "Chinmaya," the supreme Reality. It is only when each one of us is pure at heart and feel the fulfillment — born of Wisdom — that we can become true contributors of the society we live in. Hence, the Chinmaya Mission vision statement says:

> To provide individuals from any background, the wisdom of Vedānta, and the practical means for their spiritual growth and happiness, enabling them to become positive contributors of society.

Then again, why provide the "wisdom of Vedānta"? Why not just give food, clothing, shelter, or money?

Charity by itself cannot ultimately liberate. It can only ensure short-term happiness, which is beneficial, but it is not complete or lasting. Just as education equips a child so that he can take care of himself when he grows up, similarly, the wisdom of Vedānta prepares an individual for all life situations.

Vedānta imparts the knowledge of the Self, which then reveals the true nature of all things of the world. This understanding alone can prepare an individual to live life in totality and completeness. This inner transformation alone gives lasting happiness.

Vedānta is not a religion — it is the science of all religions — the foundation of dharma. In his famous talk on "The Logic of Spirituality," Swamiji explains this science of Vedānta. He shows how Vedānta is not a matter of blind belief and acceptance, but a logical science behind all religions.

There is a famous story of the Buddha from his younger days, when he was Prince Siddhartha, which brings out this point. One day, Siddhartha went riding with his cousin, Devadatta, who shot an arrow at a swan and the bird fell down. Both boys galloped towards the bird, but Siddhartha reached it first. He found that the swan was still alive, so he gently pulled out the arrow. When Devadatta arrived, he staked his claim on the swan since he had shot it. But Siddhartha refused to give it to him. The cousins started to fight, and finally decided to ask a wise sage at court to settle the matter for them. The wise man heard both boys out, and declared, "A life certainly must belong to the one who tries to save it. A life cannot belong to one who wants to destroy it. The wounded swan by right belongs to Siddhartha." Strangely, the world often gives rights to the hunter!

Lack of clarity is the source of all unhappiness. Clarity or wisdom is to nourish and sustain all "life," which is the Self in us — Sat-Cit-Ānanda, Existence-Consciousness-Bliss. If an individual goes against his (own) Self, he will naturally have to face the consequences.

Therefore, the motto of Chinmaya Mission is:

> To give maximum happiness to the maximum number for the maximum time.

"Maximum happiness" indicates lasting happiness, and this is made possible through the various activities of Chinmaya Mission, for example, Jnana Yagnas, Balvihar, CHYK, Study Groups, Vanaprastha Sansthan, and so forth. Once again, it must be emphasized that all these activities are to serve a higher goal — Self-knowledge.

SHARPENING THE VISION

Time and again, Swamiji brought the vision of Chinmaya Mission sharply into focus. Devotees all over the world invariably received a letter from him reminding them to keep the higher goal in mind when serving in the Mission. A few excerpts:

Chinmaya Mission will never teach you anything, but it is an organization where we all come together to learn. The science of Reality and the path of God-realization are the main subjects that you will learn in the Chinmaya institution.

There are subsidiary attempts such as sharpening your personality, blazing up your intellect, oiling your emotions, refitting your relationships, recharging your convictions, replenishing your values — in short, you'll die, and in your place a more brilliant man will be born. If you are ready for this Self-resurrection, come to the cavalry — Chinmaya Mission.

Chinmaya Mission is a nonstop course in religion. Our mission work is to replace the "beast" in us with the "best" in us.

Jnana Yagnas can be considered successful — not because some discourses have been organized, or because these discourses have been printed in paper books with printer's ink. They are successful only when the listeners get those ideas printed firmly upon the slates of their hearts with the white ink of purity; then, none of them can thereafter live for a moment even contrary to those eternal ideas of true living. Study of the scriptures should not be given up at all — that is the secret fuel that must fire up our enthusiasm, and inspire us to sacrifice and serve.

Ours is not a political organization, and we have no political program. Ours is the human problem — the problem of character — the texture of social life. To revive them is to revive man. To reinstate the Perfect Personality within each person is the goal.

Chinmaya Mission was forged, developed, and worked out essentially for the study of our scriptures and the philosophy of life which they contain; and this actually is the springboard for the great Hindu way-of-life. To propagate this Truth among the peoples of the world is our sole program. Such a plan of work should start first at home, and then must spread abroad.

On one occasion, a devotee suggested to Swamiji that Chinmaya Mission members should wear a badge to indicate their association with the Mission to the world. Swamiji remarked:

> You are not a dog for the world to know who your master is by the collar. The world must know that you are a Chinmaya disciple by your actions!

In a letter to Dr. V. K. Balachandran of Calcutta (published in *Vedānta Through Letters*), Swamiji wrote:

> Members of Chinmaya Mission are not subscription payers, or those who run after the swami, or even those who fall hundred times at his feet. All temple-goers are not religious. A pariah who stood, compelled by circumstances, outside the gopuram (temple tower), was much dearer to the deity than the pujārī (priest) who was near to Him, giving an oil bath to the idol. God is all-pervading and the Mission's hope is to make our generation more conscious of the God-principle. Thus, all our friends who are sincerely practicing self-purification and mental purification are faithful Mission members, more than those who pay a donation or wear a badge on their chest. So long as you are practicing — not outwardly only, but mainly inwardly — you are a dearer member of the Chinmaya family than anybody else.

The escalating growth of Chinmaya Mission centers and projects all over India required the formation of a new Trust, "Central Chinmaya Mission Trust" (CCMT), which was registered in Mumbai on June 27, 1964. Central Chinmaya Mission Trust serves as the head office for Chinmaya Mission, coordinating all activities and projects: Chinmaya Publications (including *Balvihar* and *Tapovan Prasad*); Chinmaya Vision Program and Chinmaya Vidyalayas; Chinmaya International Residential School; Chinmaya Diagnostic Centers in

Mumbai and Kolkata; Chinmaya Institute of Management, Bangalore; and Chinmaya Vibhooti in Kolwan. Central Chinmaya Mission Trust provides guidance, policy, and structure to all centers of Chinmaya Mission.

During his first world tour, Swamiji sent a letter dated May 21, 1965, to Jamuna Das Moorjani (Trustee, CCMT, from 1964–2000) specifying the details of the Chinmaya Mission emblem:

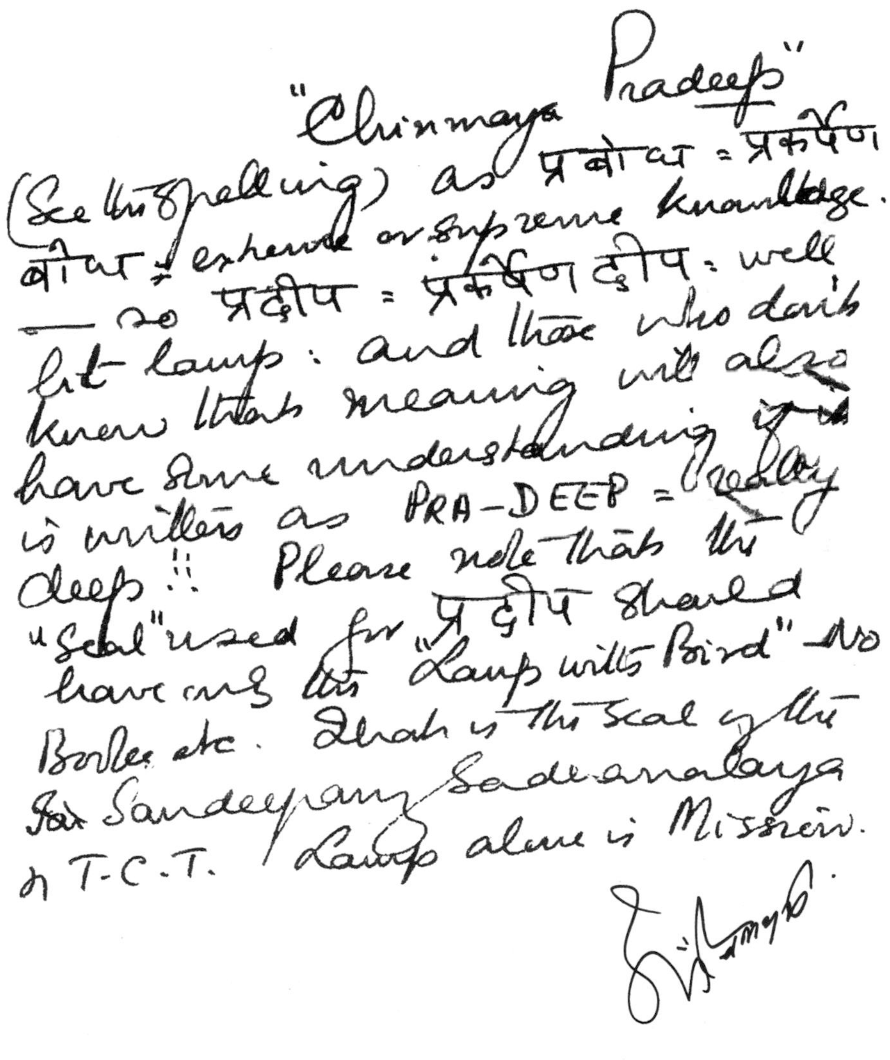
"Chinmaya Pradeep"
(See the spelling) as प्रज्ञान = प्रकर्षेण
ज्ञान = exhaustive or supreme knowledge.
— so प्रदीप = प्रकर्षेण दीप = well
lit lamp: and those who don't
know that meaning will also
have some understanding if it
is written as PRA-DEEP = really
deep!! Please note that the
"Seal" used for प्रदीप should
have only the "Lamp with Bird" — No
Books etc. That is the Seal of the
For Sandeepany Sadhanalaya
& T.C.T. / Lamp alone is Mission.
Chinmaya.

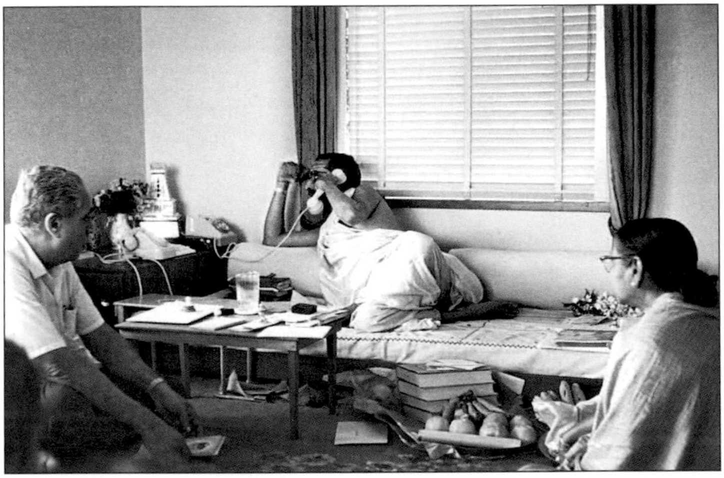

Clockwise from above:
Chinmaya Mission Emblem
Swamiji with Ram Batra, Jamuna Das Moorjani and B. M. Kamdar
Jnana Yagna audience in Ujjain (Swami Tejomayananda seated front right),
Welcome at Bhopal railway station, February 1, 1975
Swamiji answers the phone in his kuṭiyā, Powai, December 1963

Consequently, an emblem called Chinmaya Pradeep was designed for Chinmaya Mission. It consists of a lamp of knowledge, with a haṁsa (swan) bird-of-wisdom at its crown. The swan can separate water from milk, since it drinks milk, thus denoting discrimination. They together denote the spiritual and social services of Chinmaya Mission. The oil lamp symbolizes the ethical life needed to light the flame of Knowledge within. And once the spiritual seeker has lived a righteous life of noble values, he becomes fit to develop his discriminative faculty to distinguish the permanent Reality from the impermanent world — as depicted by the haṁsa bird.

HALF A BISCUIT PLUS A CHIEF EXECUTIVE

One day in 1990, I was passing by Sandeepany Sadhanalaya Powai and stopped to see if Swamiji was in the ashram. Swamiji's flight had been delayed, and he was talking to a group of people.

When I prostrated to him, he put half a biscuit in my hand, and said, "Narain, you will take over from him (indicating the then current Chief Executive, who was about to retire from the job)!"

I walked with Swamiji to his car. "Yes, Swamiji, it is possible," I said.

"If it's possible," said Swamiji, "then better ask your wife first."

All permissions were granted and arrangements made — and I began training for my new position at Central Chinmaya Mission Trust, thanks to a timely visit and half a biscuit.

Narain Bhatia
Chief Executive Officer, Central Chinmaya Mission Trust

During the All India Chinmaya Mission Workers Conference in Abbotsbury (in 1964), Swamiji dictated a pledge, in a moment of inspiration, to serve as a guide for all Mission members. On the closing day of the conference he himself administered this pledge to 140 delegates:

The Chinmaya Mission pledge:

We stand as one family, bound to each other with love and respect.

We serve as an army, courageous and disciplined, ever ready to fight against all low tendencies and false values, within and without us.

We live honestly, the noble life of sacrifice and service, producing more than we consume and giving more than we take.

We seek the Lord's grace to keep us on the path of virtue, courage, and wisdom.

May Thy grace and blessings flow through us, to the world around us.

We believe that the service of our country is the service of the Lord of lords, and devotion to the people is the devotion to the supreme Self.

We know our responsibilities; give us the ability and courage to fulfill them.

Om Tat Sat!

Here is the significance of the pledge:

The first point to note is that the entire pledge is in the present tense — "We stand … We serve … We believe …" — to highlight the necessity of present action: Start now! This moment! And not, for example, "We shall overcome … some day!"

We — not "I." Strength is in unity and togetherness. Spirituality is in sharing all that we have, that is, knowledge, goodness, talents, wealth, and happiness.

stand — not sit or lie down. Standing symbolizes activity and determination. Overcoming lethargy (physical, emotional, and intellectual) is the very first step on the ladder to success.

as one family: Not as a crowd or a mass of people. A family is one cohesive unit where each member is willing to sacrifice for the other without any conflict of interest.

bound to each other: We are bound together by the mind and intellect. All minds are connected to one another, and are also joined to the Total Mind (Iśvara).

with love and respect: Love manifesting as friendship, truthfulness, and non-violence; respect alone has the ability to bind.

We serve as an army, courageous and disciplined: Service makes a person humble, but we must be ready to serve as an army, that is, be alert, disciplined, courageous, and obedient.

ever ready to fight against all low tendencies: The scriptures list the six low tendencies as desire, anger, greed, delusion, pride, and jealousy. If we conquer desire, then the others fall into place, since anger is a result of unfulfilled desires, and fulfillment of desires gives rise to greed (we want more of the same), delusion (irrational desires create the delusion that they can be fulfilled), pride (in having achieved the desire), and jealousy (directed towards those who have achieved more of the same desire we seek to fulfill).

and false values: Values are convictions of the mind and intellect regarding the vision of the scriptures. False values are wrong convictions based on untruth. For example, only an intellectual understanding of the value of non violence will not convince us of its strength. Until we have practiced nonviolence through our own actions, we will not be convinced of its supremacy and greatness.

within: First, we should recognize the values within us and then assert it to gain a firm conviction for ourselves. The quality of our thoughts and emotions reveal the convictions within.

and without us: We must then fight against low tendencies and false values in the world outside. Great minds are required to lead reform and change the negative tendencies of society. Lord Kṛṣṇa says, "The wise, staying integrated, have to lead the world in the right direction."

We live honestly: There must be honesty in all levels of our thinking, actions, speech, and feelings. The scriptures say the path to Truth is also the Truth.

the noble life of sacrifice and service: This world is a "karma bhūmi" (realm of action), not a "bhoga bhūmi" (realm of ceaseless enjoyment). We are here to learn, and if we do not learn well, we will have to repeat the lessons in a future life. Thus, we must learn constantly, sacrificing the lower for the higher, and serving with kindness, humility, and compassion.

producing more than we consume: By doing so, we live a more efficient and purposeful life, especially since we are ceaseless "consumers" — consuming not only through the mouth, but also through the senses and mind.

and giving more than we take: To live a noble life, it is very important to keep giving. Lord Kṛṣṇa says: "If we take without giving, then we are thieves, and such a life is lived in vain."

We seek: After living a life of noble values, we take the next steps to seek the higher.

the Lord's grace: It is by His grace alone that we gain Knowledge, and through this Knowledge alone He blesses us. Lord Kṛṣṇa says: "Serve Me, be devoted unto Me, and I shall certainly bestow all that you require."

to keep us on the path of virtue, courage, and wisdom: "Keep" here implies that we have already started our journey on this path of virtue (dharma), with courage (karma yoga) and wisdom (jñāna yoga). Grace is required to keep us in steady pursuit of what we began seeking.

May Thy grace and blessings flow through us, to the world around us: Let us be instruments in the Lord's hands. May He work through us to effect the positive changes that He wishes for the world. For this, let us empty ourselves of the arrogating ego and the lower passions, since they prevent us from becoming His instrument. "Empty thyself, and I shall fill thee," is the promise here.

We believe: Belief is the strength that can change and transform. Belief is faith, and only when we have faith do we gain Knowledge.

that the service of our country is the service of the Lord of lords, and devotion to the people is the devotion to the supreme Self: If we cannot love our neighbor, then we do not love the Lord, since the Lord exists in everyone. True love for the Lord cannot be expressed in parts. Loving only a part of God cannot be loving God, for God is not "one" of the many, He is the many, omnipresent. It is only when we serve God (in all His manifestations) with love, that we gain Self-knowledge. To those who love Him fully, Lord Kṛṣṇa says, "I give them Self-knowledge" — the Knowledge that helps one realize the One in the many and see the many in the One.

We know our responsibilities: A true seeker does not lose sight of his duties and responsibilities even as he takes up multifaceted roles in the world. The seeker now has the ability to "respond" — not just "react" — to the world around. Such a wise "non-reactive" life is verily a responsible life. A pebble thrown in a still lake causes ripples. The lake ripples, and then goes back to its calm and peaceful state. A wise man is like the lake. He responds to all situations that come his way, always abiding in the calmness of the Self. A seeker practices this art of inner abidance.

give us the ability and courage to fulfill them: Merely knowing the duties and responsibilities is not the end. The seeker prays for the ability and courage to be alert and vigilant in the fulfillment of all his duties — to ever be an instrument of the Lord and to fulfill His will.

To be thus is the beginning of the journey that has no end. And it is certainly a lifelong commitment.

Om Tat Sat — These three are the appellations of the supreme Reality. Each of these words has a deep significance as explained by Lord Kṛṣṇa in the *Bhagavad-gītā*. The pledge concludes with this remembrance of the supreme Reality, for to remember Him always, is to abide in Him forever.

Spread before our eyes is a magnificent movement for the resurrection of an Indian people, and a return to the age-old values of Sanātana-dharma and the rich cultural heritage of India. In the gathering force of days ahead, Swamiji wrote about this rebirth:

In short, we are aiming at a total renaissance of our country. India needs it badly. This is the time for the culture of the Ṛṣis, to bring hope and strength, faith and courage to the dying hearts and confused heads. The Aryan culture must soak into the hearts of all everywhere; and it must beam out, spreading its glory, in all our intentions and purposes.

We must bring new meaning to our economics, a new vision to our science, a new adjustment to our social and domestic life. Then alone is philosophy justified. It will then discover its own vitality to throb with life and purpose. Our culture will be resurrected. Our country will be reawakened. Our people will discover their self-respect, their heritage, their inherent dignity of life.

In this vision we shall not limit our field to the Hindus only, nor is it only for India. Our vision shall comprehend all mankind, all nations, societies, and communities. Man is our theme of devotion, and he is our main field of worship.

We serve the Lord through the service of the people around us. Every act is an act of worship of the ever-present Sadāśiva (the ever-auspicious Lord) everywhere. To serve mankind with all that we have with us, is the yoga of service. Thus, we shall march along, silently and heroically, doing our duties to all, demanding no rights, nor any reward. Such mighty hearted, self-sacrificing, faith-clad soldiers of the Lord, heroes of Bhārata, are to be all Mission members.

This is the great Vision of our Mission. The nation expects it of all of you — shall we disappoint Bhārata?

Clockwise from above:
Swamiji addressing the Rotary Club, Surat, 1966
Portrait of Swamiji, Kolkata, 1967
Welcome on inaugural day of Jnana Yagna, Silver Jubilee year of Chinmaya Movement, (Swamiji followed by the Chief Minister, S. B. Chavan), Mumbai, March 1976
Drummers leading the way at Guruvayur temple
Swamiji being greeted at Delhi airport by Sheela Puri, Shakuntala Bindra and other devotees

Clockwise from above:
Swamiji being welcomed in Manjeri, Kerala, 1990
Swamiji watching a Balvihar program, Silver Jubilee year, Mumbai, 1976
Part of gathering during Jnana Yagna, Secunderabad, 1974
Swamiji with Ram Batra, Mumbai, 1968

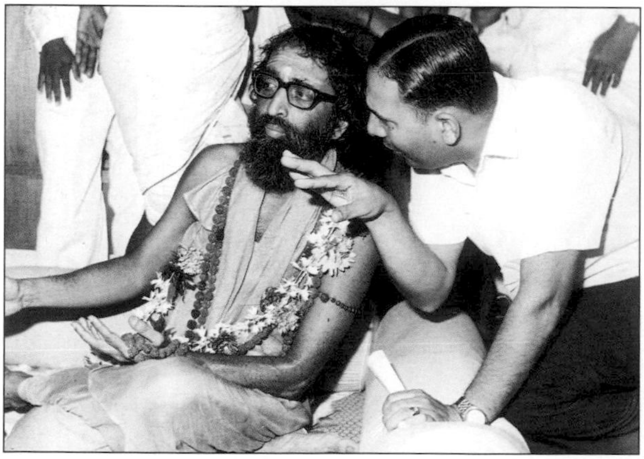

Clockwise from above:
Śrī Viṣṇusahasranāma pūjā, Delhi, February 11, 1991
Audience in Manjeri (right to left: Bina Patel, Uma Bhatnagar, Ashlesha Madhok, Swamini Apoorvananda), 1990
Part of audience, Silver Jubilee year of Chinmaya Movement, Mumbai, March 1976
Part of audience (centerfold below), Silver Jubilee Year of Chinmaya Movement, Mumbai, March 1976

◂ **Facing page clockwise from above:**
Swamiji in Jagadeeshwara temple, Powai, 1976
Swamiji garlanded on Gurupūrṇimā Day, Delhi, 1961
Part of audience, Silver Jubilee Year of Chinmaya Movement, Mumbai, March 1976
Jnana Yagna audience of 20,000 people at Oval Ground, Mumbai, 1961
Portrait of Swamiji, 1967
Portrait of Swamiji, 1973

Portrait of Swamiji, Kolkata, 1966

PART FOUR

Beyond Borders: Within and Without

◀ **Overleaf:**
Left:
Portrait of Swamiji, Delhi airport, 1979
Right:
Portrait of Swamiji, Janmāṣṭamī Day, London, 1983

XV

The World is not Enough

It is a hot summer day in June 1963 on the platform of Chennai Central Railway Station. Most such days, the heat, congestion, and chaos would intimidate a man. Most such days, the drumming noise of an Indian metropolitan would drown out the ingenious faculty in a man. But on this day, B. V. Reddy was spinning with enthusiasm and ideas for his new yoga school. As Swamiji jumped onto a train for Mumbai, he shouted out to him, "Swamiji, why don't you go overseas? I want ammunition to export yoga to America."

"Go on, arrange it," replied Swamiji, before disappearing into the compartment.

Arrange it, he did. Over the next two years, B. V. Reddy sent 18,967 letters and received 15,740 replies! He meticulously arranged every detail of Swamiji's first global tour which covered thirty-nine cities in eighteen countries: Thailand, Hong Kong, Japan, Malaysia, America, Mexico, Spain, United Kingdom, Belgium, Netherlands, Sweden, Germany, Denmark, France, Switzerland, Italy, Greece, and Lebanon. It is no wonder Swamiji called B. V. Reddy a "true karma-yoga-vīra" (heroic karma yogī) in *Tapovan Prasad* (July 1965).

On March 6, 1965, B. V. Reddy and Swamiji left the Indian shores from Kolkata, arriving in Bangkok a day later. Before leaving, Swamiji had visited the Samadhi Mandir of Swami Sivananda in Ananda Kutir, to take the blessings of this remarkable saint who had twenty years earlier, instilled the idea in him of taking the message of Vedānta beyond the borders of India.

A day earlier (March 5), a mammoth public meeting had been held in Oval Maidan, Bombay, to bid farewell to Swamiji. It was attended by thirty thousand devotees and several leaders of religious organizations — Hindu, Jain, Buddhist, Sikh, and Parsi — who drew a parallel with the farewell given to Swami Vivekananda by a group of school masters in 1893, when he had left for America to attend the World Parliament of Religions in Chicago.

During this first tour, in every city, Swamiji introduced the ideas of Vedānta in one- or two-day talks on the logic of spirituality. Many of his talks had been organized by persons who had previously met him in India. He spoke at such places like the Asia Society in San Francisco and the Vedanta Society in Los Angeles. Everywhere he went, he found that Hindus had clung to their religion even though they were away from India. But they had many misconceptions, and were mostly practicing rituals without meaning or value. As a result, Swamiji was vastly appreciated by them, and openly welcomed. B. V. Reddy describes their reception abroad:

> It was a Divine song. Everything went perfectly. Everywhere, there was such love — as if old friends, old lovers were meeting again; and all these people had never heard of Swamiji before.

This first global tour marked more than a defining moment for the revival of Hinduism — it was an inspiration. Swamiji *knew* he was in the midst of great events. Already, a greater number of Indians had turned to the ancient wisdom at home, and he had every intention of awakening the people of the world. He carefully observed the societies of the foreign land, genuinely inquisitive about their ways, and was particularly interested in understanding the American culture, and what had caused the young people to reject the values of their parents. He walked through Golden Gate Park and Haight-Ashbury (famous for its role as the center for the 1960s hippie movement), mingling and discussing the problems of the West with the common American. He would ask many questions about their outlook on life, their dreams and aspirations. One time, he even stood inconspicuously at the back of a bar, watching the typical American scene.

IN THE YEAR OF THE LONG-HAIRED HIPPY

In the days of the "hippie movement," Swamiji was invited to give a three-talk series in 1967 at Haight-Ashbury, the famous hippie section of San Francisco. He accepted the invitation, saying, "There is more seeking among the youth here than among the youth of India." He added that the spiritual thirst among the American youth was a "revolt against present imperfections and the stretching forth for perfection. What they are revolting *against* is very well known, but I don't think they have grasped what they are revolting *for*."

The audience included many long-haired hippies. One of them asked him about the use of hallucinatory drugs as a quick method of attaining illumination. "It is like taking the wrong turn on a spiritual freeway," said Swamiji. "The use of LSD, in particular, is dangerous and personality-breaking." On other occasions, he compared LSD use to forcing a rose to bloom faster by pulling on its fragile petals with one's fingers to make the blossom open up quickly.

Some years later, in 1973, he gave a talk in Golden Gate Park, a place where many hippies had gathered over the years. It was America's Independence Day, and he had entitled his talk: *What Is Real Independence?*

At the end of the talk, as I was walking with him towards his car, I said, "Swamiji, that talk was just magnificent!" He answered, "It's done, finished. When the work is finished, no more talking about it."

Rudite Emir
Chinmaya Mission San Jose
Founding Editor of *Mananam*, 1978–1985

During these three months, Swamiji found that wherever he went, people asked the same questions as Indians at home, "Who is God? Why did he create the world? What is God's grace? What is the difference between self-hypnosis and Self-realization?" But there was one new question, "Why has Christianity failed the young people of America?" Swamiji answered:

> It is not that the Christian religion has nothing to offer. It is simply that the Church is not able to satisfy the rational demand of the modern youth looking for explanations about life. It is not Christ and the Bible that have failed, but the priests and preachers and their sermons which have disillusioned the youth. Even in India, the students are not inclined to discuss the truths of life unless it is interpreted to them in a language they can understand.

In effect, the problems of the West were similar to those of Indians. When Swamiji had given his "Let Us Be Hindus" talk in 1951, he had addressed this very issue within Hinduism. The problem was not in the religion, but in understanding it. In a letter to Anjali Singh dated May 28, 1965, from New York, Swamiji wrote:

> ... For the next few lives I wouldn't dare wish for a foreign tour of this type. I am just smothered with work here. Ooofff. Do you hear my groaning pains under the pleasure of the heavy load of loving

> work? My flesh weeps in agony when my heart dances in joy, my head applauds its approbations. Between these contrariness, I am stretched and torn asunder. S-N-E-E-Z — sorry. I have such a bad cold, bad throat, bad stomach — bad-bad-bad everything except my heart, head, and character ...
>
> Here, Christianity has miserably, totally, completely failed to inspire the youth of this country. Instead of turning atheistic, they are sincerely seeking Truth in the Eastern philosophies. There are people here to explain clearly, to expound dynamically, all religions — Buddhism, Chinese systems of thought, Japanese variety of Buddhism as Zen, and so on, Sikhism, Jainism, Islam. But for the true one — Vedānta — there is none to explain, none to advocate. What a sad state. Without Vedānta, the American growing generation is not going to be benefited.

The logical science of Vedānta holds a universal appeal. Whether it is Hindus or people from other religions, everyone is benefited; everyone is able to bring out the best within themselves and the translation of their religion. And this is one of the aspects that most endeared Swamiji to Westerners. Christians were not asked to become Hindus, but by the study of philosophy, their own understanding of Christianity would be enhanced, and their own personal relationship with Christ and his teachings would deepen. So much so, that at the end of this tour, a Christian minister from Trinidad, Dr. Baldwin George, came back with Swamiji to study Vedānta at Sandeepany Sadhanalaya Powai, joining the first course midway.

On May 19, 1965, Swamiji arrived in Europe. Later, he again writes his first impressions of Paris and London:

> In France, there is a sizable group of students. Talks are translated daily. In four days, we had some six meetings and innumerable group discussions, private talks, interviews, and so forth. Altogether,

> I must have met some two-to-three thousand Parisians. Also, being my first visit, I have a lot to roam about and see. Everything here is majestic, king-size, arresting.
>
> In England, also, meetings were successful — but they are indeed a cold set of people. They wouldn't laugh — nor smile — nor even nod their heads. And after the meetings, they roar their sides away in peals of laughter among themselves at my jokes! This is unfair indeed. Always an artificial "delayed action."

From Athens, Swamiji wrote a letter dated June 15, 1965, to all members of Chinmaya Mission:

> I am now almost on the shores of India; I can almost hug her from here. From March 7th when I left, till today, never was a day spent in rest or idleness. There were two or three meetings every day, besides group discussions, newspaper and radio interviews, and television appearances. I met politicians, economists, historians, poets, writers, publishers, professors, and teachers. We visited museums, schools, colleges, clubs, hotels, restaurants, supermarkets, and hospitals. In between all these, we had to pack and unpack, travel, and catch the next plane. There were no invitations for bhikṣā, so we had to hunt for vegetarian food. There were reports to be prepared, letters to be answered, and instructions to be given to the directors of Central Chinmaya Mission Trust.
>
> Altogether, there was no time to worry or to feel the fatigue. No, in fact, there was no time to even assimilate what I have gone through. Everything seems to be a maze of misty memories and marching experiences.
>
> Now, we have to cover only Lebanon and Jordan, and on the 27th, I will touch the sacred land of India. I can already smell her mangoes, her rain-soaked earth, her fragrant peace and sweet tenderness. There is no place on the face of the earth like my country.

PHONE : 581824

SANDEEPANY SADHANALAYA

TARA CULTURAL TRUST

SAKHI VIHAR ROAD
POWAI, BOMBAY,-70.

28. 8. '66.

Amomomom! Salutations!!

It will be very interesting — glad they didn't want the 12-days Yagna — I am forcing myself on them. Hurrahh!! Their fears — 12 days will people regularly come? 2 or $2\frac{1}{2}$ hrs will everybody be able to give? Where will you stay? Where is money? .... And Poor ME! What can I answer. But I did "Narayana-Narayana". Result! Money somebody loaned — place somebody in Calcutta offered voluntarily by himself → first 3 days hall is available!! By then I will be there in London for 3 days won't I? Place will be found — else what are the Soap-boxes for!!

Books could not be sent. From our sacred harbours no ship leaves for London for the last $1\frac{1}{2}$ months!! See the "Ohe Boye" expatriate your progress!! "Kino" & "Meditation & Life" & I am flying my "Geeta" XII. What else can I do?

Thy Own Self

Chinmayananda

Clockwise from above:
Swamiji boarding a flight, 1966
Addressing a gathering at Golden Gate Park, Haight-Ashbury, Independence Day, San Francisco, July 4, 1973
Speaking on the BMI chart, Arizona, 1973
Swamiji in an achkan ready to travel abroad, Delhi, 1965

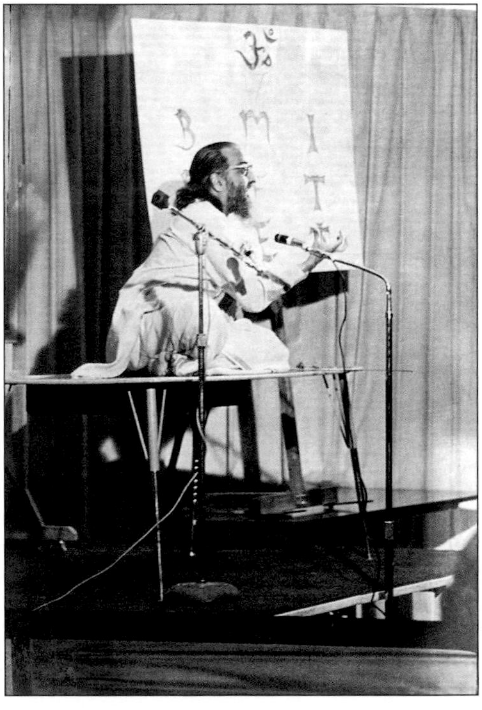

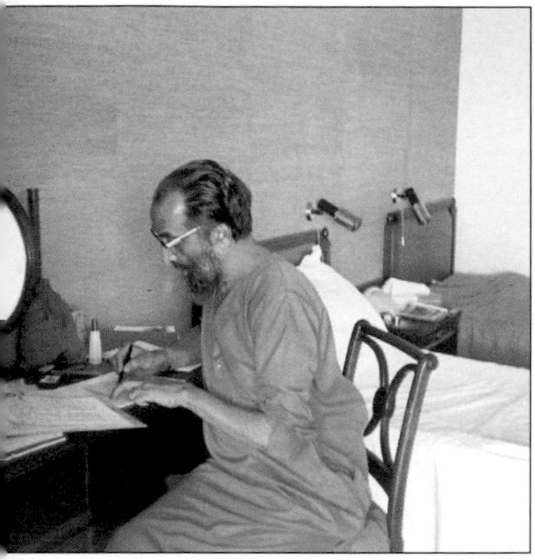

Clockwise from above:
Working at his desk
in a hotel room, Spain, 1973
During the All California
Sonoma Spiritual Camp,
Sonoma State College, 1973
During the All California
Sonoma Spiritual Camp,
Sonoma State College, 1973
During a Bhagavad-gītā discourse
in Orvis Auditorium, University of
Hawaii, Honolulu, 1972
Addressing a packed hall at the
University of British Columbia,
Vancouver, 1976

Clockwise from above:
Swamiji in a western suit with Luis Jauregui
Addressing a gathering at Golden Gate Park, San Francisco, July 4, 1973
At the All California Sonoma Spiritual Camp, Sonoma State College, July 1973
Swamiji with Nalini Browning
Swamiji with Uma Jeyarasasingham
Walking towards morning class, Humbolt University, California, 1973

Clockwise from above:
Swamiji makes a point under the mammoth cross in Chapel Hall, Mount College, San Francisco, 1974
Morning class on Īśāvāsya-upaniṣad, San Francisco, 1973
Jnana Yagna organized by the East West Center in Honolulu, Hawai, July 26, 1972
Rudite Emir welcomes Swamiji, San Francisco, 1975

All in all, the doors of the West had been thrown wide-open, and the four-month global tour in 1965 served as a testing ground in several countries. It not only allowed Swamiji to understand the mindset of many diverse societies, but also planted the seed for subsequent years — Indians and many foreigners began to wait for Swamiji's annual return after this first tour. Students of Vedānta carried their sleeping bags and followed him from city to city. In several towns, there was a small house available for Swamiji to stay in, so everyone else camped out in the backyard. If there was no house available, Swamiji would stay in a motel. A group of sincere American students gathered in San Francisco to meet weekly and study the *Gītā.* One of these was Evelyn Vrat (later known as Mother Sadhana), who organized several introductory talks in 1965, including one at Dr. Chaudhuri's "Cultural Integration Fellowship." It was here that Nalini Browning, Bob Berg, and Solange Berg met Swamiji. Nalini Browning would play a key role in the formation (and growth) of Chinmaya Mission West in 1975, and Bob and Solange Berg would help Evelyn Vrat organize Swamiji's 1st Jnana Yagna in the U.S.A. in 1966, held in the downtown Bellevue Hotel in San Francisco. Swamiji was also regularly invited to give talks in many state universities. Some of the more prominent names were: Stanford University, University of California (Berkeley), Cornell University, University of California (Medical Center San Francisco), University of Hawaii, University of Washington, Harvard University, Boston University, Massachusetts Institute of Technology, and Mesa Community College.

In the early years, Swamiji's audiences were largely composed of Westerners; and among his first devotees and workers in the U.S.A were: Nalini and Bill Browning, Rudite Emir, Byron Hayes, Leo and Bernadina Graves, Bill Sheldon, Leonard Richardson, Luis Jauregui, Dorothy Brooks, John Haring, and Alan Shifman Charles. In addition to Luis Jauregui, who was originally from Mexico, the first Spanish-speaking devotees were Luisa Bravo from Colombia and Imelda Rosenthal from Guatemala. Luis Jauregui later translated the Chinmaya Lesson Course (a correspondence course on Vedānta introduced by Swamiji in 1966 for foreign students) into Spanish, and he and his twin brother, Manuel Jauregui, held the first Study Group in Spanish at Imelda Rosenthal's home. The Spanish Lesson Course was also taken up by many seekers in the Mexican cities of Durango, Guadalajara, Tepic, Tijuanan, Mexicali, Toluca, and Tuxtla Gutierrez. Then, the Inchauspi sisters from Argentina were regular attendees of Swamiji's Jnana Yagnas in America, traveling from Argentina to be with him. The only two "visible" Indians at the time were Sulochana and Maya Menon, who accompanied Swamiji from city to city.

The central activity from 1965–73 was Jnana Yagnas and Study Groups, which were initially dedicated to the mutual study of the Chinmaya Lesson Course. Only later did they branch into the study of main texts. Another key activity was book distribution, which was first accomplished through the efforts of Nalini Browning and Leo Graves in Napa, California.

The San Francisco group wanted to continue the camaraderie created by their common interest of Vedānta. And, for a brief interlude in 1972, when the Quaker faith offered them some land in Oakhurst near the Yosemite mountain terrain to build a commune, everyone sold their properties, packed up, and headed for the mountains. As it turned out, the local zoning authorities did not give them permission to build separate cottages for each family. The distraught group wrote to Swamiji for encouragement. To their utter amazement, he ordered them back to society. "Americans have the misconception that they have to give up the family and job for the spiritual life," he replied.

At this time, a few Americans had also set an ideal of somehow combining the materialism of America with the spiritual wisdom of India, for the *best* of all possible worlds. Robert Hoblin of San Francisco wrote to Swamiji with this idea in June 1968. Swamiji replied with a most beautiful and striking letter:

> Dear Robert,
> Om Om Om
> Salutations!
>
> I received your letter yesterday. It was a joy to hear from you in this quiet mountain retreat. I hear from Bombay that they have sent extra copies of the preview to our correspondence lessons to Nalini Browning, and therefore you must have received it by now.
>
> To serve as a bridge between the East and the West, the individual must have an inconceivable height, and his arms must have the widest possible embrace. Remember your geography; he will have to stand in the middle of the Pacific Ocean to hold California and Madras together or stand in the mid-Atlantic to hold New York and Bombay in one embrace... Supposing Mr. Hoblin acquires the necessary height to stand safely in the Atlantic, and let us hope that he has cultivated the embrace sufficient to hug both Boston and Badrinath — still, remember Mr. Hoblin, that the entire traffic has to run over the crossroads of your shoulders.
>
> When an individual has grown to such a height and such an arms' length and has lost his head in the heights of meditation, he becomes the All-pervading, because where the ego has ended, the Spirit alone exists. The Spirit needs neither the Eastern spirituality with its values of life, nor the Western materialism and its all-annihilating

missiles of death and disaster. In the Eternal Heart, there are no continents, there are no peoples, there is only love. Cultivate such an all-embracing love which seeks no distinction, sees no differences, knows no East and West — and you will bring the whole universe into your palm.

Complete the study course sincerely and seriously. Absorb the lessons until they become the very essence of your spiritual existence. Live every word conscientiously. Even though some ideas may look impractical and absurd, live them all. Live the ideas without any compromise. You can. And you must.

It is urgent. Perhaps you don't see how urgent it is. A wonderful civilization is slipping into a devastating destruction. The symptoms are obvious: You are a people who have no control over your passions, who live in an atmosphere of hatred and mutual incrimination, who are sinking into tribal levels, despoiling your culture and spoiling your civilization. This destruction is a tragedy. In the psychological cataclysm that is taking place in America, saner islands of quiet and peace are to be discovered, so that some can hold their hands together and form at least a Noah's Ark!

Life survives. It has got a tenacity, and a larger purpose than modern man has ever even suspected. The Roman and the Greek civilizations were wiped out because of their own excesses. Yet, life did not cease. India may rot, America may decay, Europe may be blasted, Asia may be wiped out, but life will survive. The world and its continents are only platforms on which mere individuals for a few hours flicker, dance, and jump about, making what they call history. But if this good old globe of ours, so consistently moving around its own axis once a day — moving now at an angle to the vertical — if it were to take into its head to straighten itself, the existing continents would get submerged and equal amounts of new land would rise from the ooze of the sea. Thus, life will continue.

Man, as he is today, has no control over himself. He has been given a freedom to evolve, and in this attempted evolution, he is also allowed to do some mischief. A very considerate, old, and generous heavenly Father loves all these childish pranks of man, and apparently even allows man to spread his chest in his empty vanity!

But let us not, at least in our saner moments, forget that at our level of consciousness today, we are not masters; neither over ourselves, nor over the world. Vedānta points out the way to self-mastery, a great grand path, an expressway to higher Consciousness.

Ardently wish to embrace the whole universe. Never plan to make a crazy quilt of the world by bringing together the spiritual experience of the East and the material wealth of the West. This cannot be done. Where one is, the other cannot be.

Study the lessons. Study yourself.

Start the pilgrimage. Reach the goal.

With Prem and Om,
Thy own Self,

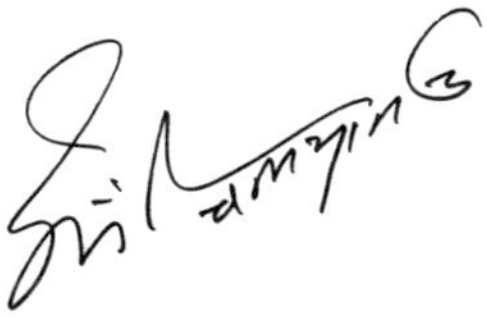

After several trips to the U.S.A., Swamiji decided that the introductory time was over. By now, the Indian community had also begun to attend his talks, many of them taking an active role in organizing Jnana Yagnas. He began an intensive schedule: in the morning, a text such as Ādi Śaṇkarā's *Bhaja Govindam*; and in the evening, one-and-a-half-hour sessions from the *Gītā*; then, after a ten-minute break, a class began on the Upaniṣads. Afterwards, there was a period of meditation. This schedule allowed the working people of America to attend most of the functions, since they were held after-work hours. In later years, Swamiji did change and improve on this program, inculcating other activities.

The early devotees from the Indian community were Uma Jeyarasasingham (now Acharya, Chinmaya Mission San Jose) who had begun listening to Swamiji's talks in Kuala Lumpur (in 1965); Rajendra and Malti Prasad, Pranji and Lalita Lodhia in California (in 1967), and Gulu and Indra Advani (in 1975). Later, they were joined by active members: Ram Kripalani in New York (in 1972), Br. Krishnamoorthy in New York, Gaurangbhai and Darshanaben Nanavaty in Seattle (in 1975 — they relocated to Houston in 1982), and Dr. Apparao Mukkamala in Michigan (in 1977).

In 1973, devotees organized a spiritual camp at California State College, Sonoma. This was the first retreat camp to be held outside India, and Swamiji described it saying, "The camp at Sonoma, though started with much hesitation and dread — only as an experiment — ended in a brilliant glow of an experience. The entire campus took the form of an Ashram! It was an unimaginable transformation in the entire area. And there were some sixty-four ardent seekers, every one of them a Gem." At the end of the camp, he wrote a letter to the organizers: "Only in the future will you come to recognize the significance of this event."

After the 1975 camp at Humboldt State University, "Chinmaya Mission West" (CMW) was incorporated. The principle goal of CMW is the same as the Chinmaya Mission statement, but it also aims to reach people of all faiths with a philosophy which is neither Eastern nor Western, but simply Truth. Chinmaya Mission West includes the United States, Canada, Trinidad and Tobago, Mexico, Central and South America. Its thirty-seven regional centers sponsor Jnana

Yagnas, spiritual camps, Study Groups, Balvihars, and many other spiritual activities. Also, CMW currently publishes a semiannual book called *Mananam* — meaning "Reflections upon Truth" — which is dedicated to promoting the ageless wisdom of Vedānta with an emphasis on the unity of all religions. Each *Mananam* focuses on a selected, contemporary theme, with diverse writings by authors from various philosophical and spiritual traditions. Some of the more recent authors featured are: Fritjof Capra, the Dalai Lama, Huston Smith, Ken Wilber, Paramahansa Yogananda, Hazrat I. Khan, Jack Canfield, Vimala Thakar, Eckhart Tolle, Desmond Tutu, and Thich Nhat Hahn. In addition, CMW puts together a bimonthly newsletter which carries the latest news and events from all its regional centers.

In one incident in 1975, Swamiji arrived in San Francisco just in time to be driven straight from the airport to the Civic Center to participate in an open forum of all religions, organized by the Sufi master, Pir Vilayat Khan. Many members of the audience were impressed with Swamiji's insightful answers to their questions on love, life, sex, and drugs. As a result, a group of fast-track "guru hunters" drove fifty miles down to Stanford University in Palo Alto, for his lecture series. At the end of the first talk, one of them asked Swamiji, "What is your *technique*?"

"What is my technique? My technique is to stand on my nose and meditate," said Swamiji. "But I only practice it in private."

He gave a mischievous laugh, and then thundered seriously, "If you are looking for shortcuts in spirituality or instant psychedelic happenings, you have made a mistake today. But don't repeat it — don't come tomorrow!"

Everyone got the message. They returned every day to hear the discourses on *Bhagavad-gītā,* Chapter 12 in the evening, and *Kenopaniṣad* in the morning.

INOPPORTUNE DEATH

I joined a study group in California, even before meeting Swamiji. And after the first lecture series in Stanford University in 1967, I invited Swamiji for bhikṣā at my house.

After the meal, I asked him a question, "How do you explain that a very good person dies very tragically — at a very inopportune time?"

Swamiji looked at me thoughtfully and replied with another question, "Inopportune for whom?"

Pranji Lodhia
Chinmaya Mission San Jose;
Treasurer, Chinmaya Mission West

BACK ROW TO SUPERFAST LANE

It was by His divine will and grace that I was asked by a couple of senior colleagues to accompany them to Ottawa, Canada, on their visit to meet a Swami Chinmayananda, who was giving discourses at the University of Ottawa in June 1977.

Since I had only gone to oblige my colleagues, I sat in the back row. The next day, we went to meet Swamiji.

"Why were you sitting in the back row?" he asked me.

I didn't know what to say, except that I came in the capacity of a driver, and was not really interested in religion, and I was going back to Michigan that evening.

Swamiji gave a surprised look. "Then why did you drive 600 miles just to attend one lecture?" he asked. He took me inside his room, took out his calendar, and gave me dates in July 1978. He told me to organize a Jnana Yagna!

Dr. Apparao Mukkamala
Chinmaya Mission Flint;
President, Chinmaya Mission West
[Apparao and Sumathi Mukkamala are Chief Sevaks, Chinmaya Vijaya]

PRINTING, NOT PRINTING BUSINESS

During the course of his lecture series in Napa, California, sometime in the 1970s, Swamiji instructed me to "learn printing." So I began to learn printing by apprenticing to established printers, eventually purchasing my own business in Napa called Family Press. I spent ten years running the business, battling with faulty equipment and struggling to keep the business afloat while fulfilling most of the printing requirements for Chinmaya Mission West.

When I talked about the difficulties with Swamiji many years later, he said, "I said to you 'learn printing' not 'learn the printing business.'" (Meaning, when working in the field, a higher vision must be kept at all times.)

Bill Browning
Krishnalaya, Piercy, California
[In 1973, Bill and Nalini Browning bought "Family Press," which for many years printed CMW publications and publicity materials.]

The most significant motivation for Chinmaya Mission West is Balvihar. Everyone presumes that second generation children born abroad are ABCDs (American Born Confused Desīs), easily interchangeable with BBCDs (British Born Confused Desīs).

Nonsense. Certainly that is one way to go, but it isn't the only way. Balvihar in the West challenges this myth. Each and every one of the thirty-seven centers under CMW have multiple Balvihar classes each week for children — and many of the bigger centers like Ann Arbor, Boston, Chicago, Dallas, Los Angeles, San Jose, Washington DC, and Tristate have opened four-to-six "satellite centers" (in schools, community halls, and temples within a sixty-mile radius) to accommodate the growing demand of parents wanting to give their children Indian values in a fun way.

In the early 1970s, Swamiji had voiced his concern for Indian children growing up in the Western culture to Sharada Kumar (now Acharya, Chinmaya Mission Ann Arbor and one of ten directors on the CMW Board). During a bhikṣā at her home in New York, he said, "I am not worried about the adults who grew up in India, because they will know where to find the answers for their problems in the scriptures. But I am worried about these young ones, who will be lost in the dual culture. Why don't you start a Balvihar for them?" Sharada Kumar was hesitant. "But I don't know how to start one!" she said. Swamiji handed her a letter for Nirmala Amma in Mumbai (who was successfully running a Balvihar in Chembur), saying, "Go get trained!"

In 1974, Sharada Kumar went to Mumbai for her training with Nirmala Amma. She returned to the U.S.A. with all the necessary materials, and with the guidance of Br. Krishnamoorthy (Acharya, Chinmaya Mission New York, called the "swami in white" by Swamiji), she started the first Balvihar in her home in Long Island in 1976. Sharada Kumar describes the initial reaction from the Indian community:

> It was tough to convince people to bring their children to Balvihar, as people had no concept of what it was. Whenever I spotted Indians in the supermarket, I would make my five-year old daughter, Aruna, run up to the parents, and ask them, "Aunty, Uncle, can you bring your children to the house, *please?*" Some of them would feel bad and couldn't say "no" to a child, so they brought their kids. On the day of the class, I would make all kinds of Indian savouries and sweets as "prasāda" to lure the parents. And soon, the word spread, and people started coming on their own.

Today, Balvihar is an outstanding success in the U.S.A. It would not be stretching a point to suggest that it is a cultural phenomenon within the Indian community. Over 250,000 children are currently enrolled in Balvihars all over the country, and more than 100,000 have graduated in the last thirty-four years. Many ex-Balvihar children now bring their kids to study in Balvihars. Sharada Kumar says that "we have had to appoint a National Balvihar Coordinator for the past ten years because there are so many enquiries from all over the country. I attribute all the success to the three G's — grace of Pujya Gurudev (Swamiji), Guruji (Swami Tejomayananda), and God!"

Within a few short years, Swamiji made an unprecedented impact on the people. His unorthodox approach to scripture was exciting, to say the least. He was logical, practical, and supremely fascinating. Some stories that quickly did the rounds:

> Swamiji was cutting a cake with the birthday girl. A man walked up to him and asked in an American drawl, "Swamiji, when desires get exhausted, then the ego is not there. Then who realizes?" Keeping his eyes focused on the cake cutting, Swamiji replied, "There is an ant fallen inside this cake. He looks to the right and finds there is cake. On top of him and below him is cake; it is all cake-o-cake. The intellect is like the ant."

In another incident:

> A young boy asked Swamiji, "What made you renounce the world? You were a postgraduate in English Literature and Law, and a very successful journalist." Swamiji asked him in return, "When will you

> spit that thing out?" referring to the chewing gum in the boy's mouth. "Oh! I am just about to spit it out. There's no juice left in it," said the boy. "Ah! I, too, did just that," laughed Swamiji. "I had chewed the world sufficiently and did not find any more juice in it."

Then again:

> One skeptic asked, "Whatever you teach is there in the books. What do I need a Guru for?" Swamiji replied, "Why don't you ask this question to the books."

And again:

> A plump devotee came up to Swamiji, and referring to another devotee, she said, "Swamiji, it isn't fair! She eats so much at every meal and still doesn't put on an ounce of extra weight, whereas I starve myself to death, just living on the bare minimum — and look at my size!" Swamiji immediately clapped his hands and beckoned everyone standing around him to come forward, "Come and see! Here is a wonderful example of an effect without a cause."

THE BEAUTY OF THE GURU

There was something extraordinary about Swamiji, his charisma that pulled us immediately towards him. At the end of my first Jnana Yagna in 1975, I asked him, "Will you be my Guru?"

"Let's pretend that you have never seen the moon," replied Swamiji. "Now look through the window and see the tree. Now see the branch, and follow the branch to the end, and what do you see? You see the moon. Similarly, a Guru shows you the Truth, and after that you don't need the branch or the window."

On another occasion, I had made a mistake, and asked Swamiji for advice. "How do I make it right?" I said.

"You must say you are sorry," said Swamiji.

"But sorry doesn't cut it," I replied.

"In the beginning it does not cut it. But, after a little while, it becomes a habit to say sorry; and, all of a sudden, it becomes part of your psyche and you will never do it again."

Meena Bhaga
Chinmaya Mission Halton

AN ENIGMATIC SWAMI

During Swamiji's talks at MIT in 1972, I went to see him at his place of residence. There were 4-5 people in the room. He asked me, "And what do you do?"

I had just quit my teaching job, hence I said, "I am not doing anything right now. I was teaching, and I love kids, but I don't like the system."

Swamiji closed his eyes. When he reopened them after a minute, he said, "All the stars, the sun, and the moon work in a system. They don't complain!"

Sheela Kripalani
Chinmaya Mission Boston

LARGE BLESSINGS IN SMALL THINGS

A poignant incident from Swamiji's second Jnana Yagna in San Francisco (in 1967) was my first encounter with his unexpected, spontaneous, and merry ways. I was driving down a San Francisco street in the late evening toward the hotel where Swamiji was giving his talks. It was dark, but the streets were still busy with traffic. All of a sudden, I saw a movement to the left, and looked at the car next to me. There was Swamiji! He was looking at me through his car window and smiling broadly at me! He then rolled down his window and motioned for me to do the same. I did, and Swamiji reached through the window (with both cars still in motion) and handed me a small memento, laughing merrily the entire time.

Then there was his stern side, which many of us learned to know. After I had asked him in a letter whether there couldn't be an exception or two to his directive not to give out his address to anyone, Swamiji answered in a letter dated September 14, 1972: "When I say, even with a wink, in the most jocular mood, 'No!' it means 'No,' please! Why should a false idea come out of my mouth? So don't give my addresses to anyone. Just say, 'No instructions' or declare that you have not the address with you to give!!"

Rudite Emir
Chinmaya Mission San Jose

PLAYING THE MIND

Swamiji wanted us to learn to be detached, so he would "play" with my and other's attachments. In hindsight, I often saw him doing this. In the summer of 1981, I traveled with him as his secretary while he was in the U.S.A., and during this time he taught me a great lesson.

From the first to the last Jnana Yagna, he was changing his mind back and forth about whether I should come to India that year to video his discourses. My emotions were swinging from great excitement to disappointment. One day, he commented, "Why doesn't Vilasini come to India in the fall and video the talks?" The next week, he said, "What is the hurry, why rush, she can come in a few years." A week later, it would be, "Why don't you come now?" My mind was going up and down like a roller coaster, getting excited and despondent, until I finally realized what he was doing. I told myself to let go and surrender, and say to myself, "Okay, whatever happens is fine."

Then, Swamiji instructed someone, "Vilasini is coming to India in the fall. Buy her a ticket!"

Vilasini Balakrishnan
Acharya, Chinmaya Mission Washington, DC

BLAME IT ON THE CAT

A large classroom in Boston University was filled to capacity as Swamiji began his first Jnana Yagna in Boston in December 1971. The text was *Bhagavad-gītā,* Chapter 12, dealing with the path of devotion. A group of enthusiastic individuals rushed to the front, and placed multiple tape recorders on the dais. Swamiji shook his head. "Only if the recorder and the tape had the capacity to record the whole talk without interruption, it is allowed," he said. "When you return to change the side of the tape, it will create a distraction in the minds of the listeners. It is not just the words that convey the subtle beauty of the sacred scriptures. The words are the carrier of the message through a connection created by focused concentration."

Swamiji then related an incident which occurred in Uttarkashi, when he was studying with his Guru, Swami Tapovanam. Just as they had begun class by chanting the traditional śānti-mantra (peace prayer), invoking the blessings of the teacher and disciple's combined efforts to discover the knowledge of Truth, creating stillness and peace on all levels conducive to the process; just then, when everything seemed in place, Swami Tapovanam announced, "Class is over."

"Why?" asked the surprised disciple.

"Did you see the cat?" asked Swami Tapovanam.

"Yes," replied Swamiji.

"So did I. Lesson over," said Swami Tapovanam.

The unexpected appearance of the cat had defocused the students' attention, creating a distraction, and causing a drop in the level of concentration and harmony which the teacher was striving to create.

Mimi Robins
Chinmaya Mission Boston
[She was Swamiji's "official photographer" in the U.S.A. and clicked the last picture of him before his mahāsamādhi.]

BE, ALWAYS BE

Swamiji was a very energetic, fiery speaker. But it was much more than that. When he spoke, an energetic inner transformation occurred within the listener. For instance, when he said you are Sat-Cit-Ānanda (Existence-Consciousness-Bliss), the mind dissolved into sat-cit-ānanda. For me, it was *That* which was underlying his words — which was most remarkable.

During my first meeting in Lancaster in 1981, he said in his talk, "And then Lord Kṛṣṇa said to Arjuna you are my channel." Suddenly, there was a transportation into another dimension. After the lecture, I was in the house where he was staying, and he casually walked by me and said, "Don't try to understand it, just *be* it." In seemingly ordinary transactions, he was always pointing to *That* which is transcendent.

Suresh Balakrishnan
Chinmaya Mission Washington DC

◀ **Facing page clockwise from above:**
Portrait of Swamiji, 1982
Portrait of Swamiji, 1982
Portrait of Swamiji, 1982
Portrait of Swamiji, 1982
Welcome address at Humbolt State University, California, 1975
Swamiji gives an introduction to Vedānta using the BMI chart, San Francisco, 1975

Clockwise from above:
Swamiji with devotees in U.S.A.
Swamiji addresses a gathering, U.S.A., 1975
Swamiji leading the prayer of all faiths, Department of Religions, Harvard University, Massachusetts, 1971

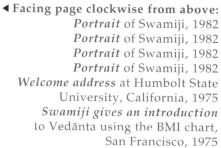

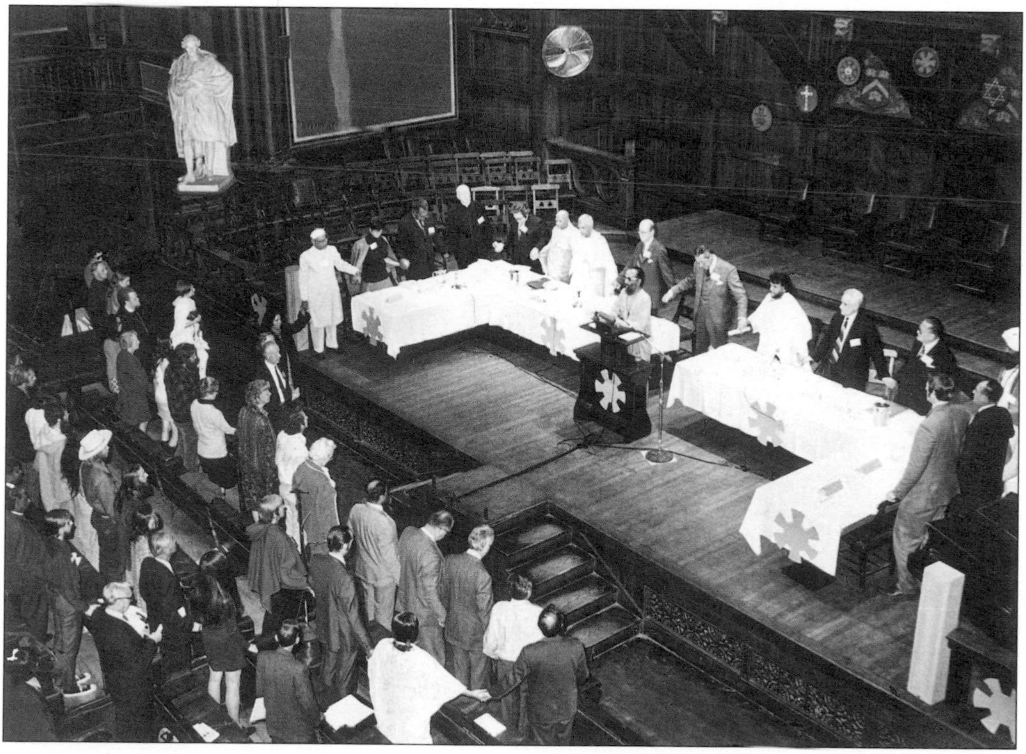

Clockwise from above:
Swamiji with Darshanaben Nanavaty
Annette Wilkes bowing to Swamiji, U.S.A.
Swamiji with Suresh and Vilasini Balakrishnan, Virginia Beach, June 14, 1985
Swamiji with Sharada Kumar, and daughters, Aruna and Vidya, Long Island, 1976
During Gurudakṣiṇā ceremony and prasāda distribution, Trinidad 1975

▸ **Facing page clockwise from above:**
Swamiji's daily satsaṅga under a tree, Olivet College, Michigan, 1982
Swamiji in the Redwood Forest with Swami Purushottamananda and Brni. Pavitra, California, 1983
Swamiji with devotees, Redwood Forest, 1983
Satsaṅga in the Redwood Forest, California, 198
Swamiji "playful," in the Redwood Forest, 1983
Looking at the Grand Redwood's, California, 19

62

Clockwise from above:
Swamiji guides Swami Tejomayananda on the installation of Lord Kṛṣṇa at the gate of Krishnalaya, Piercy, 1991
Swamiji with children, Houston, 1982
Swamiji with Gaurang Nanavaty
Swamiji with Jim Coffin and wife, Humbolt University Camp, 1986

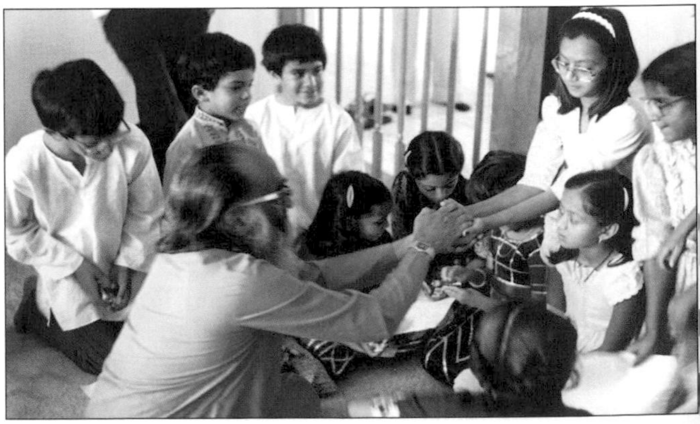

Clockwise from above:
Swamiji leads the way
(Swami Tejomayananda is a charioteer to Lord Kṛṣṇa in a golf cart, driving to the site of installation), 1991
Swamiji hands out prasāda to participants of a children's cultural show, Piercy, California, 1991
At a bhikṣā by a Canadian group, (clockwise from above: Brni. Robyn, Brni. Arpita, Swamini Shivapriyananda, Swamini Sharadapriyananda, Swamiji, Swami Tejomayananda), Piercy, 1991
At Washington airport with Swami Dheerananda, Vilasini Balakrishnan, Ashlesha Madhok, and others
Pūjā in front of Lord Śiva in the presence of Swamiji, San Jose
Swamiji at a bhikṣā by Rudite and Rustom Emir, and daughters, Laila and Minta, Piercy, 1991

Clockwise from above:
Swamiji being welcomed back to India after global tour, Mumbai airport, 1969
Portrait of Swamiji, Switzerland, 1971
Swamiji welcomed back to India after global tour, Mumbai, 1971
Swamiji being welcomed with garlands back to India, Mumbai, 1969

Swamiji continued to return to the U.S.A. each year, with the exception of 1976, when his passport renewal was mysteriously delayed after he had publicly criticized Indira Gandhi's emergency program. In 1979, an eight-acre plot of land was purchased in the redwood country of northern California by the river Eel, to serve as an ashram-school in the style of Sandeepany Sadhanalaya Powai. It was named "Krishnalaya," and on November 7, Sandeepany West was officially inaugurated with forty students from the U.S.A., Europe, and Australia. In the opening address to the students, Swamiji said:

> A great dream is coming true on this auspicious day. Twenty-five years ago, the idea sprang up that we must have an up-to-date, modern, organized institute where young people of the technological age could be intelligently introduced to the in-depth significance of life itself. This subjective science of Vedānta was our true birthright, but in the march of society under the propulsion of history, we were exiled from this inherent self-mastery and have come to roam about in sorrow and dejection in the forest of shameless sensuality.
>
> Twenty-five years ago when the idea exploded in me, nobody took me seriously; even the priests looked at me aghast, with silent sympathy, wondering how such a bright, intelligent young man could so early in life, go so totally crazy!
>
> There have been years of struggle, of uphill climb, of meeting objections, of bulldozing opposition, then fearlessly marching ahead against insufferable odds and painful inertia. It is incomprehensible even to the faithful and religious how barriers have broken down due to our spectacular success in India. An immeasurable flood of dynamic devotion has gushed out from the Hindu community in India. It is on the crest of that wave that Chinmaya Mission reached America to be born as — Chinmaya Mission West.
>
> We expect from you hard and sincere work, selfless dedication, total surrender, admirable discipline, and industrious sādhanā

(spiritual practice). We are not asking you to change, but we shall ask you to watch the transformation of your outer lifestyle taking place as a result of your inner unfoldment.

SHIVALAYA TO KRISHNALAYA

"Krishnalaya" was first named "Shivalaya" by Swamiji. But when the Śiva mūrti arrived, we found that it had been broken in transit. Swamiji promptly renamed the ashram "Krishnalaya," and made arrangements for a Kṛṣṇa mūrti, which arrived in due course.

There was a huge motorcycle gathering just up the road from Krishnalaya in 1978, during the time of a Chinmaya Spiritual Camp when Swamiji talked on the *Vivekacūḍāmaṇi.* It meant that we would be hearing motorcycles roaring by on a regular basis. When the camp attendees arrived and found their assigned rooms, on each bed, the attendees found a note by Swamiji that said, "There is a large gathering of motorcycles nearby. This gives us an opportunity for better concentration in meditation."

Narrated by Rudite Emir
Chinmaya Mission San Jose

From then on, Chinmaya Mission centers started to open in many major cities in the West. Veronica Hausman (Chinmaya Mission San Jose) says, "It was like popcorn, one center after the other came up. First, the ground had to be prepared. Then the fields had to be ploughed. Then the seeds could be sown; then fertilized. Finally, being nurtured with the passing of the seasons of rain and sun … the fruit! Ah, the patience of a saint!"

Uma Jeyarasasingham reports a time from the early 1980s, when Swamiji announced that he was going to share that year's gurudakṣiṇā with all the centers in the West. In those days, Swamiji's gurudakṣiṇā was the main source of income for Chinmaya Mission West. Since Uma Jeyarasasingham was CMW Treasurer during this time (1975–90), she also joined in, asking for funds for the headquarters:

> Swamiji looked at me, and asked, "Are you running low on funds? Are you not receiving contributions from devotees? After all, you are doing the Lord's work."
>
> After a brief pause, he suddenly sat up in his chair, and said, "Examine yourself again, and look for what you may have done to displease the Lord. When He is displeased or unhappy, Lakṣmī (Goddess of Wealth) will turn her back on you. She will not send wealth in your direction."
>
> I did not understand the full import of Swamiji's words, and looked at him questioningly. Swamiji explained, "You (that is, Mission workers) must carry out the Lord's work without ego or ego-centric desires, dedicating every thought, word, and deed as an offering to Him. And above all, you *must* treat the Lord's devotees with great respect, love, and kindness. That will please him more than any offering you can give to Him. When He is pleased, He will smile at you, and Lakṣmī will rain wealth on you through your roof."

Dr. Apparao Mukkamala (President, CMW) says Swamiji told him, "The Chinmaya Mission should never have surplus funds, as there would be no incentive and pleasure to perform and serve society. If the Mission lives only on Trust funds and interest, this will mark the beginning of its downfall."

And, Darshanaben Nanavaty (Acharya, Chinmaya Mission Houston) says:

> Whatever Swamiji instructed us about Chinmaya Mission Houston, word by word, everything has now come true. He wanted a separate standalone temple for Lord Śiva in front of the property, with a big

liṅgam (a traditional symbol of Śiva) on top. We have this now. He named our center "Chinmaya Prabha"; we did not like the name at the time, but did as he said, especially since he told us, "It will be my glory."

When Swamiji had given this name, the center was a small metal building of 5,000 sq. ft. Now, we have a hall, a Balvihar building (which is 45,000 sq. ft. under one roof), and a standalone temple in the property of twenty-one acres.

FULL STOP BEYOND HEAVEN

In 1993, Swamiji visited our ashram in Langhorne (Pennsylvania), "Chinmaya Kedar." He had recently gone through a cataract operation for his eyes, and the procedure had been organized by a devotee, Dr. Jaswant Patel. The operation was performed in the Wills Hospital in downtown Philadelphia, after which Swamiji spent a few days recovering in Dr. Patel's apartment, before continuing on to his Jnana Yagna in New Jersey.

Before leaving, Swamiji thanked everyone, including Dr. Jaswant Patel. But the doctor said, "Please do not thank me. When you go to heaven, please recommend my case."

Swamiji laughed, and said, "But, my son, the problem is that I do not stop there. I go beyond heaven!"

Narrated by Swami Shantananda
Acharya, Chinmaya Mission Tri-State

THE HOUSE IS SINKING

Swamiji had just landed at Chicago's O'Hare airport, and had literally walked in, straight into the maṇḍap (platform) for the bhūmi pūjā (earth-breaking ceremony invoking the blessings of the Lord for ensuing construction) platform which had been prepared for Chinmaya Mission Chicago's newly acquired, beautiful seven-acre property, "Chinmaya Badri." At the time, the only structure on it was a landscaper's little home, the "Little House on Prairie." That night, Swamiji slept in the "Little House on Prairie" for the first time.

At breakfast the next morning he informed us, "This house is sinking!" There was complete silence. We did not know what to think, or say!

We asked an American devotee who knew about construction work to look into the matter. He went into the "crawl space" under the building, and sure enough, when he came out, he said; "Yes. The house is sinking on the north side! The foundation was not properly reinforced on that side, and the crawl space is actively deepening as we go north...!"

Afterwards, the devotees themselves reinforced the foundation, and now Swami Sharanananda (Acharya, Chinmaya Mission Chicago) resides there quite safely.

Nimrita Dholakia
Chinmaya Mission Chicago

TOO MANY COOKS IN AN INDIAN BROTH

Swamiji had come for his heart treatment at the Bircher-Benner Clinic in Zurich in 1972, but he was also giving lectures in the clinic auditorium. The text was *Kenopaniṣad,* and there were many interested listeners from Holland, Germany, England, and Switzerland.

Towards the end of his stay, we invited Swamiji to our home. He came in November 1973 when it was snowing. He entered the kitchen before eating food. I was surprised, so I asked him, "Do you want to wash your hands, Swamiji?" He chuckled. "No, no, it is my habit in India to see how clean it is."

On his way out, he wrote in our visitor's book: "A home is a place where man lives and strives for his security and satisfaction — but the same becomes a temple when in and through our efforts we discipline ourselves to grow in our inner purity and balance. Your house is a temple. Keep it always so."

In 1985, we organized a spiritual retreat camp in Switzerland. The Pashoud couple had found a suitable place in Les Avants (near Montreux), and Laju and Kavita Chanrai had flown Swamiji's cook Govinda Nair from Sidhbari, to take care of the vegetarian requirements of the camp attendees, many of whom had come from India. This turned out to be really challenging for the Swiss cook and his team. He was not used to so many lengthy preparations, involving the use of so many utensils and spices. And he complained that too many Indian ladies were coming into his kitchen. But, the Les Avants camp was a great success!

Ammini (Annemarie) Padiyath
Chinmaya Mission Zurich

Europeans and Australasians alike fell into the intimate dale of Truth, tripping over Swamiji's riveting elucidations. Every generation, from those obsessed and overwhelmed with the riches of the world to those in search of wealth within, began to seek and find peace in the ancient wisdom of Vedānta. In France, Evelyne Mathews says:

> I was dazzled with Swamiji's commentary on *Kenopaniṣad*. He literally stunned me, unseating my atheism, removing all my previous notions. When he revisited Bitche in 1985, I was determined to learn more of Vedānta, and followed his teachings whenever he came to Europe, whether in London or St. Gallen. I also went to the marathon camp in Sidhbari (in 1991) to study the *Bhagavad-gītā,* Chapters 13–18.

Swamiji conducted two spiritual camps in Bitche in 1983 and 1985. His discourses were simultaneously translated in French during the class. When Brni. Bhakti Chaitanya (now Swamini Umananda) returned to Paris after completing the 7th Vedānta Course in Sandeepany Sadhanalaya Powai in 1991, she formed Chinmaya Mission France as an official organization in July 1992 with the help of Nicole Gibourdel, Evelyne Mathews, Alix Sevagamy, and Odile Voichet.

Swamiji's last visit to France was for three days in June 1993. On June 11, he gave a talk on the topic "Why God?" And during this visit, he spoke to Nicole Gibourdel for the first time, by simply asking her name, "Nicole, Swamiji," she answered. "Nickel, nickel," he repeated several times, then asserted, "No, not nickel, but silver." Nicole Gibourdel has never forgotten these words.

At the end of three days, Swamiji left for London, where he had a Jnana Yagna. On the last day of the London Jnana Yagna, when the gurudakṣiṇā was given to him, he announced from the dais, "This money will go for the newly formed Chinmaya Mission France."

"But why is the money going to France?" enquired some members from London. "Chinmaya Mission France is my little bud. It will grow and give a beautiful fragrance," said Swamiji.

Chinmaya Mission France purchased a property in Paris in 2004, where all their activities are now held. Swami Tejomayananda visited the newly-purchased center a year later, and immediately informed the members that he wanted to see "everything." After seeing the kitchen, the satsaṇga hall, and the residential room, he saw a trapdoor on the floor. "What is this?" he asked. The members explained that it was the access to the cellar. He said he wanted to see that *also.* The trapdoor was opened and Swami Tejomayananda disappeared into the cellar. Then, he came back and lovingly said, "Congratulations! I am very happy to see our center in Paris."

London was the first city to organize an "International Spiritual Camp." Laju and Kavita Chanrai, who had been regularly hosting Swamiji in London, arranged the international camp at the Crystal Palace in London in August 1986. This became the catalyst for establishing a Chinmaya Mission presence in the United Kingdom. In subsequent years, Swamiji returned several times, and also brought with him a dynamic disciple, Swami Swaroopananda, from the Far East. Thereafter, Chinmaya Mission U.K. (CMUK) has grown many times over, with active CHYK and Balvihar activities, Study Groups and Swaranjali, and an assortment of cultural events. The London CHYK is famously tagged around the world as "supremely hardworking and devoted (and intelligent)"! They are invited to address hundreds of people on Vedānta, and spirituality in the modern world, at the House of Commons, Morgan Stanley, Goldman Sachs, KPMG, PricewaterhouseCoopers, Kings College London, and the London School of Economics. CMUK has over fifty classes running each week; the attendance sheet for a class in the financial district alone shows two hundred names.

In September 2001, Swami Swaroopananda conducted a Hanuman Chalisa Maha Yagna in London. Overnight, CMUK went from attracting a few hundred people to close to two thousand persons during their annual Jnana Yagnas. It is told that the road leading up to the yajñaśālā was blocked and crowds thronged outside trying to gain entrance. Two years later, the CMUK website (chinmayauk.org) went live on the internet; it has since evolved to become a wonderful resource for Chinmaya Mission articles, online magazines, global and local news, and events. The site records thousands of hits every month.

On May 24, 2004, the center building "Chinmaya Kirti" was inaugurated. Satellite centers now exist in Leicester, Nuneaton, Cardiff, and Kent. In addition, CMUK Balvihar is highly acclaimed for teaching the GCSE Course in Hinduism; and hundreds of children have achieved top grades in recent years. All of this, from an inconspicuous beginning in May 1965, when Swamiji first landed in London and was greeted with a "delayed action"!

The Orient is often called "the treasure chest of the world." Its timeless wealth and wisdom has been a constant source of wonder and awe. But for thousands of Indian settlers in the Far East, Swamiji was the real treasure. He came, he liberated, and he unlocked hidden treasures within.

Swamiji's first trip to Hong Kong was on March 10, 1965. He had a Western suit made at this point, to take with him to America (the suit is now in Chinmaya Jeevan Darshan, Chinmaya Vibhooti). He returned six years later for a Jnana Yagna in 1971, after which the first Study Group, CHYK group, and Balvihar class were started. But since there was no Chinmaya Mission registered in Hong Kong, he was unable to send them an ācārya to advance their enthusiasm and activities. Hong Kong law stipulates that only if you have a business, were you eligible for a long-term visa. There is a famous joke to describe the mentality of the people here. It goes somewhat like this: In most parts of the world, people greet each other by saying, "How are you?" But in Hong Kong, they say, "How is your business?" Not surprisingly, Swamiji invested in a long-term plan.

He sent Br. Raghavan Chaitanya (now Swami Shantananda, Acharya, Chinmaya Mission Tri State) to Taiwan in 1981, from where he was to begin a business and simultaneously guide and take care of Hong Kong activities. Once in Taiwan, Br. Raghavan found himself a Chinese partner and set up a trading business, the *Trans Oceanic Enterprise Ltd.* — all of this with Swamiji's complete blessings, of course. But what does a brahmacārī know about business? It was not long before the two partners lost all their worldly possessions to a Jewish trading company. Swami Shantananda relates the tumultuous events:

> I was utterly depressed and wrote to Swamiji with the whole story. After a few days, he sent me a reply: "Why are you getting so agitated and worried. The whole of life is a game. Play it well! Take the loss with the spirit of a sportsman. You *will* succeed." His words gave me so much relief at the time and changed my entire outlook to the whole drama I was playing as a businessman!

Br. Raghavan Chaitanya did succeed. And whilst in Taiwan, he started Vedānta classes over the weekends (Friday–Sunday). Swamiji visited Taiwan for a Jnana Yagna in June 1987. Quite fittingly, he changed the brahmacārī's name to "Br. Shanta Chaitanya" (peaceful Awareness).

Meanwhile, a youngster in Hong Kong had been inspired to join the 5th Vedānta Course in Sandeepany Sadhanalaya Powai (1984–86), and when he returned at the end of two years as Br. Susheel Chaitanya (now Swami Swaroopananda, Regional Head, Australasia and U.K.), the center expanded, with multiple Balvihar, CHYK and study classes, Devi and bhajana groups, cultural programs, and a teacher's training program.

Swamiji began to make frequent visits to Hong Kong, and conducted Jnana Yagnas on a regular basis from 1988 onward. On April 21, 1991, he formally inaugurated the Chinmaya Seva Ashram. Since then, many distinguished personalities have visited the ashram, including Sant Asaram Bapu in 1991, Sri V. Ganeshan of Ramanashram, Swami Satchitananda of the Integral Yoga Institute (and guru bhai of Swamiji), Swami Govindananda of Gangeshwara Veda Dham, Dada J. P. Vaswani of Sadhu Vaswani Mission in 1992, and Swami Chidananda of Divine Life Society in 1995 (he was also guru-bhāī of Swamiji).

In March 1966, Swamiji traveled the 300 miles from Kuala Lumpur to Singapore for his first address at a hall in Perumal Koil, where he spoke on the topic, "Do we need Religion?" Five hundred people attended the talk. The following year, Swamiji returned in February to conduct a Jnana Yagna. In the following years, all grassroot activities were introduced in Singapore, with a Balvihar class starting immediately after the conclusion of the Jnana Yagna in 1967. When Swamiji came for his 2nd Jnana Yagna in 1973, there were 240 children across Singapore who regularly attended Balvihar. In 1990, during a camp called "The Vedānta Intensive and Meditation Retreat" in Singapore, Swamiji's step-by-step instructions on the practice of meditation were recorded and compiled into the book, *The Art of Contemplation*.

Swamiji's first visit to Manila was in 1979. He had been invited by Dave Sahijwani, who had previously been attending Jnana Yagnas in Hong Kong. Subsequently, Swamiji made seven visits to Manila (during 1981–90). During a visit in 1983, he himself taught the first Balvihar class at the home of Deepak and Pooja Daswani. The children gathered around Swamiji whilst he told them a Kṛṣṇa story:

"What color is milk?" asked Swamiji.

"White!" answered the children in unison.

"What color is the cow?" he again asked.

"Black!"

"What does it eat?"

"Grass."

"What color is the grass?"

"Green!"

"Who makes the green grass eaten by a black cow to come out as white milk?"

The children were silent.

"Kṛṣṇa!" said Swamiji. "It is Lord Kṛṣṇa who makes the impossible possible!"

Indonesia was another story altogether. Although Swamiji had briefly visited the country in 1987, he was barred from reentering Indonesia by President Suharto since it was a predominantly Muslim country. However, Harish Hiranand somehow managed to bring Swamiji into the country in February 1993, and he conducted a full-house satsaṇga for three days at Hotel Indonesia in Jakarta. Today, the Chinmaya Family Jakarta is vibrantly active, and, interestingly, it is run and funded by women. Everything from the organization of Jnana Yagnas to the running of classes and the financial aspects of the center is decided by woman sevikās.

The first time Swamiji went to Australia was in 1984. He was invited by a longtime devotee, Dr. K. T. Ganapathy, who had met him in Rewa during a Jnana Yagna in 1956. She relates the events leading up to Swamiji's trip to Melbourne in 1984:

> I had written to Swamiji after my husband passed on in 1980, and asked him if I could come and live in Sandeepany Ashram in Bombay. He wrote back and said, "No. Sandeepany is not for you. You have a daughter living in Australia and grandchildren being brought up in a different society who need the comfort of your presence. Also, there is no Chinmaya Mission in Melbourne, so it would be best for you to go there and start one. You have been following me for years at many Yagnas. What you already know is more than enough. Go and share it with others."
>
> I settled my affairs in India and moved to Melbourne in 1981, and from then on, I started to write to Swamiji asking him to come to Australia. He wrote to say that he was going to London in June 1984, and would fly straight to Melbourne, and I should try and arrange for a Yagna.
>
> Swamiji was immediately very popular, as people had never experienced such an erudite speaker. All the time the hall was ringing with laughter. Months before, when we were planning the event,

I was worried about the morning classes, thinking that no one would come at six o'clock. I wrote to Swamiji and suggested that perhaps we could arrange to hold the morning session in our house. But he wrote back asking me to take a public place, saying, "You just never know what may happen." Of course, he was right.

The next day, the morning lecture hall was full, and the following day we were unable to accommodate everybody, so we had to change to a larger hall.

Since that time, activities have started in Sydney and Perth as well. Swamiji also gave talks in Brisbane; and, following a camp in Melbourne in 1987, he flew to Canberra and gave two talks there. He was accompanied by Christine Grimmer and my daughter, Chitra.

Christine Grimmer heard of Swamiji from a friend who had attended his first day's talk in Melbourne in 1984. "What's he like?" she had asked the friend after the talk.

"Well ... he's amazing ... he's brilliant, very logical, very funny, he's incredibly energetic, ahhh ... actually, he has a long pointer with a pompom on the end ... he uses a kind of chart ... it's very interesting ... you'll really have to go and find out for yourself."

So the next evening, Christine Grimmer went to the talk:

Back there in 1984, in that slightly shabby lecture hall in Melbourne, the little band of us who had the good fortune to meet Swamiji, realized that we had struck gold. By 5 A.M. the next morning we were on the road to get a good seat for the next verses of *Kenopaniṣad,* the exquisite discourse on the absolute Reality and the Knower. The early start was also to avoid the missile glance that was directed at any latecomers! This was serious business, and nothing should interfere with the subtle mood built between the teacher and student.

Swamiji was highly amused by the way — to his ear, the nasal Australian accent mangled the pronunciation of English words.

He was asked in a heavy Australian accent if he had just arrived "to die"! After responding with stunned silence, he then realized the person had actually said "today." This inspired Swamiji to create all sorts of jokes and puns to use during his discourses — "To die, we meditate"!

AN ELABORATE AFFAIR

After attending the evening and morning talks for a few days, I somehow felt compelled to go and meet Swamiji in person. When I went to the house in Templestowe where Swamiji was staying, Dr. Ganapathy invited me to stay for lunch along with a few other visitors.

In a kind of buffet style, delicious Indian food had been put on the table and a pile of plates at one end. Swamiji was just standing around the kitchen area making humorous quips to the host, who then asked everyone to take a plate. At that time, I didn't know that most hosts would have a special plate — sometimes silver — set aside for Swamiji. Without knowing the etiquette in this situation, I instinctively picked up one from the pile and offered it first to Swamiji. He smiled and said with eyes wide, "Oh no! The swami has his own eee...laaab...orate plate!" followed by a boisterous shoulder-cracking chuckle. I was beginning to understand that this amazing teacher was very different from any image I had ever had of a Guru.

David Buchholz
Chinmaya Mission Melbourne

I'M COMING TO SYDNEY, WITH LOVE

A dear friend loaned me a copy of the *Bhagavad-gītā* with a commentary by Swami Chinmayananda in Hardwar. When I opened it, the words leapt out of the page. On returning to Australia, I wrote to the Mumbai headquarters of Swamiji's organization, expressed my appreciation of his books, and also asked if I could call by the next time I was India.

I was surprised and delighted when a letter came back, handwritten in an almost unreadable script saying, "You don't have to come to India. I am coming to Sydney in July. Why not join me?" It was signed "Chinmayananda."

I arrived in Sydney in July and was feeling very skeptical, wondering if I was wasting my time and why this swami would be any different from all the others I had met in India. Then, something he said in the second morning's class struck me to the core: "Everything that can be modified or changed cannot be the Truth." In one statement, everything I had imagined to be the Truth was now temporary and the only permanent reality was God. It was something that would take time to sink in, but the seed was sown.

Howard Thomas
Chinmaya Mission Melbourne

Swamiji returned to Australia most years, conducting Jnana Yagnas in Melbourne, Perth, Brisbane, Canberra, and Sydney. Chinmaya Mission was incorporated as a charitable organization in Australia in 1990, and the first ashram, Chinmaya Dham, was inaugurated in Melbourne in 1994. Later, Chinmaya Sannidhi ashram was established in Sydney in 2004. Over the years, Chinmaya Mission Australia has sent five youngsters for the Vedānta Courses in Sandeepany Sadhanalaya Powai, four of whom returned to their respective cities and are serving as ācāryas of Melbourne (Br. Gautam Chaitanya), Sydney (Brni. Sujata Chaitanya and Br. Gopal Chaitanya), and Bendigo (Brni. Nivedita Chaitanya), and one is in Hong Kong (Brni. Nishita Chaitanya). Swami Swaroopananda spends several months each year conducting Jnana

Yagnas in many regions of Australia, which include New South Wales, Victoria, Brisbane, Canberra, Perth, and Adelaide.

Chinmaya Mission also has a center in Nelson, New Zealand. The Acharya is Swamini Amritananda, who met Swamiji in Sidhbari in 1986. At the time, she was a New Zealander in search of a teacher, and had arrived at the gates of Chinmaya Tapovanam, Sidhbari. When Swamiji saw her near the entrance, he told her to go straight to Sandeepany Sadhanalaya Powai, saying that she would find her teacher there.

In 1977, Swamiji went to Mauritius on the invitation of Br. Pranava Chaitanya (now Swami Pranavananda), a student of the 5th Vedānta Course in Sandeepany Sadhanalaya Powai (1972–75). Thereafter, devotees in Mauritius saved five lakh rupees and bought one and one-half acres of land for an ashram. They wrote to Swamiji with the news; and he named the ashram "Parna Kuti." But one day in 1986, Swami Ranganathananda of Ramakrishna Mission visited the ashram and asked Br. Pranava if Swami Chinmayananda had ever visited the Chinmaya Mission Mauritius ashram. The answer was negative. The brahmacārī immediately sent a request to Swamiji to please come to the Mauritius ashram. The reply came, "O.K. I'm coming!" Swamiji stopped for twenty-four hours in 1987, while on his way from Singapore to Africa, and blessed Chinmaya Mission Mauritius. He returned in 1989 and 1990 to an audience of five thousand people for his evening talks. Currently, Swami Pranavananda divides his time between Mauritius and the French-speaking Reunion Islands, where Chinmaya Mission also has a center.

On May 27, 1986, Swamiji landed in Nairobi, Kenya, for a Jnana Yagna on *Bhagavad-gītā Chapter 12* (evenings) and *Kenopaniṣad* (mornings). The Nairobi audience was hearing Swamiji for the first time; so for three days, he gave them an elaborate introduction on the fundamentals of Vedānta. Chinmaya Mission now has centers in four countries in Africa: Kenya, Nigeria, Tanzania, and South Africa. Chinmaya Mission South Africa was founded on January 27, 1979, and the center in Durban was officially completed in 1986. Currently, Swami Abhedananda is Acharya, Chinmaya Mission South Africa. He is a student of the 9th Vedānta Course in Sandeepany Sadhanalaya Powai (1994–96).

The Middle East was no exception to Swamiji's presence. In 1971, he went to Bahrain and Kuwait, followed by a forty-one day trip to the Middle East in 1972. In August 1972, Swamiji had a Jnana Yagna in Kuwait, and subsequently visited the country eight times; his last Jnana Yagna was in February 1989.

Chinmaya Mission Bahrain was inaugurated by Swamiji on April 6, 1971. His second visit was in August of the same year, and his discourses became known as "chalk talks," since he used a blackboard and a piece of chalk in all his lectures to explain the basics of Vedānta. He delivered three "chalk talks" at a local school auditorium in Manama. In 1979, a ten-day Jnana Yagna was organized in Dubai, followed by another Jnana Yagna in May 1981. Swamiji's topic was "The Man of Perfection Downtown," and he drew an audience of seven hundred-fifty listeners on the first day. Thereafter, Swamiji went to Muscat in 1989 and 1993. Ever since, "Chinmaya Family Muscat" regularly conducts all the grassroot activities of Chinmaya Mission.

Swamiji had a very large following in Sri Lanka, since many devotees had previously heard him in Chennai. His first visit to Colombo was in 1979. A year later, dedicated devotees registered Chinmaya Mission

Sri Lanka as an "Act of Parliament." They also identified ten acres of land in a plantation section in Rambodha. Swamiji visited this site in November 1980, and was struck by the scenic beauty of the area. It is said that this is the exact place where Śrī Hanumān landed when he went in search of Sītā. As a result, Chinmaya Mission Rambodha has a 16-feet tall idol of Śrī Hanumān in the Śrī Bhakta Hanumān Temple in Rambodha.

Chinmaya Mission Colombo acquired their center building in 2007. Swami Tejomayananda officially inaugurated the building on April 29, naming it "Chinmaya Pragati." The presiding deity of "Chinmaya Pragati" is Bhaktavatsala Śrī Rāma. In the inaugural address, Swami Tejomayananda said:

> "Pragati" means "marching ahead." This center is for the progress of society and the nation at large. It should meet the physical, emotional, and spiritual needs of the devotees, fulfilling Swamiji's vision of giving maximum happiness to the maximum number of people for the maximum amount of time. With Śrī Hanumānji presiding over the hills at Rambodha and Bhaktavatsala Śrī Rāma at the seashore shrine in Chinmaya Pragati, the members should march ahead without fear, for the Lord is always near!

Here remain the memories of a golden age, of a glory that spanned six continents, of a giant visionary who united East with West — and the magic lasts, drifting across America and Eurasia and down the decades to the far corners of the world. Every city wanted its handful of Swamiji's magic dust; and long after he left his mortal frame, Chinmaya Mission marched right into the twenty-first century as a worldwide phenomenon.

PROGRAMME

GEETA GNANA YAGNA

Conducted by : H.H. SWAMI CHINMAYANANDA

Tuesday,	15.1.1980,	19.30 Hrs.	Inaugural Address by H.E. Ustad Ebrahim Al-Arrayedh, Ambassador-At-Large, State of Bahrain. Followed by Commentary on Geeta Chapter XIII by H.H. Swami Chinmayananda.
Wednesday,	16.1.1980,	19.30 Hrs.	Introduction by H.E. Musa A.H.L. Keilani, Ambassador of the Hashemite Kingdom of Jordan to the State of Bahrain.
Thursday,	17.1.1980,	19.30 Hrs.	Introduction by H.E. Dr. Hussain Mohamad Al-Bahrana, Minister of State for Legal Affairs, State of Bahrain.
Friday,	18.1.1980,	19.30 Hrs.	Introduction by Fr. Edmund Fonseca, Sacred Heart Church, Manama State of Bahrain.
Saturday,	19.1.1980,	19.30 Hrs.	Introduction by H.E. Robert H. Pelletreau Jr. Ambassador of United States to the State of Bahrain.
Sunday,	20.1.1980,	19.30 Hrs.	Introduction by H.E. Mr. H.K. Mahajan, Ambassador of India to the State of Bahrain.
Monday,	21.1.1980,	19.30 Hrs.	Introduction by Mr. Adnan Dseisu, General Manager, Financial Affairs, Gulf Air, Bahrain.
Tuesday,	22.1.1980,	19.30 Hrs.	Introduction by Dr. Diaeddine Saleh, Former President of the Supreme Administrative Court of Egypt (Conseil d'Etat).
Wednesday,	23.1.1980,	19.30 Hrs.	Introduction by H.E. Mr. H.B. Walkar, C.M.G., Ambassador of United Kingdom to the State of Bahrain.
Thursday,	24.1.1980,	19.30 Hrs.	Introduction by Rev. Harold J. Vande Berg, Pastor, National Evangelical Church of the State of Bahrain.

Chairman Atma Jashanmal will introduce Guest Speakers on all days prior to the commentary by H.H. Swami Chinmayananda.

Place : Children & Mothers Welfare Society Auditorium, near Sulmaniya Hospital.

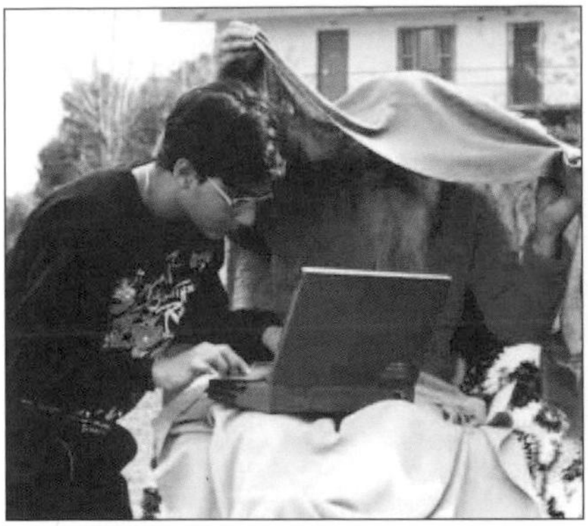

Clockwise from above:
Dheeraj Bharwani instructs Swamiji on the laptop, Singapore
Gurudakṣiṇā offering and prasāda distribution ceremony, Bitche, France, 1983
During a Spiritual Camp, Bitche, France, 1983
Swamiji with Cristiane Madeline (right of Swamiji; now Swamini Umananda) Bitche, France, 1983

Right: *Swamiji with* devotees at Singapore airport, 1989 **Center Left:** *Audience during* Swamiji's talks at Melbourne University, 1984 ▸ **Center right and below:** see overleaf

◀ **Overleaf center right:**
Swamiji with devotees at Melbourne Airport, 1987 (left to right: Kate Hallpike, Christine Grimmer, Dr. Roger Sworder, Raja Rishi,, Dr.Michael Hallpike, Anita Jayashri, Dr. Natteri Chandran)
Below:
With Dr. K. T. Ganapathy, and Australian devotees at her home in Melbourne (which is now Chinmaya Mission Melbourne), 1984

Clockwise from above:
Swamiji with Br. Shanta Chaitanya (now Swami Shantananda), Taipei, 1987
Lighting an "Om" during CHYK Camp, 2007
Jnana Yagna audience, Singapore
Celebration during Ganesh Chaturthi, Chinmaya Sannidhi, Sydney

▶ **Facing page clockwise from above:**
Swamiji with Br. Susheel Chaitanya (now Swami Swaroopananda), Hong Kong, 1987
Swamiji with Br. Siddha Chaitanya (now Swami Siddhananda)
Swamiji with Swami Dheerananada

Below:
Swamiji with Balvihar children,
Hong Kong

Clockwise from above:
Swamiji emphasizes the need for moral life to the five sons of H. E. Sheikh Mohamed Bin Alkhalifa, nephews of the King of Bahrain, 1971
Dig-vijaya yātrā, Japan, March 1965
Swamiji with devotees, Manila
At the Great Wall of China with K. P. Daswani, 1986
Talking to Ethiopians in Addis Ababa, Ethiopia, 1973
In discussion with H. E. Sheikh Mohamed Bin Salman Alkhalifa, brother of the King of Bahrain, 1971

XVI

A Possession Lost is Paradise Found

Deep in the Kangra valley, during the evening sun's slow passage into twilight, the Dhauladhar Mountains rise to a glittering sky, painted in thick translucent hues of red, orange, and yellow. Within the stone-built hall of Sidhbari ashram, illumined by the pale shimmers of dusk soaking through an open wall, Swamiji sits cross-legged alongside this stunning landscape. His words resonate against the grand mountains:

> You are looking for water in the desert. Poor desert! It does not *have* water to give you. If it had, it would give! All it has is a mirage. It is not the desert's fault. You are looking for water where it does not exist. You want happiness from this world? But it is like the desert. It does not have any happiness to give you. You are looking in the wrong direction. If you want happiness, take a right about-turn and look within!

Swamiji had himself begun looking for land at the foothills of the Himalayas in the late 1970s. He wanted to build an ashram that would bring out a batch of "pahāḍī" (hill-folk) brahmacārīs, who would be taught the *Rāmāyaṇa* in Hindi, and be given some knowledge of cooperative farming and medicine. They would then go into the Himalayan valleys, and teach the *Rāmāyaṇa* to local hill-folk. They would also treat common diseases and show them how to develop their own cooperative farming and cottage industry. In effect, when this plan went into operation, Swamiji would have discharged his debt (and that of ṛṣis through the ages) to the hill-folk, in whose shelter they had been able to pursue their spiritual goal without being disturbed.

In 1977, Swamiji went to Jammu for seven days. He stayed in Rajouri with General Narinder Singh and his wife, Indu. In the evening, he took classes for the officers on *The Logic of Spirituality*, and during the day, he traveled to various camp sites right up to the Pakistan border, in search of suitable land for the proposed ashram.

Eventually, it was an incident earlier that year that led to success. Swamiji had arrived at Jammu airport on a February morning, where he had asked General and Indu Narinder Singh to meet him. The General had then driven Swamiji in a jeep to Nurpur, where they picked up Colonel Pathania, who carried a bundle of maps and papers with him for a piece of land called Sidhbari. Colonel Pathania was a devotee from the 1950s who had implored Swamiji to come to Himachal. When Swamiji said, "then you find me a land!" Colonel Pathania had taken Swamiji to Dadh, a village three to four kilometers from Sidhbari, from where the whole plateau was visible. Swamiji stood looking at the plateau. "There! That's where I want the ashram!" he said, pointing towards Sidhbari. Driving an old ambassador car, the colonel had then traveled up and down, from army offices in Palampur to government offices in Pathankot, until he was finally able to locate the papers relevant to the piece of land that Swamiji had indicated to him.

When the party approached its destination in the late afternoon, the road disappeared and gave way to a winding pathway. General Narinder Singh describes the scene:

> On reaching, we stood on a hilltop where Swamiji's kuṭiyā stands today. The winds swirled and whirled. Sidhbari was a bald patch, with a single simbal (cotton) tree. On one side were pine forests, and to the north we could see the entire expanse of the Dhauladhar. Swamiji was standing to my right looking at the mountains, when he said, "Oh! The ṛṣis who used to come to these mountains to seek the Lord — they must have looked at the Dhauladhar and got lost! I am going to do the same!"
>
> Swamiji looked around, and we discussed where to build the cottages. I suggested that they be built of natural stone, and the ground in front of where we stood could be leveled to become a rose garden. Swamiji listened and planned very intently. On that day, he made us feel that the land already belonged to Chinmaya Mission.

Chinmaya Tapovan Trust was registered as a society on March 24, 1977, and on May 22, 1979, the Sidhbari land was allotted to Chinmaya Mission. According to legend, Sidhbari (the abode of the siddhas or "perfected ones") was home to many saints and seers, who through their austerity sanctified all the earth they walked on. A kilometer beyond the ashram is the cave of Kapila Muni, who lived over two millenniums ago. Kapila Muni is the founder of Sāṅkhya, one of the six systems of Hindu philosophy, which uses a very rational and analytic approach to differentiate the Self from the non-Self. A small temple now stands over the spot where he is said to have meditated in a cave. Devahūti, who was Kapila Muni's mother, also has a cave in the pine forests where she did penance and received the teaching from her son. Further to the left of the Kapila temple are ancient ruins made of stone, said to be the samādhi-sthalas of twelve to fifteen siddhas from olden times.

Question: What is an ashram?

Answer: A place of peace and tranquility.

Wrong.

Next answer?

A place of spiritual rules and practices; it may or may not have a temple.

Wrong again.

New question: What is the purpose of an ashram?

A place to train students in the teachings of Scriptures.

Wrong!

Next answer?

Answer: I don't want to play this game any longer!

Swamiji's explanation:

An ashram is a point of guidance, a place to develop on the path of Self-discovery. If we have a legal problem, we look to the courts for justice. If we are ill, we go to a hospital. If we have money problems, we ask a bank to help us with a loan. But if we are searching for inner peace, for the unfolding of our real Self, then we need someone or someplace to help us on our path to enlightenment. We need some guiding factor — an institution, a concept, or a person — to show us a glimpse of light in the surrounding darkness. An ashram provides this light — it provides a support system for a sincere seeker — it may or may not have a temple, it may or may not have a teaching program.

Many think that ashrams are heavens of peace and tranquility. That is the ideal, but often not the reality. An ashram is not a structure or a cluster of buildings, but the people who inhabit them. Seekers from all walks of life come here to reflect, rediscover, and revitalize on their spiritual journey. They are under tremendous strain, especially since they have given up the worldly life, but have not yet reached the contentment of spirituality. In the process of purifying the mind, their impurities surface to discolor and distort everything. Such projections are inevitable, and are to be expected in an ashram. But then, it is here that they "repair" themselves, and move a higher notch in their spiritual evolution, thus going further in the spiritual sojourn.

Once the contractors reached Sidhbari and actually started work, they found that the land was completely inappropriate, even impossible to build on the site. Since the land was on a hillock overlooking a vast open plain, strong hurricane-like winds could lift away entire buildings. The contractors plainly told Swamiji the impossibility of the project.

Swamiji remained long in meditation on the site. When he opened his eyes, he said, "We will have an ashram here. But first, let us bring Lord Hanumān. When the father sees his son, Vāyu-bhagavān (God of Wind) will calm down." And so it happened! Once the forty-foot Hanumān idol was installed, the winds stopped.

All through the construction of Sidhbari, during the early 1980s, Swamiji spent many hours guiding and watching every detail of the construction. Day-in and day-out, he would sit outside and watch the workers lay brick-after-brick. On a trip to Delhi, he personally selected the exquisite wood carvings that adorn the inner walls of Tapovan

Hall. And then, he decorated the outer walls with apsarās (celestial nymphs) — and had them painted gold!

Once in 1981, when he was holding a class on *Vivekacūḍāmaṇi,* the delegates had to stay in makeshift accommodations. A problem developed with the camp's bathroom facilities. The camp organizers were discussing the problem with Swamiji when the time for class arrived. Swamiji arrived five-minutes late to the lecture, very unusual for him because he was always extremely precise and prompt. The subject of the lectures was vāsanās, the inherent tendencies that rule our lives. While explaining the nature of vāsanās, Swamiji said, "Vāsanās make you do everything. They are very powerful. When Swami Sivananda was suggesting I take sannyāsa, I went to Badrinath for forty days to make the big decision whether or not to take sannyāsa. Ultimately, I decided to take sannyāsa. For what...?"

Swamiji made a dramatic pause.

"...to worry about your toilets and bathrooms!" he announced with a big laugh.

Jairam Jaisinghani, the ashram manager of Sandeepany Sadhanalaya Powai (later Trustee, Tara Cultural Trust), said that Swamiji would advise him that the money of the ashram is the sacred money of the devotees and must be spent with the utmost care. He would study the expense statements for the ashram in detail, and inquire about any figure that he felt was not acceptable. He was extremely particular that the receipts should be sent out in time, and that all donations be reported to him. Jairam Jaisinghani notes:

> Once, I had bought two sets of dhotis for the brahmacārīs, as I had gotten them very economically in Kerala, at one-half the Mumbai

prices. Swamiji immediately said, "This is short-term economy. The investment in soap and effort to wash these will have to be doubled until they are torn."

At another time, he saw that several rounds of cappala (sandal) purchases had been made within a two-month period. After inquiring about the purchase, Swamiji said, "If the brahmacārīs lose their cappalas or misuse them, let them walk barefoot until the next lot is due to them."

In the earlier days, Swamiji had himself kept a detailed expense list of every item he used. Even the stamps he used for his daily mail were individually accounted for in his own handwriting. An expense list (dated 1966) shows the exact amount, indicated by 15 NP (nayā or new paisā), along with the name of the devotee and the place where the letter was sent:

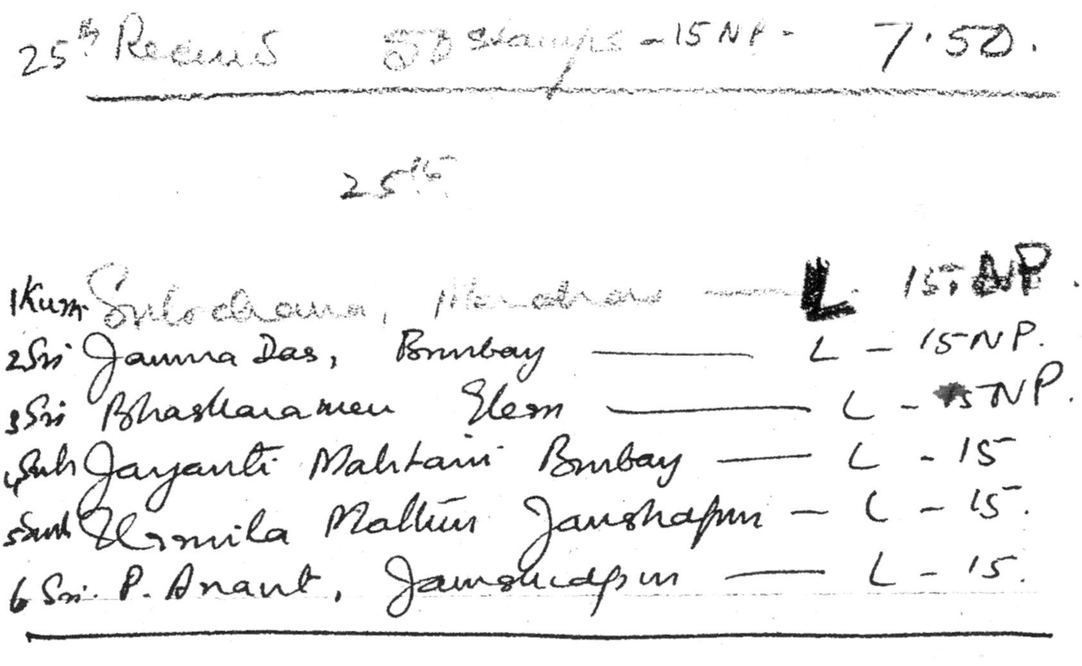
25th Recd 50 stamps – 15 NP – 7.50.

25th

1 Kum. Sulochana, Madras — L 15 NP.
2 Sri Jamna Das, Bombay — L – 15 NP.
3 Sri Bhaskaramen Elem — L – 15 NP.
4 Smt Jayanti Mahtani Bombay — L – 15
5 Smt Urmila Mathur Jamshedpur — L – 15.
6 Sri P. Anant, Jamshedpur — L – 15.

▶ **Facing page above:**
Swamiji with the forty-foot Śrī Hanumān idol in Sidhbari, June 5, 1993
Below:
Festivities on the inauguration of Śrī Rāma temple, Sidhbari October 10, 1983

Clockwise from above:
Swamiji steps on Sidhbari soil for the first time, 1978
With the Chinmaya Nursing Van following behind, Sidhbari
Swamiji oversees the construction work of the trellis, Sidhbari, March 1983
Swamiji watches the construction of the sanctum sanctorum of Śrī Rāma temple, Sidhbari, June 1983
Swamiji climbs up the makeshift ramp during construction, Sidhbari, 1983

Clockwise from above:
The digging starts for the construction of Kamala Hall, Sidhbari, 1991
Swamiji with Swami Brahmananda, Sidhbari, December 1991
Group photo of devotees, 1st Spiritual Camp, Sidhbari, 1982
Swamiji with devotees (Jamna Batra, Uma Shergill and daughters, Vasant and Sukhmani, and others) sit around Swamiji for a discussion, Sidhbari, 1983

Clockwise from above:
During an open air discourse, Sidhbari, 1989
During an open air discourse, Sidhbari, June 1983
Satsaṅga in the courtyard (outer walls of Satsaṅga Hall adorned with gold apsarās), Sidhbari, June 1983

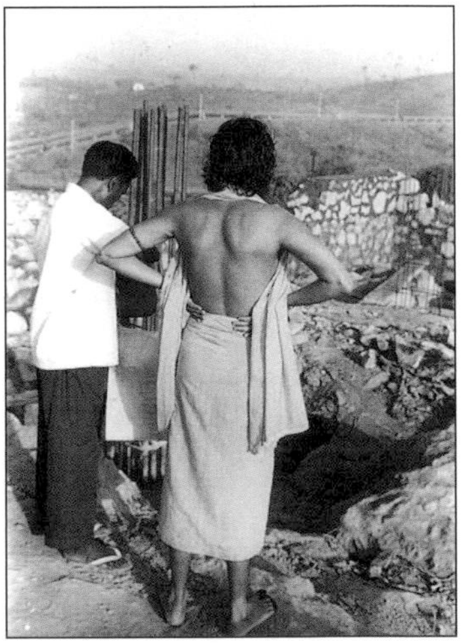

Clockwise from above:
Jagadeeshwara temple under construction, Powai, 1967
Construction of the gopuram at the Jagadeeshwara temple, Powai, 1967
During the construction of Jagadeeshwara temple, Powai, 1967
In consultation with Ram Batra and others during the construction of Jagadeeshwara temple, Powai, 1967
During the construction of Jagadeeshwara temple, Powai, 1967
Swamiji reviews construction of the Jagadeeshwara temple, Powai, 1967

Above left:
Swamiji at the gates of Jagadeeshwara temple, Sandeepany Sadhanalaya, Powai 1984
Above right:
View of entrance to Jagadeeshwara temple, Sandeepany Sadhanalaya, Powai
Center:
Swamiji during pūjās before the consecration of Jagadeeshwara temple, Powai, 1968

Right:
Swamiji prostrates to his Guru after the unveiling ceremony of Swami Tapovanam's idol, Sandeepany Sadhanalaya Powai, March 27, 1978
Extreme right:
Swamiji with Swami Tejomayananda, Mumbai, 1981

SURPRISE INSPECTIONS

When I was first assigned to the Sidhbari ashrams, Swamiji gave me the following advice, "If you want to administer, be unpredictable!"

We had to keep everything here in total readiness at all times, because Swamiji would appear anywhere at any time — in the kitchen, the bookstore, the office. He liked to drop by for "surprise inspections." This habit of Swamiji prevented slacking on our part.

Swami Subodhananda
Acharya, Sandeepany HIM, Sidhbari;
and Regional Head, Chinmaya Mission Uttar Pradesh,
Himachal Pradesh, Uttarakhand, Punjab, and Haryana

On February 8, 1982, Swamiji went to Ellayapalle — a remote village in Andhra Pradesh — for the bhūmi pūjā of a new ashram, Chinmayaranyam. The villagers had given twenty-two acres of land to Swamini Sharadapriyananda (student of the 1st Vedānta Course in Sandeepany Sadhanalya Powai) in the drought-prone Cuddapah district. The land was barren, undeveloped, and in a burial ground. It was so isolated that an ox cart would pick up visitors on a road one mile away. The village had two wells, one of which was dry, and the second was expected to go dry at any moment. Many attempts to find water had been unsuccessful. Against this background, Swamiji began to visualize a forest around the ashram.

Swamini Sharadapriyananda wanted to start a social welfare project for the poorest of the poor in rural Andhra; and when she discussed the water problem with Swamiji, he pointed to two banyan trees standing on either side of the land with his walking stick. "Dig along the line that connects the two trees. Water is sure to come," instructed Swamiji.

Workers began the digging, and water was found along the exact line indicated by Swamiji, even though they had earlier dug in the same area with no success. Chinmayaranyam has since been transformed into a beautiful green ashram with sixty acres of newly forested land surrounding it. Multiple welfare activities were initiated, including free medical clinics and homeopathic medicines, free schools for Harijan children, orphanages and a home for the aged, wells, and self-employment craft and trade programs for the villagers. In recognition of this work, the government granted a hillock surrounding the ashram for development. And, a number of the projects and activities at the Ellayapalle ashram have been replicated at another camp site, Chinmayaranyam Trikoota, also in rural Andhra Pradesh.

Swamiji had an answer for every problem. When Chinmaya Gardens was being developed in Siruvani, Tamil Nadu, the Managing Committee had trouble meeting the costs of construction. Chinmaya Gardens is spread on one hundred acres of lush, green land, (twenty-six kilometers from Coimbatore) and surrounded by the Nilgiri or "Blue" Mountains in the Western Ghats. A member of the Managing Committee, H.R. Pandurang, reports:

> In the Managing Committee Meeting it was mentioned by the Secretary that the budget for the proposed ashram was coming to three crore rupees. In those days, this was a sizeable sum and the members were worried as to how to raise this amount. Swamiji closed the discussion by saying, "Getting the money is my problem, and the Committee need not worry." He followed this up by launching the "rupee a day" scheme. The money was raised in no time.

Chinmaya Gardens offers two unique programs. First, is the Dharma Sevak Course, which is typically a two-to-six-week residential

Clockwise from above:
Satsaṅga Hall in Tapovan Kutir under construction, Uttarkashi, 1969
Pūjā before the inauguration of Sarveshvara temple on Śivarātri, Tamaraipakkam, (near Chennai), 1990
During Purohit Course in Chinmaya Gardens, Siruvani, October 2009
View of newly-forested Chinmayaranyam, Ellayapalle, Andhra Pradesh

◂ Facing page clockwise from above:
Swamini Sharadapriyananda oversees construction of Chinmayaranyam, 1972
During Swamiji's first visit to Chinmayaranyam, February 1982
Swamiji sitting on the terrace, Surat, 1966
Swamiji advises villagers where to dig for water on barren land, Chinmayaranyam, February 1982
Swamiji with Swamini Sharadapriyananda, 1991
Swamiji in front of main CCMT office building during construction, Powai, March 1984

Vedānta Course for householders. The students are instructed in the knowledge of scriptures, and the skills which they develop can later be used to conduct Study Groups. At the end of the course, the householders are encouraged to share their knowledge with society as dedicated workers of dharma (righteousness). On a more profound level, dharma is the essential nature of a thing, for example, the dharma of sugar is to be sweet, without which it would not be sugar. Thus, the Dharma Sevak Course is an intensive program for householders who seek their own true nature to help them turn within. This course is a regular feature in most Chinmaya Mission ashrams (including Krishnalaya in the West), and is conducted through the year at various times and places.

The second program is the Purohita Course, which is a distinguishing feature of Chinmaya Gardens, Siruvani (Tamil Nadu) and Chinmaya Sandeepany, Chokkahali (Karnataka). While philosophy is the theoretical aspect of religion, rituals form the practical aspect, and there is a scientific and spiritual rationale for each of the rituals as prescribed in the Vedas. In order to facilitate the practice of rituals, which today, have become by and large a mechanical exercise, the Purohita Course trains young priests over a one and one-half-year period in the knowledge and practice of rituals, enabling them to perform the rituals with right understanding. The priests are also taught Sanskrit, Astrology, and English, so they can explain the significance of all practices to the community to bring about the desired effect.

Over the years, Swamiji also continued to make several trips to Tapovan Kutir in Uttarkashi, often holding week-long camps in the newly-built, extended ashram. The original kuṭiyā of Swami Tapovanam, with its small verandah and mud-plastered walls has been preserved, and the ashram is built around it, keeping Swami Tapovanam's kuṭiyā as the central shrine. Even today, the main door of Tapovan Kutir (below the steep steps) creaks when the latch is opened, and the bell overhead tinkles in welcome. Swami Tapovanam's kuṭiyā represents the years of austerity of an enlightened Master. This is not the austerity of spiritual practice, but the austerity of Self-realization in which the Master abides. The intensity of this austerity recharges the atmosphere making the ashram a spiritual haven for the seeker.

Tapovan Kutir also represents the guru-śiṣya paramparā (the lineage of the Guru and the disciple). This is the sacred place where our Parama Guru, Swami Tapovanam, handed the knowledge of the Self to Swamiji. Actually, Swami Chinmayananda is the real "Tapovan Prasad."

The ashram in Sidhbari was further built in 1992, with a larger hall — called Kamala Hall — to accommodate delegates. In the final stages of construction, Swamiji decided to cut one of the two wooden antique pillars that had been a present to him from the palace of the Maharaja of Cochin. He had wanted a base on which to place the Lord Kṛṣṇa idol in Kamala Hall; and after discarding many options made from inferior woodwork, he directed Shivaraman to send one pillar out of the pair of antique pillars lying under the staircase in his own satsaṇga room.

Devotees were shocked. Swamiji wanted to cut a smoothly carved, beautiful one-piece pillar of teak wood in half! What's more, it was an antique, and part of a pair! If Swamiji showed little respect for heritage and history, then what could one hope from others? But Swamiji was on a single-pointed search for a pedestal for Lord Kṛṣṇa. "The Lord must have the best," he said.

The very next day, the pillar was brought to the hall along with a carpenter holding a saw. A horde of scandalized devotees collected in the hall, and watched the execution, so to speak. The antique was sliced in half. Then, Swamiji had the smoothly polished outer surface covered with muddy olive green enamel paint!

On the third morning, when the devotees were still out of sorts, Swamiji said, "It is alright to disagree with your Guru on intellectual matters. But it is not alright to disagree with him on spiritual matters. Or else, when the time comes for him to say to you, *Tat Tvam Asi (That Thou Art),* you will not understand it!"

On that day, it was very foggy and the Dhauladhar Mountains could barely be seen. Swamiji pointed to the mountains and continued, "We cannot see the Truth, but the ṛṣis and your Guru say it is there. Reasoning can take us up to a point, but after that it is our faith in the āpta-vākya (a scriptural text or statement of the Guru) that guides us along. If you tell Govindraj (an ardent devotee who had just arrived from South India, and was known to look *only* at Swamiji) that there are mountains here, he won't believe it!"

Quite appropriately, there's some poetic justice here — the muddy olive green pillar beneath Lord Krishna is seen and prostrated to along with the Lord, by all devotees who visit Sidhbari. The other pillar is still lying somewhere in Swamiji's kuṭiyā, unnoticed and unappreciated.

Ashram-life during camp with Swamiji included one special feature — the pāda-pūjā (worship of the Master's feet) followed by "Swamiji-style prasāda distribution." This was always an elaborate affair. Swami Ramananda (previously K. R. Pai, the manager of Sidhbari ashram) relates the event:

> Nobody missed the pāda-pūjā. During the recitation of the 108 names of Swamiji, rupee coins were offered along with flowers at his pādukās. Swamiji would sit in deep meditation, and when the pūjā finished, he would give prasāda. His style was unique — he would take a fistful of rupee coins that had been offered during the arcanā, and throw it at the audience in all directions. Then he would throw the fruit, with excellent aim, often directing it specifically at devotees sitting at the back. Everybody would scramble for "prasāda" and it was great fun.

> One devotee had collected many such rupee coins from the pāda pūjās, and when I asked her what she intended to do with them, she said, '"These are no longer rupee coins of commercial value, but priceless blessings. I will give them to my children to be kept in their pūjā rooms."
>
> Another elderly lady was unable to compete with the others and had not picked up such "prasāda coins." The next day, four coins landed straight in her lap. When she looked up at Swamiji, he was smiling at her. "Got it," he seemed to be saying.
>
> The children were very excited during the prasāda throwing. One child told me that these were magic coins and she was going to use them to make wishes.

Bhikṣā with Swamiji was equally memorable. An incident with Swamini Umananda portrays the sentiments of many:

> In the Indian tradition, the meeting with such a master is the fruit of our past lives. One day in Sidhbari in March 1989, Swamiji was taking his breakfast and I was with him. He took a piece of apple and put it in my mouth, saying to me, "What must be your prārabdha that I have to feed you!"

At a marathon camp in Sidhbari, a devotee asked Swamiji during a satsaṇga, "Swamiji, what does one have to do to invoke an experience of brahmaloka (heaven)?"

Swamiji gave no answer. Pin drop silence followed. One could hear the leaves rustling outside.

Then, looking at the questioner, Swamiji said, "Buddhū (you fool), where do you think you've been for the last three weeks?"

Every five years a Mastāk-abhiṣekaṁ — a bathing ritual, with holy water poured on the head of the deity — is held in Sidhbari for the forty-foot Lord Hanumān statue that presides over the ashram. The first abhiṣekaṁ was organized on October 10, 1982, and Swamiji directed R. Krishnamoorthy of Chennai to make the arrangements:

> The very first one was very tough. We had to construct our own ramp. On the top, a platform was made. There were two hand-rails, and not more than two or three people could walk up at a time. Swamiji was also going to walk up to do the abhiṣekaṁ, so we were looking into all details. When the platform was constructed, my wife said it looked terrible. She suggested we put an arch (South Indian style) behind Hanumānji's head. She used the plantain trees with the banana, and tied them to a pole. Swamiji had especially brought saplings of these trees from Kerala and planted them in Sidhbari. This was our first mistake.
>
> When Swamiji looked at the ramp, he said, "Everything fine, Krishnamoorthy, very good! (Looking at the arch) Ha! Who cut my plantain tree? You should not have cut it. You go and plant ten more of those trees!"
>
> Nevertheless, the first abhiṣekaṁ went off so well, that at the end, Swamiji said, "When this has been done, Lord Rāma cannot be far behind." I didn't understand what Swamiji meant, so he explained to me, "We will build a Rāma temple in Sidhbari."

Swamini Nishtananda remembers that when Swamiji decided to build the Rāma Mandir (temple) in Sidhbari, he remarked, "I have no will of my own. If a saṅkalpa (resolve) has come, it is Nārāyaṇa's will. It will fulfill itself."

The Rāma Mandir was built in six months during the summer of 1983. Swamiji sat at the construction site for hours at a time, going over every detail of the temple. He also sent a letter to all devotees of Chinmaya Mission, requesting them to write a likhita japa (the writing of the Lord's divine name) to be placed in a crypt below the altar:

> I have requested you to devotedly write *Om Śrī Rāma Jaya Rāma Jaya Jaya Rāma* some one-to-two pages a day in any script. With steady concentration, the hand writes, the eyes watch, the mouth repeats in murmurs, and the ears listen to the sound of the mantra. Thus, more than one sense organ is brought into one and the same act. See that your heart is empty of any personal desires. Attention is given for the cleanliness of the page, the symmetry of the letters, and the sanctity of the book.
>
> Thus, you write for one hundred days. Collect it from all, and send them to Sidhbari. Lord Rāma and Sītā have decided that they will have a crore and more likhita japa in the basement of their altar. We hope to get such sincere sheets, soaked in the devotion of the people from all over the world, to be deposited in the sanctum sanctorum.

Once, Swamiji was asked, "What is a temple?" He answered:

> Exactly what is the udder of a cow — milk! Is it only the udder of a cow? No! It is all over the body, and it is the essence of a cow. It is the strength of a cow. It is the nutritive final end product of a cow. But, we get milk only from the udder, even though milk is everywhere in the cow. Nārāyaṇa is present everywhere. God is all-pervading, but if you want to contact him, run to the nearest temple.
>
> Where is the government of India, please? Is it not everywhere, behind every one of you? It is a democracy — government of the people, by the people, for the people. But, to contact the government of India, one has to go to Delhi. And even in Delhi, all cannot sign all papers. Papers pertaining to a particular department should go

to *that* particular department, to *that* particular officer and that too, through a proper channel. If your papers fulfill all the requirements and have gone through all the required rituals, then they come back to you with a signature on it.

If this is true, then what is there in a temple? Same Nārāyaṇa is sitting there to bless you. The government of India cannot bless you, but the minister can. According to your demand you must go to that department. Department of Commerce cannot help a man who wants to get something from the External Affairs Ministry. If you go and do tapas (austerity) there, Bhagavān will come and tell you, "This is the wrong department, apply there!" Therefore, in the early morning, when you are going for your final examination, coconut for Gaṇeśa — nobody else! He is the department head.

A temple is a place where you practice what you have studied in the text-books. They are the gymnasiums for the mind. "Every day I go to the gymnasium, but my health is not improving, Swamiji." All that I can tell you is that you go for another six months. If after that your health has still not improved, naturally I will ask, "What do you do there in the gymnasium?" "Swamiji, I go there and sit down and watch everybody."

Similarly, if you go to the temple and watch who all come there, there is no chance for your mental ailment to improve or get cured. You must go there, apply your mind — remember, it is a mental gymnasium. Surrender the mind in devotion unto Him. He will purify it and return it back to you.

Bhagavān says, "Surrender your mind, I will retune it and give it back to you." But because of our desires, we do not give the mind! We say "Kṛṣṇa Kṛṣṇa," and then our mind goes back to the world, and we add "My father is not well. Please make him alright. This is not surrendering the mind.

So, a temple is necessary. A temple is a place where His presence can be contacted directly. Think! A receiving set is necessary to hear

> a broadcast from Delhi. The sound waves are available everywhere. But if you want to receive it, you have to have a set and tune it up properly to that particular station. You must go to the temple, tune up your mental equipment in order to receive the Divine message.

Chinmaya Mission has sixteen ashrams and fifty-eight temples around the world. And although Nārāyaṇa is everywhere — "I'm Śiva, I'm Kṛṣṇa , Jesus, Devī , Buddha, Mohammad, and much, much more," said Swamiji before disappearing into his kuṭiyā — yet, Sidhbari is unmistakably where his presence is most overwhelming — in the Rāma temple where he sat for hours while it was being built; in Lord Hanumān who came up with such detailed perfection; in the black oil lamps that criss-cross along the driveway; in the railing he would hold as he walked into his kuṭiyā; in the umbrella under which he was brought for pāda pūjā; in the satsaṇga hall which he would enter each morning in sublime beauty for meditation class; in his bedroom that wonderfully gives out his fragrance; and in the samādhi shrine where he rests amidst a rose garden overlooking the Dhauladhar Mountains. Swamiji had himself said, "I am in every leaf and tree in Sidhbari."

◀ **Facing page clockwise from above:**
Swamiji giving a discourse in the Satsaṅga hall during a camp, Sidhbari, 1983
Swamiji unveils Lord Kṛṣṇa's idol placed on a wooden antique pillar in the newly constructed Kamala Hall, Vivekacūḍāmaṇi Camp, October 6, 1992
Campers seated in Kamala Hall amidst Lord Kṛṣṇa, Sidhbari, May 1993
Swamiji applies ṭikkā on his forehead, Sidhbari, 1991

Above:
Pāda-pūjā in the Satsaṅga Hall by Indira and Meera Rokia, and Dr. Leena Bahrani, Sidhbari
Center:
During a Youth Camp (Swamiji's last camp in Sidhbari), May 1993
Below:
Satsaṅga in the courtyard, Sidhbari, October 1988

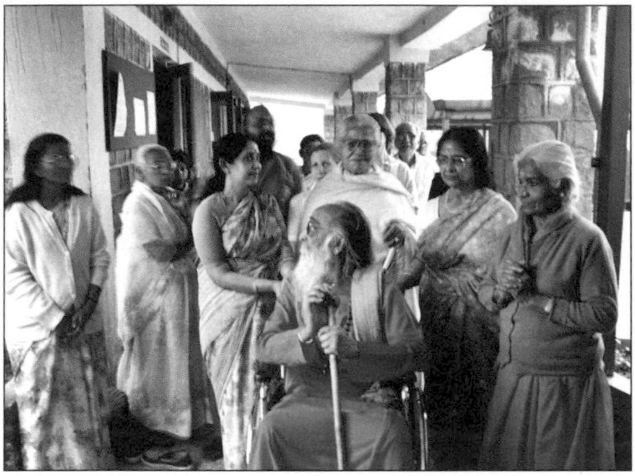

◄ **Facing page clockwise from above:**
Swamiji and devotees waiting for Śrī Rāma and Sītā ji's idols to arrive in front of Swamiji's kuṭiyā, Sidhbari, February 1983
Satsaṅga in front of Swami Tapovanam's idol, Sandeepany Sadhanalaya Powai, March 1984
Swamiji walks as devotees are seated for a Viṣṇusahasranāma pūjā, Sidhbari, June 1983
Swamiji in a wheelchair at the end of the Vivekacūḍāmaṇi Camp (right to left: Bhanumati Rao, Swamiji's half-sister Malti, Leela Nambiar, Rajeshwari Pillai), Sidhbari, 1992

Above:
Swamiji throwing the fruit of grace during bhikṣā, June 11, 1983
Center:
Dr. Akhilam (now Swamini Nishthananda) honors Swamiji on Onam, Sidhbari, 1992
Below:
Swamiji being led for pāda-pūjā amidst chants, sprinkling of flowers, dīpam, and a special umbrella (in front of Swamiji's kuṭiyā), Sidhbari, 1991

Above left:
Swamiji carrying a kalaśa on his head for the first abhiṣekam of Śrī Hanumān, Sidhbari, October 10, 1982
Above right:
Swamiji walking on the ramp built by the army for the abhiṣekam of Śrī Hanumān, Sidhbari, October 10, 1982

◀ **Facing page center:**
Devotees performing Śrī Viṣṇusahasranāma pūjā, Jamshedpur, 1974
Below left:
Swamiji shades himself in the open courtyard, Sidhbari, March 1983
Below right:
Śrī Hanumān's Mastaka-abhiṣekam, Sidhbari, 1997

Clockwise from above:
Swamiji flings both arms in joy before unveiling the idol of Śrī Hanumān, Sidhbari, October 10, 1982
Ācāryas and devotees in the procession during inauguration of Śrī Rāma temple, Sidhbari, 1983
*Śrī Hanumān Mastaka-*abhiṣekam, Sidhbari, 1997

◀ **Facing page clockwise from above:**
Swamiji leading the crowds during the consecration of Jagadeeshwara temple, 1968
During the installation of Lord Kṛṣṇa (and Gaṅgā jī) at Jagadeeshwara temple, Nov 17, 1976
Swamiji does the first abhiṣekam of Lord Sarveshvara on Śivarātri, Tamaraipakkam, February 23, 1990
Śrī Rāma temple, Sidhbari
During bhūmi pūjā of Śrī Rāma temple, Sidhbari, 1983

Clockwise from above:
Swamiji does abhiṣekam of Kāliyā-mardana Śrī Kṛṣṇa at Deenabandhu Devasthanam, Bangalore
Swamiji in Śrī Rāma temple, Sidhbari, 1988
Swamiji relaxes during a bhajan session by student nurses in the rose garden (which later became the Samadhi Sthal)
Portrait of Swamiji, Janmāṣṭamī Day, London, 1983

ASHRAMS

Chinmaya Mission's thirty-five ashrams (twenty in India and fifteen others around the world) are located in extremely beautiful surroundings. They are ideal places for spiritual practice, mental relaxation, and rejuvenation. All ashrams offer boarding and lodging facilities. Various spiritual and cultural activities, such as Spiritual Camps, frequently take place at these ashrams.

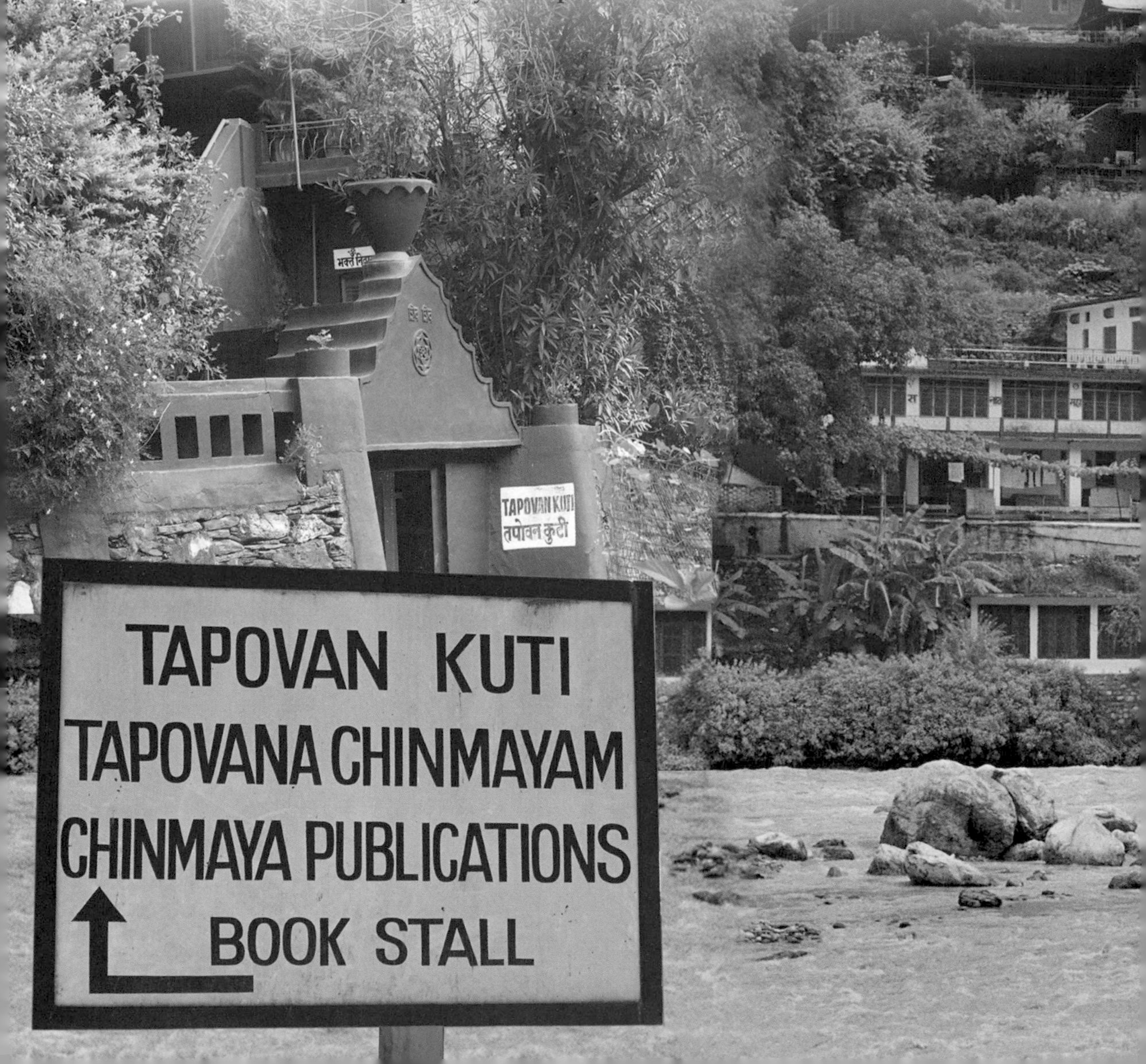

ASHRAMS

Chinmaya Mission Ashrams:

- **Chinmaya Geeta Ashram** (near Renigunta), Andhra Pradesh, India
- **Chinmaya Sarada Tapovan,** Kothapatnam, Andhra Pradesh, India
- **Chinmaya Seva Ashram Nyas,** Allahabad, Uttar Pradesh, India
- **Chinmaya Vidya Ganapathi Ashram,** Chittoor District, Andhra Pradesh, India
- **Chinmaya Yoga Ashram,** Chittoor District, Andhra Pradesh, India
- **Chinmaya Ashram** Lakshmanpur, Madhya Pradesh, India
- **Chinmaya Ashram** Mangalore, Karnataka, India
- **Chinmaya Gardens,** Siruvani (near Coimbatore), Tamil Nadu, India
- **Chinmayaranyam,** Ellayapalle, Andhra Pradesh, India
- **Chinmayaranyam,** Tirkoota, Andhra Pradesh, India
- **Chinmaya Sandeepany** Chokkahalli, Karnataka, India
- **Chinmaya Sandeepany** Kolhapur, Maharashtra, India
- **Chinmaya Sitaram Ashram,** Krishna District, Andhra Pradesh, India
- **Chinmaya Udaya Ashram,** Latur, Maharashtra, India
- **Krishnalaya,** Piercy, California, U.S.A.
- **Chinmaya Tapovan Trust,** Sidhbari, Himachal Pradesh, India
- **Sandeepany Sadhanalya** Powai, Mumbai, Maharashtra, India
- **Sarada Brahmavidya Sadhana Ashram,** Mulavaram, Andhra Pradesh, India
- **Sarveshvara Dhyana Nilayam,** Tamaraipakkam, Tamil Nadu, India
- **Tapovan Kutir,** Uttarkashi, Uttaranchal, India

| CONTACT US |

Visit the website at www.chinmayamission.com,
www.chinmayamission.org (in North America)

TEMPLES

A TEMPLE IS A SOCIAL CENTER AND MUST BECOME A PLACE OF CULTURAL REVIVAL. IT IS A SACRED PLACE OF REVERENCE (SAṄGAM), WHERE LOVE OF THE MIND AND RESPECT OF THE INTELLECT (GAṄGĀ AND YAMUNĀ) COME TOGETHER.

| SWAMI CHINMAYANANDA |

SHRINES

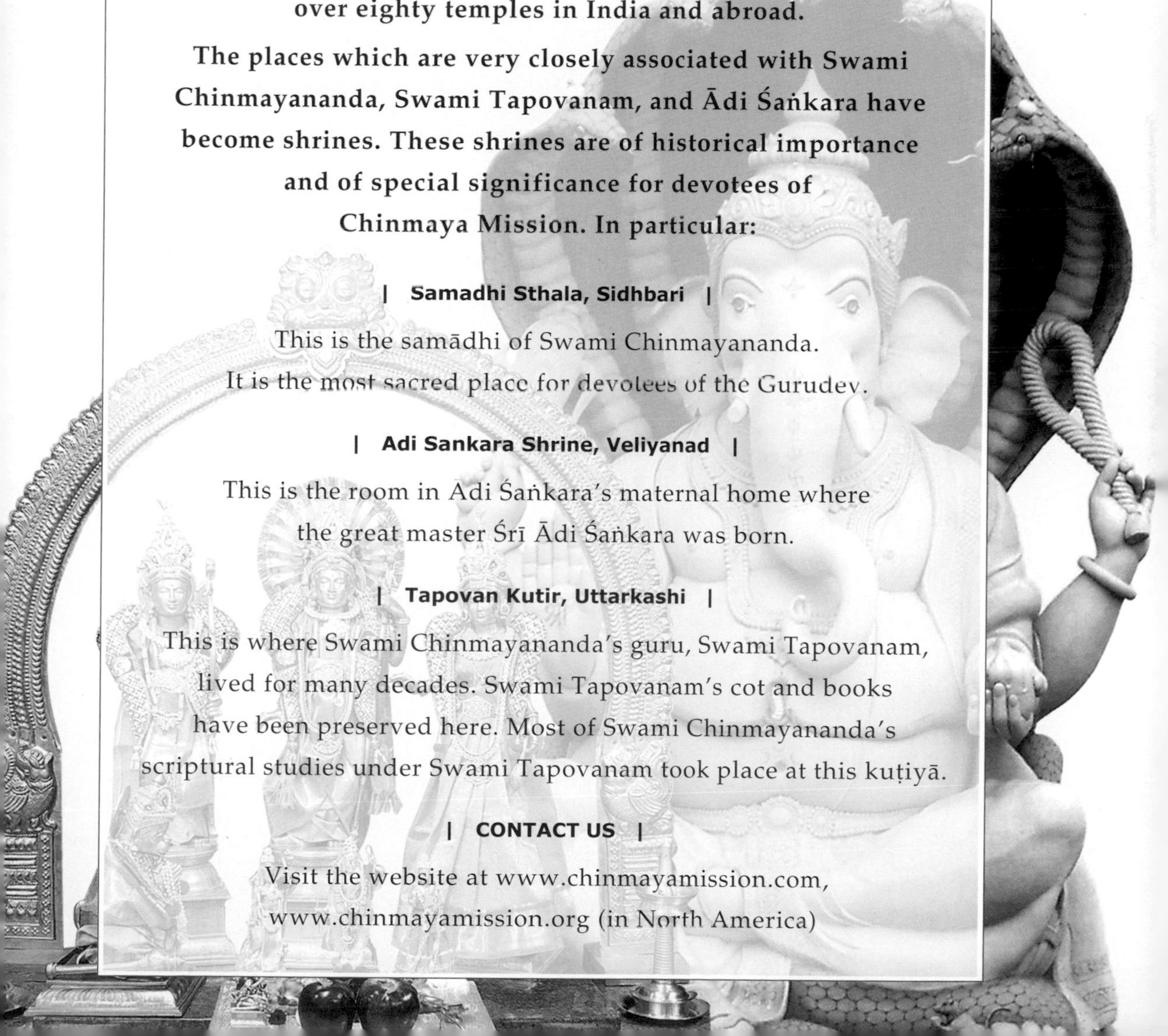

Traditionally, temples have not just been places for worshiping deities, but also have been venues for discourses, celebration of festivals, and the expression of music and arts as a form of worship to the Lord. To serve all these purposes, Chinmaya Mission has built over eighty temples in India and abroad.

The places which are very closely associated with Swami Chinmayananda, Swami Tapovanam, and Ādi Śaṅkara have become shrines. These shrines are of historical importance and of special significance for devotees of Chinmaya Mission. In particular:

| Samadhi Sthala, Sidhbari |

This is the samādhi of Swami Chinmayananda. It is the most sacred place for devotees of the Gurudev.

| Adi Sankara Shrine, Veliyanad |

This is the room in Ādi Śaṅkara's maternal home where the great master Śrī Ādi Śaṅkara was born.

| Tapovan Kutir, Uttarkashi |

This is where Swami Chinmayananda's guru, Swami Tapovanam, lived for many decades. Swami Tapovanam's cot and books have been preserved here. Most of Swami Chinmayananda's scriptural studies under Swami Tapovanam took place at this kuṭiyā.

| CONTACT US |

Visit the website at www.chinmayamission.com, www.chinmayamission.org (in North America)

XVII

Perfection is in Higher Ideals: The Chinmaya Vision Program

The Gaṅgā is a perfect symbol of unwavering determination to reach its goal. Her flowing waters find the easiest way around an obstacle to reach the sea. She will acquiescence to limits imposed upon her by the river banks unless a harsher impediment of earth and rock should obstruct her path. The Gaṅgā is not responsible for the resulting flood that breaks boundaries, because she cannot forever be held in abeyance. She will wait. She will lie down against the weakest point of defiant earth, until the weight of her surrender to gravity brings forth a new pathway to her unalterable oceanic destiny.

Similarly, a spiritual seeker must be a person of great determination. Not only is determination necessary for continuously moving towards the goal, but it is very necessary as armor against negative influences that may try to draw the seeker away from his path. Determination is a great boon; and when directed toward a goal, it is a guarantee against all failure.

In addition to his great love for Knowledge, Swamiji had an enduring love for India's rich cultural heritage, where, for example, Mother Gaṅgā is given an exalted and holy place in Hindu mythology because she represents all the dynamic and creative ideals required by man for living a holistic, fulfilling, and complete life.

In contrast, let's look at an example of a narrow, limited mindset:

Swamiji: "... REMOVE THE DARKNESS. Light a candle..."

Man: "But Swamiji, the wind keeps blowing out the candle."

Swamiji: "... Here is the place, in the temple in Rastha Peth, where my mission began..."

Man: "Swamiji, it's so small. How difficult it must have been!"

Swamiji: "...The Mahāvākyas which expound the central teachings of the Scriptures reveal the identity of the Self as Brahman. With this knowledge, when we experience the Self, saṁsāra or the realm of bondage comes to an end..."

Man: "But Swamiji, *practically*, what can *I* do!"

Practically, Swamiji visualized the Chinmaya Vision Program to improve our understanding of the world, and life at large — *yathā dṛṣṭi tathā sṛṣṭi* — as the vision, so the world appears to us. The one who has a vast vision, infinite is his potential and capabilities in the world. But if the vision is narrow, the world will appear stifling, constricted, and depressive. If the right vision can take us closer to our goal, it is only smart to work towards such a vision of life.

On February 18, 1989, Swamiji gave a talk to the delegates of the National Institute of Personnel Management at the Taj Hotel in Bombay where he scientifically analyzed the logic behind inculcating a higher ideal and the right values in life. This logic is at the center of all value-based programs initiated by Chinmaya Mission. An abridged version of Swamiji's talk is given here (the full talk is available on DVD with Chinmaya Publications):

> Life is a series of challenges. We are not given the freedom to choose the challenges, nor are we free to run away from the challenges.
>
> Challenges come in the form of situations, problems, or crises. Endlessly, they come to each and every one of us, one after another,

until the day we die. To meet them is called "life." If we don't meet them, the challenges quietly crush us, whether we are individuals or institutions.

Those who have the guts to meet them — they are the real managers, managing their affairs and problems. In meeting these challenges, a certain amount of education or technical knowledge is useful. But make no mistake, this is only information, and this outside knowledge has to be applied when meeting challenges. This is where many of us fail.

After an unsuccessful incident, many of us become very wise and say, "I should have done it this way." If we have failed, it is not because we did not have the capacity or the proficiency to succeed, or the knowledge to meet the challenge; but because at *that* moment, the right solution did not strike us. Before the challenge we were very wise, and after the challenge we are very wise — but at the time of meeting the challenge, we became a fool. Why?

Look at your own life. You will find that whenever you have failed, you were always able to say, "I should have done it this way!"

The science of management, as expounded even in great institutions like Harvard University, only explains what needs to be done *externally* to improve efficiency — keeping the right accounts, having a public relations department, a beautiful office, wall-to-wall carpeting, filing cabinets, computers — but these are all external improvements. Objective science thinks that all actions are performed by the body; and if my mouth is working, it means the job is being done. But are you listening to just the words from my mouth or to the swami who is speaking with the mouth? The mouth and ears are necessary, but they are the instruments with which my mind is trying to reach your mind. It is only when my mind has the right ideas that I am able to express these ideas, and if your mind is with your ears, then the communication becomes complete. Yes, the mouth and ears need to be healthy, but they are the tools of the mind.

The entire body is the tool through which I express myself. I use this body to express myself in facing challenges and finding solutions to my challenges. The body is necessary and it must be looked after, but more importantly, it is to be used by the mind.

If my mind is dissipated, despondent, desperate, agitated, worried, tense, stressed, strained, or worried — such a weakened mind, in its fatigue, can never act in the world outside. With such a mind being the doer in me, my performance through the body can never be dynamic, and the action can never become excellent and creative.

The mind is the man, not the body. Thus, it is the mind that is the true criterion of management, not the equipment. The mind is the doer, and the body is the toolkit to do the job.

The question now is: How to make the mind dynamic and full of energy?

You all know that the mind is thoughts. Think! Don't accept anything that I am saying. Your idea must be, when looking at me, "The longer the beard, the greater the suspicion!" Question it!

The mind is nothing but a bundle of thoughts. In deep sleep the mind is at rest, and there are no thoughts. The moment you wake up, thoughts gurgle and there is the mind again. In effect, the mind is "thought-flow."

These thoughts in each one of you are constantly sparkling away from you to the object (of thought) in distant time and place. Newton tells me that nothing can move in this universe without expenditure of energy, which means that with every thought that is moving from you (and you must have inestimable energy to push it out), in our present natural condition this is about 30,493 thoughts per day. This is your mental condition from the moment you wake up till you sleep — every day, 365 days a year till you die. Think!

When your mind is worried and anxious, and the flow of thoughts is more than usual, the mind is naturally more dissipated, which means you will have less energy to be dynamic.

Since our actions (by the body) are determined by the mental condition (of the mind), this would mean that the mental condition is directly linked to the quality of thoughts. That is to say, the mental dissipation of the mind is a result of the false values that we have recognized, thus creating the agitation and dissipation. If the thoughts are healthy, the mind is healthy; and the expression outside gathers a new momentum of excellence.

What can we do?

The thoughts you entertain are determined by the values you hold in life. Suppose you are convinced that money can buy you anything. If you are convinced that money is the highest ideal — and if this ideal is absorbed by you — then it *will* create a mental dissipation. For example, even if you are casually introduced to a friend, you will constantly be thinking how to get money from him. See, how the mind dissipates itself! *Once we have accepted money as the ideal, our thoughts become synchronized with the ideal.*

Therefore, there are certain values of life that you must maintain in your life. This is not an exercise for half an hour; it must be a complete transmutation of your life, a complete revolution of your thoughts. If you can do this, your mental dissipation will become next to zero. When your energy is conserved, the mind becomes a magazine of power. With such a mind, whatever you tackle in the world can never be a problem that your intellect cannot solve.

In the 1930s, newspapers always reported everything as a "situation" — a political situation, an international situation, a social situation. From the 1950s, the language changed; it was not a situation, but a "problem" — an international problem, a national problem, a communal problem, a state problem. The situation was gone and everything became a problem. Starting in 1965 onwards, the situation was gone, the problem was gone — everything was a "crisis." Even in the home today, everything is a crisis!

Let us say you are hungry and go into a restaurant. You order three or four vegetable dishes and maybe two or three sweet dishes. Now suppose, you suddenly find that your wallet has been lifted. Since you have ordered the food, this is a problem, but with a little effort you can explain this to the management and cancel your order. Now suppose: You ate the food; then you ordered a cigarette, and then you ordered the bill; and when the bill came, you read it three times. You added everything, and languorously inquired what each item was, and then you checked your wallet. This is not a situation, it is not a problem; it is a crisis!

When you were hungry and you knew the restaurant was open, it was only a situation, right under your control. But when you ordered the food, and then found that your money was gone, the same situation became a problem. Now, when you have eaten the food — *and don't know what to do* — this is when a situation becomes a crisis. The situation or the challenge remaining the same, your ability to face it makes a challenge a situation, a problem, or a crisis. In the modern world, the younger generation has become so dissipated that everything is a crisis. They don't know how to handle their problems and are running from pillar to post, from divorce to depression, from drugs to suicide.

When the mind is exhausted, it makes you incapable of facing the challenge. But if the mind is peaceful or serene, there is no problem under the sky for which man cannot find a solution.

If you read the lives of great people, you will find they were born just as any other child. Once they got the mental poise to face all situations in life, their performance and behavior in the world outside became so excellent that they became an ideal for others to follow, and be adored and worshiped by the world. Their achievements were considered blindingly brilliant.

The greater the responsibility you take up in life, the more careful you must be with your mind. To quieten the mind, the only effective

> way is faith — faith in something higher than you — in God. It need not necessarily be God. It can also be your profession, an ambition, or an ideal. But it must be something higher to hold on to and to inspire you with right values. Wherever success is achieved, it is because of these higher values obtained through higher ideals that have inspired people at all levels. This is the only way the mind can be made beautiful and efficient — through the exercise of religion and through the moral and ethical values that bring minimal disturbance in the mind.

At another time, in an interview with *The Sunday* in December 1981, Swamiji was asked:

> You are often urging young people to search for a new ideal that will give them motivation for self-sacrifice and dynamic action. Where do you think we can find such an ideal?

Swamiji answered:

> Each one will have to find such an ideal. Our culture is full of them. For example, look at Mahatma Gandhi. So long as he was M. K. Gandhi, he was a man with no hope of any success. All he achieved was a barrister's degree. In Africa, nothing happened. But when he came back to India, he got an ideal to pursue — freedom for 400 million people. Once he got that ideal, and was ready to sacrifice everything for it, look how his personality grew from week to week. Out of him came brilliance, and history is not complete without a chapter on Gandhiji. Where did he get it all from? One ideal, and everything changes.
>
> Swami Vivekananda must have been there in Narendra. But as Narendra, he was an ordinary, university student. But once he got an ideal, and started to pursue it, in five years a magnificent unfolding of his personality took place. Out of Narendra came a Vivekananda.

> Look at Prince Siddhartha. Once he got an ideal and held on to it, out of that ignorant man beamed the eternal prince of compassion, the Buddha. Without an ideal to hook yourself on, the depth of possibilities in you cannot be unearthed. An ideal is necessary.

The Chinmaya Vision Program (CVP) is a comprehensive educational program initiated in schools, which integrates the best in Indian culture with the philosophy of secular education. The aim is to give children higher ideals and a true vision of life, to help them face challenges in a positive and dynamic manner, so they may wholeheartedly contribute to society. Although the child is the focus of the program, nevertheless, the program also embraces the school management, teachers, and parents. Through them, the light of this higher vision will spread to society, country, and the world.

Swamiji emphasized that "training the mind is the essence of education." What better way than to begin this transformation when the mind is young, uncluttered, and open to larger horizons.

Back in 1965, he had said:

> Children are the very cream of our generation and they are the rulers and makers of tomorrow. Upon them depends the future of the nation and the safety of our culture and tradition. Let us give them a healthy physical and mental atmosphere for growth (integrated development), ingrain in them respect for life and love for all living creatures (universal outlook), team spirit and national fervor (patriotism), and pride in our hallowed, divine culture (Indian culture).

Present-day education is generally thought to be a function of how much we know. It is well-suited to produce a fine professional but can it guarantee a fine human being? No, not if the education system is not designed to do so. A narrow understanding of education makes it appear to be nothing more than a stepping-stone to a vocation. But education, in its true and complete sense, is more vast and encompassing. It has the larger purpose of transforming the child into an individual with full potential. This is why even great thinkers have been disillusioned with the mere material focus of contemporary education:

I have never allowed schooling to interfere with my education. —Mark Twain.

Men are born ignorant, not stupid; they are made stupid by education. —Bertrand Russell.

Nani Palkhivala often refers to the college-educated youth of today as "educated illiterates."

A well-educated man is he who is best equipped to bear the fortunes and misfortunes of life. —Jean Jaques Rosseau.

DON'T JUST INVEST ON THE CHILD,

ALSO INVEST IN THE CHILD.

"INVESTMENT ON" GIVES OUTER PROSPERITY.

"INVESTMENT IN" ENSURES INNER UNFOLDMENT

AND LASTING PROSPERITY. TRUE EDUCATION

IS "INVESTMENT ON" COMPLEMENTED

WITH "INVESTMENT IN" THE CHILD.

| SWAMI CHINMAYANANDA |

Clockwise from above:
The Chinmaya Vidyalaya flag
Swamiji being welcomed by school children at the inauguration of the 3rd National Jnana Yagna, Jamshedpur, 1974
Swamiji with school children and NLC officials, Tamil Nadu
Swamiji with children at the inauguration of Chinmaya Nursery School, Mumbai, January 1967
Chinmaya Nursery school children in action, Mumbai, 1976

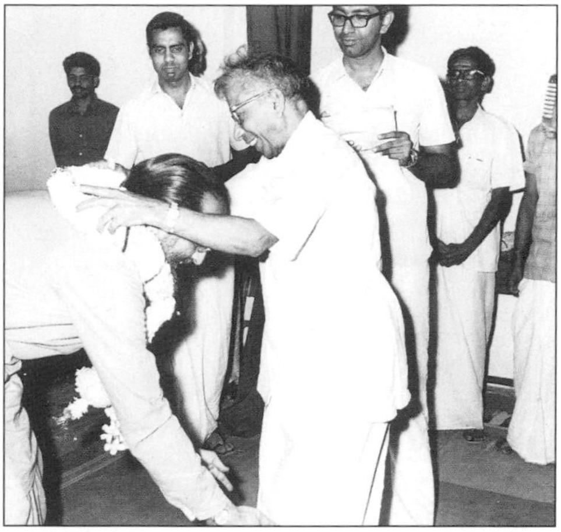

◀◀ **Overleaf from above:**
Chinmaya Vidyalaya assembly, Ernakulam
Swamiji sitting with an audience of school children, Hubli, 1976

◀ **Overleaf clockwise from above:**
Swamiji with 220 Balvihar members from 21 centers in Kerala at the 6th All Kerala Chinmaya Balmahotsav, Trichur, 1974
Swamiji touches the feet of his former teacher, Gopal A. Menon, who garlands Swamiji at the 6th All Kerala Chinmaya Balmahotsav, Trichur, 1974
Children of Chinmaya Vidyalaya Koramangala during Sports Day
Swamiji being welcomed at the yajñaśālā, Mumbai, 1986
Swamiji pointing high, Coimbatore, 1979

Above:
Swamiji at the opening of a Chinmaya Nursery School, Mumbai, 1967
Center:
Swamiji with CHYK, Medha (now Swamini Vimalananda) as a camp delegate, Sidhbari, June 1983
Below:
Swamiji inspects the model for Delhi Chinmaya Vidyalaya building with Swami Jyotirmayananda

▶ **Facing page above:**
Swamiji reads scrap books made by students of Chinmaya Vidyalaya Delhi
Below:
Swamiji with Chinmaya Vidyalaya students, Tripunithura, 1990

Clockwise from above:
Swamiji sitting outside his office in Sandeepany Sadhanalaya Powai, 1976
Swamiji at a Chinmaya Vidyalaya function, Delhi, November 14, 1980
Swamiji addresses a gathering of Managers, Mumbai, 1964

AN EDUCATED MIND

by Swami Chinmayananda

An individual who has controlled his mind is the most educated man. He may not be instructed much, but he is an educated man. This is neglected in our modern education around the world.

Many think that if they are specialized in computers and are able to earn a good livelihood — that is enough. Merely earning a livelihood and filling the stomach — any animal can do. Even a buffalo does that! Then why is education necessary?

Education means the ability to see the world in unison — macrocosmic vision. That kind of purity of mind is to be cultivated, to be educated. The purpose of education is to help you gain control over your mind with which you are going to work in your profession or in service of the society. If your mind is educated in all your contacts with the world outside, there shall be an extra beauty, an extra dynamism, an extra grace — and that grace is the result of education.

The Chinmaya Education Movement is one of Swamiji's most valuable contributions to society. It began in 1967 with a small nursery school in Kollengode (Kerala) and gradually grew to eighty Chinmaya Vidyalaya (schools), eight Chinmaya Institutes of Higher Learning, and a Chinmaya International Residential School in Coimbatore.

The Chinmaya Education Movement has seen almost two million students graduate through its halls. In 2010, there were eighty-thousand students enrolled in Chinmaya Vidyalayas across India and Trinidad alone. This success is primarily due to the unique vision of offering education enhanced with spiritual knowledge, which is made possible by the Chinmaya Vision Program.

The Chinmaya Vision Program is applied to all education programs within Chinmaya Mission. Consequently, Chinmaya Institute of Management (CIM) is educational in context, philanthropic in spirit, logical and technological in action, and humanitarian in vision. It is dedicated to the evolution of human resource as the primary factor for an individual or organization. In the last two decades, CIM has had an impressive success in the corporate sector, benefiting industry leaders, entrepreneurs, and field personnel.

The apple never falls far from the tree, and in 1990 Swamiji gave Anil Sachdev, a former Balvihar student, the final nudge to start Eicher Consultancy. For fifteen years, Anil had dreamt of contributing to the cause of holistic, economic development in India. When he finally approached Swamiji during a drive in his car, his mother who was sitting in the back seat expressed her concerns:

> "Swamiji, Anil is doing so well, and he is getting an excellent salary with very good perquisites. They have given him two cars and everything free! Should he take a risk by setting up a consulting business when he is a serious candidate for becoming the chairman of Eicher?"
>
> "Amma, do not worry," said Swamiji. "One day, he will give cars to many others! Anil is inspired to do the Lord's work, so you surrender all your worries to Him."
>
> Then turning to Anil, Swamiji said, "Accept Eicher's offer to start a separate consultancy unit, but don't get too attached to it. In the long run, you must create something of your own."

Anil Sachdev founded *Grow Talent* in 2000 with the motto, "Enabling people and organizations to realize their full potential." Thereafter, the *School of Inspired Leadership* (SOIL) was established in 2008 based on Swamiji's vision, "to build leaders with character, competence, and enthusiasm."

LEFT RIGHT LEFT, OM NAMAH ŚIVĀYA

In December 1965, I wrote to Swamiji that I had declined a seat in the Indian Institute of Technology and joined the National Defence Academy in Kharakvasla since I wanted to be an army officer. Promptly, I received a handwritten letter from Swamiji, congratulating me on getting where I wanted. He advised me that my aim should not be to seek military promotions, but to serve the nation. Swamiji wrote:

Blessed One!

Om Om Om. Salutations!

I am writing to you in between my sessions of meditation. To a real army man, character is his armour. Remember Him always as you march in your line of duty, "Left, Right, Left, Right... Om Namaḥ Śivāya! Om Namaḥ Śivāya!"

Thy own Self,

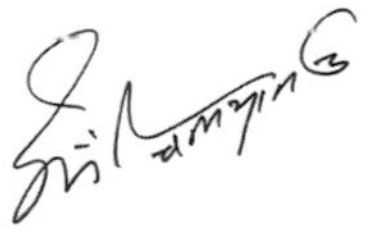

Col. Rakesh Sachdev (Retd)
Chinmaya Mission Mumbai

THE LORD GIVETH AND THE LORD TAKETH AWAY

During a Jnana Yagna in Bangalore in 1990, a local businessman came to meet Swamiji and handed him an envelope with gurudakṣiṇā.

Next, an administrator from one of the Chinmaya Vidyalayas came to see him. He complained about their lack of finance for a project they were undertaking. Swamiji gave him the envelope (which had 10,000 rupees in it).

He then turned to me and said, "He gives, and He takes away." Turning his hands inside out, Swamiji laughingly showed me his empty hands. "Nothing stays in these hands! If you remain empty, you will be His vehicle to serve the world."

Swami Ishwarananda
Acharya, Chinmaya Mission Tustin and Bakersfield

In the 1970s, it was unheard of to think of bringing an Indian child back to the Motherland for an education. No matter, Swamiji was not intimidated, and forged ahead with a fiery sprit. In a public speech in Sangli on January 6, 1979, he said:

> The pressure of demand from twelve million Indians who are now successfully living outside India and want to give Indian values to their children has compelled me to start a ten-acre residential campus in the salubrious climate of Coimbatore, where we have already started building an international institution. In this school, we propose to bring American teachers in sufficient numbers, to procure accreditation for our school with the American Educational system, so that Indian students abroad can be transferred from age 12–18 for their continued education in India.
>
> The students will be with us for six years. At age eighteen, they will return to the U.S.A. to join colleges there. During this time, they will be brought up with Indian values; they will be taken on study tours around the country each year with a special theme, geography, history, art, architecture, pilgrim centers. During their vacation they have an option of living as guests in a lower-middle-class family, so that they will get a feel of the Hindu family traditions — the endless love that parents bear for their children, the extraordinary concern for all members in the family, relatively poor but extremely cheerful people, the inordinate respect that the youngsters have

towards the elders, and the love that the children bear towards the parents and religious festivals. Our foreign-born children will have a chance to experience all this.

It has not been very easy for me to organize the campus. But I am doing it in order to avoid seeing a mongrel generation of Hindus being spawned all over the world as a byproduct of intelligent Indians! In our youth we may think in terms of "international relationship" and allow our children to adopt a false education, generated by a misguided reverence for science and technology, and the material prosperity of the suffocating and restless West. We may appreciate such parents and their large-heartedness, but we must condemn their lack of foresight to see what would become of their children's future. We have ignored the peaceful cheer and joy, the mutual concern and family integrity, which are the distinct beauties of the Hindu culture.

I have been rather open-hearted. Generally these are thoughts we never express so loudly, but only whisper among ourselves and secretly worry over them! I have spelt them out shamelessly, because the disease is growing rampant, and the diagnosis will have to be elaborate. It must be openly discussed, and the remedy to be discovered urgently and quickly. I have done my best. If you all cooperate, I see clear possibilities of a complete cure and healthier future. Our children, with a Western education and a touch of Indian culture, can grow as ideal men and women in that country — or any other — materially successful outside and spiritually peaceful within. You are welcome to think, "The swami is wrong." But, I am sure, "The swami is right!"

Eight years later, the plan was bigger and better. The "Chinmaya International Residential School" (CIRS) covered one hundred acres of land. The American teachers were not *that* necessary. Instead, world-renowned specialists combined the best teaching strategies from the East and West, and the school was affiliated to the Central Board for Secondary Education (CBSE), New Delhi, India, and the International Baccalaureate Organization (IBO), Geneva, Switzerland.

However, the years leading to its success were not without toil. When the plan for the residential school first originated in 1976 in Coimbatore, it was thought that the five acres of land purchased by Chinmaya Vidyalaya, Vadavalli (in Coimbatore), was too small. Then, in 1983, Somasundaram of the *Everest Group of Companies* took Swamiji to see one hundred acres of land in Siruvani, but this land was riddled with another problem. It was owned by many people, and, as it turned out, it would take eight years before it was all procured. Meanwhile, Swamiji had begun to consider other locations, the Andamans, Sidhbari, and Lucknow. Swami Swaroopananda (Director, Chinmaya International Residential School) narrates a conversation from 1990 in Hong Kong when Swamiji received an urgent letter which he read out to everyone:

> The Executive Committee in Lucknow have met and decided that the land in Lucknow, where we just did bhūmi pūjā, is not large enough for the prestigious Chinmaya International Residential School. Hence, we have decided that we will sell the plot and buy a larger plot, a good distance away from the city, with the same money.
>
> Swamiji put away the letter and said to us, "They may decide, and they are also right that the land is small, however, the final decision is mine. I will veto the decision. Either the school will be built on that plot which was given to me by the old village farmer to build the school, or the school will not be built in Lucknow!"
>
> There were a number of businessmen from Hong Kong sitting near Swamiji. One of them said, "Swamiji, if we know that the decision is wrong, then should we not change it before venturing upon it?"

> Swamiji looked straight at him, shaking his legs, and said, "You business people will not understand. You see everything commercially. I have been looking for a land for the international school. This elderly farmer came up to me and offered me his land saying, 'I have not been educated, but I hear you build good schools, please take my land and build a school.' The committee in Lucknow was over-excited to have the school in their area. We quickly went ahead with the bhūmi pūjā. We should have thought before, whether it was suitable or not. Even I did not."
>
> Swamiji paused, and then continued, "Don't ever allow your mind and intellect to get away with such mistakes. Teach it to never repeat the mistake again. Be firm."

Swamiji's commitment was to the "intention" and not to commercial gain. He had accepted the gift of the land from the farmer with the intention of building a school, and he did not renegade on his moral commitment.

Once, Swamiji had said, "Some act till they meet obstacles, others act in spite of obstacles; but some act without fear of meeting obstacles that might arise en route." Swamiji worked in spite of obstacles. It is with such a pure mind and fearless intellect that Swamiji laid the foundations for an institute of learning, to produce citizens of the world with clear thinking, right decisions, strong convictions, and steadfast values.

In the end, the international school was not built in Lucknow (or near-about). By 1992, Chinmaya Mission had acquired all one hundred acres of land in the foothills of the Pongacherri and Velliyangiri hills in Siruvani (26 km from Coimbatore), which became the campus for Chinmaya International Residential School. The Siruvani land is one of the seven largest biospheres in the world; the surrounding forest is rich in wildlife, with elephants, deer, wild boar, peacocks, and monkeys. Elephants are occasionally seen grazing on the hillside, and peacocks and deer come right into the school campus to drink from the waterhole.

Chinmaya International Residential School was officially inaugurated on June 6, 1996 (three years after Swamiji's mahāsamādhi), by Swami Chidananda of Divine Life Society, who was also Swamiji's guru-bhāī from Ananda Kutir. During his inaugural speech, Swami Chidananda said, "Actually Swami Chinmayanandaji had come and not me, because the name on the train ticket from Chennai to Coimbatore was in the name of Swami Chinmayananda and not Swami Chidananda." This had been a genuine slip on the part of the person who had made the train ticket.

Currently, the residential school has 550 students from 23 states in India and 19 countries abroad, with an academic and administrative staff of 200 members. The campus has seven residential blocks for students, five residential blocks for teachers, a beautiful swimming pool, a state-of-the-art gymnasium and fitness center, a 400-meter track and field ground, and a multipurpose auditorium; and all class rooms have been upgraded to hi-tech digital systems. The children train in rock-climbing, paragliding, yoga, cricket, badminton, tennis, water-polo, athletics, swimming, and so much more. The academic standard of the school is at par with any top international boarding school in the world. Students have graduated to universities like Stanford, Harvard, and the National University of Singapore.

Upon signing off on his prefaced promise in Sangli (January 6, 1979), Swamiji had trusted that time and fulfillment of events would be his judge. Looking back now, we must concur: The Swami is right! Chinmaya International Residential School is a unique fusion of two distinct cultures — the ancient and rich cultural heritage of the East blended with the creative and independent thinking of the West. Effectively, Swamiji had carved out a vivid vision of the future, creating perfect citizens of the New World.

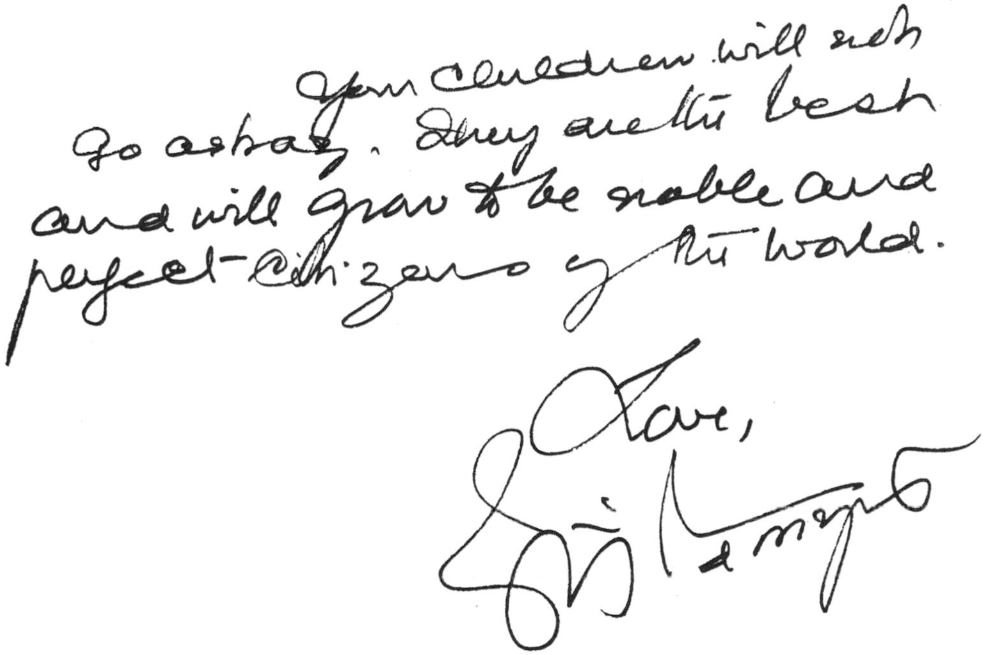
Your children will reach
[illegible]. They are the best
and will grow to be noble and
perfect citizens of the world.

Love,
[illegible]

Above:
A saṅkalpa on the bare-land of Chinmaya International Residential School, Siruvani, March 1991
Center:
Inauguration of Chinmaya International Residential School by Swami Chidananda (President of Divine Life Society), Siruvani, June 6, 1996
Below:
Aerial view of CIRS campus, Siruvani

▸ **Facing page clockwise from above:**
Swami Swaroopananda with students of CIRS in Indian attire, Siruvani
Swami Swaroopananda with students of CIRS in the office building, Siruvani
March past of Vashistha House, on Sports Day, CIRS, Siruvani
Campus of CIRS, Siruvani
Students of CIRS offer pūjā, Siruvani

VASHISTHA

CVP CVP CVP

Chinmaya Mission offers schools and colleges with a difference. The difference is the Chinmaya Vision Program (CVP) which complements the normal curriculum. CVP has been so successful that over 500 schools in India, which are not affiliated to Chinmaya Mission, have also used it to enhance the quality of their education.

CVP is a comprehensive educational program which envisages that children must come out of the education system not merely as literate people, but as truly educated, balanced, and fulfilled individuals. CVP is divided into four heads: (a) Integrated Development to develop the physical, mental, intellectual, and spiritual personalities of children. (b) Indian Culture to give the children a wide exposure to India's rich culture. (c) Patriotism to foster national pride in the children and educate them in citizenship and civic consciousness. (d) Universal Outlook to make children appreciative and sensitive to world issues and the environment.

VIDYALAYAS

Under the guidance of CVP, Chinmaya Mission is running:

- HARI HAR SCHOOLS
  These are free schools for village children. They provide vocational education in addition to the academic curriculum. The vocational education enables children, once they are older, to start their own craft industry units using local raw materials.
- CHINMAYA VIDYALAYAS
  There are eighty Chinmaya Vidyalayas (regular schools) spread all over India and one in Trinidad, affiliated either to the All India Central Board of Secondary Education (CBSE) or to their local state board. There are currently eighty thousand students enrolled in these schools.

| CONTACT US |

CCMT Education Cell
Chinmaya Gardens,
Nallur Vayul Post, Siruvani Road,
Coimbatore 641 114, Tamil Nadu, India
Tel: +91 (422) 261 5663, 261 3495
Email: ccmtec@gmail.com
Website: www.chinmayavidya.org

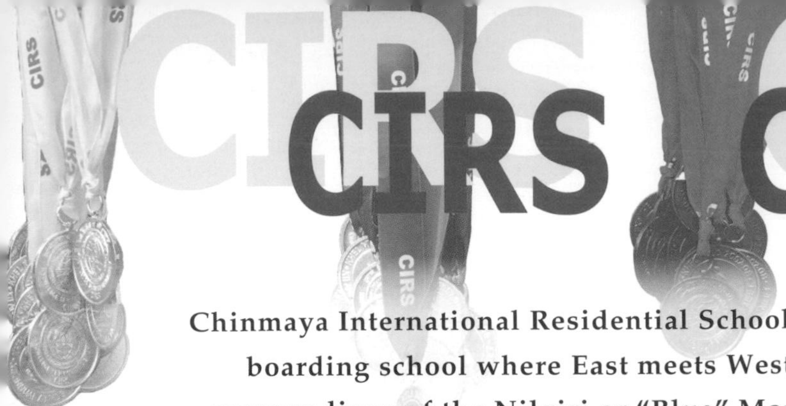

CIRS CIRS

Chinmaya International Residential School (CIRS) is a co-educational boarding school where East meets West. Located in the serene surroundings of the Nilgiri or "Blue" Mountains, CIRS is a unique fusion of the ancient and rich cultural heritage of the East and the creative and independent thinking of the West. The curriculum is based on the ancient and well-tested Indian traditional gurukul concept (teacher and student living together in a residential system) adapted to suit the modern and dynamic academic environment.

MANAGEMENT

Vedāntic scriptures carry an incredible amount of information on the art and techniques of management. The tips on management provided by old seers are extremely practicable. Chinmaya Mission regularly conducts activities for the modern corporation managers, so that they may understand and usefully apply the wisdom of the old seers in the hustle and bustle of today's corporate world, and in the area of human resource development. The activities are organized under the aegis of Chinmaya Institute of Management (CIM) in Karnataka. The main aim of CIM is to integrate core values into the field of management. CIM's courses and services integrate this approach into standard management topics.

CIM CIM

INSTITUTE

| CONTACT US |

Chinmaya Institute of Management
7 D'Costa Layout, 1st Cross, Cooke Town,
Bangalore 560 084, India
Tel: +91 (80) 4125 2084
Email: cihl2000@airtelmail.in
www.chinmayamanagement.com

Clockwise from above:
Portrait of Swamiji, Kathmandu, June 1990; ***Portrait*** of Swamiji, Sidhbari, December 1991; ***Swamiji at his desk,*** Chinmaya Vidyalaya Delhi, October 1989; ***Portrait*** of Swamiji, Sidhbari, March 1983

XVIII

The Elusive Ego Strikes a Cord

You cannot become something which you eternally are, which you have never *not* been, at any time of eternity. Liberation, which is the Realization of the Self, is not a result of any action, for if anything is a result of action, it means there was a time when it did not exist and has since come into being. Butter does not have to do anything to be soft. Ice will be cold. Fire will burn and be hot. It is their nature. To be what one is, does not require any action.

Yet, the simple fact is that without sādhana (spiritual practice), Self-realization is impossible. Sādhanā removes the veil of ignorance that prevents the Self from being recognized. It is a kind of discovery, whereby we come to perceive that which was already present. And this discovery takes place within the individual's personality. Any real and authentic sādhanā must inevitably bring about the destruction of ignorance and the discovery of the Self within.

All methods of sādhanā, be it selfless service, dedicated performance of one's duty, repetition of the Lord's name, or devoted listening to the Guru's teachings; they all seek to accomplish one thing: to expose the ego, which otherwise takes shelter and support from anything and everything, and thus ever remains elusive.

All sādhanā, by enabling action to reduce the ego, become methods of self-purification, which in turn enables Self-discovery.

Although the method to Self-realization is easily put in words, to *actually* realize the Self is not a little thing; it requires the utmost humility. It is in dying to the little self that we attain everlasting life. The death of the ego is the one and only way of attaining immortality and eternal bliss. Hence, the great master Jesus said, "Whoever clings to his life shall lose it, and whoever loses his life shall save it."

Time after time the spiritual history of the world illustrates the downfall of many seekers who have risen very high, only to have terrible falls because they did not give importance to reducing their ego. The sage Viśvāmitra spent many years performing austerity in seclusion. He became dominated by his ego, drunk with the pride of self-conquest. What happened? He lost his alertness, and when the celestial nymph Menakā came — *finished*. All his austerity was lost.

NOT AN IOTA OF THIS

CAN BE SMUGGLED INTO *THAT*.

YOU HAVE TO DIE TO RELIVE AS BRAHMAN.

THE EGO HAS TO DIE!

THE EGO MUST DIE TO REALIZE THE WAKER.

| SWAMI CHINMAYANANDA |

NARAYANA IS WORKING THROUGH ME

by Swami Chinmayananda

The song of success sung by the ego ever hums in the heart of a materialist. Under the spell of its lullaby, the higher instincts and divine yearnings in man go into a sleep of intoxication. The highest form of renunciation is the renunciation of the ego. Name and fame must also be ultimately renounced, if one is to attain liberation.

When man is able to temporarily overcome his baser tendencies, he develops an ego that *he* did it, forgetting that it was Nārāyaṇa's grace that made it happen.

In these times of intense, nonstop action, the easiest method of self-purification is selfless service, where our very actions are surrendered unto the Lord. When serving in the world, the thought process is: *I am His servant*. In this way, the action is no longer ego-directed or desire-directed activity; it becomes God-governed, God-directed activity.

With a vision to provide a platform for individuals to perform selfless service, Swamiji started a rural healthcare and development program in Sidhbari. This program was also to benefit the rural people of the Himalayas, and in particular the womenfolk. "For many millennia, the women of the Himalayas have served the ṛṣis and munis (sages and saints). I, too, have taken all my teachings in the Himalayas — this is an opportunity to do our bit for them," said Swamiji when apprised of a USAID proposal for maternal and child care services in Sidhbari. The Government of India was also keen to set up primary health care services in inaccessible and remote areas, and to train female multipurpose health workers (MPWFs) to meet the State's requirement for community nurses.

Clockwise from above:
Swamiji outside the Chinmaya Nursing Home on inaugural day, Bangalore, September 12, 1962
Dr. Akhilam (now Swamini Nishtananda) in the OPD in Sidhbari, 1985
Swamiji invoking the Lord before opening a dispensary at Sidhbari (students of the 1st Vedānta course in Hindi at Sidhbari also present), February 1983
Swamiji riding a cycle donated for the disabled by the Lion's Club, 1974

Although Swamiji was initially reluctant to get involved with a government welfare program, but the clincher for him, was the remark "that the women will benefit the most."

BEDROCK OF VALUES

In 1982–83, the Government of India issued a directive for the selection of an NGO for family planning services and maternal health care. Swamiji was clear that he wanted to help the women of the State. I prepared a project report on behalf of Chinmaya Mission.

Your project is worth Rs. 64 lakhs. You give me one lakh and I will clear your proposal." This request was quietly conveyed to me by the official looking after governmental clearance.

When I relayed this request to Swamiji, I tried to soften the blow, but ended up adding fuel to the fire. "We will take the money from a contractor to pay this official, or the project will not go through," I said to Swamiji.

"Throw the project out," said Swamiji. "I will not bribe my way through. There is no need to start a project under such circumstances." I had to assure Swamiji that no bribe would be given.

All was quiet for a month. Some officials eventually came for inspection, and the request was again repeated, but we refused to entertain it. By then, USAID had also sent a representative from Delhi. The official waited for 6–8 months, and finally gave up.

The right means symbolize a solid foundation. And there was more. Swamiji was categorical and clear that the yardstick for admissions to the nursing school would strictly be merit and need, not political pressure. This directive followed after another request had been made by an MLA, who had forwarded the names of ten girls when the second batch of training was to start in 1987. We politely informed the MLA that the policy was "Merit and Nothing Else." This incident had a short-term impact — the renewal of registration was delayed by a year. But it had a deeper, more meaningful long-term impact — values were chiseled into the foundation.

Dr. S. Chakra
Trustee, Chinmaya Tapovan Trust, Sidhbari

Discussions were spread over two years, and due to a number of reasons including delaying tactics, the Chinmaya Rural Primary Health Care and Training Centre was formed on April 10, 1985, under Chinmaya Tapovan Trust. Later, in 2003, a separate trust for development was formed, called Chinmaya Organization for Rural Development (CORD), and, therefore, throughout this chapter this program is referred to as CORD.

The first steps were an Out Patient Department (OPD) clinic in Sidhbari and community-based health services through six health sub-centers, as well as outreach domiciliary services. The emphasis was on maternal and child health care. The OPD services came under the aegis of USAID, and immunization, family planning, domiciliary antenatal, intranatal and postnatal services were added. The first director was Dr. Jayanti Mahimtura, followed by Dr. J. S. Sharma who had retired as Deputy Director of Health Services, Himachal Pradesh. For a brief period in 1987, K. R. Pai (now Swami Ramananda) took over, followed by Dr. Kshama Metre taking over in late 1987. Under her stewardship, the "Project", which primarily represented the health-related activities including the MPWF training from 1985–92, became the "Program" that would go on to create history in the Kangra District.

Fascinatingly, the project found it difficult to put together the first batch of thirty girls to be trained as Multipurpose Health Workers. The cause — an imaginary tunnel! When Sidhbari ashram was set up in 1981, it found acceptance on the face of it, but only because it was not commercial in any way. Four years later, when it announced a project that would train young girls as nurses, the villagers' imagination soared. A buzz went around that the bābās (ascetics) in the ashram would attract young girls with the promise of training, but then bundle them off through a tunnel to China or America. No other destinations came to mind, since the villagers only knew the names of these two countries.

As a result, very few local girls applied, and almost all who applied were enrolled. And yet, by the time the second batch started in 1987, the efficacy of the training had been established, and there were nearly 1,500 applications. The number shot up to 2,400 by the third and fourth batches.

While implementing outreach domiciliary services in the villages, the doctors, nurses, and students came into close contact with the villagers, and that's when it became clear that the link between primary health care and the reality of village life needed a more intense scrutiny and intervention. Dr. Kshama Metre says, "Unless communities are mobilized for resolving local issue, health care for all can never become a reality. It was this focus on the comprehensive development of the village that allowed us to engage the women and tackle the challenges they faced — poverty, low self-image, illiteracy, low status, and so on. I would say that even emptying an entire ocean of medicines on these villages would not break the vicious circle of ill-health and poverty. I strongly feel that sub-primary health services are a convergence point for all developmental issues. That is the only way to bring about relevant, realistic, and meaningful change."

swami chinmayananda

Camp: Rourkela
20 November 1990

Dr. Kshama
Chinmaya Rural Primary Health Care
And Training Centre
Chinmaya Tapovan Trust
Sidhabari 176 057

Blessed Self:

Hari Om! Hari Om! Hari Om!
Salutations!

Your note of 16th November has reached me here today through Sarada Kumar. If there are so many applications, the best thing would be to give them a test. Eliminate the older girls by age-bar restriction and you call the rest of the girls for a written exam. and eliminate 50 or 60% of them through that exam. Invite the rest of the people about 50 or 60 for an interview. In the interview eliminate another 20 or 30 and get that core of 30 students that we can entertain.

I am sure that our girls of this batch in their state examination from 18th December will score.

Even after the exam, wherever they be, let them come back for the Camp and be with us for that one month, free of all charges. This earlier batch and the new batch when they mingle and mix together, it will be a great experience and discipline for the new batch. Also they will learn all the Keertans and Bhajans from the old one's.

With Prem and Om,
Thy Own Self,

CHINMAYANANDA

P.S.: Read out the last paragraph to Trilokinath.

Share letter with Ram Kripalani

THE HEART OF THE MATTER: WELFARE VERSUS DEVELOPMENT

India is considered a developing country — the underlying meaning is that we are currently "underdeveloped" and in the process of "developing." Yet, when it comes to implementation, we do not succeed because of a failure to make some very important distinctions between welfare and development.

There is an oft-repeated saying: "If you give a poor and hungry man a fish, you have helped him for a day; if you teach him how to fish, you have helped him for a lifetime." This manner of help underlines some of the major differences in approach between welfare and development. Giving a person fish is "welfare," while taking the time and trouble to train the person to fish is "development."

Welfare addresses the immediate, apparent problem (for example, of being hungry) with a direct but short-term benefit to the person or society. The real issue (for example, the incapacity of providing for oneself) is not addressed; hence, the problem remains, needing even more "charity" by the welfare-minded.

For development, one would address the root of the problem and seek a long-term solution. It involves training and building up the capacity of the people; hence, the involvement of the people becomes an essential part of the solution. As the underlying issues are addressed, the people themselves become capable of handling their problems; in the process, they become self-reliant.

For those who want to help or do charity, the welfare approach appears to be easy — set up a free kitchen, the hungry will come and eat. Whereas, in the development approach, the beginning is more difficult.

One may need to set up appropriate training in consultation with the "beneficiaries". Sustained effort is required to build sufficient capacity to make the people and society independent. Let me clarify — development does not mean that when people are hungry, we should give them seed and land and send them for agricultural training. It means we should not stop at just giving them food.

Dr. Kshama Metre
National Director, CORD, and Padma Shree Awardee 2008

The formative years of the program were particularly difficult. Swami Ramananda expresses the frightful dependence on USAID for funds:

> Once, in 1987, there was no money, and a huge bill for construction was pending. We decided to pledge our fixed deposits, and thought that we would wait for two-to-three days. If, by then, the money did not come, we would close down the project. But the money arrived. The funds crunch, besides other struggles, in terms of voluntary manpower, was constant in such a development project.

By the time USAID support came to an end in 1990, a NORAD representative came to Sidhbari. Dr. Kshama Metre reports the event:

> A big tall gentleman came over from Norway to see the Mahila Mandals. He noticed the income generation schemes we had started, and was quick to realize that we needed sewing machines. He asked me if I'd like to start a sewing program. I declined, as we were too full.
>
> That evening, while calling on Swamiji, this Norwegian gentleman was singled out by him. "Who are you?" asked Swamiji.
>
> "My name is Brad Hopland, and I am the Deputy Representative, NORAD. I was impressed by the reputation of your project, and came to see for myself. What I saw was even more impressive,

and I offered a sewing program to Dr. Metre, but she refused."

I was summoned, and stated my reasons for refusing.

"Take it," Swamiji advised gently.

"But we are too full, Swamiji." I maintained.

A brief pause followed, after which Ajay Singh Mankotia (Trustee, Chinmaya Tapovan Trust) was summoned. "He'll help you," Swamiji said firmly.

This is how Chinmaya Seva Centre, a sewing training unit, was born on December 12, 1992.

THE SIGNIFICANCE OF BREAKFAST

Just before Swamiji was to arrive in Manila in 1988, we received a letter from Chinmaya Mission requesting us to avoid organizing the morning bhikṣā since Swamiji was not well.

But when Swamiji saw the daily schedule we had planned for his trip, he asked, "Why is there no breakfast bhikṣā?"

We explained that we wanted Swamiji to rest and be well.

"I have many children in India who need to eat! So open breakfast bhikṣā!" said Swamiji.

Dave Gopisahijwani
Chinmaya Mission Manila

In the late 1980s, Swamiji had said to Dr. M. Akhilam (now Swamini Nishtananda), "Wait and see what I will do to this program." Indeed, the program grew beyond belief. One thing led to another:

Health & Sanitation: Doctors in outpatient clinics, village midwives, immunization, family planning, nutrition, hygiene, sanitation and health education.

Clockwise from above:
Sheila Kripalani in a workshop with nurses trained by CORD, Sidhbari
Swamiji with Urmila Devi
Swamiji with the nurses of Himachal Pradesh trained by CORD, (the matron, Brni. Shanti, in yellow), October 1992
Mobilizing Farmers and Men's Club in a village in Himachal Pradesh

Clockwise from above:
Health check-up by MPWF in a village in Himachal Pradesh
Village girls being given vocational training at CORD, Sidhbari
Hari Har school children studying in Sidhbari
Swamiji with the nurses of Himachal Pradesh trained by CORD

Clockwise from above:
Natural Resource Management work being done by CORD
Mahila Mandal Group in Sidhbari
Swamiji welcomed at headquarters of CORD by MPWFs, Sidhbari

Swami Chinmayananda

First Chinmaya Spiritual Camp

The Queens Hotel
Church Road
Crystal Palace
Londan SE19 2UG

August 20, 1986.

Dr. Kshama
Chinmaya Tapovan Trust
Sandeepany (HIM)
Sidhabari

Blessed Self,

Hari Om! Hari Om!! Hari Om!!!

Salutations!

Your kind and elaborate letter so beautifully written has reached me. Every idea there is true and acceptable. The education of the villagers must come through the activities of the health workers. It would be impossible for the ashram to contact all the villagers individually.

I have written today itself to Swami Jyotirmayananda to contact the Association and get me 30 copies of "Where there is no Doctor" (in Hindi) -- if not free, then at a concessional rate. You may write to Swami Jyotirmayananda for more details about it. If the copies are available, I will bring them with me.

Prem and Om,
Thine Own Self,

Mahila Mandals: Empowering women to discuss personal and economic concerns and actively participate in common interests and concerns of the villages.

Yuva Mandals: Empowering young men to communicate, question, face fears, and voice concerns rather than look for crutches like alcohol, tobacco and drugs; development of education and trade skills to create opportunities within the community; channeling the energy of youth positively.

Yuvati Mandals: A platform for young girls to discuss and promote education and trade skills; girls learn about health issues which are not openly discussed in the family or community.

Farmers and Men's Clubs: Upliftment of the small farmer and laborer by mobilizing them into groups to prevent them being marginalized; issues related to farm and allied sector, as well as economic, social, and environmental issues, and their role in local self governance are also given focus.

Balwadis and Balveers: Nurturing Children through Balwadis or play groups for growth and development of children (two-to-six years). Young minds are exposed to spirituality, physical education, the alphabet and numbers; Balveers are for children over six years and includes mothers who discuss issues concerning children and women in their immediate environment.

Adult Literacy: Basic reading, writing, and arithmetic for villagers.

Social Justice and Informal Legal Assistance: For example, fighting alcohol abuse awareness, domestic violence, gender discrimination, and child abuse.

Self-help Groups: A form of micro-banking within the community which allows villagers to access finance without any collateral from banks, instead sponsored by an NGO like CORD.

Income Generating Activities: Mobilizing sustainable livelihood through, for example, agriculture, horticulture, dairy, small shops, food products, fabrics (weaving, sewing, embroidery, and knitting), traditional arts and crafts, and bamboo and non-timber forest crafts. Ensuring self-reliance, building operational management, and mainstreaming the micro entrepreneurs into the local markets, is an integral part of the process.

Community-based Rehabilitation: Therapeutic management, inclusion, and integration of the disabled into the community.

Local Self Governance: Strengthening the democratic process through general village councils and empowered participatory involvement of the villagers.

Natural Resource Management: Motivate and train people to develop, implement, and sustain their natural resources. For example, water and soil conservation, vegetation measures, human resource development, and solid-waste management.

CORD has touched the lives of over one million villagers directly, and over one-half million villagers indirectly in 600 villages in four states of India. The work of CORD Sidhbari in District Kangra of Himachal Pradesh is being replicated at the following sites:

Orissa:

CORD Lathikata, 25 kilometers from Rourkela in District Sundergarh.

CORD Deuladiha, 200 kilometers from Rourkela in District Keonjhar.

Tamil Nadu:

CORD Tamraipakkam, 40 kilometers from Chennai in District Thiruvallur.

CORD Siruvani, 25 kilometers from Coimbatore.

They all run a comprehensive integrated rural development program.

Since 1999, CORD Training Centre in Sidhbari has provided Self-help Group trainings to five northern states of India (Himachal Pradesh, Haryana, Punjab, Jammu & Kashmir, and Uttarakhand) in close collaboration with NABARD (National Bank for Agriculture and Rural Development). More than 30,000 government, NGO, and bank functionaries have been trained, to make micro-finance accessible to the poorest of the poor.

In the immediate aftermath of the Tsunami disaster in 2004, Chinmaya Mission Sri Lanka established a project titled *Tsunami Relief and Rehabilitation.* The initial objective was to provide immediate relief measures to the victims. In 2005, CORD Sri Lanka was formed, with the wider objective of complete rehabilitation (including trauma support). CORD Sri Lanka has established work in three areas: Batticaloa, Rambodha, and Jaffna.

In 2007, Chinmaya Vijaya Orphanage in Kaza (near Vijayawada), Andhra Pradesh was formed under the patronage of CORD. Built on five acres of land, Chinmaya Vijaya is committed to the care of orphaned and homeless girls. It provides them with a family, a home, and a strong foundation to lead an independent and secure life.

In 2009, CORD USA was created to work with CORD India, as well as local, social welfare organizations in the U.S.A. It raises funds through Walkathons and other events and coordinates programs in Chinmaya Mission centers; the funds are intended for social welfare both locally and internationally.

The work of CORD has been supported by various agencies and people from different corners of the world: United States Agency for International Development (USAID), Ford Foundation, Norwegian Agency for Development (NORAD), Canadian International Development Agency (CIDA), Abilis Foundation (Pentagon Foundation Trust), People's Science Institute, Sir Ratan Tata Trust, National Bank for Agriculture & Rural Development (NABARD), Orissa State Government, and Grow Talent Company Ltd.

Dr. Kshama Metre has been acclaimed as one of India's modern social transformers, along with legends like Baba Amte. She has won several awards and recognitions for her contribution to society: Person-of-the-Year Award in the national magazine *The Week* (1993); Ojaswini Award for Excellence in Service (2000); National Women Commission Award for Women Empowerment (2002); featured in the book *Prophets of India* (2004); Sadguru Gnanananda Award for Manav Seva Dharam Samvardhani (2005); Nina Sibel Award for Commendable Work with the Differently-abled (2006); nominated as a member of the 11th Planning Commission (Primary Health Care) by the Government of India for 2007–12; Padma Shree Award for Social Services given by the President of India (2008).

Dr. Kshama Metre was a pediatrician in Delhi, one of the umpteen doctors in the capital city. In a chance meeting with Swamiji in 1984, he had asked her, "Are you attached?"

"No," replied Dr. Metre, mistakenly thinking that Swamiji had referred to her marital status. Swamiji threw his head back and laughed.

She understood his remark a year later, when in Sidhbari, Swamiji asked, "Do you want to come here?"

"Yes," replied Dr. Metre.

By just listening to her Guru, Dr. Kshama Metre had rewritten her entire future destiny.

Swami Chinmayananda
10, Shrungar Society, Parle Point, Surat-395 007.

Dr. Kshama.
Sadhabari.
Hari Om!
Salutations.

Read! I liked
your plan of serving the people.
May all your schemes thrive
and grow into a large shelter for the
worried hearts of people.
I will never
Your plan.
say No. You have the Chinmaya
spirit of service well ingrained
in your heart.

Love,
Chinmaya

(461st.) Geeta Gnana Yagna-(Jan. 15 to Jan. 22, 1989)

at Vanita Vishram, Athwa Gate, Surat.

Time and again, Swamiji encouraged devotees to take up a concrete project to give shape to their concerns for society, and to express their talents as a means of self-purification. He encouraged Anil Sachdev to pursue his dream of holistic economic development in India; building leaders of character, competence, and enthusiasm.

He made Rudite Emir the founding editor of *Mananam*. She went on to serve Him by writing several books: *Swami Chinmayananda: A Life of Inspiration & Service*; *At Every Breath, A Teaching*; *Stories about the Life and Teachings of Swami Chinmayananda*; and *Undoing: Returning to Simplicity*.

When Christiane Madeleine (now Swamini Umananda) met Swamiji during his first Jnana Yagna Camp in France in 1983, Dr. Mahesh Ghatradyal had introduced her saying, "Swamiji, she is Christiane, she will translate." Swamini Umananda went on to translate *The Holy Gītā: Commentary by Swami Chinmayananda* in French (published in 1998). She says, "The months of translation were really a meditation. The total immersion in the text and in the ideas was a deep sādhanā for me." The French translation of Swamiji's commentary is a reference in bookshops in France, reprinted in pocket format in 2008.

Sheela Sharma was a writer of Hindi books. She was unsure whether she should author more of her own books or translate Upaniṣad commentaries. Then Swamiji said to her, "Your salvation lies in doing Upaniṣad translations." Sheela Sharma translated eight Upaniṣad commentaries to Hindi, and the commentary on *Nārada Bhakti Sūtra*.

Shivaraman served Swamiji as his personal attendant from 1970 onwards. He took care of his daily medicines, clothes, and other personal needs. After Swamiji's mahāsamādhi, Shivaraman was asked, "Now that Swamiji has gone, how do you feel?" Shivaraman replied, "Where has he gone? He is still here. That is why I am here and still serving him!" Shivaraman said that Swamiji gave him this advice, which became his single "mantra" while serving Him,

"Whatever happens in the ashram, whoever comes or goes, you must remain a witness."

Sharada Kumar met Swamiji as a college girl during a Jnana Yagna in Bombay in 1963. At the time, she had thought, *I wish I could chant for Him.* Not long after, Swamiji gave her many opportunities as the lead chanter in many of his Jnana Yagnas, giving her the nick-name "HMV" (her Master's voice). *"Dharmāviruddho bhūteṣu kāmo'smi bharatarṣabha"* says Sharada Kumar. "Lord Kṛṣṇa says in Chapter 7, 'I am that desire in beings that is not opposed to Dharma!'"

In the early 1970s, Anjali Singh had grumbled to Swamiji, "I don't know how to serve you ... I can't sing, I can't type. I can't cook, and I can't chant!" When Swamiji next returned from Hong Kong, he brought with him a present — a Canon camera. "You can take photographs," he said. Anjali Singh clicked 12,000 photographs of Swamiji, and documented 20,000 photographs of him in the Chinmaya Photo Archives. Swamiji's altar pictures all over the world, and most of the pictures in this book are the result of this sādhanā.

When Sita Juneja (now Swamini Gurupriyananda) was introduced to Swamiji as an interior decorator, Swamiji threw up his arms in delight and said, "Oh! You must be very special if you can decorate the interior. Most people I meet usually decorate their exterior with great dexterity!" In 1992, when the Kamala Hall was being built in Sidhbari, Swamiji informed Sita Juneja that he wanted large glass windows behind the stage, so that the Dhauladhar Mountains would be visible from inside the hall. Later, Swamiji again reminded her, "Have you thought about this?" Before she could come up with a plan, Swamiji attained mahāsamādhi. Sita Juneja then did the woodwork of the Samadhi Sthala, but made one change: she added large glass windows to the beautiful Kerala style architecture designed by Maithili, thereby making the snow-peaked mountains visible in all their majestic glory from Swamiji's resting place. Sita Juneja then oversaw the building and interiors of the monumental Chinmaya Centre of World Understanding in Delhi, including Chinmaya Chetna, an interactive multimedia exhibit on Swamiji's life and teachings.

Br. Radhakrishnan Chaitanya (later Swami Jyotirmayananda) wanted to serve Swamiji. He was not adept at public speaking; hence, Swamiji put him to work in overseeing the construction of Tapovan Kutir in Uttarkashi (in the 1970s). Swami Jyotirmayananda also looked after the building of Chinmaya Vidyalaya Delhi and Unchahar. It was also because of Swami Jyotirmayananda's persistent efforts over twenty-five years that Chinmaya Mission Delhi was given the prestigious land on Lodi Road — in the heart of city — where Chinmaya Centre of World Understanding proudly stands.

Swamini Sharadapriyananda had wanted to start a social welfare project for the poorest of the poor in rural Andhra Pradesh. Thus, on February 8, 1982, Chinmayaranyam Ellayapalle ashram was formed for the underprivileged in Andhra, with multiple welfare activities. It was during Swamiji's first visit to Chinmayaranyam, that the celebrated "water story" took place. "Dig along the line that connects the two trees. Water is sure to come," he had instructed the villagers, who had until then not been able to find any water on the twenty-two acres of barren, undeveloped land. When Swamiji returned in March 1988, he addressed the villagers:

> Just as the sun and sunlight are not two things, God and God's grace are not two things. The light in the sun is the sun. The sun can never be without light. Similarly the grace of God is the nature of God. God has no existence without His grace. But, I must come out of my house and go in to the sun to enjoy the sunlight. If I sit in my house and close all the windows and doors, and then complain that there is no sunlight in my house, I am a fool! Even when the windows are closed, just behind the windows, the Lord (the sun) is waiting for you to open the windows. And sunlight

is a very decent guy; he will not open windows which are closed, and enter uninvited. He will wait patiently until you open the window. In the same way, because we don't open the windows of our heart, therefore, God's grace does not reach us. The only way to open the windows is to roll up your sleeves and come out and serve some other human beings in society. This is the greatness of puruṣārtha (self-effort). Without puruṣārtha, Īśvara kṛpā (the Lord's grace) can never come. Even if God wants to give you His grace, He cannot give it to you unless you start puruṣārtha.

Do you mean to say that the Īśvara kṛpā was not on this land before? When the Swamini came and started work, look at the puruṣārtha-Īśvara kṛpā (self-effort effected Lord's grace) on all sides. We villagers were never working; we thought that there is no water. But when we saw that the Swamini is getting water, we started digging wells. Because of this effort, Īśvara kṛpā came, and water came. With the waters, the fields have become green. But if you don't work harder and harder, Īśvara kṛpā will dry up.

TO GIVE LOVE IS FREEDOM; TO DEMAND LOVE IS SLAVERY.

IN NATURE, THE SUN, THE RAINS, THE SPRING

AND THE RIVERS WORK IN A RHYTHM OF GIVING.

SOME OF US LOVE ONLY IF WE ARE LOVED IN RETURN,

LIKE A COMMERCIAL TRANSACTION.

VERY FEW ARE RICH IN LOVE. HOW CAN THEY LOVE

WHEN THEY HAVE NONE IN THEMSELVES?

SERVICE OF OTHERS IS THE EXPRESSION OF LOVE IN ONE'S HEART.

THE DAY YOU TAKE UP THE POLICY OF GIVING LOVE,

INSTEAD OF DEMANDING IT; THAT DAY, YOU WILL HAVE

REWRITTEN YOUR ENTIRE FUTURE DESTINY.

| SWAMI CHINMAYANANDA |

Such enlightened Masters, ever-established in the Self, and thus instruments of the Lord, are few upon this earth. Their mere presence purifies the atmosphere wherever they go. Like a spring whose waters never fail, like a breeze that enters a house whose windows are open, such Masters instantly refine those with whom they come into contact.

Grace turns back from the hearts of those hardened with egoism and selfishness. If we want grace, we must face the Divine. As long as our attention is diverted to things exterior (of the world), we deprive ourselves of His grace. When the windows are closed, sunlight may be everywhere else, but the inside of a home will still be in darkness.

Grace, expressing as self-effort, bears fruit in the form of the highest blessedness. The greater the devotion, and the greater the reverence for the Guru, the greater is the inflow of the Guru's grace.

Reality is everyone's property. Therefore, it is said, "Ask and it will be given to you; seek and you will find; knock, and the door will be opened." (*The Holy Bible, Mathew: 7.7*) — for it is yours by birthright. The tragedy of this world is that no one asks. They ask for what they can see — passing unrealities. No one realizes the worth and value of that which cannot be seen. There is no lack of *THAT* which we are seeking. But, there is a lack in the seeking.

TO REALIZE THE SELF IS ITSELF THE
GREATEST WORSHIP THAT ONE CAN OFFER
TO THE SELF. THE GREATEST ADORATION
THAT WE CAN GIVE TO THE SUPREME,
OR TO A TEACHER, IS TO BECOME *IT*.

| SWAMI CHINMAYANANDA |

Clockwise from above:
Swamiji watches cultural show by nurses trained at CORD, Sidhbari
Swamiji with nurses trained by CORD after their cultural show, Sidhbari
Swamiji with Sita Juneja (now Swamini Gurupriyananda)
Swamiji with Dr. Apparao and Sumati Mukkamala and their daughter, Aparna, Flint
Shivaraman taking care of Swamiji's clothes

Clockwise from above:
Swamiji with Dr. Kshama Metre (on the right of Swamiji), Sidhbari
Swamiji leaving the Satsanga Hall in Sidhbari with nurses trained by CORD
Swamiji being photographed by Anjali Singh, Uttarkashi, 1984
Hari Har School children sitting with Swamiji during a spiritual camp in Sidhbari, 1983
Portrait of Swamiji, 1991

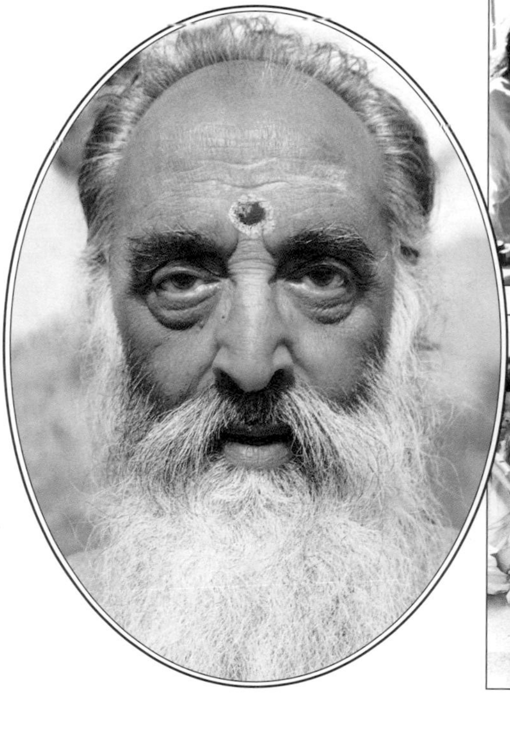

CORD CORD

Chinmaya Organization for Rural Development (CORD) is the service wing of Chinmaya Mission to facilitate participatory and integrated sustainable development for the poor and to harness human resources, and enable the poor to transform their lives through programs driven by themselves. The holistic programs of CORD for the rural and impoverished of India have crossed countless social, economic, and political boundaries, touching over one million villagers directly, and over one-half million villagers indirectly in 600 villages in four states of India: Himachal Pradesh, Orissa, Tamil Nadu, and Andhra Pradesh.

"CORD is a bond of love and understanding between the 'haves' and the 'have-nots' so as to empower the 'have-nots,' to take charge of their life to become makers of their own destiny. It is not a favor shown to them but only our duty fulfilled towards them. In this process of giving and serving, the giver grows spiritually and the receiver is blessed with the power of transformation." Swami Tejomayananda

CORD CORD

The programs and activities of CORD are:

- Mahila Mandals: Empowering Women
- Yuvati Groups: Encouraging Self-Confidence in Young Girls
- Balwadis: Nurturing Children
- Fighting Social Injustice: E.g., Gender Issues and Domestic Violence
- Yuva Groups: Channeling Energy Positively in Youth
- Self-Help Groups: Accessing Financial Resources through Micro Banking
- Sustainable Income Generation Activities: E.g., Agriculture, Horticulture, Dairy, Weaving, Sewing, Traditional Arts, and Bamboo Crafts
- Primary Healthcare Services
- Rehabilitation for the Differently-abled
- Natural Resource Management: Creating Awareness and Sustaining Natural Resources
- Strengthening Local Governance

| CORD & YOU |

India, home to one billion people, is also home to the largest number of the world's poor. CORD welcomes your help in reaching out to as many people as possible.

| CONTACT US |

CORD Head Office
2nd Floor, Chinmaya Mission,
89, Lodi Estate, New Delhi 110003, India
Tel: +91 (11) 24616291, +91 9899107730
E-mail: cordheadoffice@gmail.com
Website: www.cord.org.in

CORD Resource Centre, Sidhbari
Kangra District, Himachal Pradesh 176 057, India
Tel: +91 (1892) 234322
Email: cordsidhbari@gmail.com, nationaldirectorcord@rediffmail.com

PART FIVE

Twilight Triumph

◀ **Overleaf:**
Left:
During the 75th birthday of Swamiji celebrated with Swarna Tulābhāram, Sidhbari, 1991
Right:
During pāda-pūjā, Mumbai, 1984

XIX

It's Only My Heart!

Up until 1970, on a few occasions, Swamiji had been ill with high fever or a minor sore throat. He took it as a warning that his body would not be able to continue at its usual pace. In fact, during one attack of high fever in 1960, the devotees (in their anxiety), overdid their care, giving Swamiji not a moment's peace. When the doctor came to check him, Swamiji asked him with dignified seriousness, "Is there a nursing home available where I can get some rest!"

By 1970, all the principal scriptures of Vedānta had been taught in large cities; they had been translated and published in several languages; Swamiji's students were teachers in major cities — conducting Jnana Yagnas, taking classes, and organizing activities. Thus, Swamiji mentioned that he would slow down, since his body was not able to continue at its usual pace. But, this was not immediately possible. Chinmaya Mission and the numbers of devotees all over the world had grown — extensively — and the multiple projects and activities seemed to necessitate that Swamiji continue with his exhaustive schedule of work. Then, on March 21, 1970, just five days into a Jnana Yagna in Mysore — Swamiji suffered a heart attack.

He was immediately taken to a hospital, but there was not a single vacant bed available. A temporary ward was set up on the hospital

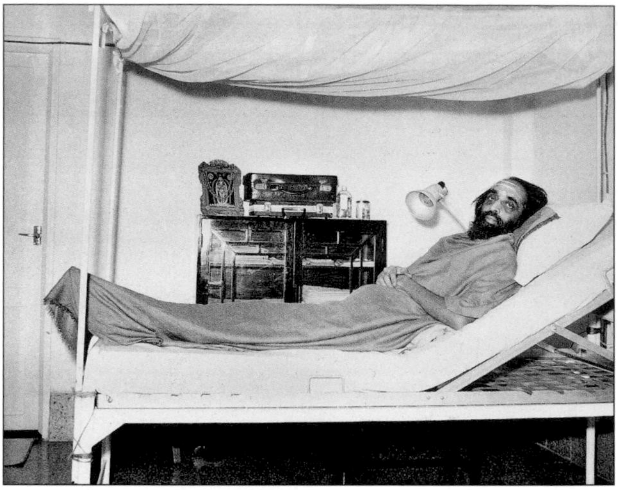

Clockwise from above:
Swamiji in hospital after his heart attack, 1970
Part of Jnana Yagna audience, Bangalore, March 1993
Swamiji with the Chinmaya Mission Hospital Committee, Bangalore, 1967
Foundation Stone Ceremony of Chinmaya Mission Hospital, Bangalore, February 4, 1968

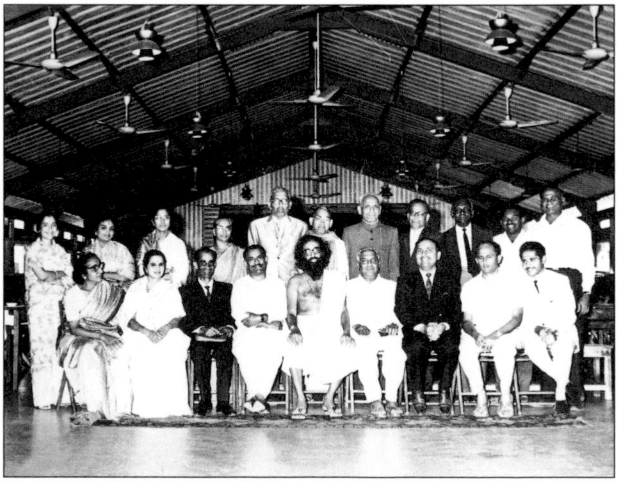

verandah for Swamiji, and Mission members brought in supplies, everything from bed to curtains. Everyone waited in suspense for signs of improvement as experts in cardiology came from all over India to be of service to Swamiji.

After three days, signs of improvement were visible, and two days later, a room became available in the hospital. With the exception of a couple of relapses in the following month, Swamiji continued to recover. On May 10, he was discharged and traveled to Bangalore. Devotees there waited for him at the new "Chinmaya Mission Hospital" — Swamiji would be the first patient. He greeted everyone with his usual sense of humor, "I inaugurated the out-patient ward in Mysore, and today I inaugurate the inpatient ward here!"

The Chinmaya Mission Hospital in Bangalore was conceived as an arena of service for local Mission members. In 1960, a small group of Mission devotees hired a room in a slum area in Murphy Town, Bangalore. They began conducting a biweekly medical clinic for the poor and needy. When Swamiji heard about the Murphy Town project and its volunteers, who included Sushila Purushottam, Kamala Reddy, Prafulla Iyengar, Smt. Dassanchar, and Smt. Yogam, he was very pleased. He gave them a check of Rs. 500/- and said, "Why not! This gives me the idea of starting a hospital."

Once the saṅkalpa had been made, funds were collected, land was purchased, and construction planned and executed. When Swamiji checked in as an inpatient in 1970, scores of devotees trooped in and out of the hospital each day. The number of visitors was particularly large given that the annual audience at Swamiji's Jnana Yagna in Bangalore regularly numbered over 10,000 people. The result — Chinmaya Mission Hospital quickly became famous! Yet again, another platform for selfless service had been thrown wide open.

During this time, at the invitation of several Mission members, Sri Satya Sai Baba of Puttaparthi came to visit Swamiji in the hospital. And three years later, in 1973, Swamiji personally invited him to preside over the opening ceremony of the National Jnana Yagna held in Bangalore.

Throughout his life, Swamiji came in close contact with many holy men, saints, and sages. In 1956, Swamiji had been invited by Swami Nirmal Maharaj of Punjab to attend and address the All India Vedānta Conference in Amritsar. Leaving at midnight, Swamiji traveled three hundred miles by car to address the assembly in the morning. He then traveled all day to return for the 6 P.M. lecture in Delhi. The next year, in 1957, Swami Nirmal Maharaj — who was known as the "lion of Vedānta," while Swamiji was called the "tiger of Vedānta" — inaugurated Swamiji's first Jnana Yagna in Mumbai.

In 1975, Swamiji traveled to the Shringeri Math to pay his respects to the presiding Śrī Śaṅkarācārya Abhinava Vidyatirtha Mahaswamigal. The Śaṅkarācārya presented Swamiji with a double rudrākṣa seed encased in gold. This sacred seed is from the fruit of the Elaeocarpus tree, beads of which are used to make a rosary for prayer. The double rudrākṣa seed is quite rare and holds a special significance since it symbolizes the marriage of Lord Śiva and Gaurī (Puruṣa-Consciousness and prakṛti-matter) — the two aspects of creation joined into one. This pendant was presented to Swamiji in recognition of his service to mankind in propagating the most ancient knowledge of Sanātana-dharma.

In 1978, Swamiji met with the Tibetan Buddhist leader, the Dalai Lama, in Dharamsala. The Tibetan government-in-exile has its headquarters in McLeod Ganj, a suburb of Dharamsala in District Kangra, Himachal Pradesh. Situated in the Dhauladhar Mountains at an elevation of 2,082 meters, McLeod Ganj is often referred to as "Little Lhasa" by Tibetans. Swamiji had come to the same district to view the proposed building site of the Sidhbari ashram.

"Why don't you come down to the plains of India with the great Buddhist ideas?" Swamiji had asked the Dalai Lama.

"We always wait for students to come to us," replied the Dalai Lama with a shy grin.

"Yes, yes...I know...but they're not coming! So we teachers have to go to them," Swamiji rejoined with a chuckle.

The Dalai Lama nodded in agreement. "I will think it over," he said. Then he joked with Swamiji, "You are an impatient one!"

Swamiji gave an expansive gesture by throwing out his arms, and said, "Yes! I am very impatient to arouse the world to their divine nature."

They proceeded to have a discussion on certain Sanskrit and Buddhist terms, after which the Dalai Lama announced, "Okay. If you plan something, I will go down and talk." On January 25, 1979, Swamiji invited the Dalai Lama to come to Allahabad to inaugurate the Vishwa Hindu Parishad Conference attended by one thousand Hindu leaders from two dozen countries. Decades later, in 1998, during an International Camp in Sidhbari, the Dalai Lama came to pay homage at Swamiji's samādhi and spoke to all the delegates of the camp in the Kamala Hall.

In the spring of 1979, Swamiji was among a group of distinguished swamis who were invited to speak at the 83rd birthday celebration of Anandamai Ma held in Bangalore. It is said that Anandamai Ma showed great affection for Swamiji on that day. Swamiji also reciprocated with much reverence and affection. He had previously met Anandamai Ma on two occasions: She had been a guest at Sandeepany Sadhanalya

Powai in 1975; and, although the exact date of his first meeting with her is unknown, it was sometime during his days in Ananda Kutir when he was a student of Vedānta. Swamiji had developed a problem with his practice of prāṇayāma (breath-control exercises advocated in Yoga) and Swami Sivananda had sent him to Anandamai Ma for assistance. Prāṇayāma had led him to be constantly hungry, no matter how much he ate. It is reported that Anandamai Ma asked for four roṭīs to be brought, and directed Swamiji to eat a bit from each. She then asked him to place the roṭīs on his head and also place his right hand on top of the roṭīs. The problem got cured! In later years, Swamiji related this incident in Delhi, and said, "Which śāstra says that you keep jhūṭi (already tasted food) roṭīs on the head and the jhūṭā hand on the roṭīs, and it will reduce hunger?" Swamiji was indicating the greatness and divinity of Anandamai Ma.

In 1989, Swamiji dedicated a Jnana Yagna to honor Swami Gangeshwarananda, who was 108 years old. Swamiji had great respect for this elderly mahātmā and would visit him whenever he could. One time, Swamiji (with his pādukās on) had just walked across some wooden planks over a canal and arrived at the mahātmā's side without informing anyone. Although Swami Gangeshwarananda was blind, nevertheless, he immediately recognized Swamiji.

"Chinmayananda, so you've come," he said.

Swamiji was curious how he had known that it was he who had arrived.

"The way you walk." answered Swami Gangeshwarananda. "Only one swami walks like that, and it is Chinmayananda. You walk like an army general!"

Swamiji had an especially beautiful friendship with Swami Chidananda, the second President of the Divine Life Society (after Swami Sivananda's mahāsamādhi in 1963). They had struck a bond when they were both students in Ananda Kutir in 1947, and their love and respect for each other would last their lifetimes. On August 1, 1993, just two days before Swamiji's mahāsamādhi in San Diego, Swami Chidananda had immediately come to see Swamiji, despite his own frail health, when he heard of Swamiji's critical condition. In his urgency to reach Swamiji's bedside, he had taken a flight from Washington, DC to San Diego by himself, without even informing any of his own devotees who later followed him. After Swamiji's mahāsamādhi, Swami Chidananda continued to bless and inaugurate many Chinmaya Mission events all over the world — he came to Sidhbari in August 1994 for Swamiji's first Puṇya-tithi-arādhanā; he inaugurated Swamiji's life size "pratimā" statue in Sandeepany Sandhanalya Powai in March 1995; he inaugurated Chinmaya International Residential School in Siruvani in June 1996, where he lovingly called Swami Tejomayananda his "spiritual nephew."

Swamiji and Swami Chidananda were a unique contrast in their outward personality. Swamiji was majestic — grand — with an aristocratic bearing, he walked tall. He was also beautifully attired, with immaculately ironed, flowing robes. Swamiji was always on time for all appointments — one could set one's watch to his entrance.

Swami Chidananda was humility personified. He was quick to touch anyone's feet. His dhotī would be tied above ankle length — more for convenience than decor. His evening satsaṅga was usually accompanied by two rather large (ancient-looking) alarm clocks that would be placed on the table in front of him. Both were to remind him to finish his lecture on time. Often, one alarm would ring in the middle of his talk. Swami Chidananda would switch it off while continuing to talk. Then, some minutes later, the second alarm would ring.

Clockwise from above:
Swamiji visits Anandamai Ma in her Dehradun ashram (accompanied by Mr. Kharbanda and Sheela Puri) October 1968
Swamiji with Sri Satya Sai Baba during inauguration of the Bangalore Jnana Yagna, 1973
Anandamai Ma's visit to Jagadeeshwara Temple, Powai, 1970
Anandamai Ma's visit to Jagadeeshwara temple (Swamiji climbing the steps with Ma), Powai, 1970

▸ **Facing page above left:**
Swamiji greeting Swami Abhedananda during Gītā Jnana Yagna, Trivandrum, 1962
Above right:
A meeting of two mahātmās, one touches the feet; the other garlands (Swamiji prostrates to Śrī Avadhoot ji) Swamiji has written behind this photo: " Be humble at the feet of the great and thus loot them!" Surat, June 1966

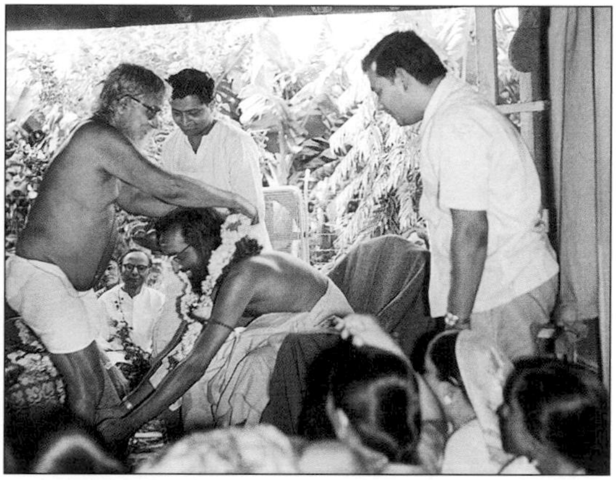

Clockwise from center:
Swamiji welcoming the Pejawar Math Swamiji who came to inaugurate the Jnana Yagna, Mysore, 1967
Swamiji being honored by the famous Bhagawatar of Guruvayur, Guruvayur, 1967
Swamiji with Nisargadatta Maharaj

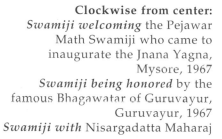

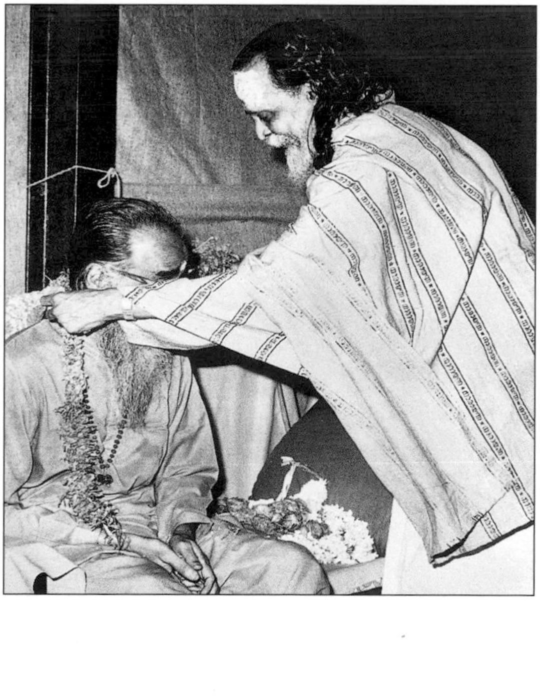

Left:
Swamiji with Swami Satchitananda of Yoga Vedanta Forest Academy, Coimbatore, 1967

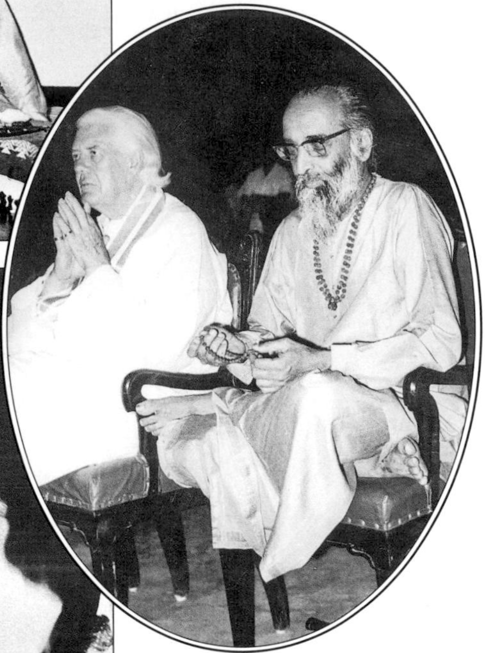

Above:
Swamiji with Professor Coats, President, Theosophical Society, 1978
Center:
Swamiji with Cardinal Gracias who was the chief guest during Mumbai Jnana Yagna, November 1964
Below:
Swamiji with Swami Krishnananda of Divine Life Society, Rishikesh, February 1981

Above:
Swamiji with the Dalai Lama at the Vishva Hindu Parishad Conference, Allahabad, January 25, 1979
Center:
Seated with guru-bhāī Swami Chidananda, President, Divine Life Society, Rishikesh, 1985
Below:
Swamiji visits Mata Brahmajyoti at her ashram "Ganga Tat" (just below Tapovan Kutir) Uttarkashi, 1984

▸ **Overleaf above:**
Swami Narsinghgiriji Maharaj of Sanyaas Ashram inaugurates Swamiji's 1st Yagna in Delhi, 1953
Below:
Swamiji speaks to devotees after the installation of Lord Kṛṣṇa in Kamala Hall, Sidhbari, October 6, 1992

In the summer of 1980, when Swamiji was in the United States for a series of Jnana Yagnas, his heart condition required attention. Several doctors in Detroit noted that both his blood sugar and pulse were erratic. Cardiac catherization revealed blockage of more than eighty percent in all of the four main arteries supplying blood to the heart. Devotees contacted the world-famous heart surgeon, Dr. Denton Cooley, at the Medical Center in Houston, who performed Swamiji's multiple bypass surgery on August 26, 1980.

After recuperating for two months in Houston and Detroit, Swamiji pushed up his sleeves, rubbed his palms together, and declared, "Now I have ten more years, let's see what I can do!" Twenty-four hours later, he was on a flight to India with a full itinerary for 1981.

Upon arriving in Bombay, Swamiji met with CCMT Board members and put forth a plan of giving more independence to Mission Centers. Up until this point, all ācāryas posted at various Mission Centers in the world had been answerable to CCMT for the coordination of activities, expense accounts, and ironing out problems. But now, Swamiji decided upon a new plan where the Mission Centers would be independent and responsible for organizing and coordinating all activities according to the needs in their communities. This new system gave the ācāryas, as well as the householder devotees, the opportunity to work in unison and own collective responsibility for their Mission Centers. It would also challenge them to serve society selflessly and thus evolve spiritually.

Would the householders take up Swamiji's challenge? Would they have sufficient insight to run a spiritual organization for the greatest benefit of all? But most importantly, would they have the courage to pursue their own divine goal, to fulfill their inexorable destiny, by making each of their lives a manifestation of God?

Swamiji was certain. *They would.*

In 1974, Swami Govindagiri had come from Uttarkashi to Chennai for medical care. After his recovery, he attended a Jnana Yagna by Swamiji, after which he said:

> Swami Chinmayananda, as well as Swami Tapovanam, have been Gurus to me. Yes, I have learned a lot from Swami Chinmayananda. He has the capacity to enable one to see the Truth. When you listen to him speak, you walk away thinking you know everything there is to know. If we have failed, it is in our inability to keep the brightness of that Knowledge in our minds to blind out all doubts. We allow the clouds of our old tendencies to come back and settle in.

One need not leave one's home, family, or profession in order to lead a divine life. What has to be given up is the ego — the idea that *I am so and so;* that *I am the doer* — which is based on a wrong understanding of ourselves. To make our life divine requires an inner change, not an outer one.

A human life is a rare and invaluable gift — for a human embodiment is only one among eighty-four lakh possible embodiments of life on earth. As such, it is not to be wasted in suffering from egoism, selfishness, fears, anxieties, desires, and cravings — or any other passing unrealities.

The spiritual seeker, who has had enough of the outside world, will not waste his time on the trifles of the day, but will seek the eternal Truth within. This is the serious business of life. All other things are secondary. Making a living is necessary, but it is not the purpose of life. If making a living is meant for life — then what is "life" meant for? Can there be anything which is more lasting in value and purpose than realizing the Self, the Reality, and transcending all pain and discontent? This moment, this concept, this Truth, is the most tremendous Truth of life.

What is this Truth?

The full moon is the reality, not the eclipse. Silence is the reality, not the sound that comes over it. Even as butter is present in milk, as silence is present in the midst of sound, which is only superimposed over it; even so — invisibly — the Truth is present in the midst of untruth. The Scriptures declare: *Brahma satyaṁ jaganmithyā jīvo brahmaiva nāparaḥ* (Brahman alone is the Reality, the world is an illusion; and the jīva — individual ego — is nothing other than Brahman). It means, the Truth alone prevails in all three periods of time, without hindrance and without change, always in its full. All plurality is only an appearance, like a rope mistaken for a snake. It is Brahman alone that appears as the jīva. It is One without a second. It is the Reality. It is the Truth.

Swamiji said:

> Reject all hairy men if you are looking for a bald-headed man. Reject everything of the mind when looking for the Self. You know what is decaying — try to know, what is God, the undecaying. You know what is changing — now turn your attention to the permanent, the changeless.
>
> When, exclusively, you want IT — and IT alone — IT happens.
>
> It is not an exaggeration.
>
> There is the authority of the Upaniṣads and the great mighty Masters who have reached the citadel of Truth and declared, *"Asti, asti, asti — there is, there is, there is!"*
>
> Have faith in yourself and in the goal, and put forth effort in what you believe in. As you go ahead, it *will* get confirmed.
>
> God never created you to fail.

Those who have drunk this honey, this bliss, have declared, "Sweetness, sweetness, sweetness, everything sweetness, sweetness beyond description; all is beauty, auspiciousness, bliss" — *Ānando brahmeti-vyajānāt* (He knew bliss as Brahman) — that peace, that bliss, that fullness, that Light of lights alone exists, and I am THAT.

Swamiji seated in the verandah of Tapovan Kutir, Uttarkashi, 1985

HOSPITAL

Chinmaya Mission Hospital is a modern 200-bed hospital in Bangalore, Karnataka. It has the latest equipment and a staff of highly skilled doctors and nurses. The hospital has a twenty-four hour emergency department, multiple operation theatres, an intensive care unit, and an outpatient department that offers cardiology, dentistry, ENT, gynecology, neonatology, obstetrics, ophthalmology, pediatrics, pathology, physiotherapy, and general medical services.

In order that the underprivileged patients are also able to avail of the hospitals facilities, considerable proportion of services are provided either free or at very affordable cost. The hospital also provides free immunization to many infants every week.

NURSING

Chinmaya Institute of Nursing offers a three-year diploma course in nursing which has been approved both by the All-India Nursing Council and the Karnataka State Nursing Council. Graduates follow-up their three-year course with a one-year paid internship at the Chinmaya Mission Hospital.

| CONTACT US |

Chinmaya Mission Hospital
Chinmaya Mission Hospital Road,
Indira Nagar, Bangalore 560 038, India
Tel : +91 (80) 25280 1505, 25280461, 25292062
Email: cmhblr@rediffmail.com

XX

Adi Sankara Nilayam and Footprints on the Mark

It could be said that, when confronted with a language such as Sanskrit, a language that is not commonly spoken or understood, or "domesticated" by the modern mind, we tend to contract emotionally and intellectually. Perhaps our fascination with avant-garde technology, and inventions (and weapons of mass destruction) will not tolerate the wisdom of our forefathers; our fear of each other and desire to dominate cannot grasp the beauty and supremacy of something old — and sometimes — intangible.

On November 1, 1992, during the inaugural speech of the newly built Eshwara Kripa building in Adi Sankara Nilayam, Veliyanad, in Kerala, Swamiji said:

> My attempt here is to build a study and research centre where both Eastern and Western scholars can come and stay, and thus bring out the relevance of the ancient terms and terminologies of our Sanskrit literature in the context of the modern way of life. This is the most appropriate place to do such research, because it is here that the great commentator of the Upaniṣads, Śrī Ādi Śaṅkara, was born 1,200 years ago.
>
> In India, many who are deeply learned in Sanskrit cannot communicate the wisdom enshrined in Sanskrit to the modern

world. And those who know English have hardly the entry into the depths of Sanskrit. We must therefore identify those scholars who know Sanskrit in depth, and also have the skill to communicate that wisdom in English. In the West, there are scholars who want to get initiated into various facets of Vedic lore. If we bring the Eastern and Western scholars together on one platform, we can vitalize modern education with the rejuvenating ideas of our ancient philosophy, and the fruits of this will percolate down to benefit the common man.

We have numerous disciplines of science in Sanskrit which the world is yet to know. Apart from the philosophy of our spiritual heritage — which to some extent I have succeeded in bringing out through the Jnana Yagnas over the last forty years — we have yet to explore the various knowledge systems in Sanskrit language in architecture, medicine, alchemy, astronomy, astrology, various systems of yoga, and so forth. By churning the knowledge contained in such ancient texts, the secrets can be brought out to save and serve humanity from the present ditch of pollution into which it has fallen, both externally and internally. The world will then be able to derive inspiration and guidance from the Indian heritage. Unfortunately, all our ancient text books are in Sanskrit. Therefore, the deep thoughts contained in them and the technical terms employed by our forefathers have to be pragmatically interpreted. Although it is a time-consuming and laborious task, we are hopeful to accomplish this.

Thus, Chinmaya International Foundation has been set up with a view to bridge the fully-developed, time-tested, trusted, ancient science of the East and the modern developing branches of science in the West. It is a meeting ground for Eastern and Western thinkers to open up new channels of world-saving thoughts.

Three years earlier, on April 24, 1989, "Chinmaya International Foundation" (CIF) had been registered as a Trust in Cochin with the explicit aim of establishing a center of excellence for the study, research, and dissemination of knowledge in the areas of Indian philosophy and culture, art and science, and business management (both modern and ancient). "Chinmaya International Foundation would be a bridge between East and West, past and present, science and spirituality, pundit and public," declared Swamiji.

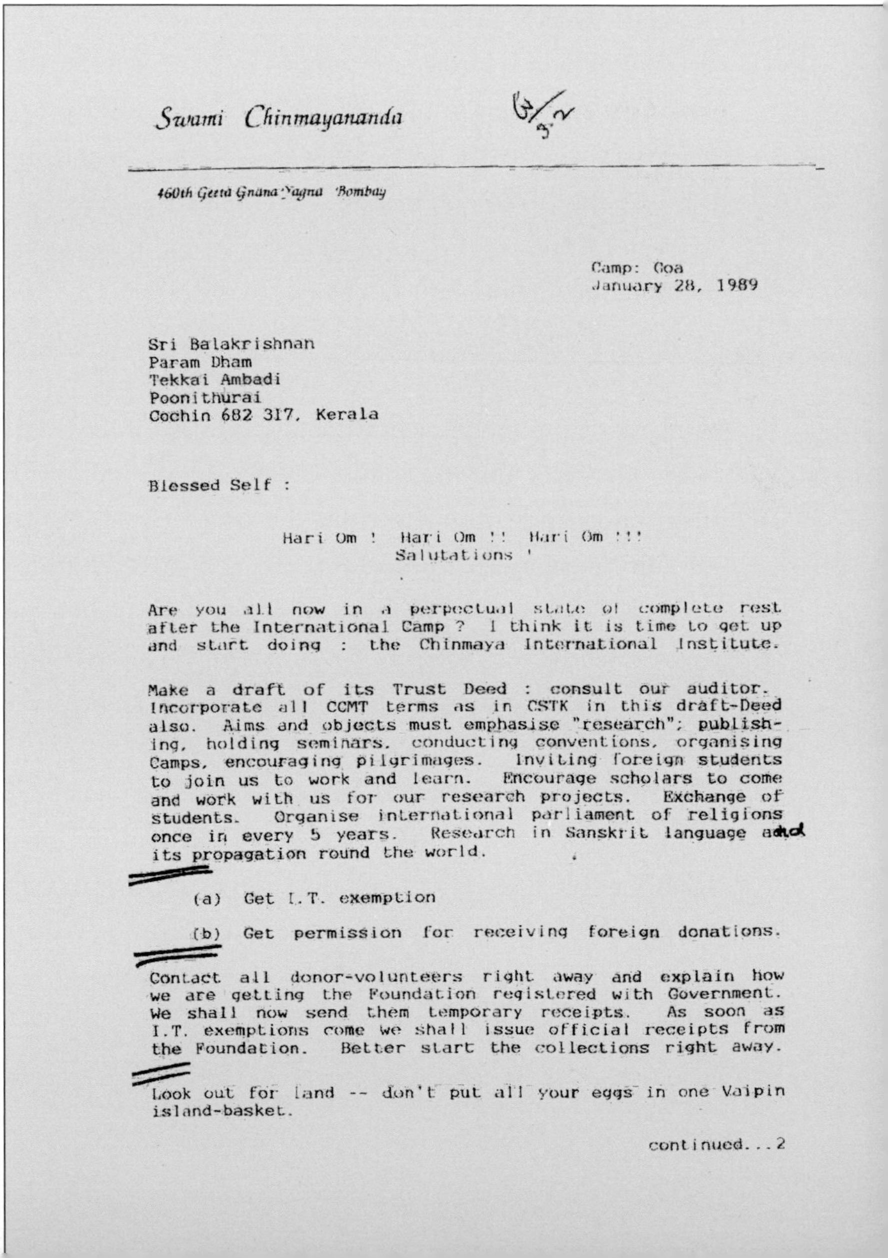

Swami Chinmayananda

460th Geeta Gnana Yagna Bombay

Camp: Goa
January 28, 1989

Sri Balakrishnan
Param Dham
Tekkai Ambadi
Poonithurai
Cochin 682 317, Kerala

Blessed Self :

Hari Om ! Hari Om !! Hari Om !!!
Salutations !

Are you all now in a perpectual state of complete rest after the International Camp ? I think it is time to get up and start doing : the Chinmaya International Institute.

Make a draft of its Trust Deed : consult our auditor. Incorporate all CCMT terms as in CSTK in this draft-Deed also. Aims and objects must emphasise "research"; publishing, holding seminars, conducting conventions, organising Camps, encouraging pilgrimages. Inviting foreign students to join us to work and learn. Encourage scholars to come and work with us for our research projects. Exchange of students. Organise international parliament of religions once in every 5 years. Research in Sanskrit language and its propagation round the world.

(a) Get I.T. exemption

(b) Get permission for receiving foreign donations.

Contact all donor-volunteers right away and explain how we are getting the Foundation registered with Government. We shall now send them temporary receipts. As soon as I.T. exemptions come we shall issue official receipts from the Foundation. Better start the collections right away.

Look out for land -- don't put all your eggs in one Vaipin island-basket.

continued...2

Every structure has a story to tell, a story that gives it shape, depth, and mission. This story unfolded, even as it was being constructed, starting at the beginning — with Swamiji's saṅkalpa of Chinmaya International Foundation — which found its way to Melpazhur Mana, to a village named Veliyanad in Kerala, where the great saint and revered Advaita Vedāntin, Ādi Śaṅkara, was born.

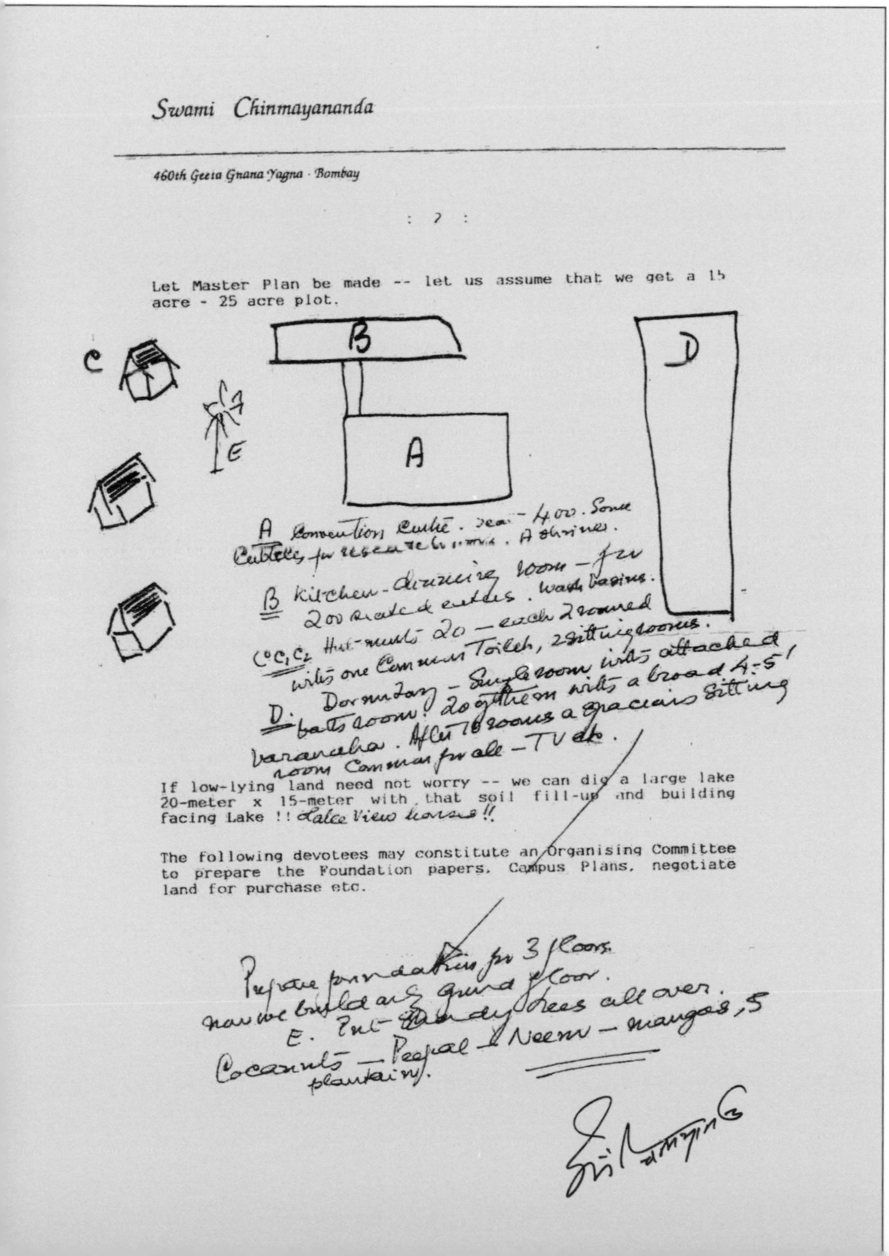

Swami Chinmayananda

460th Geeta Gnana Yagna · Bombay

: 2 :

Let Master Plan be made -- let us assume that we get a 15 acre - 25 acre plot.

B D C E A

A Convention Centre. Seat - 400. Some Cubicles for research [illegible]. A shrine.

B Kitchen - dining room - for 200 seated [illegible]. Wash basins.

C, C1, C2 Hut-ments 20 - each 2 roomed with one common Toilet, 2 sitting rooms.

D. Dormitory - Single room with attached bath room! 20 of them with a broad 4-5' varandha. After 10 rooms a spacious sitting room common for all - TV etc.

If low-lying land need not worry -- we can dig a large lake 20-meter x 15-meter with that soil fill-up and building facing Lake !! Lake View house!!

The following devotees may constitute an Organising Committee to prepare the Foundation papers, Campus Plans, negotiate land for purchase etc.

Prepare foundations for 3 floors. [illegible] we build only ground floor.

E. Plant [illegible] trees all over. Coconuts - Peepal - Neem - mangoes, plantain.

[Signature]

Mana is the word used in traditional Kerala to refer to the house of a person of the brāhmaṇa cast (the cast of scholars, teachers, and priests); and Melpazhur is the "house name" of Ādi Śaṅkara's mother, Āryambā. "In Kerala, we are all maternal, not paternal. So each individual, when he is born in a family, belongs to the mother's family and not to the father's family," related Swamiji. "So Ādi Śaṅkara belonged to Melpazhur Mana. Whereas, Kaladi is the place where his father was — the father was very old when Śaṅkara was born. So the community whispers began to say, how can this old man beget a child? In those days, prejudices were terrible, and they started ill-treating the couple. Therefore, the father (who had full faith in his vision of the Lord, who had said to him, 'I am coming') said to his wife, Āryambā, 'You go and peacefully deliver the baby in your mother's house.' This is the tradition in India, to deliver the child at one's maternal home. So she came to Melpazhur Mana, and there is a particular room, where she delivered the baby Śaṅkara. Here, an eternal lamp is kept, which is always burning."

After the registration of the Trust, Swamiji appointed three trustees, A. Balakrishnan, C. M. K. Marar, and K. K. Rajan, to look for a suitable plot of land for the project. Forty sites were seen and rejected; then, A. Balakishnan wrote to Swamiji mentioning the details of an eight-acre plot, Melpazhur Mana. He specifically mentioned that its present owner, Śaṅkaran Nambūtiri, was unable to afford the upkeep of the property:

> Times are tough; they are unable to maintain this place. The Shringeri Math paid an advance to buy this place, but for some reason the deal did not go through, nor did they ask for their advance back. Others have expressed some interest, but they have been reluctant to buy this place since it has a Devi Nagayakshi temple and many sarpa kāvus (smaller altars dedicated to the snake deities) which require

special and traditional attention. Not caring for them as per tradition is also damaging so they say.

A month later, Swamiji came to see the property, and immediately directed that it be acquired. He also instructed the trustees, "Don't bargain on the price. Whatever be the Nambūdirī's asking price, you pay him one rupee extra ..." In February 1990, Chinmaya Mission bought the property and named it "Adi Sankara Nilayam." Henceforward, it would be a place of pilgrimage, and the home of Chinmaya International Foundation.

Meanwhile, Dr. Krishnan, an ayurvedic specialist, had spent many hours digging into the property's antecedents, and on the eve of the property transfer, he informed Swamiji, "It appears that Śaṅkaran Nambūtiri's grandfather and your grandfather were brothers!" This stunning revelation along with the fact that this was the birthplace of Ādi Śaṅkara made Swamiji's next statement all the more overwhelming. "It's my property that has come back to me!" said Swamiji.

A DREAM AND A PROMISE

One day in 1992, Fr. Bhikshu Elinjamattom of the Satchidananda Mission of Assisi in Italy was driving over a bridge in Rome. In the distance, he saw a man standing on the curb, looking down at the river flowing under the bridge. Even from that distance Fr. Elinjamattom sensed an urgency to stop and ask after this man who appeared to be clad in orange robes.

Since Fr. Elinjamattom was of Indian origin, the orange cloth was familiar to him. But when he stopped his car, got down, and started walking toward the man, his feeling of familiarity was confirmed.

▶

"Are you Swami Chinmayananda?" he asked the man.

"Yes!" came the answer.

Swamiji and Fr. Elinjamattom spoke for a good while. Swamiji mentioned his new project, Chinmaya International Foundation, in the birthplace of Ādi Śaṅkara, in Kerala ...

"Kerala! That is where I was born!" exclaimed Fr. Elinjamattom animatedly.

"Then you must visit us!" invited Swamiji. Fr. Elinjamatton promised he would.

Months passed. In August 1993, Fr. Elinjamattom was watching the news on Italian T.V., where it was announced that India's revered spiritual teacher, Swami Chinmayananda, had attained mahāsamādhi. He made up his mind to go to Chinmaya International Foundation.

Unknowingly, he arrived at Kaladi. But what's meant to be will always find a way, and somehow, Fr. Elinjamattom was led to A. Balakrishnan (Trustee, CIF), who guided him to Adi Sankara Nilayam. When Fr. Elinjamattom reached his destination, he declared: "I want to do something for CIF, as I had promised Swamiji on the bridge ..."

Fr. Elinjamattom kept his word. The residential block where the scholars live today — called the Scholars Block — is sponsored by him.

Then, in 2008, his disciple, Fr. Massimo de Orlando, arrived in Adi Sankara Nilayam with a group from Italy. He wanted a camp on *Vivekacūḍāmaṇi* for his team! He himself gave talks on *Vivekacūḍāmaṇi* in Italian, and chanted the Sanskrit verses with a clarity, precision, and diction seldom heard even amongst Indians. Swami Advayananda gave discourses on Advaita-vedānta along with Swamini Niranjanananda, whilst Fr. Massimo translated them into Italian for the participants.

Before leaving, the group offered to sponsor CIF's entire Easy Sanskrit Online Course which was in the process of being set up at the time.

The entire cost of the website, and converting the Easy Sanskrit kit into an online course format, and making it fully functional was an offering of love from Fr. Massimo's team and the Satchidananda Mission of Assisi.

Amazingly, sixteen years ago, two great men had met by chance, on the middle of a busy street, on top of a bridge, in the city of Rome — one mentioned his dream; the other kept his promise.

Swamiji was very clear in his outline for CIF. He identified the following key areas:

> First, we must turn Adi Sankara Nilayam into a thriving center for research in Sanskrit, philosophy, and the ancient Indian Scriptures. Serious students will come here. They will be supplied books, a library, and other research materials. They can stay here. We will provide all comforts to do research. There are very many great ācāryas and paṇḍitas in this country who are not finding any patronage to do research. So they will also be coming here. The fruits of their research work will be entirely ours. CIF will have the rights to their work and will publish them and distribute the same through our Mission Centers and authorized agencies. Universities may recognize them and use them as prescribed texts to be taught to the coming generations.
>
> Second, CIF must spread the knowledge of Sanskrit in India and throughout the world. I hope to be able to start a Shankara Sanskrit University, so that all the Chinmaya Mission Centers, that are working with or teaching Sanskrit, will be affiliated. This will be a big university spread all over the country. As a beginning, we have already started a postal Sanskrit Lesson Course.
>
> Third, we must create a bridge between Indian and Western philosophers and thinkers. The more we study the modern theories

> that are coming out in cosmology, the more we learn to appreciate the vision of our ṛṣis. But these associations between the old theory or scriptural literature and the most modern technological and astronomical discoveries in the Western world are not brought together. If they are brought together, the younger generation will jump at it and feel proud that our scriptures, as understood till now, are not a cock-and-bull story; that it is not without rhyme and reason, but based upon high mathematical analysis and supreme understanding of the cosmos and its working; that enormous amount of science lies behind those simple words that they speak! This synchronization is to be brought about, which can be done only by inviting and bringing the western scholars and thinkers.
>
> Fourth, during school-college vacation time, CIF will be used for conducting teacher's training courses — training in spiritual values. We will also use this place to impart training to administrators, managers, and industrialists — they can come to CIF for a month or two, and we can give them (a course on) values!

When asked whether it was time to banish Western values and focus only on the Indian, Swamiji replied:

> No! Western values will have to live, because we have to live in the Western world. Our country, if it is to become a really great nation, has to stand in line with the technological development, which is Western. But India has got its own values, that cultural contact which we should not leave. That is why, despite all development in Japan, they have not left their culture. In the same way, we must hold onto our culture; we have a lot to teach others.

Over the years, Chinmaya International Foundation has grown swiftly and considerably. It has hosted a variety of programs, including academic seminars and workshops for students, teachers, and managers. But most noteworthy amongst its achievements is the Postal and E-Vedānta (online) and Sanskrit Courses (Foundation and Advanced) which it offers to students all over the world. The Sanskrit Online Course is the only such available course in the world where the study, as well as the checking of assignments, is done completely online. The E-Vedānta (or Home Study Course) is on top of the Google search list.

Another area of distinction is the development of "Anusaaraka," an English to Hindi translation (and language accessing) software with insights from Sanskrit grammar. This project is classified as a Natural Language Processing (NLP) tool, which is a subset in the field of Artificial Intelligence.

And, CIF has come out with a host of research publications — such as *Īśvara Darśanam, Śrī Rāma Jātakam, Gītāñjali, Holy Gītā Ready Reference, Śrīrāmakṛṣṇa-caritam, Śrīpadmapāda-caritam, Sūkti Sudhā, Laghukarṇāmṛtam,* and many more. These have received accolades from scholars and the general public. CIF welcomes research scholars to its elegantly furnished library which houses over 15,000 rare books and 30 journal subscriptions. In addition, ancient manuscripts (nearly 400 year-old, palm-leaf manuscripts and 2,000 digital manuscripts) can be seen being preserved and cured through the process of manuscriptology.

CIF is affiliated to the Rashtriya Sanskrit Sansthan, New Delhi, as a Shodha Sansthan (Center for Excellence in Sanskrit Research). It is also recognized as a research center by Kerala's Mahatma Gandhi University and as a Centre for Sanskrit Research and Indology by Indira Gandhi National Open University (the world's largest Open University) in New Delhi. In collaboration with IGNOU, CIF offers courses in Sanskrit and Advaita-vedānta.

Swamiji's vision to establish a Sanskrit University is — at present — a work in progress. It is being envisaged over the next ten years.

It is said that the saṅkalpa śakti of a mahātmā must culminate in fulfillment. He who is without ego, his identification is with the total mind-intellect (Īśvara). Thus, whatever is born of his resolve, will, and determination manifests itself as a blessing for the world. And, on that historic day in November 1989, when Swamiji went to Melpazhur Mana, his saṅkalpa had found its mark in the birthplace of Jagad-Guru Śrī Ādi Śaṅkara. K. K. Rajan, who accompanied Swamiji, describes the events of that day:

> Swamiji had been very unwell with burning fever of 104 degrees. He was to attend a function at Chinmaya Vidyalaya Ernakulam, which he said that he might not be able to attend, but he sent a message that he would still come to see Melpazhur Mana. I was extremely nervous, since the property was crumbling, broken down — it had not been maintained at all since the owners had been unable to afford the cost — there were overgrown bushes and the ground was laden with thorns, bushes, and scorpions. How would Swamiji deal with this, given his high fever?
>
> At 4:45 P.M., we arrived at Melpazhur Mana. Balakrishnan and Marar had already arrived with Śaṅkaran Nambūtiri, the owner of the property. Swamiji began to walk with distinct discomfort over the property. I rushed to his side and tried to push away the thorns with my hands. Then, I tried to stop Swamiji from proceeding further, suggesting he view the land from afar. But, Swamiji was firm. He said:
>
> "Let my footprints be here..."

Right:
Swamiji in Adi Sankara Nilayam, Veliyanad, 1990
Center:
Scorpions galore in Adi Sankara Nilayam, Veliyanad, 1990
Below:
Swamiji walks around Adi Sankara Nilayam, February 1990

Above left:
Swamiji inspects the Kṛṣṇa Temple in Adi Sankara Nilayam, (with A. Balakrishnan, K. K. Rajan, Dr. C. M. Rajan, Isabel Taylor, Bina Sutarwala, and Br. Vara Chaitanya, Veliyanad, February 1990
Above right:
Sacred birthroom of Ādi Śaṅkara where an eternal lamp is lit, Adi Sankara Nilayam, Veliyanad

Center:
Swamiji during the rounds of Adi Sankara Nilayam (with Ashlesha Madhok, Isabel Taylor, Dr. C. M. Rajan, Uma Bhatnagar, K. K. Rajan, and A. Balakrishnan) , Veliyanad, February 1990
Below:
Swamiji inside the Illom (walking towards the room where Ādi Śaṅkara was born), Adi Sankara Nilayam, Velyanad, 1990

Above:
Illom, Adi Sankara Nilayam, Veliyanand
Right:
Swamiji giving instructions, Adi Sankara Nilayam, Veliyanad, February 1990
Below:
The inaugural pūjās of Chinmaya International Foundation, Adi Sankara Nilayam, Veliyanad, February 1990

Clockwise from above:
Swamiji inaugurates Chinmaya International Foundation, Adi Sankara Nilayam, Veliyanad, 1990
Swamiji lights the lamp to mark the opening of Chinmaya International Foundation, Adi Sankara Nilayam, February 1990
Swamiji launching the "Chant Geeta Land Washington" Competition, Coimbatore, 1991
During the inaugural pūjā of Chinmaya International Foundation, Veliyanad, 1990

Portrait of Swamiji, Sarveshwara temple, Tamraipakkam, 1990

CIF CIF

Chinmaya International Foundation (CIF) is a research center for advanced study in Sanskrit and Indology. It is a cross-cultural forum for the exchange of knowledge. Swami Chinmayananda visualized CIF as a bridge between the East and West, past and present, science and spirituality, pundit and public.

CIF is located in the birthplace of Ādi Śaṅkara in Veliyanad, Kerala, thirty kilometers from the city of Ernakulam. Originally known as the Melpazhur Mana, it was named Adi Sankara Nilayam by Swami Chinmayananda, since this is the home of Āryāmbā, the mother of Ādi Śaṅkara.

CIF CIF

CIF is engaged in multifarious academic projects, such as:

- A critical edition of the *Brahma-sūtra with Śāṅkara-bhāṣya*, English translation, and commentary.
- *Sūkti-sudhā*, a compendium of proverbs from Sanskrit literature.
- *Vāda-kośa*, a compendium of ancient Indian philosophical tenets.
- Anusaaraka, a language accessing software for translation from English to Hindi with insights from Sanskrit grammar.
- Sanskrit Home Course for beginners and advanced students.
- Postal and Online Vedānta Course (Foundation and Advanced Courses).
- The collection, preservation, digitalization, and publication of rare palm-leaf manuscripts and other ancient documents.
- Research publications, such as *Holy Gītā Ready Reference, Īśvara Darśanam Śrī-Rāma-jātakam* and *Gītāñjalī*, which have received accolades from scholars and the general public.

CIF also regularly organizes camps, workshops, and programs on various aspects of Indian Philosophy, Sanskrit literature, and Indian culture, heritage, and civilization.

| CONTACT US |

Chinmaya International Foundation
Adi Sankara Nilayam, Veliyanad,
Ernakulam District 682 319, Kerala, India
Tel: +91 (484) 2747 307, 2747 104
Email: office@chinfo.org
Website: www.chinfo.org

XXI

Life to Legacy

On life's goal, Swamiji once said, "When we are born, we cry, and our relations and neighbors stand around and smile. Let us order our lives in such a way that, when we leave this world, we shall smile with satisfaction and let others be left crying at the departure of such a noble one."

Even though devotees knew this day would come at some point, it was with no small amount of dread that they actually faced the news of Swamiji's critical heart condition. On July 26, 1993, Swamiji arrived in San Diego, California. He had stopped at Venkat and Nandini Rangan's home for one day, before continuing to Los Angeles, where he was to conduct a camp (July 27–August 2). But after a short rest in the afternoon, Swamiji had trouble breathing. A doctor was called, and he was taken to Scripps Memorial Hospital in La Jolla where cardio test results showed that two arteries were completely blocked, and a third one was 90% blocked. From that night onwards, Swamiji was heavily sedated.

After consultation with a panel of doctors, Swamiji was shifted to Sharp Memorial Hospital on July 29 for emergency bypass surgery. Although a five-bypass surgery was completed the same evening, his condition continued to be critical and his heart and lungs were put on a life-support system.

Many devotees had flown in from all parts of the U.S.A. They had been given the Golden Room in the hospital, where they kept a continuous chant of the *Mahā-mṛtyuñjaya* japa. On August 1, Swami Chidananda of Divine Life Society arrived; and after spending some time by Swamiji's bedside, he met with devotees outside and told them that he had invoked both Swami Tapovanam and Swami Sivananda on either side of Swamiji's bed. The devotees asked his advice whether to keep Swamiji on the life-support system or allow it to be switched off. "Let destiny take its own time. Wait one more day. By the time we (indicating to himself and the person accompanying him) reach Washington, it will stop."

The hour came. On August 3, 1993, at 5:45 P.M., Swamiji attained mahāsamādhi in San Diego, California.

Tears and tributes poured in from the far corners of the globe. It caused not only India, but the world to stop, to stand still long enough for a period of self-examination, and to salute the glorious life of a remarkable saint. His life was a chronicle that had changed history forever. Gone were the days when a person had to leave everything and go to the mountains in search of a Guru and Truth. The common person could now aspire for a divine life in the hustle and bustle of a cosmopolitan city. The teachings of the scriptures now came directly to him. Such was the compassion and vision of this great teacher, Swami Chinmayananda.

As devotees gathered to bid Swamiji farewell, they remembered his last days. Viji Sundaram of Boston recalls:

> As I sat before Swamiji's body, I cried, too, even though I knew he was still with us — that he had only vacated, as he would have

put it — that "unholy mass of calcium, carbon, and phosphorous."

Characteristically, Swamiji never let on about his health in those last few days, sometimes even giving the impression that he was still running on all four cylinders. After bhikṣā at the camp in Piercy (July 10–17, 1993) he opted to toss fruits to those around him, instead of handing them over. After the pāda-pūjā, the hands that pitched the one dollar coins and flowers to the audience several yards away, surely could not have belonged to someone with an ailing heart. And at the banquet on the penultimate day of that camp, as Edwin Lopez belted out foot-trapping Spanish music on his guitar, Swamiji's shoulders bogeyed to the music, as he smiled and cheered him on. Swamiji sure fooled us all.

Not completely, though. There were remarks he made that hinted at things to come. On the last day of the Piercy camp, for example, Swamiji announced that his next Northern California camp would be in San Jose next year, but added with a small pause and a smile, "That is, if I come!"

A week before, during the camp in Washington D.C. (July 19–25), Swamiji told David Taylor, "The Lord has been calling me, but all these people won't let me go." Another devotee, Asha Kamdar of Mumbai, recalls that on June 8, 1993, Swamiji said to her with reference to his health, "Two months more, then I'll get an extension."

On June 7, 1993, When Padmini Nambiar of Delhi last met Swamiji at Delhi airport, he seemed very weak:

"Where is he?" asked Swamiji, indicating to her husband.

"You don't speak too much!" cautioned Padmini.

Swamiji asked her to lean toward him. He then whispered in her ear, "Don't forget. *I will always speak to you.*"

AND THE OSCAR GOES TO ...

During the last camp at Washington D.C., Swamiji had asked me to come and cook for him, and chant. The house where he was staying had separate taps for cold and hot water. So every time Swamiji would wash his hands after a meal, I would go before him, mix the cold and hot water in a jug and pour it on his hands as he washed them.

On one of the days, after he had finished washing them, he looked at both sides of his hand and commented, "Yes, nicely frozen," (meaning the water was cold!). I apologized to Swamiji.

After his next meal, I ran beforehand to make sure I had got the temperature right. When Swamiji walked in, he must have noticed my nervousness. As I started to pour the water, he jumped back screaming. I was horrified. *If the water is that hot, I deserve to suffer, too,* I thought. I poured the entire jug on myself. Then I looked up at Swamiji. He had a glint of merriment in his eye.

"I got you! Didn't I?"

I was quite wet, and no mood to enjoy the joke. "Swamiji, you are such an actor! If only you had gone for acting, you would have won an Oscar!" I said.

Swamiji looked at me straight, and said, "Who said I am not an actor?"

Sharada Kumar
Acharya, Chinmaya Mission Ann Arbor

Swamiji's body was embalmed in a lotus position. Accompanied by sixteen devotees, including Swami Tejomayananda, he was then carefully placed on a British Airways flight back to India. On August 7,

1993, at 10:25 A.M., local time, the aircraft touched down at New Delhi's Indira Gandhi International Airport.

At midday, his casket arrived, bedecked with flowers, at the Chinmaya Centre of World Understanding in Lodi Road, New Delhi. Thousands of people — devotees, Indian political leaders, and members of the general public — lined up throughout the day amidst police security to pay their homage to Him.

Television bulletins covered the public darśan. The news of Swamiji's mahāsamādhi had already been splashed across all national, and many international, newspapers. As evening descended, it was time for his mortal remains to be taken to Sidhbari, to the place he loved the most.

Dr. N. Krishnaswami of Ooty remembers an incident from the early 1980s, when Sidhbari ashram was being built. Swamiji was standing in front of Swami Tapovanam's life-size photo in the Satsang Hall. Dr. Krishnaswami walked up behind Swamiji, and quietly said to him, "Tapovan Maharaj must be very happy that his prime disciple has at last returned to the Himalayas as wished by him."

"I believe so," said Swamiji. "This will be my final abode."

Meanwhile, in Sidhbari, another few thousand devotees had gathered over the past three days from all parts of the world. At approximately 3:00 P.M., the convoy of cars carrying Swamiji could faintly be seen amidst continuous rain in the valley. Slowly, the flower-decorated car entered the Sidhbari ashram, passed by the forty-foot idol of Lord Hanumān, and, as it came to a halt, it was besieged by devotees.

His body was seated in the Kamala Hall, and as he looked upon his devotees from the stage, they sang bhajans. At dawn, the Chinmaya Aṣṭottaranāmāvhaliḥ — the 108 names of Swamiji were chanted;

and as Swami Tejomayananda led the chant, his voice broke down. Swamiji was then carried to the rose garden behind his kuṭiyā. This had been his favored resting place, overlooking the Dhauladhar Mountains; and in his last years, Swamiji had often sat in the lawn surrounded by devotees amidst the multi-colored roses. Keeping this in mind, a Samadhi Sthal had been prepared here in the previous three days.

The paṇḍita chanted Vedic prayers, and the senior Swamis of Chinmaya Mission — with Swami Purushottamananda, the senior-most disciple, leading — performed Swamiji's last rites. In the background, an unbroken repetition of *Om Namaḥ Śivāya* was chanted by the devotees. In this holiest of holy environments, with the minds of all his devotees attuned towards Him, with the serene and beautiful Himalayas all around, Swami Chinmayananda was laid to rest.

Earlier, in April 1993, during a train journey to Surat, Anjali Singh had wanted a record of certain incidents in Swamiji's life. She requested him for a question-answer session. She suggested his answers be published in a book, similar to *On Wings and Wheels: A Dialogue on Moral Conflict.* However, this time, he could show how the philosophy he had taught, had been lived by him, with qualities like fearlessness, forbearance, and so forth.

"If Swamiji does not tell us, certain details of his life would be lost to posterity," said Anjali Singh.

Swamiji agreed to answer questions, but on a different topic. He was not at all inclined to give autobiographical details. He said,

"There is enough material available for those who want to do research on it. In any case, I will be living ... I will be living ..."

Anjali Singh found the repetition of the last sentence to be very perplexing. She says:

> I did not understand what Swamiji was trying to say, so I waited; but he was not forthcoming. I assumed that he simply intended to stay on with us for a while and this was an assurance. One does not try to understand anything beyond the physical level, and I realize now that his statement conveyed something deeper.
>
> Swamiji must have repeated a few thousand times that he is not the body, and it is perhaps only after his mahāsamādhi that many of us have tried to feel his true Being. Perhaps no one felt the need to do so earlier — why make the visible unnecessarily invisible!
>
> I have found, after speaking to a lot of close devotees, that His presence and active guidance is being felt by many. This might be what he meant when he said, "I will be living ... I will be living ..." The repetition must have meant *continuous* living in the hearts of all devotees — providing guidance, strength, quietude, solace, and understanding in a silent way. The Guru that had manifested "outside" has gone back to the Guru "within" from where he came. "I will be living ... I will be living ..." is a statement of fact!

In fact, after his first ventricular failure in 1989, Swamiji made a solemn promise to devotees:

"I promise I will never leave you. Remember that!"

Two years later, after more ventricular failures, he added to this:

"If I leave you, where is 'you'? I am the very Existence, Sat. The further I go, the nearer shall I be for each one of you. This is a promise."

On August 3, 1994, a year after Swamiji's mahāsamādhi, Swami Chidananda of Divine Life Society came to Sidhbari for his Puṇya-tithi-ārādhanā. There must have been a special bond between these two mahātmās, for not only was Swami Chidananda present at Swamiji's mahāsamādhi, but he was also present for his first anniversary.

As soon as Swami Chidananda entered the ashram, he went to Swamiji's Samadhi Sthal, where he prostrated, prayed, and sang a bhajan. He then proceeded to do a parikramā (circumambulation) of the samādhi. Three-fourths of his way around, he paused briefly, then said to all the devotees present:

"A bit of Swami Chinmayananda is in each and every one of you, without exception."

This statement holds a wealth of meaning. Emotionally and sentimentally, Swamiji is in the hearts of those who love him. His presence is felt to be with those who attune their minds to Him. But the fascinating import of this statement is that it is again, a statement of fact and, confirmed by our scriptures.

Ādi Śaṅkara, in his composition *Tattva Bodhaḥ,* says something special on the āgāmi-karma of a Jīvanmukta. Āgāmi-karma, in the context of the Jīvanmukta, is the result of actions that have been performed by him in his present birth, after his Liberation. Since the Jīvanmukta has no births wherein he will get to experience the results of his actions, the question can be raised: What happens to these āgāmi-karmas performed by a Jīvanmukta?

Ādi Śaṅkara states:

> To those who praise, serve, and worship the Jīvanmukta go the results of the meritorious actions (meritorious āgāmi-karma) done

> by the Jīvanmukta. To those who criticize, hate, or cause pain to the Jīvanmukta go the results of all the unpraiseworthy and sinful actions (negative āgāmi-karma) done by the Jīvanmukta.

And, indeed, the meritorious actions done by Swamiji were enormous, beyond comprehension and praise. He had carved the spiritual destiny of millions of seekers all over the world, awakening realms of peace, joy, and happiness thought unlikely and impractical before his time. Swami Chinmayananda had left his mortal frame, but his vision — *his legacy* — had only just begun.

More significantly, his legacy endures — for those who love and revere him — in the days to come, when the overpowering might of his vision unfolds like a blissful calm, when the growing joy overflows in the midst of a generation unborn ... then, remember this hour, and think ... *It is true! A bit of Swami Chinmayananda* ***is*** *in each and every one of us, without exception.*

I PROMISE

In 1992, while looking at the sarso (mustard) fields around Sidhbari, Swamiji remarked:

> It is all a delusion.
> When the sarso was born,
> I was there.
> When the sarso became green,
> I was there.
> When the sarso flowered,
> I was there.
> Sarsos come and sarsos go,
> But I remain always.

Clockwise from above:
Swamiji while recuperating in Sidhbari, January 1992
Swamiji visits Swaṃi Tejomayananda's mother, Parvati Kaitwade, who was ill (Swamiji assured her that her son will return to India from the U.S.A. in August that year), Indore, March 1993
Swamiji visits "Paramdham", Ahmedabad Chinmaya Mission (greeted by Swamini Vimalananda, Arvindbhai Mehta and others) February 24, 1993
Swamiji on Janmāṣṭamī Day, Vivekacūḍāmaṇi Camp, August 1992

Clockwise from above:
Swamiji recuperating in Sidhbari, December 1991
Swamiji in mahāsamādhi state,
Delhi, August 7 1993
The procession of cars with cortege from Delhi to Sidhbari (nearing Sidbhari ashram), August 8, 1993
The procession of cars with cortege from Delhi to Sidhbari (nearing Sidbhari ashram), August 8 1993
Swamiji in mahāsamādhi state,
Delhi, August 7 1993
▶ **Below left:**
Ārati before bhū-samādhi performed by Swami Puroshottamananda, Sidhbari, August 9, 1993
Below right:
Swami Puroshottamananda and Swami Tejomayananda with shaven heads offer ārati, Sidhbari, August 10, 1993

Clockwise from above:
Assembled devotees during Swamiji's bhū- samādhi, Sidhbari, August 9, 1993
Assembled devotees during Swamiji's bhū- samādhi, Sidhbari, August 9, 1993
Army personnel come to pay homage from Yol Cantonment, Sidhbari, August 9, 1993
Swamiji being lowered into his final resting place by swamis and brahmacharis of Chinmaya Mission, Sidhbari, August 9, 1993
Assembled devotees during abhiṣekam, Sidhbari, August 9, 1993

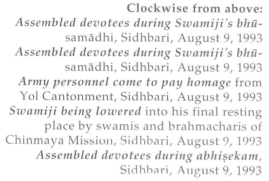

Clockwise from above:
Portrait of Swamiji, Sidhbari, January 1992
Swami Chidananda (President of Divine Life Society) pays homage at Swamiji's samādhi, Sidhbari, August 2, 1994
The Samadhi Sthala, Sidhbari, 1995
The Samadhi Sthala, in Kerala style, under construction, Sidhbari
Devotees in Sidhbari at Swamiji's samādhi on the first Puṇya-tithi-ārādhanā, August 2, 1994

Clockwise from above:
Swamiji in Sarveshwara temple during pūjā, Tamraipakkam, February 1990
The Dalai Lama pays homage to Swamiji during the International Spiritual Camp, Sidhbari, April 1998
The Samadhi Sthala, Sidhbari, 1995
Swami Purushottamananda performs abhiṣekam on the first Puṇya-tithi-ārādhanā in the presence of Swami Chidananda (President of Divine Life Society), Sidhbari, August 3, 1994
Assembled devotees for the first Puṇya-tithi-ārādhanā of Swamiji, Sidhbari, August 3, 1994

From above:
After the foundation laying stone of Chinmaya Centre of World Understanding, Delhi (left to right: Swami Brahmananda, Swami Purushottamananda, Swami Jyotirmayananda, Swami Tejomayananda, Swami Nityananda, Swamini Sharadapriyananda, Br. Atma Chaitanya, Swami Subhodhananda, Br. Manav Chaitanya, Br. Siddha Chaitanya), Delhi, 1994
Sannyāsa dīkṣā given on Śivarātrī day (Swami Shantananda front row left) Sidhbari, March 3, 1992
Below:
Group photo of swamis and brahmacharis of Chinmaya Mission on the Golden Jubilee Year celebration of Chinmaya Movement, December 31, 2001

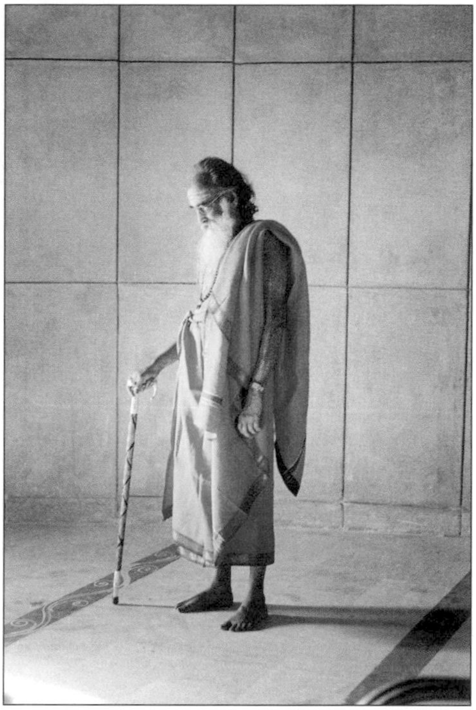

Above left:
Swami Tejomayananda performs padukā-pūjā on Divālī day, 1995
Above center:
Sacred feet of Swamiji

Above:
Swamiji inspecting the hall, Tamaraipakkam, February 1990
Below:
Group photo of Chinmaya Mission Acharyas, Sidhbari, March 1996

XXII

'Tis to Glory We Steer

A week after Swamiji's ṣoḍaśi, the religious ceremony conducted on the 16th day after the passing away of the mahātmā, a young and unassuming disciple, Swami Tejomayananda, was unanimously elected as the next head of Chinmaya Mission worldwide. In one of his first statements to devotees of Chinmaya Mission, he said:

> So far you have seen the work that Pujya Gurudev did. Now, you will see the work that his *name* will accomplish.

After his mahāsamādhi, Pujya Swami Chinmayanandaji began to be referred to as "Gurudev." This was done primarily out of respect, but it also served a very practical purpose. Chinmaya Mission now had over 100 swamis, who were actively spreading the message of Vedānta, and all of whom were called "Swamiji" — it was only sagacious to identify *the* foremost "Swamiji" by a distinct name — Pujya Gurudev. Using the same logic, Swami Tejomayananda was also named — Guruji.

Quite naturally, it took a while for many devotees to come to terms with Gurudev's physical absence. But, Guruji was very clear about his position from the start. A reporter in Kerala asked him in 1993:

"How does it feel to be in Gurudev's shoes?"

"I am not in His shoes, but at His feet."

"Are you fit to be at the helm?" asked another.

"If I am not fit, then He who has put me there, will see to it that I am made fit."

In an incident in Jakarta, a girl who was extremely attached to Gurudev did not like the attention that devotees were giving to Guruji when he came to Jakarta in Gurudev's place. She felt that everyone was behaving as if they had forgotten Gurudev! Guruji explained to her:

> Devotees are giving me attention because I am doing Pujya Gurudev's work. When you love Gurudev, you would want his work to continue.

In the last twenty-five years, Chinmaya Mission has grown astronomically, worldwide. All projects visualized and undertaken by Gurudev were completed, consolidated, and expanded. Guruji spent the first decade leaving no stone unturned in fulfilling each and every saṅkalpa made by Gurudev.

Yet, it is the collective force of the devotees of Gurudev that continues to amaze. They form the strength and spiritual glory of the Master. Many have sky-rocketed in their spiritual trajectory, inspiring greater and greater numbers through their dedication and vision. Consequently, when Guruji envisioned the "Chinmaya Vibhooti" project a decade later, it came as no surprise.

Spanning seventy acres of land and surrounded by the Sahyadri Hills in the serene and pictorial village of Kolwan (one hour from Pune and three hours by car from Mumbai), Chinmaya Vibhooti, meaning "the glory of Chinmaya," is a majestic tribute to Pujya Gurudev Swami Chinmayananda. This institute is the Vision Center of Chinmaya Mission. Its vast resources are specifically aimed towards empowerment and training of Chinmaya Mission workers so they may effectively serve society. In particular, Chinmaya Vibhooti is designed to deal with a large workforce, to support the increasing demand by Mission centers throughout the world for sevakas and sevikās to conduct programs in their communities. Chinmaya Vibhooti is often referred to as the VIP Center of Chinmaya Mission — Vision, Inspiration, Practice!

Everything in Chinmaya Vibhooti is on a grand scale. It has not one, but two temples: the Maruti Mandir at its entrance, and the Pranava Ganesha Mandir on a hilltop at the far end overlooking the entire site. A main road travels the entire length of the complex, and golf carts (named " pavana vāhanas") pick and drop-off passengers at various stops — at either one of the multiple auditoriums, lecture halls, classrooms, and residential blocks, or the 800-seat cafeteria-style dining hall with five food stations; the expansive Chinmaya Vani Bookshop spread over 4,000 square feet, or the expansive administrative offices.

The main Sudharma auditorium is fully air-conditioned and seats 1,008 people. It is the largest of its kind in the Pune area. When Pandit Jasraj came to Chinmaya Vibhooti to inaugurate Chinmaya Naada Bindu, he remarked in his inaugural address, "We don't find such large auditoriums in the city as Chinmaya Mission has here in Kolwan. What's even more astonishing is that, despite being in a remote village, it is filled to capacity!"

One of the most glorious aspects of Chinmaya Vibhooti is "Chinmaya Jeevan Darshan" (CJD). Covering 17,000 square feet,

CJD is the largest permanent exhibition on the life and teachings of Swami Chinmayananda. The depiction is done through various means, including sixteen wall frescos, a prayer dome, and modern interactive technology. But the central attraction is a lifelike wax statue of Gurudev made by Jeni Fairey, a former employee of Madame Tussauds Museum in London. This altar never fails to evoke emotion, making the remark by Swami Swaroopananda all the more potent: "We come to Chinmaya Vibhooti to *become* His Vibhooti."

Chinmaya Vibhooti is also home to a new project, "Chinmaya Naada Bindu," a state-of-the-art residential school of Indian Classical Music and Dance, formerly inaugurated on September 13, 2009.

Gurudev's love for classical music and dance was legendary. "Music is the ornamentation of silence," he said, "and the art of listening to Indian classical music is itself a meditation." At another time, he said:

> Sound is a basic disturbance. When it does not convey any meaning, it is noise. When it conveys a meaning, it is a word. And words arranged in proper syntax and conveying a fullness of thought become a sentence, in prose. The same idea expressed in metrical composition becomes poetry. Poetry soaked in emotion and cadences in its own harmony and rhythm becomes music.
>
> The audience must arrive with minds well-prepared for this great takeoff. Calm your mind. Remember the Lord in your heart. Sit completely relaxed, both physically and mentally, surrendering totally to Him who is the sole protector of this Universe.

THE SAGE DURVASA, GURUDEV, AND A POT OF RICE

My husband, Bala, invited Gurudev in 1978 for bhikṣā at our home in Atlanta. I was a new bride [just] nineteen years [old], and when Gurudev arrived with a sizable entourage, I suddenly realized that I was right in the middle of my first official luncheon party!

When he came to the table, a few ladies immediately instructed me on how to serve him. Then disaster struck. "Where is the rice?" asked one lady. The rice? I looked at my husband, then at Gurudev and slowly said, "I forgot to make it!"

The entourage burst into laughter. I was very embarrassed and wondered if this was how Draupadī felt when Sage Durvāsā came to her hut for a meal and she had no rice left in her pot.

Gurudev's voice suddenly boomed through the laughter. "Never mind. We will wait until she makes the rice and then we will eat." he said. "And do not ask questions like what is on the table. Just eat."

There have been many "firsts" in our lives with Pujya Gurudev, but through this one act of affection and compassion, Gurudev had embraced a teenager as only a father could.

As I look at his statue in Chinmaya Jeevan Darshan, my knees weaken with emotion. I kneel and speak the words once spoken to Lord Śiva by a Thamiz Shaivite saint:

My father and mother art Thou; My best friend art Thou;
The Divine form comes to ease my agitations art Thou;
What better companion can I find on Earth than Thou.

Ramaa Bharadvaj
Celebrated Bharatnatyam Dancer;
Director of Dance, Chinmaya Naada Bindu

Guruji's love for classical music is equally legendary. For years, both Gurudev and Guruji have been actively encouraging and promoting the fine arts amongst the devotees of Chinmaya Mission. Hence, Chinmaya Naada Bindu (CNB) was established with the motto:

> To develop the arts of music and dance as a means of inner purification and Self-realization, and to create artists and art lovers as the finest ambassadors of universal love, peace, and harmony.

CNB offers residential and certificate courses in vocal and instrumental music and classical dance forms. It also conducts workshops by world-renowned artistes, and organizes several concerts and festivals throughout the year.

A prominent music and dance festival is "Jai Bharati," held at the Chinmaya Centre of World Understanding in Delhi in the month of March each year. Jai Bharati initially started in 1991 as "Bhakti Sandhya" evening performances, when Gurudev urged Sita Juneja (now Swamini Gurupriyananda) of Delhi to organize regular performances of devotional music and dance by accomplished artists. Bhakti Sandhya evenings soon became hugely popular; and, in 2005, it evolved into a three-day festival, "Jai Bharati."

Another music project, which has its headquarters at Chinmaya Vibhooti, is "Swaranjali." This is a professional performing arts group that conducts classes in Indian classical music and devotional songs. Its activities initially started in 2002 in Mumbai; but within five years, Swaranjali classes were being conducted in several cities: Indore, Pune, Goa, Delhi, Noida, Bhuvaneshwar, Guwahati, London, San Jose, and Danville, as well as at seven localities in Mumbai. As a result, in 2007, Swaranjali was officially declared as a "grassroot" activity of Chinmaya Mission. The main objective of Swaranjali is to inculcate bhakti (devotion) in the hearts of its members and to provide a platform for artists of Chinmaya Mission worldwide.

With the everlasting glory of the Master ornamented by music and dance, we end an important chapter in our history. In life, Gurudev had meticulously traveled the world to shake its people out of their spiritual slumber. We now see his legacy entering a new millennium, turning present generations with inspiration and wisdom, providing them with multiple platforms upon which to envision their hopes and expectations — but above all — upon which to express their aspiration for Self-knowledge.

One thing is certain: the Chinmaya phenomenon is here to stay. Certainly, after Gurudev's mahāsamādhi, his legacy has made his name far more famous and enduring than ever before. Without doubt, Swami Chinmayananda is one of the best-known spiritual giants of our time.

Still, we might be cautious, and heed the insight of one common notion: "A purely objective and factual biography (or memory) of anyone is beyond any biographer's honest grasp." If this be true, then what can we learn from the story of Gurudev's life?

Perhaps, we can experience an inspiration for the Essential. We might gain the motivation to embark on our own quest for Self-knowledge.

A most inspiring aspect of Gurudev's life is that he was born in ordinary circumstances — most individuals can certainly identify with his childhood and youth. Who would have guessed that the boy who had once said, "I am going to find out how these holy men are keeping up the bluff," would become a revered Master in his own lifetime — that his would be a story of complete fulfillment — of a man who rose to the pinnacle of glory, and gave his gift to the world, so they might live as he did, and rejoice in what he had found bliss.

Gurudev's legacy is explicit:

He did it! And so can you.

In his own words, he said:

As much time and effort as it takes to master any profession in this world, that much time and effort it takes to gain Self-knowledge. Be sure to apply yourself single-pointedly and with diligence.

What more can I say — should I say!! I have said all that is to be said — all that can be said.

I am standing at His gate, waiting. I can enter anytime I wish, but I am waiting for you all to come with me.

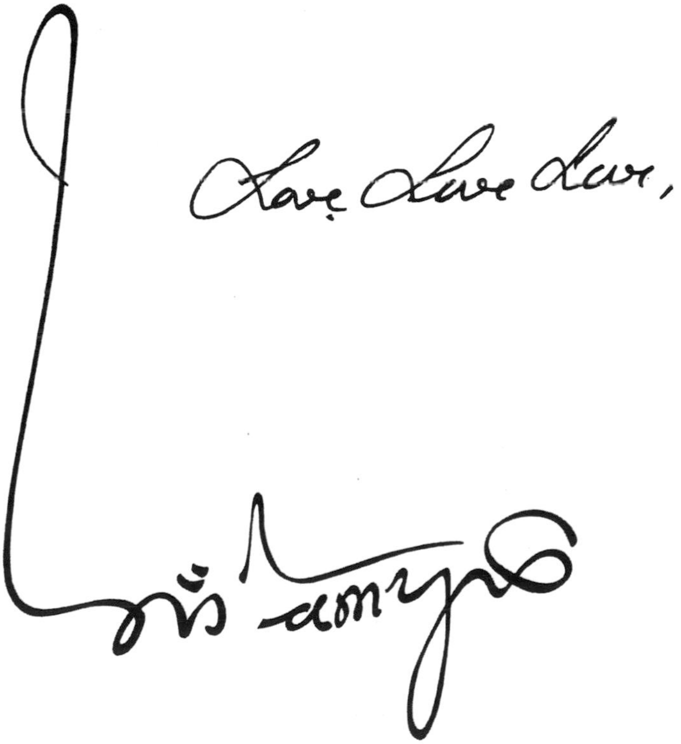

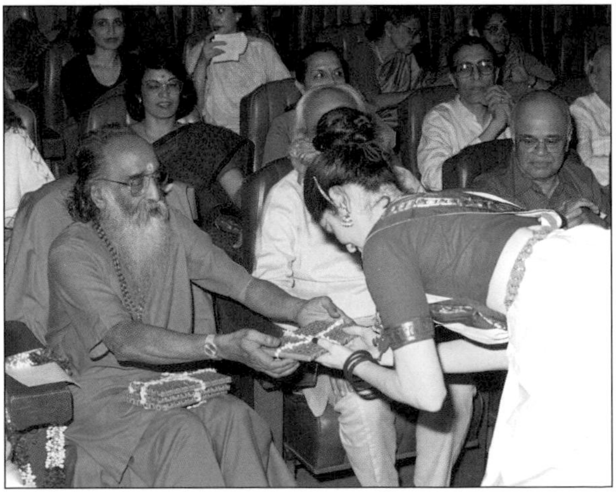

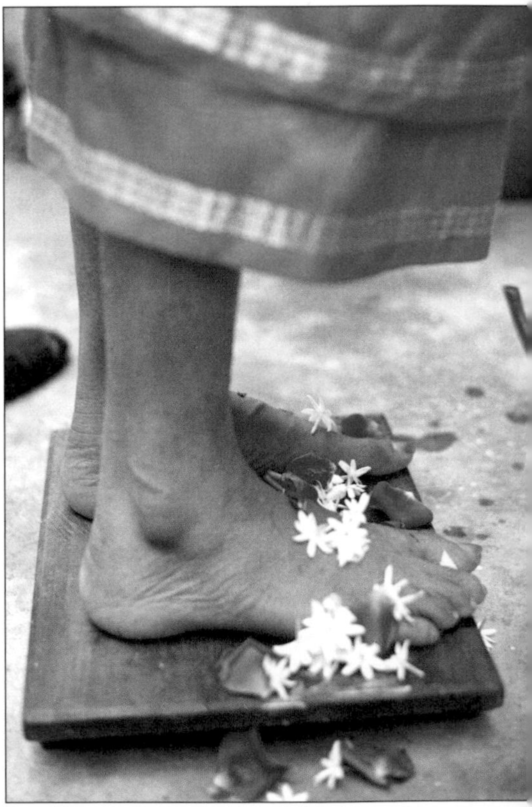

Clockwise from above:
Swamiji attends a music concert by Ustad Sultan Khan at Rajji Kumar's house, Delhi, 1983
Sacred feet of Swamiji
Bhakti Sandhya concert by Aparajita and Devi Mahatmyan, Delhi, 1990
Dr. K. J. Yesudas after singing classical devotional music for Swamiji, Delhi, October 16, 1991

Clockwise from above:
Swamiji gives his own rudrākṣa bead to Purushottamdas Jalota and a silver plate to Anup Jalota on the benefit performance in Delhi, February 8, 1990
M. S. Subbalakshmi (recipient of Ramon Magsasay Award) sings at a benefit performance for Chinmaya Mission, Chennai, 1980 (and again in Delhi on September 10, 1988)
Swamiji with Dr. Padma Subrahmanyam and troupe after a Bhakti Sandhya concert, Delhi, October 21, 1989
Swamiji during the second last Tulābhāram, Sidhbari, May 29, 1993

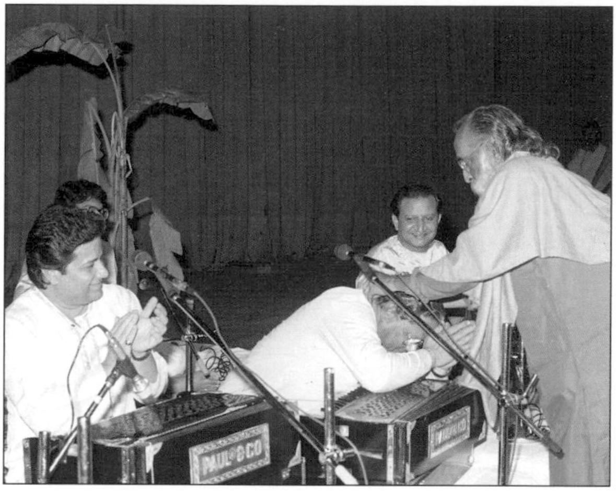

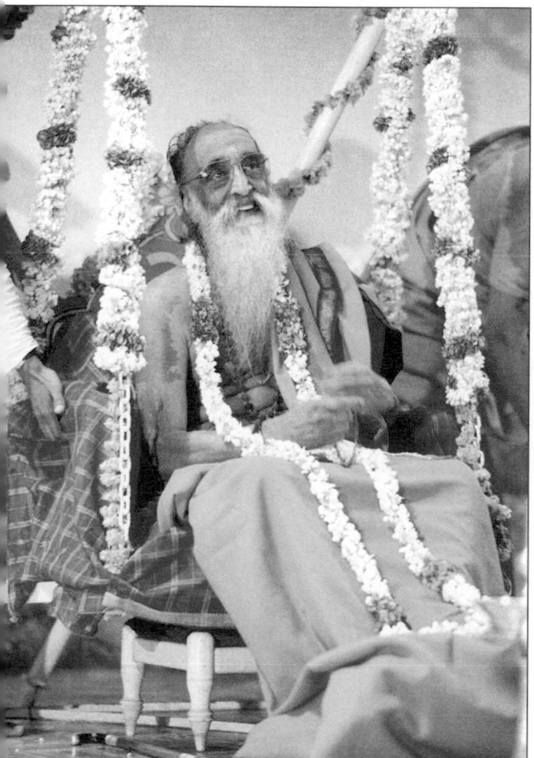

Clockwise from above:
Concert by Pandit Ulhas Kashalkar (Hindustani Vocal) and Suresh Talwalkar (Tabla) during inaugural function of Chinmaya Naada Bindu, Kolwan, September 13, 2009
Sacred feet of Swamiji
Bharatnatyam dancers during inaugural function of Chinmaya Naada Bindu, Kolwan, September 13, 2009
Concert by Kala Ramnath, Chinmaya Naada Bindu, Kolwan, 2010

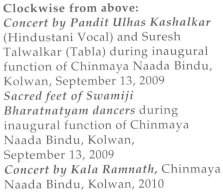

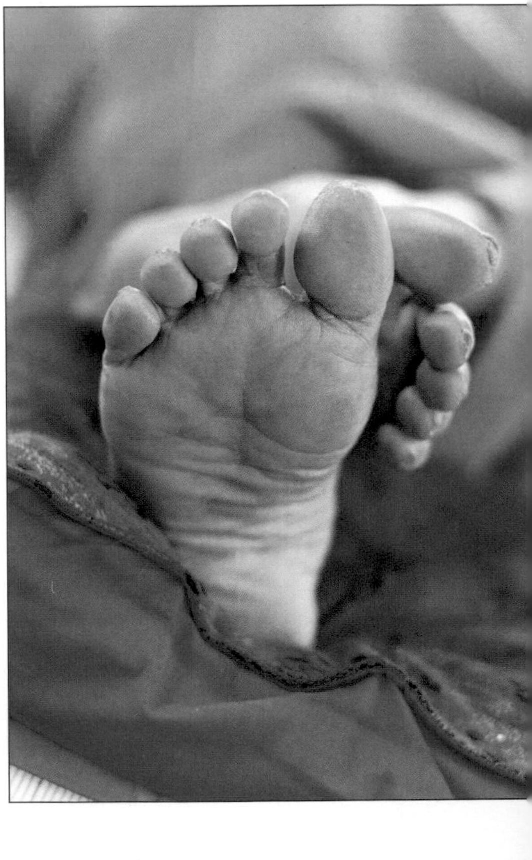

Clockwise from above:
Pandit Jasraj at the Chinmaya Centre of World Understanding, Delhi, 1998
Swami Tejomayananda and H. K. Hinduja enjoying a Hindustani classical music performance in Sudharma Auditorium, Chinmaya Vibhooti, Kolwan, November 2010
Swami Tejomayananda with Pandit Jasraj, Pandit Shiv Kumar Sharma, and Pandit Ulhas Kashalkar during the inaugural of Chinmaya Naada Bindu, Kolwan, September 13, 2009
Portrait of Swamiji, Sidhbari, 1992

CHINMAYA

Chinmaya Vibhooti is:

(a) A grateful tribute to Pujya Gurudev Swami Chinmayananda — founder of worldwide Chinmaya Mission — by all his disciples, devotees, and beneficiaries.

(b) A Vision Center to keep his vision ever-glowing and vibrant by empowering all workers of Chinmaya Mission through appropriate training courses.

(c) A means to bring awareness among all people about the life and work of Swami Chinmayananda.

Chinmaya Vibhooti spans over seventy acres of serene, pictorial landscape surrounded by the Sahyadri Mountains in Kolwan (a village in Maharashtra), two-and-half hours away from Mumbai and forty-five minutes away from Pune.

The main features of this project are:

JOURNEY WITH A MASTER: A depiction of Swami Chinmayananda's life, work, and teachings through various means, including modern interactive technology.

RESEARCH AND TRAINING CENTERS: Specific training programs, particularly for all workers of the Chinmaya Mission, are conducted here to equip them to work more effectively in their respective fields of service.

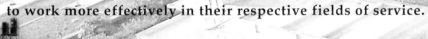

VIBHOOTI

CAMPSITE: A permanent infrastructure to conduct educative and entertaining camps for children, youth, and adults.

INTERNATIONAL CONVENTION CENTER: A facility to accommodate 1,008 people in an auditorium with a large common kitchen and dining hall. There will be an auditorium than can seat 2,000 persons.

RESIDENTIAL COMPLEX: Facilities to accommodate up to 2,000 people, with a large common kitchen and dining hall.

TEMPLES: Two temples dedicated to Lord Gaṇeśa and Lord Hanumān on the hill-top and at the entrance of the Vision Center.

| CONTACT US |

P. O. Kolwan, Taluka Mulshi,
District Pune 412 108
Maharashtra, India
Tel: +91 (20) 2296 0012, 2296 0013
Email: chinmaya.vibhooti@chinmayamission.com

CHINMAYA

It is said that the performing arts are not for everyone; they are either for an amīr (very rich man) or a fakīr (man without belongings); and only a person without any attachment to his riches or aversion to his penury can be a sincere practitioner and master of the performing arts.

Chinmaya Naada Bindu (CNB) is a state-of-art residential school of Indian Classical Music and Dance that provides a vibrant atmosphere for such sincere students and established artists so they can develop the arts of music and dance as a means of inner-purification and Self-realization, and become the finest ambassadors of universal love, peace, and harmony. Hence, the motto of CNB is: "Swara to Ishwara" (for music), and "Nartan to Paramatman" (for dance). CNB imparts world-class training through excellent faculty, conducts workshops and seminars by renowned musicologists, and organizes music and dance concerts and festivals throughout the year.

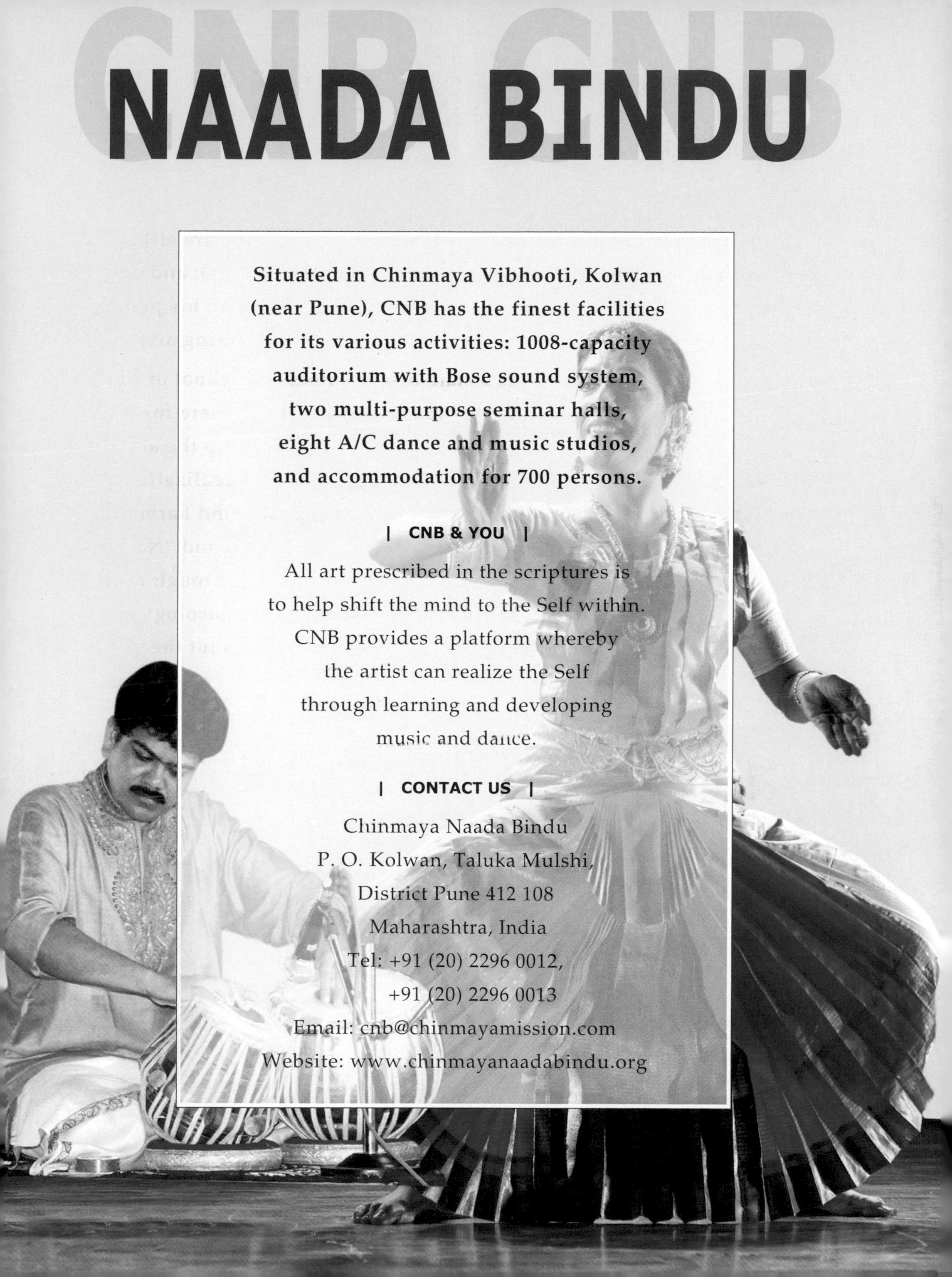
NAADA BINDU
Situated in Chinmaya Vibhooti, Kolwan (near Pune), CNB has the finest facilities for its various activities: 1008-capacity auditorium with Bose sound system, two multi-purpose seminar halls, eight A/C dance and music studios, and accommodation for 700 persons.
| CNB & YOU |
All art prescribed in the scriptures is to help shift the mind to the Self within. CNB provides a platform whereby the artist can realize the Self through learning and developing music and dance.
| CONTACT US |
Chinmaya Naada Bindu
P. O. Kolwan, Taluka Mulshi,
District Pune 412 108
Maharashtra, India
Tel: +91 (20) 2296 0012,
+91 (20) 2296 0013
Email: cnb@chinmayamission.com
Website: www.chinmayanaadabindu.org

Glossary

A	*Ācārya*	teacher
	Adharma	unrighteousness
	Adi Sankara Nilayam	maternal home and birthplace of Ādi Śaṅkarācārya
	Advaita-vedānta	non-dual philosophy of the Upaniṣads
	Āgāmī karma	results born from the actions of the present embodiment that are to be accrued to the individual in the future
	Akhaṇḍanāma-saṅkīrtana	continuous singing of the Lord's name
	Ānanda	Bliss
	Ānanda Kutīr	name of Swami Sivananda's ashram
	Apsarā	celestial nymph
	Āpta-vākya	scriptural text or statement of the Guru
	Aṣṭottaraśat-nāmāvaliḥ	108 names for worship of the deity
	Avabhṛta-snāna	ceremonial bath after completion of a yajña
B	*Bhagavān*	God, Lord
	Bhāgavatam	purāṇa which describes the story of Lord Kṛṣṇa
	Bhajan	rendering of hymns
	Bhaktavatsala Rāma	Lord Rāma, whose love for his devotees is compared to the love of a mother cow for her calf
	Bhakti-yoga	path of devotion unto the Lord
	Bhāratīya	Indian
	Bhikṣā	offering of food, especially to a renunciate

	Bhoga-bhūmi	field of sensual pleasure, enjoyment
	Bhū-samādhi	ceremonial internment given to the mortal remains of a saint
	Brahma-muhūrta	auspicious time of day-break (around 4.30 am), auspicious time for meditation
	Brahma-sūtra	text of aphorisms on the teachings of the Upaniṣads, authored by Veda Vyāsa
	Brahmacārī	one pursuing the knowledge of Brahman, who lives a student life
	Brahmacarya	celibacy; also, one who constantly engages the mind in contemplation of the Self, the supreme Reality
	Brāhmaṇa	one belonging to the class of teachers
	Brahman	infinite Self, ultimate Reality
	Brahman-vicāra	reflection on Truth
	Buddha	Gautama Buddha, the founder of Buddhism
C	*Candrakalādharā*	name for Lord Śiva, literally one who is adorned with kalā of the moon
	Cappal	footwear
	Cintana	reflection or thought
	Cit	Consciousness
D	*Dāl*	split lentil
	Darśana	vision of the Lord; this term is also used to mean a philosophical system in Indian tradition
	Devī	goddess
	Dharma	nature of a thing, duty, righteousness
	Dharmaśālā	place of rest for pilgrims
	Dhoti	lower garment draped by men in parts of India, like a full-skirt
	Dhyāna	meditation
	Divālī	festival of lights; celebrated to mark the return of Lord Rāma to Ayodhyā
G	*Gṛhastha-āśrama*	householder stage in life
	Gaṅgā	sacred river for Indians
	Gaṅgā-stotram	hymn to Mother Gaṅgā
	Gāyatrī-mantra	sacred chant for the Sūrya, the Sun God
	Gopuram	temple tower
	Guru	Teacher

	Guru Nanak	founder of the Sikh religion
	Guru-pūrṇimā	festival dedicated to the worship of the Guru; it falls on the day of the full moon in June–July (also the birth day of Veda Vyāsa, the teacher of all teachers)
	Guru-bhāī	spiritual brother by virtue of having the same Guru
	Guru-śiṣya paramparā	the lineage of the Guru and disciple
	Guru-dakṣiṇā	student's offering to the Teacher
	Gurukula	residence of the Guru where the brahmacārin stays to study
H	*Hanumān*	deity of Rāmāyaṇa fame, devotee of Lord Rāma, son of Vāyu who assumed the form of a monkey
	Himavat-vibhūti	glory of the Himalayas
I	*Īśvara*	Lord
	Īśvara-kṛpā	grace and blessings of the Lord
	Īśvara-saṅkalpa	will of the Lord
J	*Jagat-guru*	world Teacher
	Jala	water
	Japa	continuous chanting of Lord's name
	Jīva	the individual
	Jīvanmukta-puruṣa	one who is liberated even while living
	Jīvanmukta	one who is liberated even while living
	Jñāna	knowledge
	Jñāna-niṣṭha	one who abides in the Truth
	Jhūṭī	already tasted food
K	*Kalaśa*	pot
	Kamaṇḍalu	begging bowl
	Kṛṣṇa	a beloved incarnation of Lord Viṣṇu
	Karma-bhūmi	the field of action
	Karma-yoga	path of selfless and dedicated action
	Karma-yoga vīra	one who excels on the path of selfless and dedicated action
	Karma-yogī	one who lives a life of selfless action
	Kaunteya	Son of Kunti, another name for Arjuna of the Mahābhārata fame
	Khākhī	muddy brown colour

	Khaḍāu	wooden sandal with a knob between the first and second toe usually worn by monks
	Kṣatriya	ruler class
	Kula guru	spiritual perceptor of the household
	Kuṭiyā/Kuṭīra	small house, hut
L	*Lakṣmī*	Goddess of material and spiritual wealth, consort of Lord Viṣṇu
	Laḍḍu	Indian sweet, fresh Indian sweet
	Liṅgam	literally means "indicator", form used for worship of Lord Śiva
	Likhita-japa	repeatedly writing the Lord's divine name or a mantra
	Lord Viṣṇu	Lord as the sustainer and nourisher of the Universe
M	*Madhavācārya*	founder of Dvaita (dualism) philosophy
	Maṇḍap	covered platform, usually that of a temple
	Maharaja	King
	Mahā-mṛtyuñjaya-mantra	particularly well-known Vedic prayer to Lord Śivā as the destroyer of ignorance
	Mahāsamādhi	end of physical being of a great Master
	Mahātmā	holy person or Master
	Mananam	reflection
	Mantra	chant, slogan
	Maunam	silence
	Māyā	cosmic delusory power of the Lord, illusion, ignorance of the Self
	Muni	sage
N	*Nārāyaṇa*	Lord, name for Lord Viṣṇu
	Nārāyaṇīyam	devotional composition on Lord Guruvāyūrappan (Lord Kṛṣṇa) written by Nārāyāṇa Bhaṭṭatiri
	Nayā paise	smallest Indian currency, 100 nayā paise is one rupee
O	*Om Namaḥ Śivāya*	prostrations to Lord Śivā
P	*Pādukā*	sandals
	Pāda-pūjā	worship of the Master's feet
	Pahāḍī	from, of the mountain regions
	Panḍita	priest
	Parama-guru	Guru's Guru

	Parikramā	circumambulation
	Pavana-vāhana	name given to small vehicles like golf carts in Chinmaya Vibhooti, Kolwan
	Prabodha	awakening, indicates Self-realization
	Pradīpa	well-lit lamp
	Prāṇāyāma	breath-control exercises advocated in Yoga
	Prasāda	that which is accepted as a token of the Lord's blessings after worship
	Prasanna-vadanam	serene face
	Prasthānatraya	Upaniṣads, *Bhagavad-gītā* and Brahma-sūtras, the three principal canonical works on Vedānta philosophy
	Preyas	path of the sensually pleasant as opposed to the path of the morally good
	Puṇya tithi-arādhanā	worship of a great soul, in coming years, on the day of their mahāsamādhi anniversary
	Pūjā	ritualistic worship
	Pujārī	priest in a temple
	Purāṇas	compositions of Śrī Veda Vyāsa enshrining the glories of the Lord with ample guidance for spiritual life through the medium of stories
	Puruṣārtha	self-effort
R	*Ṛṣi*	sage
	Rāmānuja	founder of Viśiṣṭādvaita (qualified non-dualism) school of philosophy
	Rāmāyaṇa	story of Lord Rāma, originally composed by Śrī Vālmikī
	Rasāsvāda	reveling in the Bliss of peace
	Roṭī	flat and round wheat bread, like a pancake
S	*Śānti-mantra*	peace invocation
	Śāstra	scripture
	Śāstra-cintana-pradhāna	emphasis on study and logical reflection on teachings of scriptures
	Śiva	Lord expressing as destroyer of the cosmos
	Śivarātrī	sacred night of worship of Lord Śiva where one observes a fast and keeps awake during the night worshiping Lord Śiva; it falls on the 13th night - 14th day in the waning moon of the month of Māgha

	Śravaṇa	listening to scriptures
	Śreyas	path of the morally good as opposed to the path of the pleasant
	Śruti	Vedas
	Śūdra	working class
	Ṣoḍaśi	ceremony on the 16th day after the death, passing on of an individual
	Saṁskāra-pradhāna	emphasis on inculcating noble values and right disposition in life
	Saccidānanda	Existence-Consciousness-Bliss
	Sadāśiva	ever-auspicious
	Sādhanā	spiritual practice
	Sādhu	mendicant
	Saṅkalpa	thought, will, or resolve
	Saṅkalpa-śakti	power of resolve
	Samādhi	complete absorption of mind in meditation
	Sannyāsa	path of renunciation
	Sannyāsī	renunciate
	Sarpa-kāvu	small altars dedicated to snake dieties
	Sarvajña	all-knower
	Sat	Existence
	Satsaṅga	company of the wise and pure
	Sāttvic	characteristic of Maya which expresses as knowledge and serenity
	Satyāgrahī	freedom fighter following the non-violent movement as advocated by Mahatma Gandhi
	Saumya	pleasant and calm
	Sevikā/Sevak	one who is serving
	Siddha	person endowed with siddhīs or unusual powers or a person of Self-realization
T	*Tāmasic*	characteristic of Maya which expresses as ignorance and stupor and causes the non-apprehension of Reality
	Tapas	austerity
	Tyāga	giving up
	Tyāgī	renunciate

U	***Upaniṣad***	portion of Vedas that pertain to knowlege of the Self
	Upāsanā	spiritual practice, worship
V	***Vṛddha***	old, elderly
	Vaidika-havana	fire sacrifice ordained in the Vedas
	Vairāgya	detachment, dispassion
	Vānaprastha	stage of life wherein one retires from worldly duties
	Vāsanā	habitual tendencies, impressions gained from past inclinations or tendencies dictated by past actions
	Veda Vyāsa	great sage who compiled the Vedas, authored the *Mahābhārata,* and the Purāṇas
	Vedānta	Upaniṣadic section of the Vedas that deals with the knowledge of the supreme Reality
	Vīṇā	Indian stringed instrument
	Verandah	courtyard
	Vicāra-pradhāna	emphasis on enquiry
	Vināyaka	Lord Gaṇeśa
	Virāṭ	supreme Reality with the conditioning of the macrocosm, the physical universe
Y	***Yajña-prasāda***	blessings from the yajña
	Yajñaśālā	place where yajña is performed
	Yamunā	river revered in India for its association with Lord Kṛṣṇa
	Yogāsana	postures of yoga
	Yogī	one who is practicing Yoga

Patrons and Contributors

Grateful acknowledgement and special thanks is given to the following:

DAVID & MARGARET DUKES

| TORONTO, CANADA |

JANGA & SHASHIKALA REDDY

| SAN MARINO, CA, USA |

SANTOSH & GAYATHRI BHAGWATH

| SUGAR LAND, TX, USA |

KULDEEP & NEENA DEV

| TORONTO, CANADA |

TRANSLITERATION AND PRONUNCIATION GUIDE

In the book, Devanāgarī characters are transliterated according to the scheme adopted by the International Congress of Orientalists at Athens in 1912. In it one fixed pronunciation value is given to each letter; f, q, w, x and z are not called to use. An audio recording of this guide is available at www. chinmayamission com/scriptures.php. According to this scheme:

	sounds like		*sounds like*
a	o in son	ḍh	dh in adhesive
ā	a in father	ṇ	n in under*
i	i in different	t	t in tabla
ī	ee in feel	th	th in thumb
u	u in full	d	th in this
ū	oo in boot	dh	dh in Gandhi
ṛ	rh in rhythm*	n	n in nose
ṝ	**	p	p in pen
ḷ	**	ph	ph in phantom*
e	a in evade	b	b in boil
ai	i in delight	bh	bh in abhor
o	o in core	m	m in mind
au	o in now	y	y in yes
k	c in calm	r	r in right
kh	kh in khan	l	l in love
g	g in gate	v	v in very
gh	gh in ghost	ś	sh in shut
ṅ	an in ankle*	ṣ	s in sugar
c	ch in chuckle	s	s in simple
ch	ch in witch*	h	h in happy
j	j in justice	ṁ	m in improvise
jh	jh in Jhansi	ḥ	**
ñ	ny in banyan	kṣ	tio in action
ṭ	t in tank	tr	th in three*
ṭh	**	jñ	gn in gnosis
ḍ	d in dog	'	a silent 'a'

* These letters don't have an exact English equivalent. An approximation is given here.
** These sounds cannot be approximated in English words.

Chinmaya Mission Centers

AFRICA
Durban
Kenya
Nigeria
United Republic of Tanzania

AUSTRALIA
Adelaide
Brisbane
Melbourne
Perth
Sydney

BAHRAIN
Manama

CANADA
Calgary
Halton
Niagara Falls
Ontario
Ottawa
Vancouver

FRANCE
Paris

HONG KONG
Kowloon

INDIA

ANDAMAN & NICOBAR ISLANDS
Port Blair

ANDHRA PRADESH
Adoni
Akivedu
Allur
Anantapur
Bapatla
Bhimavaram
Brahmamgari Matham
Chebrolu
Chennur
Chilakaluripet
Chirala
Emmiganore
Erdandi
Gudivada
Gundugolanu
Guntur
Hanmakonda
Hindupur
Hyderabad
Kaikalur
Kavali
Kongareddipalli
Kurnool
Machlipatnam
Narasaraopeta
Nellore
Ongole
Pakala
Parchur
Piler
Proddatur
Pulicherla
Railway Kodur
Rajampet
Rajupalem
Rayachoti
Renigunta Mandalam
Sankarapuram
Secunderabad
Siddipet
Sircilla
Sompeta
Srikalahasti
Sunnapuralapalle
Tadipatri
Tekumatla
Tenali
Tirupati
Vijayanagaram
Vijayawada
Vikarabad
Visakhapatnam
Vizianagaram
Yelurupadu

ASSAM
Guwahati

BIHAR
Gaya
Patna

DELHI
New Delhi

GOA
Vasco
Curchorem
Madgaon
Mapusa
Panaji
Ponda

GUJARAT
Ahmedabad
Bhavnagar
Jamnagar
Rajkot
Surat
Surendranagar
Vadodara

HARYANA
Chandigarh
Panchkula

HIMACHAL PRADESH
Sidhbari

JHARKHAND
Chas
Bokaro
Jamshedpur
Ranchi

KARNATAKA
Bengaluru
Belgaum
Bellary
Davangere
Hubli
Mandya
Mangalore
Mysore
Nanjagud
Sagar
Shivamogga
Tiptur
Tumkur

KERALA
Alleppey
Calicut
Changanassery
Ernakulam
Kanhangad
Kannur
Karugaputhur
Kasargod
Koduvally
Kollam
Kollengode
Kottayam
Manjeri
Mattencheri
Nileshwar
Ottapalam
Palakkad
Pallasena
Pallavur
Parli
Payyanur
Poinachi
Puthenkavu
Quilandy
Sreekandapuram
Taliparamba
Tattamangalam
Thalassery
Thiruvananthapuram
Tirur
Trichur
Tripunithura

MADHYA PRADESH
Bhopal
Gwalior
Indore
Jabalpur
Rewa
Satna

MAHARASHTRA
Ahmednagar
Akola
Amravati
Aurangabad
Chandrapur
Chinchwad
Dombivali
Ichalkaranje
Jalgaon
Khopoli
Kolhapur
Miraj
Mulund
Mumbai
Nagpur
Nanded
Nasik
Pune
Pusad
Ratnagiri
Sangli
Solapur
Tarapur
Thane
Wardha
Yavatmal

MEGHALAYA
Shillong

ODISHA
Angul
Aska
Balasore
Baripada
Berhampur
Bhawanipatna
Bhubaneshwar
Bolangir
Cuttack
Deogarh
Deuladiha
Dhenkanal
Jagatpur
Jatni
Lathikata
Paralakhemundi
Rourkela
Sambalpur

PUDUCHERRY
Puducherry

PUNJAB
Amritsar
Hoshiarpur
Patiala
Ludhiana

RAJASTHAN
Jaipur
Jodhpur

SIKKIM
Gangtok

TAMIL NADU
Chennai
Coimbatore
Kodaikanal
Kotagiri
Madurai
Nagapattinam
Pollachi
Pollur Taluka
Salem
Tiruchengode
Tirunelveli
Tirupur
Trichy

UTTAR PRADESH
Aligarh
Fatehpur
Ghaziabad
Jhansi
Kanpur
Lakhimpurkheri
Lucknow
Meerut
Muradabad
Muzaffarnagar
Noida
Pratapgarh
Roorkee
Saharanpur
Sultanpur

UTTARANCHAL
Dehradun
Uttarkashi

WEST BENGAL
Kolkata

INDONESIA
Jakarta

MALAYSIA
Kuala Lumpur

MAURITIUS
Plaines Wilhems

NEPAL
Kathmandu

NEW ZEALAND
Auckland
Nelson
Wellington

OMAN
Masquat

PHILLIPINES
Manila

REUNION ISLANDS
Saint Suzanne

SINGAPORE

SRI LANKA
Colombo
Rambodha

TRINIDAD & TOBAGO
Trinidad

UNITED ARAB EMIRATES
Dubai

UNITED KINGDOM
London

UNITED STATES OF AMERICA

ALABAMA
Birmingham

ARIZONA
Phoenix

ARKANSAS
Bentonville

CALIFORNIA
Bakersfield
Los Angeles
San Diego
San Jose
Tustin

CONNECTICUT
Fairfield

FLORIDA
Miami
Orlando
St. Augustine
Tampa

GEORGIA
Alpharetta
Atlanta

ILLINOIS
Chicago

INDIANA
Merrilville

IOWA
Iowa City

MARYLAND
Washington D. C.

MASSACHUSETTS
Boston

MICHIGAN
Ann Arbor
Boston
Flint

MINNESOTA
Minneapolis

NEW JERSEY
Princeton

NEW MEXICO
Rio Grande Region

NEW YORK
Buffalo
New York

NORTH CAROLINA
Raleigh-Durham

OHIO
Columbus

OREGON
Portland

PENNSYLVANIA
Philadelphia
Pittsburgh

TEXAS
Austin
Beaumonth
Dallas
Dulles
Houston

WASHINGTON
Seattle

Chinmaya Mission Ashrams

CANADA

Toronto

INDIA

ANDHRA PRADESH
Ellayapalle
Trikoota
Kothapatnam
Elamandyam
Iruvaram

HIMACHAL PRADESH
Sidhbari

KARNATAKA
Chokkahalli
Mangalore

MADHYA PRADESH
Lakshmanpur

MAHARASHTRA
Kolhapur
Udgir
Mumbai

TAMIL NADU
Coimbatore
Tamaraipakkam

UTTARANCHAL
Uttarkashi

UTTAR PRADESH
Allahabad
Mandhana

UNITED STATES OF AMERICA

CALIFORNIA
Piercy

NORTH AMERICA, CANADA, AND WEST INDIES

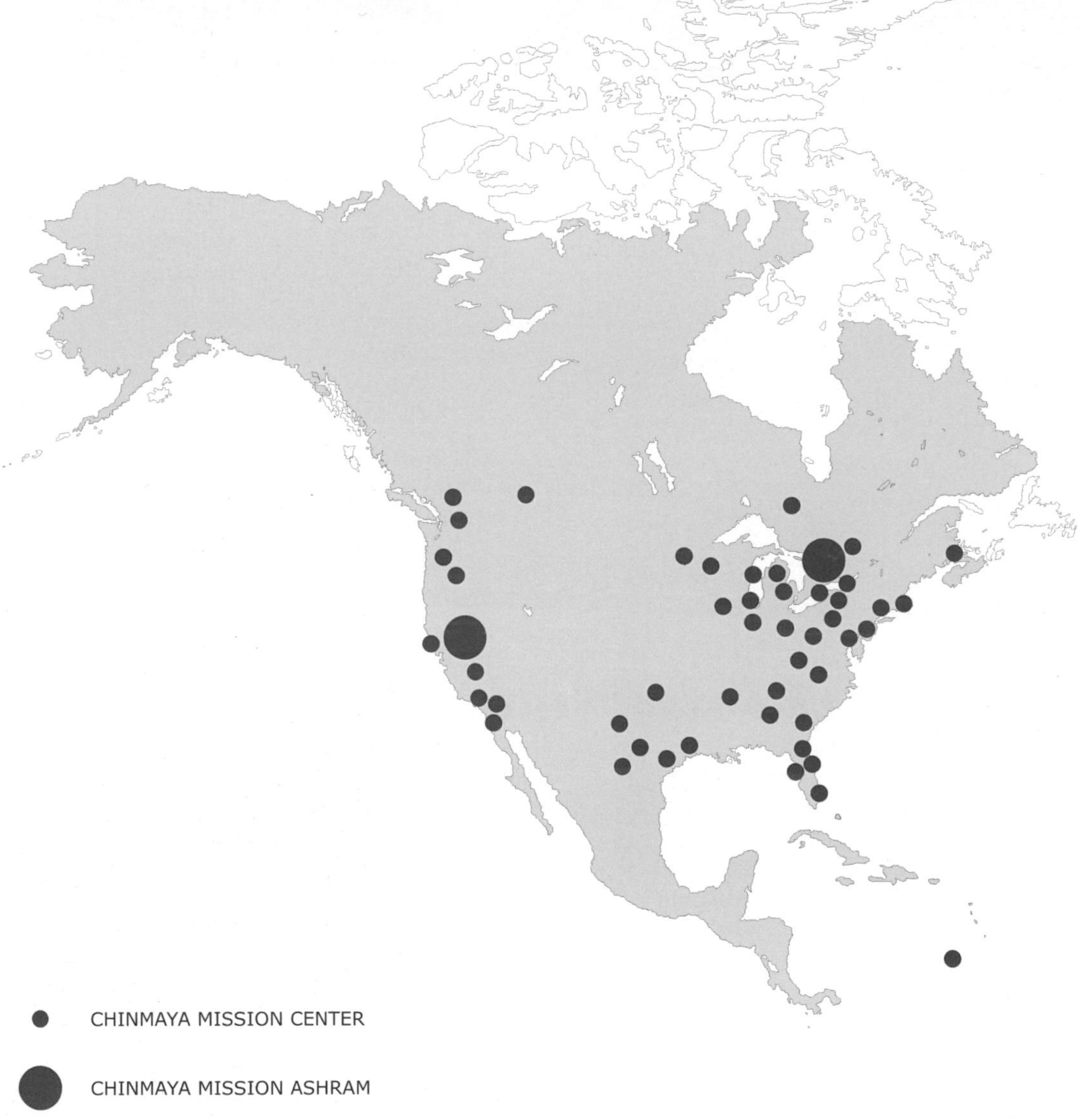